Economic Reforms and
Modernization in Nigeria,
1945–1965

Economic Reforms and Modernization in Nigeria, 1945–1965

Toyin Falola

The Kent State University Press
KENT & LONDON

© 2004 by The Kent State University Press, Kent, Ohio 44242
ALL RIGHTS RESERVED
Library of Congress Catalog Card Number 2004010975
ISBN 0-87338-801-1
Manufactured in the United States of America

08 07 06 05 04   5 4 3 2 1

LIBRARY OF CONGRESS CATALOGING-IN-PUBLICATION DATA
Falola, Toyin.
Economic reforms and modernization in Nigeria, 1945–1965 / Toyin Falola.
p.   cm.
Includes bibliographical references and index.
ISBN 0-87338-801-1 (hardcover : alk. paper)
1. Nigeria—Economic conditions—To 1960. 2. Nigeria—Economic policy. I. title.
HC1055.F355 2004
330.9669'03—dc22
2004010975

British Library Cataloging-in-Publication data are available.

For the parents of my two friends
Vik Bahl and Manuel Callahan:
L. Prem and Sulakshna Lakshi Bahl,
and Carmen Callahan

Contents

Preface and Acknowledgments	xi
1 Economy and Politics in a Colonial Society	1
2 The Political Context of Economic Reforms and Modernization	31
3 The Economy, 1945–1960	66
4 "Separate Economies": Regionalism and Development Institutions	108
5 The Economy, 1960–1965	156
Postscript: Economy and Society after 1965	182
Appendix: Statistical Tables on the Nigerian Economy	207
Notes	228
Selected Bibliography	246
Index	267

Tables

1	Earnings from Agricultural and Domestic Exports	87
2	Gross Domestic Product of Nigeria, 1952–1953	94
3	Output and Value of the Principal Export Crops in Selected Years, 1900–1959	95
4	Agricultural Investments by Regional Boards: Western Region	151
5	Agricultural Investments by Regional Boards: Eastern Region	151
6	Agricultural Investments by Regional Boards: Northern Region	152
7	Annual Average Yield of Important Food Crops, 1960–1971	167
8	Earnings from Agricultural Exports, 1960–1974	167
9	Contribution of Manufacturing Industries to Gross National Product	170
10	Growth Rates of Manufacturing Industries	170
11	Federal and Regional Recurrent Revenues, 1959–1966	175
12	Investment in Manufacturing and Processing	193
13	Oil Contribution to Federal Government Revenue, 1961–1977	193
A1	The GDP at Factor Costs by Economic Sector, 1950–1957	208
A2	Sectoral Composition of the GDP, 1960–1982	208
A3	Growth of the GDP, 1960–1982 at 1973–1974 Factor Cost	209
A4	GDP at 1977–1982 Factor Cost: Percentage Distribution	209
A5	GDP by Activity Type	210
A6	Nigeria's Term of Trade, 1949–1960	211
A7	Earnings from Commodity Trade	211
A8	Food Imports as Proportion of Total Imports and Per Capita Food Imports, 1961–1983	212
A9	Expansion of the Nigerian Road Network, 1962–1980	212
A10	Tonnage of Non-Oil Cargo Handled by Nigerian Ports, 1961–1982	213

A11	Performance of the Nigerian Railway Corporation, 1961–1965	213
A12	Electricity Demand in Nigeria, 1970–1980	213
A13	Nigeria Gas Development, 1971–1980	214
A14	Some Indicators of the Growth in Transport and Communication in Nigeria, 1945–1960	214
A15	Sectoral Growth Rates of the Economy, Selected Years 1962–1982	215
A16	Index of Agricultural Production in Nigeria, 1979–1983	215
A17	Fiscal Structure under the Nigeria (Constitution) Order in Council, 1960	216–17
A18	The Funding of Agricultural Development Projects	218
A19	Crude Oil Production	218
A20	Public Capital Expenditure in the Agricultural Sector, 1962–1985	219
A21	Proposed Changes in Revenue Allocation Formula, 1977–1981	220
A22	Recurrent Expenditure of Nigerian Federal Government, Selected Years 1959–1983	221
A23	Total Federal Government Expenditure at Current Prices, Selected Years 1959–1985	221
A24	Nigerian Federal Government Revenue from Crude Petroleum, 1961–1985	222
A25	Revenue of Nigerian Federal Government, Selected Years 1959–1985	223
A26	Federal Government's Oil Revenues and Total Current Revenues, 1969–1976	224
A27	Gross Manufacturing Contribution, 1959–1960	224
A28	Foreign Investments in the Economy, 1975–1981	225
A29	Foreign Private Capital Outflows and Unremitted Profits, 1975–1981	225
A30	Foreign Private Investment as Percent of Total	226
A31	Sectoral Composition of Planned and Actual Expenditures in the 1962–1968 Development Plan	227

Preface and Acknowledgments

This is my second book on the period covering the last years of colonial rule, a successor to *Development Planning and Decolonization in Nigeria*. After 1940 the Nigerian economy and politics were transformed so rapidly that the country began to look different in many ways than it had looked in its previous history. The first generation members of the political class inherited power in the 1950s, and the agenda of an emerging nation-state turned primarily to the issue of development. The country became obsessed with the transfer of power from the British to the Nigerians, and what the new power-holders would do with this opportunity. The country entered its most crucial stage thus far in its so-called march toward "modernization." This was an age of ideas and actions, all focused toward achieving rapid changes in the economy. The colonial administration, previously uncommitted to development, had to change course after 1940, in part driven by the fear of losing its colony, and in part forced out of its lethargy by nationalist forces. If before 1940 progress had been slow, it was a different story thereafter, as the country began to witness an expansion in its infrastructure, schools, health services, and industries. It is both the process and the outcome of the major economic changes after 1940 that form the subject of this book.

However, this book is different in two ways from its predecessor, *Development Planning and Decolonization in Nigeria*. Unlike the previous book, it deliberately seeks to reach a larger audience by combining synthesis with new research findings on various issues. The presentation is very much geared to general readers, while specialists will find newness in interpretations and data that is being used for the first time. This book deliberately provides additional analysis on politics in order to capture the general events of the period and to transcend the narrowness imposed by a strictly economic analysis. Politics determined in part how the major economic objectives of the period were arrived at. In addition, politics provided the enabling forces to initiate and implement political programs. During the period covered by this book, politics also determined the management of issues, as politicians were at that time among the major economic planners.

The book covers one of the most important phases in the history of modern Nigeria. Indeed, many regard the period as the "golden era" in the development of regional and national consciousness. Driven by the need to be free of British rule, many Nigerians, especially the elite, were proud of themselves. Nationalism emboldened them to think big about power, development, and individual achievements and self-esteem. The most commonly used word was "change." Many more people went to school, in the hope of attaining social mobility. The first university in the country, the University of Ibadan, was established in 1948. Those who could not gain admission to Ibadan sought opportunities abroad, traveling to Britain, the "mother country," also to the United States and other places. The regional governments in the 1950s made education their primary goal and contributed to the massive expansion of both primary and secondary schools. The farmers, craftsmen, market women, and others who did not go to school were also conditioned to dream of a great future: the inheritors of power promised to transform their lives within a generation. Most people expected progress, variously defined to mean earning more money, living in better houses, wearing good clothes, eating better food, and being able to send children to school. In short, independence was associated with the banishment of poverty.

The book captures the great changes of the era, and it pushes a little bit further into the period dominated by oil, if only to sketch the trends and the major issues. Several statistical tables are provided on the post–independence economy to indicate the nature of changes after independence. Two themes loom large in the study, one peripherally and the other my major concern. My major concern is with the economy, providing an analysis of the growth and characteristics of the era under consideration. I focus on the broad trends in the economy, as well as providing original accounts of the development agencies created during the period. Considerations of development plans and agencies ultimately revolve around the issues of economic growth. But, as the analysis indicates growth in Gross Domestic Product (GDP), per capita income, capital formation, aggregate savings and productivity, and also reviews the performance of the leading sectors (notably agriculture and industries), it can reveal profound changes which may nevertheless leave out the most important consideration: the betterment of people's lives. I have included aspects of development as part of the larger context of economic history. Thus, issues of standard of living and capacity of government to provide more amenities to the ever-growing population are included in my analysis. On the one hand, we see an economy showing impressive evidence of economic growth, but, on the other hand, we see that the capacity for Nigerians to improve their living standard was not always enhanced.

The second theme, albeit analyzed in the context in a single chapter, is that of politics, which involved a process of transfer of power from the British to Nigerians and the mismanagement of this great opportunity by first generation members of the political class. Chapter 2 examines the formation of political parties, the various constitutions of the era, the competition for election, and the entrenchment of ethnicity that ultimately led to the civil war in 1967. All these political issues impacted upon the economic reforms and programs discussed in this book.

Both the economic and the political issues reveal the reforms undertaken in the last years of colonial rule. In some instances, one influenced the other, as in the process to "regionalize" the awarding of loans and the execution of development programs, or as in the political rivalry over the revenue allocation formula. Whereas a single development plan was formulated for the country in 1946, the political reforms thereafter created the need for various regional development plans in the 1950s. As each region tried to assert itself and to ensure that constitutional rights were fulfilled in the early years, the formulation of plans became a means of self-assertion. It did not matter if there were overlaps or duplications, and it was not necessary for a region to relate its goals to any national economic target. To take another example, the political instability of the First Republic also impacted upon economic performance, which slowed down considerably. Yet in some other instances, there was no such "organic" linkage. Certainly, politics was considered more important than the economy, especially as the members of the political class were anxious to inherit power from the British. The point of unity between politics and economy, as I point out in chapter 1, was the attempt to reform society by creating new institutions and attempting to move the economy and politics forward. The pace in both was fast.

At the initial conception of the project, I received valuable comments from Dr. Saheed Adejumobi and Dr. Akanmu Adebayo. These two critical students of this period of Nigerian history offered a variety of suggestions. I owe the final format to the suggestion by colleagues that I should leave out a long discourse on politics, which I intend to constitute into a separate book in future. The first draft received generous comments from Professors Jeremiah Dibua and Gloria Chuku. I appreciate the interest of the Kent State University Press in the manuscript, with special gratitude to John T. Hubbell, Joanna H. Craig, and Kathy Method. Professor Felix Ekechi of Kent State never stopped assuring me that the Press would do a good job. Dr. Ann O'Hear lent her expertise in turning the manuscript into a better one. I am also grateful to Ashley Rothrock, who compiled the index. Once again, I cannot but thank the members of my nuclear family—Bisi, Dolapo, Bisola, and Toyin—and a host of friends in Austin for contributing to my rich academic and social life.

Since it is customary for scholars to disagree on various issues, even ignoring some of the wise suggestions offered by those who have taken the trouble to read their drafts, I would like to add the now common caveat that I am responsible for all my errors.

1
Economy and Politics in a Colonial Society

The last fifteen years of British rule in Nigeria were active and full of contradictions about power and its consequences. The British, with the other Allied powers, had just been victorious over Germany in World War II. Britain's victory did not bring much confidence to its country or colonies, certainly not in the consolidation of power over its empire, a contrast to what happened at the end of World War I. World War II left Britain in a state of economic crisis and with huge debts to the United States. While Britain needed resources to rebuild its economy, this was a time of rising nationalism in Nigeria and other colonies when the colonial subjects were complaining about exploitation. This is the first contradiction that contributed to shaping the historical reality of the post-1945 era: Nigerians had to deal with a colonial power whose global influence was waning.

A declining influence did not mean that Britain intended to give up its Nigerian colony. Indeed, only a few people in the mid-1940s anticipated that independence would come within a span of fifteen years. Rather, what the colonial government intended was to retain the established political and economic institutions in order to continue transferring wealth abroad. But the ferment of nationalism and the growing anticolonial sentiments in different parts of the world dictated a change of policy and a different outcome. This is the second contradiction: the colony could be retained, but far-reaching reforms had to be undertaken in order to prevent violent resistance. It was precisely at the point where the colonial system began to reform itself that it also began the final journey to dissolution.

Reforms were risky in that they exposed the ineffectiveness of the colonial system in addressing protests and demands. Here lies the third contradiction: one reform created the need for another. As the economy either expanded or modernized, it opened up opportunities in such a way that more profits and benefits were demanded by the beneficiaries. As political reforms were undertaken, nationalists were eager not to express gratitude but to demand additional changes, which meant a transfer of power and, ultimately, an end to colonial rule.

By the early 1950s an end to colonial rule could be anticipated, even if the date was still unknown. Now assured that power would be theirs, the nationalists began to spend more energies fighting one another than fighting the British. The imperial master was no longer the enemy; the enemy was now fellow Nigerians who represented other ethnic groups. The departing power that was supposed to lose influence now began to make substantial gains by manipulating the competing regional leaders against one another and, ultimately, ensuring that the friendly Northern Region controlled the federal government. This is the last of the contradictions: as ethnic conflict weakened the Nigerian political class, the British were able to manipulate one leader against another, to become more imaginative in controlling the process of disengagement, and to establish a solid foundation for neocolonialism; that is, ensuring that the end of colonial rule was not the end of British influence in the country.

These various contradictions were embodied in the major events as they unfolded between 1945 and 1960. To continue to rule, the British had to grant major concessions to Nigerians by way of reforming the economy and politics. They also had to respond to the pressure of the Cold War by preventing the rise of communist parties. Friendly Nigerian leaders were needed to manage power in such a way that established colonial interests would be maintained long after the British had left. The economic changes of the postwar era and the constitutional reforms after 1947 combined to lay a weak foundation for an independent country. In the remainder of this chapter an outline history of the period, with a focus on the landmarks, will be presented. In the chapters that follow, I will examine both the economic and the political changes and their eventual consequences.

The Colonial Era before 1939

In spite of the massive evidence of resistance that they had to confront, colonial documents portrayed British conquest and rule as easy and most welcome.[1] To the apologists of British rule, the main problem was how to change the "traditional Nigerians" fixed in their ways and attitudes to "new" men and women who were pro-market, pro-taxes, and pro-modernity. Yet kings and chiefs were forced to sign treaties of friendship, were coerced into accepting alien authorities, and, in a number of cases, were forced to succumb to greater military power.[2]

Many kings and other rulers of established precolonial states were not as ignorant of imperialism as they are often portrayed. They too had benefited from indigenous imperialism, and the empire builders among them knew the merits of efficient armies and public treasuries. Thus, al-Kanemi, who himself established a new political dynasty in Borno to the northeast during the nineteenth century, had to warn his peers in the adjacent Sokoto Caliphate to be careful of the British. Al-Kanemi was aware of the British conquest of India and saw the same thing happening in his homeland. They would come in ones and twos until they took over the entire country warned the politically astute al-Kanemi.[3]

Al-Kanemi was right in formulating what can be called a "nibbling thesis." Europeans came gradually in the fifteenth century onward, in ones and twos, eventually seizing the entire country. Originally, the motive was commercial and, for over three hundred years, contact was dominated by the transatlantic slave trade. When this heinous trade was abolished in the nineteenth century, it was replaced by agricultural crops, notably palm oil and palm kernels.[4] Politics became important to the pursuit of trade. In 1849 John Beecroft was stationed as British consul for the coastline of West Africa, although the British proclaimed that they had no interest in gaining territorial possessions. To look after commercial interests, a consulate was established in Lagos in 1851, following two battles with the people. Consulate officials meddled in local politics, and they successfully manipulated the bitter rivalries for the throne of Lagos to establish a colony in 1861.[5] The Lagos Colony enabled the British to gain a major foothold in the country, to be in a position to collect data on trade, and to have a strong base from which to participate in the partition of West Africa in the 1880s and 1890s.

Not much followed by way of territorial expansion, as the British government calculated that overseas colonies were not necessary in the 1860s and 1870s. Nevertheless, trade and political interests continued to be strong.[6] European traders and missionaries actually intensified the contacts with Nigeria, benefiting from the widespread optimism that the interactions with Nigerians were both profitable for trade and conducive to the creation of a Christian "kingdom." The missionaries merged economy and religion, in the idea of "the Bible and the Plow," which meant that converted people could become producers, which would then lead to the expansion of the market. In a calculating manner, the aggressive wave of Christian expansionism was justified in part by the need to remove the evils of the transatlantic slave trade and to spread "civilization" to "backward" parts of the world. The missionaries voiced the opinion expressed in Europe that its people and religion were definitely superior to Africans, and that the white man was at the top of a racial pyramid with the black man at the very bottom.[7] The missionaries became involved in local politics, and they were among the strongest advocates of the imposition of colonial rule.[8] Like a number of European politicians, many missionaries regarded the occupation of Africa as the right thing to do, a "sacred trust" invested in the "civilized" people to uplift so-called backward races. No wonder, then, that it was common to find many missionaries presenting Nigerians as children and the missionaries as their parents who would offer guidance and leadership. The missionary message of "civilization" also found support among a new generation of educated Africans. The offer of Western education and the "progress" that came with it encouraged some Nigerians to ask for "modernization," even if this would inevitably be accompanied by British rule.[9]

The foreign traders were equally visibly aggressive, notably in the area of the Niger Delta and largely in order to profit from the palm-oil business. They began to move to the hinterland along the Niger River and expected their government to protect them and to support their activities. The consuls in Lagos and the Niger Delta were active in promoting trade. In addition, trading companies were allowed to administer some of the areas where they conducted business operations. The most successful combination of trade and politics occurred in the Niger Delta, under the leadership of Sir George Goldie, the founder of the Royal Niger Company (RNC).

In the early 1880s the fear that the French and Germans might establish jurisdiction in some areas along the coast motivated the British to work out schemes to control the Niger and Oil Rivers. The well-known "Scramble for Africa" was now under way as Britain, France, Germany, Belgium, and Portugal competed for territories for economic and political reasons. To regulate their competition, a conference was convened in Berlin (1884–85), where the European powers agreed among themselves that effective occupation of an area was needed to justify a claim to that area.[10] The rush began thereafter to sign treaties, to conquer by force, and to use all necessary means in order to prevent a competitor from claiming a desired area. From "effective occupation" only of the Lagos Colony and a small area on the mainland in 1885, the British moved quickly fifteen years later to take over the huge territory later called Nigeria. Only a summary of the process is necessary in this study.

The British consul on the Oil River signed a number of treaties with the chiefs in the Niger Delta. In the same area the RNC, established by Goldie, held a charter to govern from 1886 to 1899, allowing the British to maintain control without having to pay for it. The RNC established an armed constabulary to perform police duties, and a court of justice, in addition to performing other administrative duties in parts of the Niger Delta. The RNC was tough and brutal in dealing with the people; it reaped enormous profits and further extended its control over the hinterland. Goldie and his company prefigured what colonial rule would be about: the company exploited local producers and traders, cheated its own Nigerian staff, was eager to use force, and was blatantly racist. The RNC used its charter to dominate trade and was thus able to make enormous profits. In addition, it engaged in treaty making and expeditions that subsequently determined some of the boundaries of modern Nigeria. Among the success stories in the quest for territorial control were the absorption of Warri in 1882, Idah in 1883, Jibu on the Benue in 1884, and Ibi, also in the Benue region, in 1885. Contacts were established with Sokoto and Gwandu, the capitals of the extensive Sokoto Caliphate, and punitive expeditions were sent in 1897 to Ilorin and Nupe, two powerful states in the Middle Belt. All this extended the company's claims to an extensive area in what later became known as Eastern and Northern Nigeria, thus ensuring that the British did not have to share these territories with the French and Germans. So successful was Goldie that pro-British accounts tend to describe him as "the founder of Nigeria."[11]

Local chiefs and kings were shocked by the activities of the RNC. The company's trading tactics undercut their profits, and its territorial extension undermined their power. Many African middlemen found themselves in trouble as the RNC imposed tax on them, while the company was hostile to chiefs and kings opposed to its activities. Frustrated by the activities of the RNC, many were to ask the question: when would the white men be banished from the land?[12]

A swift answer was given to this question: more white men would come and to all the nooks and crannies of the land. By the time the question was being posed in the 1880s, the partition of Africa was already in progress. From Lagos the British moved to the Yoruba hinterland. They meddled in the Yoruba wars, attacked the Ijebu in 1892, and signed treaties with many Yoruba kings and chiefs, notably with the Alaafin of Oyo in 1893. A resident consul was placed at Ibadan in 1893 to begin the foundation of a colonial administration. These events also brought to an end the long warfare among the principal Yoruba states, a great relief to thousands of people. The missionaries active in the region, including Yoruba converts, were eager to expand the "Christian kingdom," even among the Ijebu, who had resisted the spread of Christianity for four decades.

In the southeast the British established a colonial jurisdiction in the Niger Delta, creating a small government in 1893. Two years later an entity known as the Niger Coast Protectorate emerged with a claim over most of the Niger Delta region. The charter of the RNC was revoked in 1899, but its gains were acquired by the British government. The powerful Benin Empire was subdued in 1897, and the equally influential Aro, among the Igbo, were attacked in 1901.[13]

In the North the Protectorate of Northern Nigeria was created in 1900, again using the combination of treaties and violence.[14] Military encounters subdued the Nupe and Kano, while some other emirates surrendered to avoid battles. Wars of conquest followed until the Sokoto Caliphate was eventually subdued by 1903. Resistance continued in various parts of the country, most especially among the Igbo, but the British colony of Nigeria was now in place.[15] Due to economic considerations—the North had a running budget deficit and the surplus in the South could be diverted to the North—the southern and northern protectorates were amalgamated in 1914, all included in a huge country now known as Nigeria, the largest British colony in West Africa and the most populous British colony in Africa.[16] Administratively, the country eventually became divided into three: North, West, and East, although these were not only geographical divisions but also linguistic and ethnic entities. Each region was in turn divided into provinces.

As would be expected, the indigenous elite opposed this aggression. To uphold tradition, to defend their sovereignty, and to protect the interests of commerce and politics, it was in the best interest of many chiefs and kings to resist. Leaders such as the Jaja of Opobo, the Nana of Itsekiri, and the Oba Ovonramwen of Benin displayed remarkable gallantry. Some groups, such as the Ekumeku in Western Igboland, showed an ability to resist for a long time. In the end the British conquest was successful largely because of superior British technology, itself a product of the Industrial Revolution that put Europe far ahead of Africa. The use of force was crucial: many groups were conquered, such as the Ijebu, Itsekiri, Bini, Igbo, Tiv, and Ibibio, to mention but a few; others surrendered because they had no answer to the invading army, or, as in the example of some Yoruba states, because they were already tired of wars with one another, and there were those who calculated that it was better to negotiate in order to secure advantages in trade and to hope for possible political renegotiation at a future date.

Governance and resistance (later, nationalism) went hand in hand. Both were involved in yet another dominant ideology of the period: progress. To the British, colonial rule was about progress—the changes they brought were allegedly meant to benefit Nigerians. The resistance fighters and nationalist leaders believed that their activities would bring progress: preventing the conquest, seeking reforms, and later on achieving independence were all projected as being for the good of the country. As colonial rule became consolidated, the definition of progress by the elite began to include some of the reasons advanced to justify colonialism. Here is a contradiction that shaped Anglo-Nigerian relations from the beginning to the end of the colonial period. To many members of the emerging Nigerian elite of the nineteenth and early twentieth centuries, who were products of missionary education, colonialism was not all that bad, as it would bring social and economic changes.

Opinions, however, were divided as to how this progress would come about and what the contributions of Nigerians would be. It was not until after 1945—the main period covered in this book—that these contributions were clarified as part of the decolonization process. Before then there were controversies and ideological divisions. Just as there were pro-British people, there were also anticolonial forces. Hundreds of people were recruited into the West African Frontier Force, thus using Africans against Africans to take over their territories. Even the huge empire of Sokoto failed to mobilize its enormous resources to fight a sustained war. But there was resistance and there were lingering protests, as among the Ekumeku in the southeast.[17] A number of elite members doubted what the outcome of the conquest would be. Many turned to their gods and magic, hoping for a miracle of deliverance to happen. What was certain, however, was not the success of resistance but the new experience of colonialism.

This experience was multiple and diverse. The most immediate impact, and ultimately the most important, was the distribution of power among the white officers, the indigenous elite, and the rising educated elite. This was a source of great tension. Of course, white officials were in control of the administration until the 1950s, when power began to be devolved to Nigerians.[18] The majority of white officers never regarded themselves as total strangers to the land. Many indeed disputed the claims by Nigerians that Africa did not belong to Europeans. As an expatriate, an officer was very much connected with home and with his superior officers in London, thanks in part to the availability of rapid communication methods. The members of the Nigerian educated elite who wanted power and privileges were regarded as "savvy boys" who did not know what they were doing. Whether a Nigerian liked or disliked the British, he or she had no choice but to be part of a "colonial situation," to obey or to protest new laws, to recognize boundaries, and to realize that previous indigenous rules were inadequate to cope with a new situation based on the exercise of power by outsiders.

For the greater part of the colonial period the solution to managing the tension created by this imposition of power was a local government system known as indirect rule. In a cost-saving device, the existing political institutions would be modified so that indigenous chiefs and kings would continue to exercise some power, and a small number of British officers would supervise and regulate the conduct of politics and administration. The British officers gave advice, although some of their advice sounded more like commands. The balance of power was decidedly tilted in favor of the British officers, who had to ensure that colonial objectives were fulfilled in such aspects as the collection of taxes and the production of crops for export. In a clever manner, the tasks of collecting tax or executing public works appeared as if they emanated from the local agencies and were performed for the benefit of the local people, rather than to meet British interests. Thus, the most direct impact of British rule was presented so as to appear as if the Nigerian leaders were in control of their people. Also, certain aspects of Nigerian cultures that were considered "uncivilized" would be prohibited. Nevertheless, the colonial administration did not move quickly to abolish domestic slavery, while it benefited from forced labor and taxation. The indirect rule system was first imposed in the North, where a preexisting caliphate system, with powerful emirs and delineated authority, ensured a satisfactory arrangement.[19] Indirect rule was subsequently extended to the South, where it worked with mixed success.[20]

Indirect rule reconfigured power relations between the chiefs and their people. Instead of acting as the defenders of their traditional power as they had in the last years of the nineteenth century, many became co-opted into the new administration and profited more from obeying the colonial government than from meeting the expectations of their own people. In turn, the local chiefs were rewarded with wages and benefits, and their excesses, sometimes bordering on corruption, were forgiven.[21] The traditional mechanisms to remove or to discipline the chiefs were either weakened or eliminated, as the chiefs owed their appointments and retention to the British officers. The system favored the "traditional chiefs," who were not expected to modernize themselves by acquiring Western education and culture. The best among them were to remain "pure," steeped in traditional ways. This ensured the promotion of tradition and ethnicity in ways that would later create problems for independent Nigeria. In the North, colonial officers could stand aloof, interfering only when sufficient tax had not been collected. In the East, indirect rule encountered more problems because it had entailed creating powerful chiefs where none had previously existed. In acephalous societies without powerful kings, as among the Igbo, democratically oriented institutions were ignored and chiefs, known as warrant chiefs, were created just to ensure that indirect rule was put into practice. Regarded as corrupt and arrogant, the warrant chiefs had no choice but to rule by abusing their power and primarily as the representatives of the colonial authority.[22] Among the Yoruba, the power of some kings, notably the Alaafin, was enhanced far beyond what local customs allowed and extended over a wider territory.[23] The same was true of the Oba of Benin in relation to other chiefs in the area.[24]

Indirect rule alienated the Nigerian educated elite, who were excluded from power. Thinking that they possessed the means to modernize their country, the language to mediate between the masses and the colonial officers, and the values and tastes characterized as "civilized," the Nigerian elite wanted to be at the forefront of politics. Until the 1940s the British wanted to either put them at the very back or ignore them altogether. The majority of British officials did not hide their contempt for the Nigerian elite.[25] For one thing, the educated Nigerians saw little or no need to respect white people. These Nigerians had invested in their education, and the professionals among them, such as lawyers, even regarded themselves as better qualified than many British officers. To the officers who wanted adulation, the educated elite seemed disrespectful and rude, and the officers preferred the farmers and poor people who worshiped them. Colonial officers also regarded the elite as ungrateful people who were not satisfied with what the system had given them but were always asking for more. They should be suppressed, not even oppressed, recommended one officer, who complained in 1930 that after giving them education and a better livelihood, all they could think about was how to govern themselves. Indirect rule served to exclude the educated elite from power and prevented them for a long time from even gaining a national platform from which to operate. To the elite, indirect rule and the chiefs who served in the system were reactionary.

The next question was what to do with power. British rule had a decisive answer until the 1940s: change the existing economy in order to ensure a transfer of wealth to Europe. Where indirect rule was most effective, as in the North, the development agenda was regarded by colonial officials as secondary. They approved of minimal economic progress, supported the chiefs to maintain the status quo, and objected to the demands of the educated elite. In other places, local officials associated with indirect rule did not see power as an avenue to bring about change but as a means to accumulate wealth. Chiefs, clerks, messengers, and others simply regarded access to government as an opportunity to control others. Power was regarded as a way of generating an income that would enable them to live well and to acquire the objects associated with the new generation—cars, clothes, huge and secluded residential houses, and education.

No government or public objective is ever simple. A government can be evaluated on the basis of benefits that accrue to the people it governs. The majority of Nigerians always ignored the objectives of the colonial government in their own desire to have people-friendly and development-oriented administration. Yet, despite the fact that many colonial officers disguised their intentions, their statements clearly revealed the real colonial objectives. As the guru of colonial administration, Sir Frederick D. Lugard,[26] put it, the objectives of government were clear to see:

> It is in order to foster the growth of the trade of this country, and to find an outlet for our manufactures and our surplus energy, that our far-seeing statesmen and our commercial men advocate colonial expansion. . . . If

our advent in Africa introduces civilization, peace, and good government, abolishes the slave trade, and effects other advantages for Africa, it must not be therefore supposed that this was our sole and only aim in going there. However greatly such objects may weigh with a large and powerful section of the nation, I do not believe that in these days our national policy is based on motives of philanthropy only.[27]

Until the 1940s the government was less than ready to promote development or to accelerate the pace of welfare provision and social change. It was not a people-oriented government. Some of its policies actually brought about alienation. Forced labor was used to complete a number of public projects. Africans paid taxes in cash for the first time, and many had to produce and to sell in order to generate the funds. Thousands of people had to migrate in search of money, jobs, and new opportunities. Yet, taxation was imposed without political representation or projects that the members of the public could associate with their tax payments. The widespread perception was that the colonial government had done little to help the people. In the words of one missionary in the 1920s:

Do they not exist to pay tax, work on the railway, absorb the products of English factories, and provide them with the raw materials to produce others, with the final aim of enriching some Company Directors and providing well paid jobs for some thousands of young people without resources? Which one is primitive?[28]

It was the real "primitive," the colonial officer, who had the power to transform the lives of others! Colonialism brought many changes, even if the people complained that its positive impact on them was either minimal or not as great as they had expected. Since the people were already perceived as contented with their lives, many colonial officers praised the little that the colonial government accomplished, very often disassociating their local decisions from the larger impact of capitalism and international trade. As far as many colonial officers were concerned, they were "modernizers"; after all, many believed that Nigeria and the rest of the continent had no history and was backward before the colonial conquest. Even the enlightened scholars of the age, such as Margery Perham, who was familiar with the impressive empire of Sokoto in the nineteenth century, could still conclude that "until the very recent penetration of Europe the greater part of the continent was without the wheel, the plough or the transport animal; without stone houses or clothes except skins; without writing and so without history."[29] The stereotypes of Nigerians and other Africans were couched in the language of antidevelopment and antimodernity: many Africans were naked; their minds were dominated by superstition; they lived in a permanent state of insecurity; and they had no government in many areas. Given this attitude, even the most minute policy change was regarded as an advance.

The need to create a new economy was primary. The British would further monetize the economy to draw more people into the market economy. Indigenous currencies were phased out and replaced by new coins and paper money. As the people paid tax, bought imports, and developed tastes for new products, the market expanded, and the use of new currencies and banking facilities gained an increasing popularity. Agriculture was commercialized, as crops and rural areas were connected to the international economy. The need to earn money for a variety of reasons pressured millions of farmers to produce for the market. The establishment of an efficient transport system was a paramount need, in order to move raw materials to the coast from where they could be transported abroad, and to distribute imported items to the internal markets. Indeed, the colonial government regarded the development of a new transport system of railroads and roads as arguably its most important contribution. From scratch, the government built a railway system and many roads connected to it, thereby creating a transport revolution. The system was originally paid for with loans, which Nigerians eventually repaid through taxes and export duties. Minerals (tin, coal) and agricultural products (cocoa, rubber, peanuts) were taken out of the country, in addition to capital derived from taxes and duties. Without the railway system and roads, the import-export trade that dominated the colonial economy would have been difficult to sustain.

The golden rule was that productivity must increase in order to generate raw materials for the outside world, as well as funds to run the economy. Nigerians had to pay tax, and the government could collect export and import duties on cash crops. Taxation was regarded as an important strategy for various reasons. It would make people work, a belief that was even dominant in Britain among the members of the upper class. The idea was that if people were forced to pay tax, they would be forced to work. Lugard restated this Victorian philosophy in 1906, by linking taxation to the stimulation of industry and productivity. According to him, "there is no civilised State in the world where direct taxation has not been found to be a necessity, and African communities which aspire to be regarded as civilised must share the common burden of civilisation."[30]

By working, Africans would generate money for themselves and the government. In Lugard's view, by funding the government, the people were actually protecting themselves and creating the basis for their own progress. Very early in the colonial period, taxation was introduced in the North, without problems since the preceding indigenous administration had also had a revenue system based partly on the collection of taxes. It was a different story in the South, where direct taxation was new to many communities. After 1912 direct taxes were introduced to various places in various years. Among the Yoruba the introduction of direct taxes in 1916 led to riots in Abeokuta and Iseyin. In other parts of the South taxation was introduced after World War I, where it was met with resentment and led to the 1929 Women's War in parts of Eastern Nigeria.

In the first three decades of the colonial administration taxation was not limited to the collection of money. Men and women were forced to work, that is, to provide labor in lieu of money. People aged fifteen to fifty were compelled to work in the building of roads and railways, at least for a period of six days in one quarter. Many, of course, were paid but below the minimum wage. In building the railways, which required a large amount of labor, over 30 percent of the workforce was obtained by forced labor. In local administration, the chiefs made extensive use of forced labor to build and maintain roads. There were cases of abuse, even the use of the system to victimize critics. It was not until the mid-1940s that the practice of forced labor began to decline considerably, especially at the local level.[31]

The colonial era witnessed changes in other spheres of life. Reference has been made to the role of the educated elite. The members of this elite were essentially products of missionary schools. The creation of schools began during the nineteenth century.[32] The colonial era provided the missions with the security they needed to move to many new areas and, in some cases, provided access to money to pay teachers and to run some schools. Once the advantages of Western education were realized, persuading Nigerians, especially in the South, to go to school was not difficult. The examples of wage earners, men competent in the use of the English language, and a generation that was displaying the acquisition of new tastes in attire and manners were among the compelling visible displays of the advantages of Western education for all to see. The educated elite always wanted more of everything. Upgraded in the nineteenth century as important participants in the foreign firms and the administration, they were to be downgraded after the 1880s. In the first three decades of colonial rule, the majority of them occupied subordinate positions in the colonial administration. This upset them a great deal, and many turned their attention to seeking the means to uplift themselves or to mobilize their peers to pressure the colonial system to reform itself.

Yet another aspect of change that is relevant to this study is urbanization and its political consequences in a colonial context.[33] Older cities expanded (for example, Kano and Ibadan), and new cities such as Kaduna, Port Harcourt, and Enugu were created to meet the needs of administration, the mining industry, and the railways. Economic considerations were the most important factors in the massive movements of people to the cities. The movement of people out of the rural areas was provoked by a host of factors: the search for employment; the limited opportunities for nonagricultural occupations in the villages; the need to seek money to pay colonial taxes; land infertility and other ecological problems in some areas; and the desire to escape from one place to another so as to overcome difficulties created by either the old order or even the new ones. The migrations took various forms, many of which have continued to this day. A 1957 study revealed that thousands traveled great distances on foot in search of money, food, and opportunities,[34] suggesting that migratory patterns were tied to economic needs. Many traveled shorter distances as well, to work as migrant laborers on farms and in households.[35] Some groups moved from hill settlements to the plains, others were attracted by the new railway stations, and still others moved out of Nigeria to Ghana, Gabon, Rio Muni, and Fernando Po. In general, colonial rule led to the regrouping of people and to the creation of new population units to meet the needs of the economy and the administration. Then and now, the movements have led to greater interactions among various groups, but in more recent years (from the 1960s onward), they also have generated conflicts and violence that have consumed thousands of lives and a great deal of property.

The majority of the migrants were young men and women, who were able to create a distinctive urban-cum-youth culture in music, dress, and lifestyles. The distinction between "traditional" living and "modern" living was being defined, as the cities had their nightclubs, vices, and pleasure-oriented occupations. The challenges of city life promoted a culture of individualism, as a person sought the means to survive and to climb up the social ladder. The universal religions of Islam and Christianity spread in the cities, sometimes appealing to the need to avoid the degeneracy of city life. The cities were also the home of the educated elite, whose members were able to develop interactions based on ethnicity and even broader national or professional ties. Various ideas on different aspects of society spread rather quickly and avenues for political expression were developed.

As attractive as the cities appeared from the point of view of employment, they have always posed problems for the country in terms of slums, refuse disposal, and crime. They all contributed to the country's development problems: how can the demands for roads, houses, schools, and social services be met? As Nigerians sought answers to some of these questions after 1940, more and more people began to listen to the promises of politicians and nationalists.

Ever since, such promises have been repeated by a succession of power seekers in the same way and words, even as the problems deepened.

The intensity of the migration and population movements could suggest evidence of greater integration in the country. On the one hand, economies were being integrated, especially in the distribution of commodities. On the other hand, political integration to achieve a stable nation-state was being complicated. When groups moved in large numbers to other areas, as the Igbo of the South did by moving to the North and the Hausa did by moving to the Middle Belt, the hosts tend first to welcome them but later to resent them as economic exploiters. Thus, the Igbo became despised in some places in the North, and the Hausa were regarded as enemies among the Tiv. This element of intergroup hostility has remained a feature of modern Nigeria, although it has not halted migrations and regular movements. Within the cities, tensions and stratification began to emerge. Where people moved to older cities, there were some tensions with the indigenous people over land and control of major markets. Where migrants lived together in the same neighborhood, as the sabon garis in the North, it ensured the emergence of a separate identity that, up until today in many cases, means that strangers and hosts are not integrated.

Furthermore, urbanization instigated the rise of ethnic-based associations, such as the Ibibio Union created in 1928. This was an attempt to promote associations outside of the homeland. In later unions, some grew big enough to promote politics and business. For instance, the various associations among the Igbo federated into the Ibo Federal Union, which supported a political party and the activities of Chief Nnamdi Azikiwe in the 1950s. Secret societies, churches, trade guilds, and other organizations also emerged to promote social and cultural activities as well as to build networks. Patrons emerged, men and women of power, wealth, and influence, who built their fame through their abilities to help others obtain jobs, admissions to schools, and access to resources, and to help others get out of trouble in case they were arrested by the police. Whether real or imagined, the common people believed that they needed patrons to survive in a competitive setting.

The cities favored a new class of Nigerians: the educated elite. Indeed, the spread of Western education was one of the greatest changes of the era. The foundation of Western education was established by the missionaries during the nineteenth century.[36] The number of schools increased substantially in the first decades of the twentieth century, various communities were energized to send their children to schools, and jobs were available to those with education at whatever level. A number of elite schools emerged, notably a few secondary schools in Lagos, Katsina, Ibadan, and Umuahia all of which were able to produce a generation of junior- and middle-level workers who worked for the government. The ambitious ones among them struggled to receive higher education or moved rapidly in the civil service and inherited power in the 1950s and 1960s.

Far more than many early missionaries anticipated, Nigerians quickly understood the values of higher education and professional training. Not a few began to dream of becoming doctors and lawyers.[37] Western education also created an elite that began to combine the values of old with the new—many developed preferences for monogamy, smaller households, and tastes for Western goods. They were similarly eager to enjoy new social services, such as healthcare (hospitals, dispensaries), recreation clubs, and sports and games, and they sought more facilities where there were not enough or when racism prevented their access to existing ones. Their tastes and preferences were to influence the contents of development plans after 1940.

If Western education created opportunities, it also generated problems that feature prominently in this book. To start with, opportunities were not available to all. Investments in education were limited, and senior officers were distrustful of the products of missionary schools that reminded them of egalitarian ideas and freedom. In addition, throughout the colonial period, the spread of Western education was uneven: the South had more schools than the North; the cities more than the rural areas. The political consequence, as we shall see later on, was that the North was afraid of being dominated by the South. But there was also a social consequence as well. Those who had education and jobs were far more empowered than those without. As the lifestyles of the educated became something to emulate, Nigerians began to equate education and the creation of more schools with economic development. In the language of nationalism, education would bring progress to the individual and development to the society. The demand for educational opportunities became one of the core areas of nationalist agitation and the conception of development and the country's future.

Policies and changes instigated various discourses and demands around progress, modernity, and nationalism. Of course, there were scattered acts of violence in the first three decades of colonial rule, especially in the rural areas where people expressed their opposition to taxation and some other policies.[38] Some acts of colonial resistance took a religious dimension (as in the case of the Mahdi eschatological rebellions in the North), women's protest (as in the case of the Women's War of 1929),[39] and students' activism.[40]

The educated elite capitalized on these various protests to develop their anticolonial nationalism, both in its philosophical and practical essence. Nationalism demanded freedom, liberation from colonial oppression and white racism. After 1940, the need for self-determination became paramount.

The foundations of political parties were laid in Lagos in the second decade, as associations emerged to demand reforms.[41] Other bigger parties followed, notably the Nigerian National Democratic Party (NNDP) in the 1920s and the Nigerian Youth Movement in the 1930s. Both wanted the establishment of a university, increase in political representation by Nigerians, adult suffrage, and greater economic opportunities for Nigerians.

The tone and intentions of pioneer nationalists were moderate, compared to those of their successors in the 1940s. "Nigeria has only one AIM," declared a major address in 1925, "only one THOUGHT, and only one DUTY and that is loyalty to the THRONE and person of the King-Emperor."[42] The pioneer nationalists were not contesting the survival of the colonial system but were more worried that elite interests were not given primary consideration by the colonial officers. Why was their number so small in the Legislative Council? Were indigenous chiefs more important than the elite were? Why could the chiefs not be removed by their own people? Why was there no university for them and their children to attend? Why were the Lebanese allowed to enter the country to compete with them? These and other questions along this line revealed their motivation: the colonial system should change to meet the demands of a new educated elite. But their agitation and various demands indicated the strong desire for progress, even if there was a selfish element to some of them.

The demands and discourses could create the impression that the intelligentsia and the people were united. Far from it, as the next chapter shows. The Nigerian society began to reveal the deep divisions that have characterized its modern history. It is a country, artificially created by the British who merged many indigenous groups and states. The provinces in the South and North were amalgamated in 1914, but this did not mean that the country was better unified in the way future nationalists would have wanted. Some common cultures were emerging around Western education, Islam, and Christianity. Civil servants were coming together in the cities and workplaces.

Nevertheless, the conditions for a country that would be fragile and divided were created in the first half of the twentieth century.[43] These divisions were spatial, economic, and social. The South and North were governed as if they were different countries, a situation that later led to the adoption of a federal system of government and intense regionalism. Very early in the colonial administration, officers in the South and North resisted the amalgamation of 1914, but the need to unify the railway systems in order to be able to move goods to the port and to use the revenues of the South to run the North compelled the leading policy makers to go ahead with the amalgamation. Nevertheless, the colonial government ensured that the North and South had minimal interaction. Lord Lugard, the architect of the amalgamation, was pro-North, preferring its "traditional" kings and chiefs to the so-called arrogant elite of the South. Not only did Lugard reject the idea of breaking the North into three provinces, he sought the means to prevent the "contamination" of its people by the southern elite. The little communication of the prewar years eventually led to the big problems of the post-1940 era.

Within the regions, groups and languages were treated differently, thus promoting the culture and politics of ethnicity. Islamic areas were regarded as superior to so-called pagan ones; larger groups, such as the Yoruba and Hausa, were accorded greater respect than the minorities, such as the Ijo and Tiv. Many British officers, including the prominent ones, such as Lord Lugard, preferred the North to the South, the Islamic intelligentsia in the North to the educated elite of the South. As early as 1911, a highly respected government official remarked that the British did not want the North to become like the South in many ways that were then considered negative:

> We want no violent changes, no transmogrification of the dignified and courteous Moslem into a trousered burlesque with a veneer of European civilization. We do not want to replace a patriarchal and venerable system of government by a discontented and irresponsible democracy of semi-educated politicians.[44]

Ethnicity was promoted, as groups and peoples were treated as "ethnic objects." As the division of society consolidated along regional/ethnic lines, Nigerians also began to think and organize themselves on the basis of ethnicity. Even groups in the same region began to fight over the location of administrative headquarters, schools, and the status of their traditional rulers in the hierarchies of chiefs.[45] Ethnic consciousness began to take deep root, as the educated elite and members of the political class began to mobilize and to profit from ethnicity. The so-called semi-educated politicians from the South began to see the North as backward, and its intelligentsia as too conservative. Southerners believed that the British fraudulently manipulated the political system and elections in favor of the North. This perception became a dangerous stereotype behind the formation of political parties and alliance formations in the 1950s and 1960s. The stereotype further deepened ethnic consciousness.

Economic and social development was uneven. The provision and expansion of Western education became a critical aspect of this disparity. Before the imposition of colonial rule, the North was far more educationally ahead of the South, but in Islamic and Arabic education. As Western education spread, progress in the North was slower. Unable to integrate Islamic education with many aspects of colonial changes, Western education began to acquire greater significance. However, with the missionary penetration slower than what obtained in the South, the North began to witness a disadvantage.[46] Areas with cash crops and minerals witnessed more progress than areas without. As the port became important, Lagos and the South grew economically more prosperous than the North, which became an hinterland enclave moving its goods and people southwards. There was an emerging division along social lines, between an educated elite and the rest of the population. Those with the qualifications in Western formal school were able to obtain jobs, to earn far more wages than their counterparts could make in traditional occupations, and they developed useful networks among themselves. The elite began to see its vision as the defining one for the country.

Politics and Economy in the War Years

Britain, like other colonial powers, drew its colonies into World War II.[47] Nigeria supplied raw materials, including established ones and even new trade items such as cassava starch.[48] Nigerians served in the army, and funds were raised to contribute to the war campaign.[49] This participation in the war unleashed reforms and changes at a faster speed than ever before. New ideas and contacts further instigated the spirit of nationalism among Nigerians. The contributions to the war encouraged Britain to be open to reforms, talking as if Africans deserved to be compensated for their efforts to win World War II.

To the colonizers and the colonized, World War II was a watershed in their history and relations. Nigerians were recruited as soldiers, with many finding themselves in Ethiopia and Burma. In both places, they served well as soldiers, carriers, and in other major roles assigned to them.[50] In a well-publicized "Win the War Fund," cash donations were collected from many people to finance the war, while farmers were asked to produce the needed commodities. The elite strongly believed that Adolf Hitler and fascism were far worse than British colonialism in Nigeria, and they were later to use some of the anti-German propaganda for their nationalist cause. In seeking an alternative to the Suez route, West Africa became a landing base for American and British troops. Lagos and Port Harcourt became ports to receive foreign troops.

In many ways, the war years encouraged greater demand for reforms and anticolonial polemics and actions. The Allied Powers gave the Nigerian nationalists many words to use against their colonial masters. In an effort to fend off German radio propaganda in West Africa, the British also launched their own, sometimes recruiting prominent Nigerians to broadcast on radio. When the Germans alleged that Nigerians were being forced to contribute money and serve in the British army, the sultan of Sokoto was used to fight back. "That is a lie," asserted the sultan, "and I would also like to ask Hitler whether it is by force that we gather in our mosques and schools and offer up prayers from our hearts, day and night, for the success of the British armies and the downfall of His Majesty's enemies."[51] If the Allied Powers described Hitler as an enemy of democracy, the British were themselves reminded that there was no democracy in Nigeria. A totalitarian colonial state was criticizing Germany for totalitarianism, a contradiction noted by Nigerians. If the Germans were criticized as racists, Nigerians had to remind the British that they, too, could not use the same facilities with whites. They expressed great disappointment when they learned that the Atlantic Charter would not apply to them.

Events and policies were undertaken in such a way as to begin to alter the colonial system. Using the need to win the war as an excuse, it became less tolerant of opposition. The student leaders of King's College, a leading secondary school, were expelled and conscripted into the army for criticizing the decision to take over the school's building for war aims. Evidence of urban discontent began to show in the early 1940s, due to inflation and scarcity of imported items.

Some events indicated that a successful attack against the colonialists was possible. France was defeated and its people divided during the war. Japan demonstrated an astonishing success in withstanding Europe and the United States. Nigerians recruited into the British army were not intimidated by the idea of European superiority that had characterized the colonial regimes. One can talk of a psychology of liberation from the idea of race superiority and colonial invincibility. A new mental outlook served the cause of nationalism.

International politics, too, was changing, some in favor of nationalism in Africa, but all definitely in a way that ensured that Europeans were no longer the only players in the politics of the continent. The French failed to sustain their hold on Indochina; India obtained independence in 1947; the United States and Soviet Russia became more powerful than Europe; and in England the Labour Party came to power and promised to promote freedom. New forces began to question the role of Europe in Africa. An often-cited source has been the Atlantic Charter, signed by Prime Minister Winston Churchill of Great Britain and President Franklin D. Roosevelt of the United States, part of which promised "the right of all peoples to choose the form of government under which they live." Although some high-ranking British politicians denied that this applied to Africa, left-leaning members of the Fabian Colonial Bureau were encouraging Africans to believe that the Atlantic Charter covered the whole world. As a critic of the British government told the highly inspired members of the West African Students' Union in 1940:

I want to see the time when West Africans will be able to govern themselves. I know that you have some meagre representation in your councils, but still the official mind dominates. It is almost as though, if good, you are invited into the parlour for a piece of cake.[52]

Whether they wanted independence for Africans or not, British politicians began to talk about the future of Nigeria and other colonies. In the United States, anticolonial opinions were growing stronger. Many began to wonder why they should assist Britain in a war to keep its colonies. Nigerians seized the moment, boldly asserting that the Atlantic Charter applied to them. Even communist ideas were beginning to spread slowly, although they never established any enduring impact. Young Nigerian nationalists were then receiving encouraging ideas from different parts of the world.

Other events and war-related circumstances favored the growing nationalist consciousness and the hope that the country's politics would be altered. Nigerians realized that the power of the colonial government and Britain as a whole were weakened by the war. Britain had lost its Far Eastern colonies to Japan, it needed Africans to help in regaining Burma, but even its "subjects" in Nigeria and other colonies had to be appealed to, rather than forced, to support the war. The Nigerians who served in the war were exposed to other cultures and ideas, and many were demanding freedom for their people. And, there were hundreds of others who worked at home in new jobs created by the needs of the war. For many, the dream of high wages and a comfortable lifestyle was unfulfilled, thereby creating a class of discontented people. A new generation of politicians were coming on the scene, now eager to exploit the changing situation. When the National Council of Nigeria and the Cameroons (later, the National Council of Nigerian Citizens [NCNC]) published its constitution in 1945, it gave prominent attention to the demand for "internal self government."[53]

If prewar political activities were mainly urban-based and elitist, conditions began to lead toward some kind of popular movement, as more and more people began to listen to anticolonial messages. Some economic conditions made this possible. A scarcity of products, including basic ones such as salt, led to inflation and rationing.[54] The people blamed scarcity and inflation on the government. Although the prices of cash crops went up, the government appropriated part of the profits through the marketing boards. The economic conditions made it possible for workers and politicians to unite and to speak with one voice. The politicians, such as Azikiwe, who controlled the media cleverly presented the voice of nationalism as the voice of the workers. Since the workers had incomes and were literate, this was also a clever marketing device, as the main buyers of the newspapers were those represented in editorials and news items. The nationalists with an eye on political power regarded the workers as allies, or at least those to be manipulated while they climbed the ladder of power. The workers thought they needed the nationalists for the strategy to employ against the colonial power. To the civil servants, who were prohibited from political statements, the nationalist media served their interests. This collaboration would sustain the formation and activities of political unions after 1945.

The war equally established its impact on the economy. The demand for some items, such as rubber and tin, led to greater production. In seeking the means to increase the production of raw materials, to curtail imports, and to prevent supplies going to enemy territories, the colonial governments embarked upon several new measures. The large firms were given quotas to purchase materials, which the government in turn bought from them. A supply board was created to determine quotas and prices. Restrictions were placed on imports; licenses were required to buy items from places other than Britain. The foreign firms enjoyed greater buying power, and Nigerian businesses found it very difficult to participate in the lucrative import-export trade. From a prewar monopoly on prices, the foreign firms moved to a monopoly on buying exports and selling imports, even establishing the Association of West African Merchants.[55] This arrangement angered ambitious Nigerians, thus becoming yet another reason for anticolonial sentiments. New firms could not be created, even by non-Nigerians, since there was no assurance that they would be allowed to take part in trade. It gave more power to colonial officers and the British government to regulate commerce. The instances of the use of power included the decision by the government to buy the entire cocoa crop in 1939, to control all exports after 1942, to control the issuance of licenses to selected firms, and to place a quota on goods that could be purchased from non-European sources such as India.

The control measures and other wartime policies affected Nigerians in different ways. On paper, it would seem as if the producers were prevented from being exploited by firms, since the government was able to fix prices. In reality, the prices were low, usually below the world prices. The underpayment to the producers enabled the firms to make profits and the government to raise money to finance the war without raising taxes. As pointed out in chapter 3, the marketing boards of the postwar years continued with this arrangement, thereby ensuring that millions of producers continued to contribute substantially to public revenues. To the Nigerian business owners, wartime controls denied them access to the most lucrative trade of buying crops. However, many were able to turn to retail trade, where they were far more efficient and competitive than the big firms in penetrating various parts of the country. Indeed, the war forced a number of foreign firms to close their retail stores, either because

Students enjoying a break at the University of Ibadan, Nigeria's first university. Photo by A. Olusegun Fayemi.

many of the expatriate staff were drafted for the war or because there were no imported goods to make them profitable.

One final outcome was the discussion and, later on, policies on "welfare and development." In influential corridors of power, some officers were beginning to talk of the responsibility of the colonial governments to the people, specifically how greater efforts should be expended on development and the possibility of preparing them for an active role in the management of their communities and administration. Some officers even feared that the failure to reform the economy and politics could trigger widespread violence. A significant response was taken in 1940 to create the Colonial Development and Welfare Act, which allocated a sum of £5 million a year to the development of all the British colonies. The Commission on Higher Education in West Africa was created, and it recommended the expansion of secondary and primary schools and the establishment of university colleges in Legon (Ghana) and Ibadan in Nigeria. The education of Africans was now regarded as important to other economic and social reforms.[56] It was recognized that health services were grossly inadequate, and promises were made for greater expansion.

Labor unions, workers, and the elite had to be placated, lest they organize and mobilize against the colonial government. Guidelines were provided on wages, arbitration, and how to resolve tension between workers and the government. The government would now have "labor advisers" who would work with workers to reduce conflicts. The educated elite would now be involved in the administration. A few Nigerians would be added to the Executive Councils of Nigeria, although initially as unofficial members, to break the total monopoly by Europeans on decision making. A few, too, would be admitted for the first time into the Administrative Service, the upper echelon of the colonial bureaucracy. A serious commitment was also made to write a new constitution, a major reform that ended in the country's independence.

Postwar Developments

From the position of Nigerians, especially the elite and nationalists, the colonial system needed to correct itself. From the view of the more combative anticolonial Nigerians, the colonial regime should be terminated and power given to Nigerians. From the view of the British, only reforms were necessary. Pressures were coming from different directions, even if the goals were different: from above, that is, the colonizers, and from below, that is, Nigerians. The pressure from both ultimately led to important changes in the economy and politics. Two broad areas, which form the themes of this book, focused the discussions on change and the future of Nigeria.

The first is the economy. To the British, the economy was working well enough, but many more people should benefit through social services. In other words, it should be possible to use part of their taxes to provide schools, hospitals, and roads, and to create additional jobs. Many Nigerians wanted all of the social and welfare services, but their views were different from those of their overlords. They found the pace of new-services creation rather slow, and they believed that all Nigerians should have access to modern amenities. In other words, development, rather than wealth transfer to Europe, should be the principal objective of the economy.

The second is politics. The complaints by Nigerians were too many and wide-ranging. Many aspects of local governments were found to be unsatisfactory. "People of Royal parentage," complained a group of people among the Yoruba, "are tigers and must feed upon the flesh of common people ... what we suffered cannot all be committed to writing."[57] In the East, the warrant chiefs were disliked for being arrogant, corrupt, and ostentatious in their lifestyles.[58] The situation was not different in the North, where the emirs enjoyed tremendous power. Even the officials and followers of the emirs, generally a large number, were accused of excesses.

Yet another widespread complaint was that the gap between colonial officials and the people was too wide. The number of officers was not that large, and they expected local chiefs to do most of their work for them. Avenues to report chiefs and local public staff were not many, even a language barrier made this difficult. To take one example, allegations of bribery were rather common, especially by court clerks, messengers and court members. However, reaching the senior colonial officials was so difficult that many chose to give the bribes demanded.

If the problems were recognized, the thinking in the 1940s was how many of them could be corrected. To the colonial officers, reforms were enough. Many among them were not prepared for the dissolution of the empire. The widespread opinion before the 1940s was that the "whiteman has come to stay as long as men lived."[59] During the 1940s, the belief among many officers was that what the colonial system required was to grant many concessions by way of reforms in order to prolong British rule.

However, this was an era when the number of anticolonial Nigerians was growing and radical nationalism was becoming fashionable. Some events consolidated previous efforts, such as the formation of political parties. Others amounted to a growing nationalist consciousness and radicalism. The Nigerian Youth Movement, the major party of the late 1930s, was becoming less influential in the 1940s. In its place was the NCNC founded in 1944, with Nnamdi Azikiwe as its general secretary and leading actor. Indeed, it would appear in the 1940s as if the Nigerian elite would all unite behind one political party, the NCNC, and present a common front. This was not to be. Obafemi Awolowo, later a chief and prominent leader, formed the Egbe Omo Oduduwa in 1945, a cultural association that became a political party and a major rival of the NCNC.

If the parties before the war were mainly elitist, their membership would expand after the war. There was the pool of ex-servicemen, whose horizons had been broadened by travel and service in the army. Many among them were radical, and many were not, but they were conscious of the need to participate in political activities or at least express anticolonial opinions. There was a growing number of students, even teenagers in secondary schools, who began to regard anticolonial slogans and statements as an expression of youth identity. There was also a growing number of workers who saw a need to unite and protest. Thus, the decade of the 1940s was Nigeria's radical moment, as a combination of activities by a younger generation and an aggressive media changed the tone of discourse.

Indeed, the rising power of workers began to manifest itself in the 1940s. Between 1945 and 1950, the country recorded many cases of strikes and workers' protests. Before this period, the ability of workers to influence politics was very much limited. Unlike farmers, traders, and others in indigenous occupations, the number of workers was rather small for a long time. Even this small size was largely made up of the staffs of European firms and colonial governments. There were some strikes and protests, but these were largely to seek improvements to wages and benefits, rather than an end to the colonial system. The most active before the war were civil servants, railway workers, and teachers. They formed unions, and their leaders made moderate demands, as most feared termination, demotion, or other forms of punishment. The situation changed in the 1940s, and beyond, as the number of salaried workers and labor unions increased. Although the unions were small in membership, their number increased from five to seventy in the early 1940s, and they all came together under an umbrella organization, the Nigerian Trades Union Congress.

The most intense expression of labor power came in 1945 when the unions organized a general strike. Michael Imoudu, the president of the Railway Workers Union, was thrown into a position of national leadership, an opportunity that he used to empower the workers. Their reason was to protest inflation and demand better pay. Very quickly the strike acquired the elements of nationalist agitation. This was the first time that many unions, with a membership of over thirty thousand workers, would organize a big strike. It was long-drawn, lasting thirty-seven days. Essential services, notably the railway and postal services, were affected.

The general strike received support from the NCNC, and Azikiwe used his newspaper, the *West African Pilot*, to support the workers. Many Nigerians came to the conclusion that they could be truly powerful if they could unite. On one occasion in 1948, cocoa farmers also demonstrated what unity could achieve. Coming together under an umbrella association known as the Maiyegun—"straighten the world"—they protested the injustice of low prices. When the government decided to destroy the cocoa trees affected by swollen shoot, a bug infestation, members of the Maiyegun organized armed protest against government cutting gangs.

Arguably the most radical movement of the time was the Zikists, an organization that regarded Azikiwe as a hero. Founded in 1946, its main mission was opposition to British rule. It sought to bring together union leaders, students, and left-oriented youth. Raji Abdallah, a self-proclaimed radical, was the president of the Zikists, while Nduka Eze, a labor leader, and Mokwugo Okoye, an ex-servicemen, were other prominent members. This was a group of highly inspired young men, and the organization boasted a membership of over one thousand people.[60] They espoused a socialist philosophy, although their agenda for the country was not always specified in details. As to their anticolonial stand, no contemporary doubted the sincerity of the Zikists, even if their style did cause some stir in less radical circles. "I hate the Union Jack with all my heart," declared the fiery Abdallah in 1949, "It is a symbol of persecution and brutality."[61] Abdallah's combative speeches led to his arrest and trial for sedition. He and some other members of the Zikists headed to prison.

The peak of the radical attainment of the Zikists was reached in 1949, following a crisis known as the Enugu Colliery Shooting Incident. It started as a strike of coal miners for better pay and improved facilities. A white officer in charge of a police detachment opened fire on them, killing eighteen and wounding thirty-one. This crisis galvanized anticolonial protests led by the Zikists. In a series of anticolonial riots, more lives were lost. The government proscribed the Zikists and jailed many of their leaders in 1950. Azikiwe dissociated himself from the Zikists, even using his newspaper to ridicule those in jail. The collapse of the Zikists in 1950 meant, in part, that the organization of politics along ideological lines was in trouble. In that decade, regionalism took a stronger hold. The young radicals lost hope in Azikiwe who, according to Okoye, was himself scared of a revolution.[62]

The colonial government responded to all these pressures by initiating political reforms after 1945.[63] Some aspects of indirect rule were changed to reflect the demand to include educated elite in the government. In 1946 the Legislative Council was reconstituted to deal with the reality that Nigerians were ignored. Before the reform, the Legislative Council was dominated by ex-officio members. The Richards Constitution of 1946 introduced an unofficial majority to the council. In addition, three regional councils were established in the East, North and West, although the country was yet to have a three-regional structure.[64] Five years later, a revised constitution divided the country into three regions and led to an elected government. The 1951 Constitution instigated the formation of political parties and an intense rivalry for power.

The transfer of power witnessed an accelerated pace in the 1950s. Three major political parties contested the election to the Houses of Assembly: the National Council of Nigeria and the Cameroons (NCNC), the Action Group (AG), and the Northern People's Congress (NPC). The politicians made various complaints about the constitution and the political process. Far-reaching changes were again made to the constitution. A federal system was adopted in 1954 and Nigerians began to control the regions. Internal self-governments were granted to the East and West in 1956 and to the North in 1959. The Nigerian Independence Act granted complete independence to the country on October 1, 1960.

A new university at Ibadan was now functioning, providing the first local advantage in higher education to a tiny elite. Opportunities increased for Nigerians in most sectors. A Nigerianization program started in 1948 meant that there were jobs for those with formal skills. Recruitment into the civil service expanded more than ever before, and rapid promotion was ensured.[65] The fire-eating union leaders of the mid-1940s calmed down, and there was no serious strike until after the country's independence. Imported goods were available and at affordable prices. Nigerians began to believe that the transfer of power had enormous advantages to the elite. They would certainly become mobile. The dream was to replace Europeans and acquire their lifestyles.

Changes in the economy were equally important, if less dramatic. In the 1940s, development planning entered the agenda and colonial vocabulary. Resources were now to be allocated to social services, education, and projects that could generate jobs. A number of economically oriented projects were created. The economy witnessed an expansion, and more changes came in the 1950s as the regional governments embarked on many new programs. The export of primary products increased, and the government, through the marketing boards, was able to make more money. Imports, too, expanded, although trade terms were not still in balance. A host of local entrepreneurs began to rise and benefit in the informal sector, while wage earners saw a rise in income. New industries were being created to substitute the importation of cement, cigarettes, and beer. The industries created more jobs, and encouraged the emergence of a tiny group of industrialists. As Nigerians began to award major contracts in the 1950s, some contractors were able to grow rich. The shortage of capital that had prevented many from competing with expatriate firms was now being solved, as the politicians could reward their friends and associates with government contracts.

The members of the Nigerian political class were quick to discover how lucrative power could be. So also did they realize that power could be used to transform people's lives. In the economic programs of the 1950s, the regional governments were quick to spend the money accumulated by the marketing boards and additional revenues from exports. Small-scale farmers made this wealth possible, as the marketing boards bought from them at prices lower than what obtained in the international market. The regional governments decided to use the surpluses on what they presented to the public as development projects, a continuation of the development planning efforts of the colonial government. Some projects were visible and immediate, notably new roads, hospitals, schools, and public libraries. Some were notable for their big impact, such as the universities established in the early 1960s. The results of some were unclear, such as huge investments on mechanized agriculture. Attempts were also made to create industries; indeed, there was much optimism that heavy industries would emerge to transform the country within a limited period of time. A few industries failed in the early stages, simply because not much planning went into them or because the foreign partners cheated.

Euphoria and Caution

The years after 1945 witnessed great expectations on the part of Nigerians that they were on the threshold of change. Indeed, the mood for most of the 1940s and 1950s was one of great optimism. A review of the statements by leading politicians indicates that they regarded British colonialism as the greatest obstacle to progress. They exaggerated their own abilities and intellect to bring about rapid transformation. As the majority of the population were farmers and rural-based, they promised far more than was possible, speaking as if the countryside would be urbanized within a short time. They also exaggerated the consequences of planning.

The establishment of schools was a top priority. The people and the governments correlated educational expansion with economic expansion, assuming and planning that the establishment of schools would bring about immediate economic changes. The expansion to the educational system consumed as high as 40 percent of the regional budgets in the 1950s. This became one of the major achievements of the period, but it was not without its impact on the exaggerated expectation that development would follow rather quickly, in addition to instigating a pressure to abandon the rural areas in preference for cities.

Nevertheless, there was a huge contradiction, as the signals of trouble were becoming more and more clear after 1951. Politics was a competition with bitterness, dominated by violence, a spirit of "winner takes all," intense regionalism and an interpersonal animosity. In the social and economic sectors, it was clear by the early 1960s that the leaders would not deliver what they had promised. They seemed more concerned with their own egos, political survival, and personal enrichment than pursuing policies to liberate the poor. They deserve credit for expanding the educational system, far more than the British did, but class inequality was emerging. On the one hand, the rural areas were becoming more and more underdeveloped. Once the young men and women finished school, there was nothing for them to do in the rural areas. On the other hand, the income differential between those with higher education and those without was wide. As ordinary as it may sound, people needed the good jobs and education to have access to cars, televisions, good food, and decent accommodation. In the 1950s and 1960s, the Nigerian elite deliberately sought to re-create the privileges enjoyed by the British officers in terms of wages, pension, vacation, and benefits. Forgetting that the number of officers was small and that re-creating their conditions of work would become costly, this orientation created social and economic differentials that became hard to sustain in later decades.

There were problems far beyond the control of the new leaders to handle, but these would heavily weigh down on the country in future decades. First, as

Western medicine was gaining popularity, established indigenous means were losing more and more popularity. In addition, Western medicine requires personnel and infrastructure; and the needs of the population continually grew faster than the available facilities.

The same crisis occurred with food production. The colonial economy was based on agriculture. However, there were problems that subsequently created food scarcity and massive importation from the 1970s onward. By focusing on export crops, the economy took a decisive step in the devastation of food production. Land meant for food crop production was instead dedicated to cocoa, peanuts, and other more lucrative products. There was also the crisis of occasional drought and famine, especially in the North. Although many first generation Nigerian politicians saw the need to make agriculture the cornerstone of the economy, the reliance on oil after 1967 led to the rapid abandonment of this idea, as it became far easier to generate revenues on oil than agriculture.

The country's population grew for most of the twentieth century. Comments on growth are always based on observable data and raw estimates, as all the censuses in the country's history have one problem or another, including undercounting or "cooked" figures to make political gains.[66] That the population is large is not a point of contest, but how large it is remains unknown. A 1963 census put the population at 55 million, a phenomenal growth within ten years, as a previous 1953 figure stood at 30 million. The growth has been explained as owing to an improved standard of living, better communications, and health facilities.

Finally, the politicians underestimated the legacies of colonial rule. The assumption was that once they had power, this would translate into command of the economy and control of revenues. It was not to be. To start with, the British had ensured that independence would not bring about an economic revolution. Those who inherited power were not thinking of nationalizing the economy or even overcoming dependence. Rather, they saw Britain as a source of financial support. The colonial economic structure survived into independence. By and large, the economy still revolved around the export-import trade. As Nigeria conducted its international politics in the early 1960s, it did so merely to reinforce economic dependence on the West. Capital flight continued in the form of raw materials, foreign reserves kept in Britain, and the payment of pensions and salaries to departing colonial officers.

The chapters that follow elaborate on many of the aforementioned issues from the 1940s to the mid-1960s. In chapter 2, I analyze the political trends during the colonial period, paying attention to the major reforms after 1945 that led to the country's independence. The political system collapsed in 1966, thereby setting the stage for an era that was dominated by military regimes and the oil industry. The remaining chapters consider the economy in phases, starting with the foundation of the modern economy during the twentieth century, the changes after 1940, and the various attempts to attain development during the 1950s and 1960s. The analysis reveals a paradox: in spite of the incremental growth in the economy, the cumulative achievements did not lead to a developed nation.

2

The Political Context of Economic Reforms and Modernization

Economic reforms and changes occur in a political environment. There should be a vast difference in commitment to development between a government controlled by the British and one controlled by the Nigerians, while the approaches to economic planning can differ on the basis of political leaders' ideological leanings. How one government manages and utilizes resources for development purposes can be different from another, based on the interests of those who control power and the overall objectives of the economy. There also can be the issue of agencies that manage development programs, as in the examples provided in chapter 4. As the country moved from a "unitary" colonial system to a federal one, its leaders had to determine how to allocate responsibilities to various tiers of government and, if possible, to coordinate the works of various development agencies. The process of appointing political leaders, and the conflicts generated by the process can impact upon the economy. Whether a government is successful or not, there are agents in the society, such as churches, communities, and voluntary associations that participate in economic activities and development projects. These agents also take part in the socialization of individuals into society and inculcate values in people that may shape the way they interpret their economic values and reality. The socialization agencies and the government are expected to produce excellent "managers" who will initiate new ideas and control the economy. The inefficiency and values of managers will shape various aspects of the economy. Would they seek the means to attain rapid development? Would the country be integrated by way of bringing ethnic groups together? How would they consider the issues of culture and religion in making economic decisions? Would wealth distribution lead to widening the gap between the poor and the rich?

The impact of the international system is also part of politics: to what extent do relations with the West affect the economic development of the country? In a colonial situation, the country was subjected to exploitation and domination. Part of what independence was supposed to accomplish was to minimize that domination and to seek the means of controlling the economy. It was expected that Nigerian leaders would be in a position to negotiate better prices, to use the money they made to diversify the economy, and to expand opportunities in a way that the country would be able to consume most of its own products and rely less and less on imports.

In what follows, I identify the essential elements in the politics of the last years of colonial rule and the short-lived First Republic when Nigerians managed their own country. Two issues are worth emphasizing in order to underscore the significance of the chapter. The process of the transfer of power, as well as the experiment in handling a new country, affected economic performance. In addition, the political process should be regarded as part of the process of "modernization" itself. In other words, the progress or otherwise in stabilizing politics was regarded by contemporaries as part of "development." The following examples bring home this point with real-life experiences: if a farmer made good income from the sale of his crops, but he could not send his children to school as he had hoped, or, if a politician who had rigged an election was in power, each would be inclined to say that he and the country were not doing well. It has come to be the case with Nigeria that political mismanagement goes hand in hand with economic decline. Thus, it is even unnecessary to justify a discussion of politics in the analysis of Nigeria's economy, as its impact looms large.

Constitutional Reforms and Federalism

The dismantling of British rule began after World War II. Colonial rule did not last as long as many officers had expected, the process to end it took fifteen years, and it was mainly peaceful and through constitutional means. The first major political reaction to the various demands for change by Nigerians and also the first comprehensive initiative by the colonial authorities was to offer a new constitution. As it turned out, Nigeria's political future revolved around the various modifications to the constitution and the competition for power on the principles stated in this legal document. The nationalists were not freedom fighters who had to spill their blood or go to jail before the British decided to leave the country.

The first constitutional initiative, by Sir Arthur Richards, the governor in the mid-1940s, was greeted with much opposition, a manifestation of the growing assertiveness of the Nigerian nationalists. The subsequent constitutional changes in the 1950s brought to the fore the intensity of regionalism, as political leaders looked at issues from their ethnic or regional considerations. The constitution-making process revealed the fractured nature of the political system as well as the society itself.

Sir Arthur Richards governed Nigeria from 1943 to 1947 and gave his name to the first major constitution. To his subordinate colonial officers, he was a reform-oriented governor. To the Nigerian politicians and trade union leaders, he was a dictator, sometimes portrayed as cruel and nicknamed "Richard Iron Hand." Both assessments have a validity to them. On the positive side, Richards was less hostile to the educated elite, that is, compared to many of his predecessors. He was willing to listen to some educated men and also to reform the government in a way that would involve some elite members. To the Nigerian elite and nationalist leaders, the constitution was "unconstitutional" in that its writing did not involve them, members of the public did not discuss it, and, in England, it was passed in the House of Commons after a discussion that lasted no longer than thirty minutes.

The Richards Constitution saw Nigeria as an amalgamation of different people and groups that had to be governed separately. The philosophy of indirect rule and provincial administrations was taken for granted, as the constitution actually fragmented the country. The country was divided into the three regions of East, West, and North, each under a chief commissioner. This division introduced the idea of regionalism that created problems in later years. The regions were not equal in size or population: the North was three-quarters of the entire country and represented half of the population; the West and East were almost equal in size. There would be three Regional Houses of Assembly, located at Enugu in the East, Ibadan in the West, and Kaduna in the North, each to comprise an almost equal number of official and nonofficial members. The House could discuss general legislation and pass the budget for its region. In addition, the North would have a House of Chiefs, to give a forum to the emirs and high-ranking traditional dignitaries. The constitution also made room for a central Legislative Council, again comprising official and nonofficial members. The nonofficial members would be nominated by the governor and a few would be selected by the local governments. Only four members in the Legislative Council (one from Calabar and three from Lagos, as in previous years) would be elected.

The Nigerian leaders and newspaper publishers criticized various aspects of the Richards Constitution.[1] They complained that they were not involved in its formulation, and criticized various aspects of the constitution. The Nigerian leaders, especially those based in the South, believed that the constitution unsuccessfully balanced the requirements of indirect rule and those of parliamentary democracy. While they sought power, some also wanted a united country and complained that the idea of regionalism was a policy of "divide and rule." However, in the North, the distribution of power was found acceptable simply because they feared that the elite from the South could use a unitary constitution to control them. The Nigerian elite also complained that the constitution did not give them ministerial appointments or make provision for democratic representation.

The Richards Constitution enabled the National Council of Nigeria and the Cameroons (NCNC), then the only major party in the country, to turn the opposition to the constitution into a major political advantage. The NCNC rejected the idea of regionalism and called for greater unity. The party mobilized resources to attack the constitution both within the country and in England. Azikiwe showed his skills as a political organizer, orator, and critic. He raised money to campaign against the Richards Constitution, including a delegation to England. Little was achieved from the trip, which generated the first major discourse on political corruption, as the NCNC was accused of using the protest to raise money that ended up in private pockets. Azikiwe and the party had to beat a retreat, and both went into silence from 1948 to 1951.

The Richards Constitution did not last the nine years anticipated by its originator. When Sir John Macpherson came to power in 1948, one of his immediate programs was to revise the Richards Constitution. Determined to involve Nigerians, the government formulated fourteen questions and requested people at the various tiers of government to consider them and respond in writing.[2] A revised constitution emerged in 1951. As recommendations diverged remarkably between the South and North, the Macpherson Constitution adopted a compromise by retaining the three regions, not just with administrative power as before but as political entities with large legislative and executive powers. The judiciary and the public service were retained as unified agencies. The idea of a tri-regional framework was acceptable to the North and the West. The Northern Region had dominant representation in a central house, equal in power to the rest of the country. The regional bodies were invested with legislative power on issues spelt out in the constitution or delegated to them by the central authority. The country would have a Council of Ministers, whose job was to advise the governor on various issues.

The southern politicians criticized the Macpherson Constitution. To Awolowo, a southern politician, the power of the North would make federalism difficult to operate. A widespread criticism was that the Macpherson Constitution failed to define the relationship between the regions and the central government. There was no provision to resolve possible conflicts between tiers of government, especially in situations in which a regional government decided to embark upon a course different from that of the center. It was unclear whether the Macpherson Constitution wanted to promote a unitary or federal system, and the blending of both left confusion as to how to allocate functions to the federal and regional governments.

In spite of the various criticisms, the British and the Nigerian politicians were now agreed that independence was visible. Power would be gradually transferred to Nigerians. A general election was held in 1952. On the last day of March 1953, Anthony Enahoro, a member of the Action Group (AG), tabled a motion in the House of Representatives: "That this House accepts as a primary political objective the attainment of self-government for Nigeria in 1956."[3] Alhaji Ahmadu Bello, the sardauna of Sokoto and leader of the Northern People's Congress (NPC), called for an amendment to change the date from 1956 to "as soon as practicable." The disagreement generated by this difference in date created a major political uproar and violence in 1953. The North threatened to secede, and the Kano riots of 1953 instigated the revision of the constitution.

The Federal House of Assembly did not work as well as anticipated by the Macpherson Constitution. Each regional assembly was to send a certain number of delegates to the central house. Two major constitutional conferences were held in 1953 to discuss a better federal constitution.[4] The outcome was the Lyttleton Constitution of 1954, which gave more power to the regions in a federal system. The Lyttleton Constitution gave the federal government the power to make law on a wide range of subjects: aviation, census, banking, customs, citizenship, defense, copyright, currency, external relations, deportation, immigration and emigration, various aspects of higher education, railways, mining, police, interregional commerce, interregional water, trunk roads, weights and measures, radio, and television. The power of the regions was defined in a concurrent list, and should the federal government legislate on any item in this list, it would be up to a regional government to adopt it or not. These included matters on antiquities, bankruptcy, electricity, commercial combines, labor, some aspects of higher education, national parks, surveys, tourist traffic, public safety, and water power. Where the federal government was not empowered to act on an issue, the assumption was that that power would be exercised by the regions. The financial relations between the center and regions

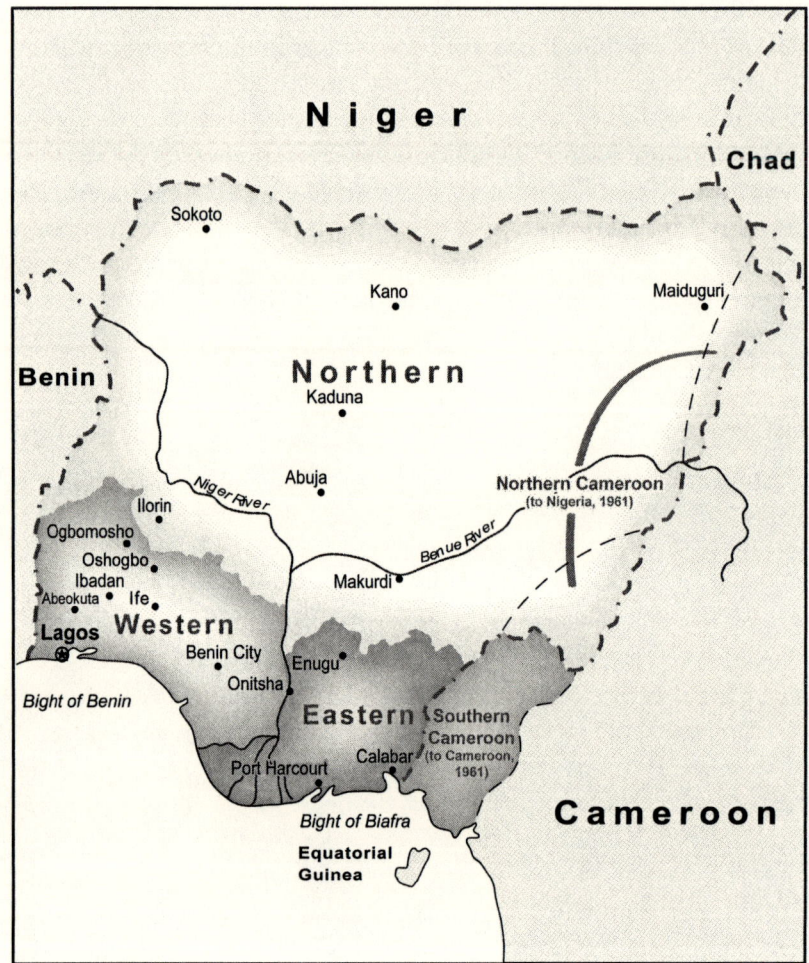

Nigerian States, 1955–1963

were also altered: statutory grants to the regions would end, the main revenues would be shared, and part of the country's reserves would be distributed to the regions. Other than the army, the foreign service, and the federal civil service, all other institutions were regional.

To reflect the new changes, the country was to be called the Federation of Nigeria, headed by a governor-general, and the heads of the regions would be known as governors. The federal cabinet would be comprised of the governor-general, the chief secretary, the attorney-general, the financial secretary, and ten Nigerian ministers, three from each region and one from the Southern Cameroons. The ministers would also be members of the legislature, each would head a government department that he would direct. The federal legislative body, the House of Representatives, would then be selected by popular elections. The Southern Cameroons would no longer be part of the East, now constituted into a quasi-federal territory with its own leader.

The regional governments acquired considerable autonomy in economic and social matters. They were free to initiate and plan their economic programs. The fiscal and judicial systems were reorganized to conform to a federal system. Events now began to move rapidly toward independence. Other constitutional conferences were held that granted power to Nigerians.[5] Each conference was a pressure on the British to leave and on Nigerian leaders to negotiate power among themselves. The Eastern and Western Regions obtained internal self-government in 1957, and the Northern Region did so in 1959. Complete independence was granted in 1960, with a new constitution that repeated the provisions in the previous one. The federal government was under the leadership of Alhaji Sir Abubakar Tafawa Balewa, the prime minister, who presided over a weak coalition of two political parties. On October 1, 1960, the country attained its full independence.

The choice of federalism was partly predicated on ethnic differences. The assumption was that Nigerian groups were too many and so divided that a government that would keep them apart as much as possible would be the best for them. As to the diversity of the groups, there can be no doubt. Of the more than 250 groups, three are large: the Hausa-speaking people in the North, the Yoruba in the West, and the Igbo in the East. As political parties were being formed, the identities of these three were also becoming solidified in a way that a major political party represented each of them.

Eager to attain power, the politicians focused their primary attention on how to obtain power. And, eager to depart, the British were less willing to invest time in solving the major problems that the colonial government and the constitution-making process had created. To start with, the process of attaining independence did not ensure or put in place adequate conditions for the country to become united. The constitution wanted to minimize interregional conflicts, but politics attained the opposite. Rather than a nationalism that would build one nation taking hold, what happened was ethnic nationalism. No national party emerged, no national statesman was produced, and no strong national movement came to the fore. To keep the various ethnic groups together, a federal constitution ensured the distribution of power among the regions. However, for the constitution to function in practice, the political leaders needed to be skillful and able to compromise.

The inability to overcome ethnic divisions gave rise to a host of other problems. One concerned how to divide the country's national revenues. The constitutional changes that led to the adoption of a federal system created the need to examine the allocation of revenue. Thus in 1946, the government appointed Sir Sydney Phillipson, the country's financial secretary, to provide a formula to share revenues following the implementation of the Richards Constitution. Phillipson recommended that the revenues of a region should come from a block grant allocated by the central government and the taxes and fees collected in each region.[6] Four years later, a commission was established to revisit the issue, and its recommendations were enacted into law as the Nigeria (Revenue Allocation) Order in Council of December 4, 1951. In addition to the revenues they were able to generate, the centrally collected revenues were to be distributed on the principles of derivation (the area that generated the income), needs, and national interest.[7] The regions were vested with the power of fixing and collecting tax, and they were to collect grants to cover the expenses of the police.

Six years later, the Fiscal Commission was appointed to review the formula, following some changes to the constitution. The commission rejected the principles of derivation, but its recommendation still recognized the need to reward areas that generated the income. Duties collected on crops and hides and skins were to be returned to the regions that produced them. Derivation was to be used to distribute revenues made from tobacco, diesel oil, and motor spirit. Where money was made from minerals (rents, mining royalties, and fees) 50 percent would go to the region with the deposit. The regions would control income tax. An innovation was the creation of a "distributable pool" of central funds, comprising funds collected from mining revenues (30 percent) and import revenues (30 percent). The distributable pool was to be divided into three: the West was to receive 24 percent, the East 31 percent, and the North 40 percent. The remainder would be used as grants to meet some special needs.[8]

Political Parties and Leadership

Political parties occupied a central position in the events leading to independence and the politics of the First Republic. They started as small associations in the second decade of the twentieth century, concerned with the need to seek reforms, to protest a number of colonial policies that the elite did not like, and to fight cases of racial discrimination. At the forefront of the nationalist politics and associations were the members of the educated elite. In their various writings and political ideas, they began to define the nation, describing themselves as Nigerians, proposing ideas to change the country, and arguing that power should belong to them rather than to the traditional elite supplanted by the British. They accepted many European ideas and values, without being hostile to local cultures.⁹ If nationalism was defined strictly to mean a demand for independence, this group would not have qualified as nationalists, as their main concern was how the colonial system would improve. But they expressed great patriotic positions, such as love for the black race and its culture, and they also identified with the spirit and ideas of Pan-Africanism, which sought the unity of the blacks in fighting white domination and racial injustice.¹⁰ Their methods were nonviolent; they preferred to write, send delegations, explore the channels opened by the colonial government, and publish anticolonial ideas in the media. Those who worked with the church also used religion to empower themselves by creating independent ones, free of European officers and with messages more adapted to the Nigerian culture.¹¹ The hostility between the colonial officers and the elite served to deepen nationalist consciousness. Those of them interested in business found it hard to compete with European and Lebanese firms. Those in the church had to accept the control of European senior clergy. Those who sought jobs in the civil service could not move to senior positions, and the enterprising ones had to seek avenues in law, medicine, and other services outside the domination of the government.

Arguably the most important protest movement in the early years was associated with the National Congress of British West Africa, formed in 1913 but inactive for seven years because of World War I. It was formed by members of the educated elite based throughout the West African coastal cities, and it attested to the relationships that many had forged, in spite of their different locations, on the basis of family connections, attendance at the same college, and reading similar literature. The congress held its first meeting in Accra in 1920, with delegates from the four British West African colonies.

In a brilliant manner, the delegates consolidated all the wishes and demands of members of the educated elite, a long list that included the establishment of a West African university, the creation of a West African Dominion (similar to that of Australia, India, and Canada) able to speak with one voice, the creation of municipal councils for cities, the establishment of a House of Assembly with power over budget and taxation, and the election of Africans to the colonial legislative councils. When the congress sent a delegation to the secretary of state for the colonies in London, the colonial officers on the spot believed that they had gone too far. The fear of the so-called power-hungry elite could become real, and an attack came from the governor of Nigeria, Hugh Clifford:

> a self-selected and self-appointed congregation of educated African gentlemen ... whose eyes are fixed, not upon their own tribal obligations and the duties to their Natural Rulers which immemorial Custom should impose upon them, but upon political theories evolved by Europeans to fit a

wholly different environment, for the government of peoples who have arrived at a wholly different stage of civilization.[12]

Although the congress was successfully challenged by the British, political expression and associations by the elite did not come to an end. Politics was still dominated by elite members. Either in collective associations or as individuals, concerns were mainly about the empowerment of this minority: they wanted to participate in the administration; they were not happy that traditional chiefs had more power than they did; they demanded the creation of schools in order to reproduce themselves; and they wanted more access to business opportunities.

In 1922 the colonial government allowed Nigerians to have four of the forty-six seats in the Legislative Council, three to be elected from Lagos and one from Calabar, that is, in addition to another smaller number of nominated members. Members of the educated elite were now represented, albeit by a small number; however, the governor could dismiss their views at meetings. Herbert Macaulay, now one of the country's political heroes, established the Nigerian National Democratic Party (NNDP) to contest the three seats in Lagos. Essentially based in Lagos, the party was only national in name. However, it performed the functions of a political party, even if not always in a democratic manner. Macaulay was deeply involved in Lagos politics, especially in the prolonged and bitter fight that led to the deposition in 1925 of a high-ranking chief, the Eleko, as well as his restoration in 1931.[13] The NNDP had a manifesto that demanded the establishment of a university, the introduction of free compulsory primary education, and the abolition of provincial courts. The NNDP was successful in all the elections until 1938, and it was able to win the respect of many people, including traditional chiefs, market women, and members of the educated elite. Throughout the 1920s and 1930s, the wishes and grievances of the pioneer politicians were clear: they did not like the indirect-rule system, which they regarded as preventing the most enlightened members of the country from being involved in politics; they believed that the pace of "modernization" was slow; they wanted more Nigerians to serve in the civil service, especially in senior positions; and they accused the British of racism and discrimination.

The beginning of a radical political orientation began in the 1930s, with the formation of the Lagos Youth Movement (LYM), later renamed the Nigerian Youth Movement (NYM). From this decade onward, politics began to move beyond the restricted membership of the Lagos elite to involve others in different locations. The issues began to broaden into wide-ranging reforms, even to asking the British to leave the country. A new generation began to criticize the previous ones for their conservatism. The increase in the number of Nigerians in institutions of higher learning in the country and abroad enlarged the membership of political associations.

The NYM was established to protest the inadequacies of the Yaba Higher College as an institution of higher education in the country. Yaba was opened in 1934, but many members of the Nigerian educated elite were not satisfied with the diplomas that it would award; they regarded them as inferior to those of a British university. With a firm belief that education in general, and higher education in particular, was needed to fight the British and, ultimately, to end their control of the country, the Nigerian critics of Yaba used the opportunity to create a political platform. Yaba was competitive because only a small number (about thirty each year) could be admitted. After gaining admission, the weeding out was ruthless, as a high percentage was asked to withdraw after the first-year examination. To those who survived, their professional degrees were regarded as less worthy than the British ones. Thus, rather than becoming an engineer, the product of Yaba could only get a job as an engineering assistant. Those with the resources or the necessary survival skills to travel later went abroad. Those without saw nationalist agitation as one way of overcoming colonial subordination.

In the Lagos election of 1938 the NYM won all the three seats, thereby ending the fame of the NNDP. The NYM was more national and more radical than the NNDP, but its manifesto was not so much different. Nigerian students were also mobilizing abroad, connecting themselves to the broader, socialist-oriented platform of the Pan-Africanist Movement. Some were followers of Marcus Garvey, the radical Jamaican Pan-Africanist who died in 1940. Unlike the NNDP, the NYM was very aggressive in criticizing the British and in describing many Nigerian elite as rather timid. Nnamdi Azikiwe, who joined the NYM in 1937, added to the combative polemic of the period. In 1938, he warned the British that

> all is not well and that the era of submission, without constitutional opposition and all the concomitants of Uncle Tomism, is gone. And that the Nigeria of today and tomorrow must realise that it is part of the Sleeping African Giant who must be awakened from its deep sleep, in order to harness its energy and usher in a New Nigeria.[14]

This mood continued into the 1940s, leading to the General Strike of 1945. However, radicalism was not sustained in the nationalist movement. The NYM itself was split by personality rivalry and, by 1941, had become an essentially Yoruba party. Rather than pursue collective national politics, the new leaders began to solidify their cultural and ethnic base.[15] Indeed, by the 1950s radicalism became the ideology of a minority. The radical members among the trade unions had limited impact on the outcome of the political struggles. And although many people and groups now identified themselves with the nationalist cause, the rural side was not well integrated with the political process. Indeed, nationalism was dominated by a tiny elite, with the support of trade unions and organized commercial interests, such as women traders. The dominant actors in the process, the politicians of the 1940s and 50s, did not pursue a radical ideology, but very quickly regarded independence as an opportunity to promote self-interest. Parties and leadership were strongly entrenched in regions, and ethnicity became a major issue.

The major players who emerged were Nnamdi Azikiwe and the NCNC, Obafemi Awolowo and the AG, and the Sardauna Alhaji Ahmadu Bello and the NPC. Although they all cast themselves in the mold of national leaders, their rivalry and strategies of political mobilization reveal very clearly that they were ethnic and regional leaders. By 1960 these three major political parties were in existence, each representing a region of the country. They were the National Council of Nigeria and the Cameroons (later, the National Council of Nigerian Citizens, NCNC), the Action Group (AG), and the Northern People's Congress (NPC). Since the country practiced a multiparty system, there were many small parties and, arguably, the most significant, largely in terms of its leftist tendencies, was the Northern Elements Progressive Union (NEPU).[16] The three leaders and their parties are examined in turn.

The NCNC and Chief Nnamdi Azikiwe

The first post–World War II political party was the NCNC, which called for a political democracy that would unify the country. The leading figure in the NCNC was Chief Nnamdi Azikiwe. He was born in Zungeru, a railway station town in Northern Nigeria. His father was a first generation Igbo educated elite who worked as a civil servant. The senior Azikiwe complained of discrimination in the service, which was the main reason why he encouraged his son to seek higher education in the United States.[17]

The theme of racial discrimination was even further pursued in the accounts on his college life, presented by Azikiwe as one of great difficulty and injustice. In spite of this, he obtained three college degrees, and in future years was to receive a series of honorary doctorates. Failing to obtain a job in Nigeria, he went to the Gold Coast (later Ghana), where he stayed for three years and escaped being convicted for sedition. On his return to Nigeria, he became a newspaper publisher and politician. He joined the NYM and rose quickly to become one of its most influential members. As an Igbo in a party dominated by the Yoruba, he broadened the ethnic base while he used his newspaper to publicize party activities.

Azikiwe was an instant hero in Lagos and, later on, in different parts of Southern Nigeria. To the young and impressionable, his use of English—notably a deliberate choice of multisyllabic words and long sentences—was a source of great attraction. To the Igbo people, Azikiwe was a symbol of success and his hard work had made it possible for one of their own to obtain a higher degree. To the anticolonialists the careful but combative editorials in his newspaper, the *West African Pilot,* founded in 1937, were always admired. He demanded freedom, and in a major petition to the secretary of state for colonies in 1941 he asked Britain to embark on a fifteen-year program to transfer power to colonial subjects. In 1944, due to the pressure by the Nigerian Union of Students, Herbert Macaulay and Azikiwe joined forces to establish the NCNC. Azikiwe would dominate this party, until its demise in the 1960s.

The Action Group and Chief Obafemi Awolowo

Awolowo was the undisputed leader of the Action Group, the party that controlled power in the Western Region in the 1950s and whose members wielded considerable influence for most of the twentieth century.[18] The AG championed a federalist democracy that would empower all the regions and ethnic groups. Like Azikiwe, Awolowo's career was extraordinary for its prodigy and monumental accomplishments.

Born in 1909 to an Ijebu-Yoruba family in the city of Ikenne, Awolowo struggled hard in his early life. He was a man of great versatility and accomplishments. After one year of secondary school, he worked as a primary school teacher, stenographer, college clerk, and a newspaper reporter. He also tried a number of small businesses, as a moneylender, produce buyer, and motor transporter, but he never grew rich from any of them. He obtained a degree in business as an external candidate of the University of London and also began his political career as a member of the NYM. In 1944, at the age of 35, he had saved enough to travel to London where he obtained a law degree in 1946. While abroad, he also wrote books to outline his vision of Nigeria, and became involved in political activities. He wrote a successful book, *Path to Nigerian Freedom,* which presented a case that Nigeria is an agglomeration of diverse nationalities, each with its own constitution that the British had destroyed. His vision was to empower the various cultural-cum-linguistic nationalities. He believed that power should reside in a new educated elite, rather than with the chiefs and kings at the local levels. His political philosophy was unabashedly regional: each ethnic group should be culturally united, then politically reformed by its elite. All cultural groups can come together in Nigeria, in a federal constitution. In 1945, he and others founded the Egbe Omo Oduduwa—the Society of the Descendants of Oduduwa—limited only to the Yoruba. This was the beginning of a political move that would make him a hero among the Yoruba during the twentieth century.

Awolowo returned to Nigeria in 1946 and launched into law, journalism, and politics. His strategy was to unite the Yoruba elite, and he turned a cultural organization into a political one. He was very successful in this strategy. He regarded the Yoruba intelligentsia as the leading vanguard in the fight against colonial rule. In 1948, he became the general secretary of the Egbe Omo Oduduwa, which brought into its fold prominent chiefs, Obas, and elite. The Egbe Omo Oduduwa began to offer ways to reform local authorities and to develop the Yoruba.

The long and sometimes bitter conflict between Awolowo and Azikiwe began in the late 1940s. By the time Awolowo returned to Nigeria, Azikiwe had already acquired considerable influence in Lagos politics and among the radical elements. His advocacy of a great deal of political autonomy to each ethnic group went against the politics of Azikiwe, who wanted to bring diverse associations together. To Azikiwe, Awolowo's strategy of uniting the Yoruba would undermine the NCNC. The formation of the Egbe Omo Oduduwa galvanized the Yoruba elite, and the Ibo State Union (ISU) similarly became stronger. The conflict became pronounced in the media. When Azikiwe became the leader of the ISU, the Yoruba politicians accused him of wanting to turn the NCNC into an Igbo party. The Egbe Omo Oduduwa became a political party, the Action Group, in 1951, and it recorded an immediate electoral success in the election of that year.

Awolowo knew that politics required money. However, unlike many of his peers and successors, he built his extensive financial empire through his business and investments rather than stealing from the public treasury. He was also able to use state revenues in a creative way to empower the Yoruba intelligentsia. Thanks to the favorable price of cocoa in the 1950s, the Western Region was prosperous. The AG was able to embark upon an impressive economic program. As more and more public revenues were spent on these projects, a class of successful Yoruba emerged as traders, contractors, bankers, businessmen, and industrialists. The majority of them, even when they were not actively involved in politics, supported the AG with money. The alliance between politics and commercial patronage enhanced Awolowo's status.

The NPC and the Sardauna Bello

As with their southern counterparts, the members of the northern intelligentsia began to come together in the 1940s to organize a political platform. Part of the goal was to modernize indigenous authorities and use them for administration and development. The Northern People's Congress (NPC) was a regional party, with the motto, "One North, One People Irrespective of Religion, Rank or Tribe." The NPC was strongly committed to defending Islam and traditional chiefs.[19] It was successful in cleverly adapting indigenous institutions to modern needs, and in incorporating emirs and chiefs into the contemporary power structure, even within a secular framework.[20] During the nineteenth century the successful jihad led by Uthman dan Fodio created the Sokoto Caliphate, a huge theocratic government divided into various emirates, each headed by an emir. During the colonial period, the British policy of indirect rule enabled the emirates to constitute centers of administrative power. As before, the emirs held allegiance to the sultan of Sokoto and were still respected in their areas. Islam provided a cultural unity. The leaders of the NPC continued with this trend of according recognition to the emirs and the unifying agency of Islam.

Ahmadu Bello's career followed a path different from that of his southern peers. Like Awolowo and Azikiwe, he received Western education. Bello was trained as a teacher and administrator, although he did not develop the consummate passion to seek higher education abroad. If his southern counterparts put too much emphasis on developing new institutions based on Western ideas, he chose to fall on the past of his people. If the chieftaincy titles of Azikiwe and Awolowo were honorary, that of Bello was hereditary. Born in 1910 to a royal family, he was a descendant of dan Fodio, the founder of the Sokoto Caliphate. His bid for the throne of the sultan was unsuccessful, but he had a traditional title, the sardauna, that is, one of the leading councilors to the sultan. If Azikiwe and Awolowo were Christians, Bello was a Muslim, an Alhaji who had performed the pilgrimage to the Holy Land (Mecca) and committed to the spread of his religion. And unlike both Awolowo and Azikiwe, his grip on power was stronger, and the loyalty to him was more enduring.[21] He served as the only premier of the North, from 1954 to 1966, when he was killed by the military in the first coup. If Awolowo and Azikiwe had the major ambition of controlling federal power, Bello allowed his deputy, Alhaji Tafawa Balewa, to do this, thereby creating an arrangement that the country's political leader was actually subordinate to the premier.[22]

Although the NPC controlled the federal government in the 1950s and 1960s, the party and its intelligentsia acted under suspicion from the South. For them to control the North and retain power at the center, the NPC believed strongly in regionalism, a policy of one dominant political party in each region. In trying to forge alliances, they made statements to the effect that they did not seek to dominate the South, but only to support those with similar aspirations as their own. Certainly, they were not opposed to the emergence of other parties in the North. Indeed, there was a credible one, the NEPU, founded by Alhaji Aminu Kano, who advanced a philosophy of egalitarianism. What the NPC was opposed to was the spread of southern parties, such as the NCNC and AG, to the North. The assumption was that the parties formed by the northerners would not be strong enough to undermine the NPC or traditional authorities such as the emirs. The assumption was also that the founders of alternative parties in the North would still be Muslims, and their philosophy was unlikely to undermine the Islamic civilization. Southerners were perceived as dangerous for the ideas that they would bring to the North. The northern intelligentsia also feared that the withdrawal of the British could lead to the control of their schools and civil service by the southerners. Thus, they also had to deal with technocratic domination.

The Consolidation of Regionalism

Regionalism was consolidated in the 1950s and 1960s. From 1951 to 1962, the NCNC controlled the East, the AG the West, and the NPC the North. In many ways, each was also associated with the major ethnic groups: the NCNC with the Igbo, the AG with the Yoruba, and the NPC with the Hausa and Fulani. Events during this period were also dominated by three regional leaders: Azikiwe, Awolowo, and Bello. From 1954 to 1959, the three served as the first premiers of their regions, while retaining the chairmanships of their political parties. The three leaders were the spokesmen of their parties, ethnic groups, and even the emerging social classes.

All the political parties resorted to the strategy of mobilizing ethnic and regional resources to strengthen themselves. Political leaders saw their regions as more important than the rest of the country, and many wanted federal power because of the advantages it would bring to their respective regions. The careers and activities of the three major figures began to shape the course of history. If the rivalry in the 1940s was between the Yoruba and Igbo in the South, other complications were added in the 1950s. A North-South division began to emerge and it affected all important discussions. The General Conference at Ibadan in 1950 revealed that the divisions in the country were becoming stronger and more threatening. The delegates from the North even threatened to secede from the rest of the country, if the power of regionalism was not fully asserted. The southern politicians began to present the North as antiprogress, and its politicians as too conservative to lead their region, not to talk of the country. In the North the fear of the South was real. A major editorial in the well-read, local-language newspaper concluded in 1950 that "it is the Southerner who has the power in the North. They have control of the railway stations; of the Post Offices; of Government Hospitals; of the canteens."[23] Each region regarded itself as the best, others as backward, and opposition leaders were portrayed as unreliable. To the NCNC, the Igbo were the most hardworking and driven Nigerians, who, given the opportunity, would transform themselves and the rest of the country. The dissatisfaction of the Igbo political class began quite early, as their attempts to create a transregional and transethnic political party failed to materialize. In the 1950s the Action Group quickly eroded the influence of Azikiwe and the NCNC in the West. Regarding the Yoruba politicians as hard to deal with, the NCNC moved to the NPC in a coalition that did not succeed in the long run. The NPC found the means to acquire the majority in the House of Representatives without needing the NCNC. As the NCNC and NPC party leaders fought and pathways diverged, the crisis became, in the 1960s, one between the Hausa and the Igbo, which ultimately resulted in the tragedy of the massacre of the Igbo in many northern cities in 1966 and 1967.

Ethnic conflicts, or at least resentments, were also becoming part of the political landscape. Where Igbo small-scale traders and civil servants predominated, as among the Efik in the Southeast or the Hausa in the North, they were becoming targets of verbal attack. Among the Yoruba, some politicians were using anti-Igbo resentment to rally their own supporters. The embattled minority government in the West, in alliance with the NPC, warned its members not to allow the creation of an "Ibo Empire":

> More and more Ibo business interests are pouring into Lagos and Ibadan, and the Ibos are striving might and main to penetrate the Western economy thereby exploiting our wealth and riches for the benefit of themselves.[24]

The Igbo, too, directed their resentment to their alleged rivals, and complained of persecution. In the Middle Belt, Hausa and Igbo traders and middlemen were disliked for their control of local trade. These and various other examples do show the perception that one group had of the other, the failure of the government to build a united country. Indeed, the first generation of Nigerian politicians and their successors were astute in the manipulation of ethnicity for personal gains.

Political Parties and Regionalism

As already indicated in the preceding sections, additional parties were formed in the 1950s. The formation of these new parties and the activities of the NCNC reveal the deep cleavages in society. To start with the NCNC, the image of a national party in the 1940s was shed in the 1950s as the party began to be projected as an Igbo-led, Igbo-dominated one. Azikiwe emerged from a temporary obscurity to energize the party in 1951. Unlike an association that was previously based on members drawn from trade unions, ethnic associations, and others, the NCNC moved quickly to become a regional party. Against the wishes of the radical members of his party, Azikiwe became the premier of the Eastern Region in 1954, no doubt to create a formidable political base for himself and to be able to participate in the vigorous competition of the time. Antiregionalism suffered a major setback.

In the West, Awolowo began to consolidate his own political base along regional lines. In a political maneuver that would be repeated many more times in his career, Awolowo spent months in secret meetings, planning the formation and structure of his political party. In 1951 the Action Group announced its formation in the hinterland city of Owo with the primary aim of bringing together all Yoruba nationalists. The AG won the majority seats in the 1951 election. Its principal members became ministers, including Awolowo, who was appointed the leader of government business in the Western Regional House of Assembly and the minister of local government.

The AG clearly reveals the tension between provincialism and antiregionalism. On the one hand, Awolowo cleverly manipulated the Yoruba identity to forge a political party. As he united an emerging Yoruba intelligentsia, they alienated their Igbo counterparts, all in a bid to gain control in the West. On the other hand, Awolowo, like Azikiwe, never abandoned the nationalist orientation of forging a united Nigeria. Although both could be champions of regionalism, they advocated pan-regional ideas in their writings and even in their political calculations.

In the North, the Northern People's Congress was established in 1949. The NPC never claimed to be a national party, and it was able to establish a quick grip on power. It won a decisive victory in the regional election of 1951 and controlled the North until the fall of the First Republic. As far as the NPC was concerned, the parties from the South offered a threat to the survival of the North.

The three parties were the lead contestants in the country's first general election in 1952. The results show that the parties maintained strong regional strongholds. In addition, the results and party structures also show that the large ethnic groups were also in control of the regions: the Yoruba in the West, the Igbo in the East, and the Hausa-Fulani in the North. When the major political offices are analyzed along ethnic lines, the domination of these groups also becomes clearer.

The federal elections were held in 1954, with the NPC having the majority of seats in the House of Representatives. The NCNC won the majority of seats in the South, thereby ensuring that it could appoint six of the nine federal ministers. In anticipation of future federal elections and the appointment of the first prime minister, the parties worked hard to consolidate themselves. The NPC continued to maintain its hold in the North, the NCNC wanted to strengthen itself in the North, and the AG wanted to eliminate the influence of the NCNC among the Yoruba and reach out to minorities in the North and East. The constitutional provision in 1957 created the office of the prime minister with the power to choose his cabinet. Alhaji Sir Abubakar Tafawa Balewa, the vice president of the NPC, became the first prime minister. His government drew his cabinet from all the parties. In the power-sharing arrangement of 1958, in the North, the Hausa and Fulani share in the executive positions was 50 percent; in the West, the Yoruba had 68 percent; and in the East, the Igbo had 49 percent.

In 1959 a second federal election was held, with the NPC emerging with a majority of seats, 142 of the 312. The NCNC and its NEPU allies had 89, and the AG 73. The nonpartisan cabinet of the previous year was hard to re-create. The NPC and the AG found it hard to work together, as the latter insisted on the creation of new regions in the North, to the annoyance of the northern leaders. The NCNC and NPC formed a coalition that saw Azikiwe emerging as the ceremonial president and Balewa retaining his prime ministership. Awolowo was the opposition leader, further damaging the relations with the NPC. The politics of regionalism had become fully consolidated.

Regionalism was not just a political ideology, it was also an economic and social one. As each political party attained dominance, those who controlled it constituted a powerful class with the ability to award contracts, scholarships, and jobs, and to distribute largesse. They expected their followers to think in regional-cum-ethnic terms in order to participate in the system. A younger generation became incorporated into this ideology, as they began to see their future as determined by regional affiliation and the ability of their ethnic representatives to gain power at the center. Regional and class interests merged in ethnicity, thereby enhancing its relevance as a social and political tool.

Party competition within the regions was rather difficult, in view of the dominant strength of one party in each region. Indeed, each region could be described as a one-party state. Given the patronage system and the abuse of police power, an opposition party could easily be destroyed, and its members could be deprived of access to public resources. One tragedy was that once a major party was excluded from federal power, as in the case of the AG after 1959, it would take the form of the exclusion of an entire ethnic group, thus fueling a desire for secession.

The parties often disguised their regional strategies by speaking in national terms or hoping to transform themselves into national parties.[25] The NCNC tried hard in the 1950s, still continuing to play the strategy of party formation of the 1940s. In 1951 the party even advocated a unitary government, rejected in preference for a federal system. Azikiwe put himself on the ballot for the Lagos seat in the 1951 elections. Among the Yoruba, the NCNC was still a formidable party and it succeeded in winning the majority in the 1954 elections. In the neighboring Edo-speaking areas, the NCNC also recorded impressive electoral successes. The NPC attempted to run a modern government by using traditional authorities. As there were many non-Hausa and non-Fulani in the region, especially in the Middle Belt, the groups were sometimes seen as a threat to the consolidation of northern interests. Thus, attempts were made to incorporate them into the NPC in order to prevent southern political parties from gaining influence.

In the case of the AG, the adoption of a socialist ideology was to create a national platform with members drawn from everywhere. By the mid-1950s, the AG had also become the favorite party among the minorities in the East and North, as its commitment to ethnic autonomies in a federal system was appealing. As Awolowo became a leader of opposition after 1959, so too did he and many members of his party become stronger in their antiregionalist beliefs, if only to prevent the domination of Nigeria by the NPC.

The dominant parties sought to project themselves as "national" in some other ways. The most common was to forge alliances with the political representatives of minority groups or between two big regional parties. These alliances were many and unstable, but they reveal class interests and attempts to move beyond the ethnic divide. From a class perspective, all the prominent members of the political parties profited from power, by being able to award contracts, enjoy privileges, and reward supporters. Opposition was despised, as it would undermine them. Since regionalism and ethnicity enabled them to protect their interests, they were always ready to manipulate both of them.

Similarly, alliance formation reveals the need to protect established privileges. Given the population of the North and the greater electoral control that it enjoyed, the NPC only required a minimum alliance in order to govern at the center. Within the North itself, there was no need for the NPC to form any alliance. In stretching to the South, the goal was not to sell the NPC to them but only to forge alliances with their conservative elements. In the West, the socialist claims of the AG meant that working with the NPC was almost impossible.

In the East the NCNC cooperated but only at the risk of serving as a junior partner in a federal government.

Following the parliamentary election of 1959, the NPC and the NCNC forged an alliance to create a coalition government. Alhaji Sir Abubakar Tafawa Balewa, the vice president of the NPC, became the prime minister, a position he held for the entire duration of the First Republic. The NPC also had the majority of seats in the House of Representatives. The AG became the opposition party, extremely critical of the federal government. To acquire a mass appeal, it seized every opportunity to show that the NPC was a feudal party, the NCNC opportunistic, and that both lacked the ability and ideas to develop the country.

Interregional Rivalries

The regions regarded one another as rivals. The political leaders in all the regions promoted this rivalry for both ethnic and personal interests. Indeed, as early as 1953, the first major crisis broke out, with the North threatening to secede. The crisis was generated over the motion by Anthony Enahoro to ask the British to concede self-government by 1956, and the objection to this date by the North. The sardauna and his party regarded 1956 as too early and a ploy by the South to dominate the North. He pleaded for more time because: "We in the North are working very hard toward self-government although we were late in assimilating Western education yet within a short time we will catch up with the other Regions."[26] When the members from the South pressed further on the issue, the sardauna closed with the remark: "The mistake of 1914 has come to light and I should like to go no further."[27]

The southern politicians and media portrayed the northerners and their politicians as too backward. As the northerners headed home, the Lagos crowd insulted them with words that labeled them as collaborators and stooges of the British. The AG, to extend its political base, turned itself into an agency to educate northerners about the need for independence. Acting on the assumption that the leaders were too traditional and the people uneducated, the AG organized a political campaign in the North. While in the North, the AG was bold in describing the NPC as a reactionary party and its leaders as hiding the truth from their people. Political violence followed this campaign, with riots in the city of Kano. Official records put the number of the dead at thirty-six and the injured at over two hundred. More blood would be shed in future years, unnecessary in view of the reasons that led to them. The outcome of the crisis was the Lyttleton Constitution of 1954, which allowed the regions greater autonomy. The general elections in 1959 were eagerly contested, and the results and coalitions reflected the intensity of regionalism. The NPC won the majority of seats with 143, with all but 8 from the North. The NCNC and its NEPU allies had 89 seats (58 from the East, 8 from the North, 2 from Lagos, and 21 from the West). The Action Group had 73 seats (a large number of 33 in the North, 25 in the East, and 25 in the West). A coalition was necessary in order to form the federal government. The intense negotiations found the NCNC and NPC in alliance and the AG in opposition. The coalitions led to less peace, as the country moved from one crisis to another.

When the major ethnic groups gained control of their regions, the minorities began to be afraid of political marginalization, discrimination in civil service appointments, and limited allocation of projects to their areas. In the East, the major area of protest was among the people in the Calabar-Ogoja Rivers area (the COR) who feared the domination of the Igbo. In the West, the groups in the Mid-West (notably the Edo) were afraid of Yoruba domination and began to advocate the creation of a separate region. In the North, the zone of protest was in the Middle Belt. A minority political party emerged, the United Middle Belt Congress (UMBC), to prevent the complete domination of the region by the NPC. The Tiv became eager for independence and subsequently resorted to violence.

The minorities believed that one way to solve their problems was to create states, that is, break the big regions into smaller units. The idea of state creation began with the politics of decolonization in the 1940s. In 1943 Azikiwe had advocated the creation of eight states, and Awolowo wanted even more, arguing that each ethnic group, irrespective of size, deserved a separate state. Agitation for new states was made in the 1950s, especially in the Benin Delta area and the Middle Belt. In 1957 fifteen claims for states were put before the constitutional conference in London. In response, the Minorities Commission was established to ascertain the fears of minorities and seek the means to allay them. Only the AG was adamant in demanding new states. With the British also reluctant, the commission decided against the establishment of new states.

The Crisis of Regionalism, 1960–1966

> We all have our fears of one another. Some fear that opportunities in their own areas are limited and they would therefore wish to expand and venture unhampered in other parts. Some fear the sheer weight of numbers of other parts which they feel could be used to the detriment of their own interests. Some fear the sheer weight of skills and the aggressive drive of other groups.[28]

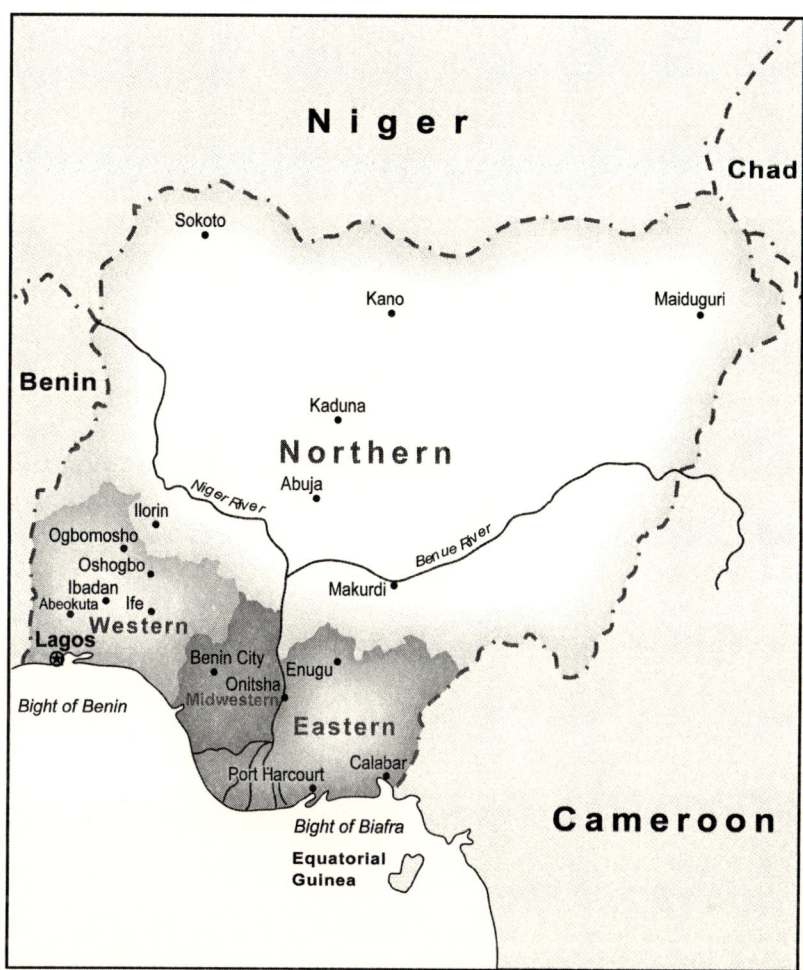

Nigerian States, 1963

Independence came as a mixed blessing. On the one hand, Nigerians were now in power, and nationalism was proclaimed as triumphant. On the other hand, there were various unresolved problems that the country had no leaders or respected statesmen to handle. The issue of ethnicity loomed large, both at the level of interethnic and regional relations and within each region as minority elements were largely dissatisfied with the political arrangement. There was the North-South divide: the South regarded the North as too big and politically dominant, thereby making federalism unworkable; the North regarded the South as too aggressive and its elite rather ambitious, thereby making it difficult to build a coherent nation-state. As the quotation above effectively captures, one region was afraid of the other. The North had the opportunity to control power at the federal level and within its own region. However, educational and economic power resided in the South. Due to the faster spread of Western education, the South produced the majority of the country's professionals and educated citizens. This enabled the South to control virtually all the modernizing sectors—the civil service, railways, trading firms—in a way that the North felt threatened. To the South, giving too much political power to the North would endanger the federal system.

Regional and ethnic competition became so bitter and violent that the general populace began to wonder whether independence was necessary in the first place. Whether in the North or South, the politicians were manifesting self-interest, expressed in the ambition to accumulate wealth. Politics was becoming a lucrative avenue to wealth and business. Corruption was becoming common, although smaller in scale than what happened under military rule in the years that followed. Indeed, regionalization and all its troubles were actually articulated as a political model. In what one scholar has called "the principle of regional security," the idea was to regionalize political institutions and for the representatives of the regions to limit themselves to their boundaries and negotiate at the center primarily to distribute largesse.[29] In practice, regionalism became difficult to manage, and there were also challenges from opposition forces that advocated a national philosophy.

Federalism and the constitution of the 1950s ensured that Nigeria would be governed in a multiparty system. The government would be a parliamentary democracy modeled after that of Britain. In five years, the system collapsed.[30] When the issue of democracy was revisited in the 1970s, much blame was heaped on the parliamentary system. The substitute, an American-style presidential system, also collapsed within five years. Both constitutions read well; indeed certain passages on the distribution of power between the various organs of government actually read perfectly. A constitution operates in a political and cultural context; but the Nigerian one turned out to be debilitating.

Perhaps, the place to start the analysis of failure lies in the linkage between politics and wealth. Then and now, government is a lucrative business to the participants, especially to those who struggle hard to obtain crucial appointments. Nigerian politicians are mainly entrepreneurs who see politics as nothing but an avenue to money. Although far less greedy than their successors, many politicians of the First Republic were driven by the desire for money. A few acquired money the hard way, through their own personal business drive, and only sought power for ego and what it could contribute to society. Arguably Chief Awolowo would belong to this category. A few were also so well connected through established aristocracy, as in the case of the Sardauna Bello, that they therefore needed little or no public money. However, the majority wanted to accumulate money, and politics made it possible.

Although the thesis sounds like a justification of corruption, it may be argued that one of the overriding objectives of the first generation politicians was to escape poverty and be proclaimed as patrons. As patrons, they would need money to maintain an army of dependents, to bribe their way in consolidating their hold, and in projecting the lifestyle of success. Essentially, most of the careers of the politicians read as cases of peasant success—village-born kids who went to school by accident, got lucky to have power, but promised themselves never to return to the village. As examples of peasant success, they needed to show that they were successful to the extent that they could solve the problems of others, and they could spend money anyhow and at any time. Although the members of the public knew that the politicians were spending public money, this knowledge did not translate into a revolution to change the political culture. Rather, many joined in celebrating the peasant success, in praying that their own time too would come.

The methods of self-validation damaged politics. As a politician must always be in the loop to benefit from power, it was bad business to contest and lose an election. To win an election and be outside the center of action was bad business as well. Thus, one must win and cleverly calculate to be where power to award contracts was, in order to touch big money. If opposition was too strong, it could damage access to power and wealth. Thus, opposition was like a cancer that must be removed. The killing or incarceration of the opponent became a wise move. Devoid of ideology, and always self-serving, a politician need not show loyalty to a political party that did not make it possible for him to enrich himself. Rather, he would change party, or cross the floor in the legislature because of self-interest.[31]

Ethnicity was thriving in a polity driven by elite self-interest. The regionalism of the 1950s became more complicated until things fell apart. Important major policies and political decisions were shaped by regional and ethnic considerations. The public and media were drawn into many conflicts, politics received a bad name, and the country moved rapidly toward disintegration.[32] The major issues included the rivalry over the census, violence in the Middle Belt, and the political crisis in the Western Region.

The decennial census conducted in 1962 and 1963 created a major political row because of allegations that the figures were "cooked." To the southern politicians, the census offered an opportunity to restructure national politics and the balance of power. They believed that the British had inflated the population of the North in order to give the region a political advantage. The parliamentary seats allocated to each region were based on population proportion, thus the North had 174 seats, the West, 62, and the East, 73. The sharing of revenues from the distributable pool was also based in part on population figures. In an accurate census, the southern politicians believed that the population of the South should be more than that of the North, thus allowing them to establish control on the federal government. The southern politicians were to be disappointed, both with the census and the outcome. Initial unofficial results in 1962 gave the South more people than the North: the population of the North increased by 12.3 million over that of the 1952 census (a 30 percent increase); that of the West by 6.08 million or a 71 percent increase; and that of the East from 7.2 to 12.3 million, an increase of 71 percent. Fearing that figures for the East and West were inflated, the federal government called for a recount in selected areas in 1963. Although the verification did not dispute the numbers for the South, it altered that of the North, increasing it from the previous 30 percent to 80 percent. It was clear that politics had shaped the outcome, and the federal government cancelled the results and ordered a recount in 1964. The new results gave the North 30 million people and the South 26 million, an increase of 67 percent in the North, 65 percent in the East, and 100 percent in the West.

To the southern politicians, the population figures for the North were regarded as too high, and a deliberate attempt to maintain political dominance. In spite of its alliance with the NPC, the NCNC rejected the census figures. The southern intellectuals and the media alleged fraud.[33] However, the NPC and its allies in the West led by Chief S. Ladoke Akintola, the premier, and his new party supported the result. The western wing of the NCNC became divided, and a majority faction used the census controversy to identify with Akintola to form yet another party, the United Nigeria Democratic Party (UNDP).

To turn to the other issue of violence, major political riots broke out among the Tiv in 1960.[34] They were again repeated in 1964, leading to the death of almost four hundred people. The Tiv were opposed to the tactics of the NPC to dominate them, and they believed that the Hausa-Fulani political class wanted to incorporate them by force into their own political party. Among the allegations made by the Tiv were that the loyalists of the NPC were appointed as traditional chiefs, members of the local government, and given scholarships, while their own people suffered great discrimination in the award of scholarships and appointments to the northern regional civil service. The Tiv riots offered great challenges to the government and showed that the incorporation of minority elements was very difficult indeed.

Minority elements in all the big regions were dissatisfied with the political arrangement. Put together, they were many, about 40 percent of the population, but their scattered locations in different areas had prevented the forma-

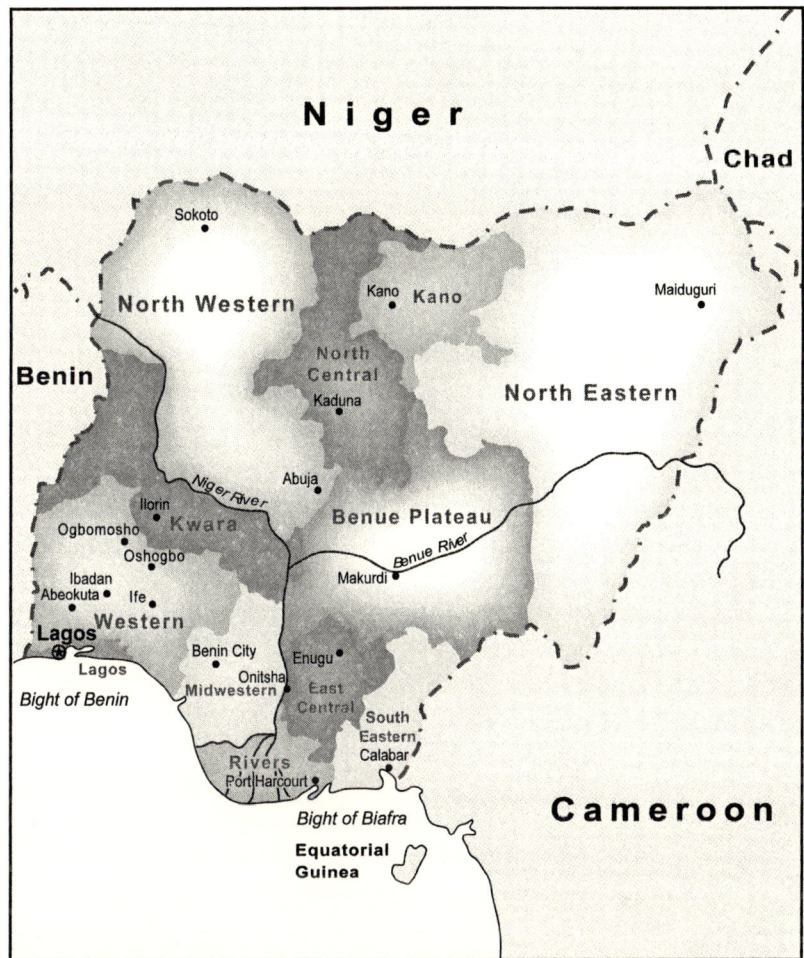

Nigerian States, 1967

tion of a strong political platform. Where the members of the minorities could operate within political parties, they did so. But they also sought other means to advance their political interests. Trade unions, the army, and political radical-oriented associations all provided the means to articulate nonregional political ideas that enhanced their participation in government. In the East the groups in the Niger Delta resisted Igbo domination, and after 1967 were even hostile to the idea of secession and the formation of the Republic of Biafra, which incorporated them into a new country without their consent. In the North, the Tiv riots were one manifestation of intraregional troubles. Other minorities in the Middle Belt were equally hostile to what they regarded as the attempts by the NPC to allow the Fulani and Hausa to dominate them and to spread Islam among their people in order to use religion to further the interest of politics. In the West, a new region—the Mid-West—was carved out, thus becoming the only state created during the First Republic.

Most of the volatile crises took place in the Western Region, soon after independence. Some aspects involved the national contest for power in which Awolowo was a leading figure.[35] Some were about bitter interregional power between the South and the North, as in the case of the census. One was ideological: should the AG adopt socialism as a party manifesto? And others were just about the rivalry for power within the AG itself. In 1962 the AG split, and the party and the region did not recover from it throughout the First Republic. Personality clashes between two leaders, Awolowo and his deputy, Chief S. Ladoke Akintola;[36] the controversy over alliance formation; the relevance of the adoption of a socialist ideology; and the rivalry between Yoruba subgroups (notably the Ijebu and Oyo) were the four leading issues in a conflict that was so bitter that some of its consequences remain today.

The public face of this rivalry revolved mainly around the politics of regionalism and antiregionalism: how should the Western Region deal with the North and the NPC, which controlled the federal government? Awolowo saw an alliance between the AG and the NPC as dangerous, even fearing that it could lead to the end of the party that he had formed. In the 1959 election, the AG was the best prepared and committed more money than the other parties to the campaign. With its success in minority areas in both the East and North, Awolowo was confident that he could do better in a later election. However, for his party to control federal power, it either had to forge alliances with the NCNC in order to create a so-called progressive platform or find the means to win in all parts of the country. As an alternative to an alliance with the NPC, he chose to transform the AG into a national party by adopting a socialist ideology in the hope that the party would penetrate minority areas in the North and elsewhere and weaken the NPC. Awolowo advocated the breakup of the North into two or more regions, and he hoped that the emergence of an articulate educated elite would undermine the power of traditional authorities. In other words, Awolowo reckoned that elitism and modernization would create northerners who think like southerners and who would thus see the NPC as antidevelopment.

Akintola, the premier who succeeded Awolowo when he relocated to Lagos to serve as the leader of the opposition, chose the path of alliance with the NPC and the coalition in power at the federal level. To Akintola and other conservatives, there was nothing wrong with this strategy as long as the southern members could be rewarded with federal support and keep appointments in the cabinet. This would keep the Western Region intact and powerful, and ensure that it was fully represented in national government comprising the representatives of all the regions. Thus, if Awolowo wanted to pursue a new antiregionalist approach, Akintola chose to remain faithful to the regionalist approach. Akintola refused the pressure from Awolowo and his faction in the AG to use the resources of the West to pursue an antiregionalist approach and to expand the AG.

Awolowo was far more clever in presenting his option to the Yoruba intelligentsia as an inevitable path to the development of the region and the liberation of the Yoruba from northern domination. He presented antiregionalism in the language of egalitarianism, with socialism as its ideology. Akintola, now the defender of the status quo, sought the option of presenting collaboration with the NPC as the best way to reward party loyalists who would be able to use party alliance to consolidate their social class. As Akintola controlled executive power and had the force of the federal government behind him, he believed that coercion and political corruption would work better than persuasion. His position was complicated by the credible history of performance that Awolowo displayed in the 1950s. If Awolowo was associated with innovations and modernization, Akintola came to manage what was already in place or decided upon. The fall in cocoa prices during the period alienated him from the farmers, thus making it difficult for him to be trusted, that is, if he was able to put his position across in an effective manner.

Were the crisis limited to these two leaders and their supporters, perhaps it could have been resolved through some of the peace-making meetings. However, the public and other political parties were drawn into it. The West was so badly divided that it affected national politics. Political violence became an aspect of politics, and the unpredictability of events and reactions to them turned the place into a volatile jungle. To the NPC, the regionalist argument that each party should control its own region and make no attempt to campaign in other areas was sufficient to support Akintola. The crisis manifested itself in various dangerous and unpredictable ways. As members of the Western House of Assembly identified with one leader or another, the conduct of legislative politics became impaired. When the pro-Awolowo faction pursued the means to impeach Akintola, which degenerated into violence in the regional assembly, the federal government declared a state of emergency in May 1962 and appointed a pro-Akintola administrator to govern the region for six months. With the NCNC and NPC behind him, Akintola was restored to power in January 1963 as the leader of his new party, the United People's Party (UPP).

More troubles awaited Awolowo. The first was an attempt to discredit him, to erode his credibility and public support. He was accused of illegal diversion of public money to the AG, partly to fund a personal campaign to become the prime minister. The biggest trouble was his arrest, together with thirty other associates, and his subsequent trial on treason charges (1962–63). He was found guilty and sentenced to imprisonment for ten years.

If the Akintola faction and the NPC believed that their enemy was gone, they miscalculated. The masses became more energized in their opposition to the Akintola regime, and party politics became far more bitter. Akintola sought a difficult coalition comprising members of the NCNC in the West and the NPC. With the support of the NPC, Akintola was able to form a government, but his party remained a minority and was widely unpopular in the West. To him, such an alliance ensured political security guaranteed by the federal government. The trouble, however, was that the tripartite structure that had stabilized the country for over ten years had been disturbed. Bello and the NPC had not originally planned to control the West, but for the region to become autonomous. With the destruction of the AG and Akintola's reliance on the NPC, the political landscape was transformed in a way that all the key participants could no longer control. The Yoruba elite were now bitterly divided, the NCNC was in full control of the Mid-West, carved out of the Western Region in 1963; the NPC and NCNC saw opportunities to extend their influence in the southwest but at great risk to the federation itself. Rather than a traditional North-South divide, politics began to move toward either the "progressives" against the "conservatives," or toward a more ethnic one in which the NPC and the Akintola supporters regarded the Igbo as the opposition.

Discontent and Protest

Two years after independence, it was becoming clear to many that the promises made by the politicians would never be fulfilled. The students, trade union leaders, and many urban workers were becoming increasingly critical of the political system and politicians. Many did not see the so-called democracy that the constitution promised. The perception was that the politicians were using the people for personal ends of attaining power and all that came with it. The people were grumbling, both in public and private, always talking about the sins of the politicians—election frauds, political corruption, bribery, mismanagement, and a limitless number of other vices. The politically conscious farmers now understood how the government and its agencies were wasting the money created by their labor. As many now believed in educating their children and enhancing their own standard of living, they attributed their difficulties to the failure of government and the excesses of the politicians. In the cities, a growing army of the unemployed was becoming restless, with some joining political parties as thugs. Many among them from minority areas interpreted their worsening conditions in ethnic terms: the big "tribes"—the Igbo, Hausa, and Yoruba—were making life difficult for them. In the Southwest, Southeast, and Middle Belt, the minorities were clamoring for their own states, in the hope that these would bring development.

There were protests of a violent nature, as in the Tiv riots. There were scattered cases of political violence directed at some corrupt or unpopular politicians. In the West, the farmers joined urban people to protest inflation and political decadence. In what was called "Operation Wet E," a number of people were drenched with petrol and set on fire. Property, too, was equally damaged. This extreme measure was visited upon people believed to have been too corrupt.

Urban workers continued to organize into unions,[37] which were becoming platforms for radical expressions. Various documents from different unions castigated politicians, and called on the people to mobilize. By far the most successful demonstration of labor power was the General Strike of 1964, brought about by a combination of factors: disappointment with the political process, the growing incidents of corruption, the flaunting of wealth by the first generation of politicians and entrepreneurs, inflation, and rapid decline in real wages. The general strike was successful. The unions were able to involve almost 800,000 workers. As they moved to the streets to protest, they were joined by thousands of students and the unemployed. After some negotiations between the government and labor leaders, a wage increase was awarded. This was a victory for labor, although it turned out to be temporary as prices of goods also increased. Yet, the unions could have achieved more, but for the division among their leaders, the failure of many unions to come together, the lack of commitment on the part of union leaders who used the unions for personal gains, and the interpretation of economic and political reality in ethnic terms.

The End of an Era: Elections and the Coup

The transfer of power and elections have always been problems in Nigeria. Indeed, major elections, as in 1965 and 1983, have served as the prelude to military coups. With the crisis in the Western Region and cracks in the NPC–NCNC alliance, the elections of 1964 and 1965 proved to be disastrous in their outcome.

The political events leading to the federal election of 1964 were marked by thuggery in different parts of the country and complicated formation of party alliances. Two major political forces eventually emerged. The first group was the Nigerian National Alliance (NNA), with the NPC as the dominant party;

Akintola's new alliance, known as the UNDP in the Western Region; and small opposition parties in the Eastern Region and the Mid-West, a new region created in 1963. The NNA believed in regionalism—each party was to create its regions—and a coalition led by the NPC should control the federal government. Their ally in the West, Akintola, was now using anti-Igbo rhetoric to rally his fractured base. The Igbo were accused of dominating various federal corporations. The other was the United Progressive Grand Alliance (UPGA), comprising the NCNC in the East and Mid-West, the AG, and a number of small opposition parties in the North. The NCNC abandoned its older ally, the NPC, over various issues, most especially the disputed census. The period of alliance formation and the weeks preceding the elections witnessed riots and thuggery in different places, blatant intimidation of political opponents, and schemes to rig the elections. Fearing that the elections would be fraudulent, the UPGA announced a boycott. As the boycott was not national, the polls went ahead and the NNA declared an overwhelming victory.

A major crisis followed, since the elections were heavily tainted, and the country appears to have headed toward total collapse. In the words of a contemporary analyst:

> Northern domination, Yoruba disunity and Eastern aggressiveness were all highlighted; as were bitter personal animosities, the ugly scramble for jobs, the resort to force and fraud, the glaring inequalities of opportunities and the growing economic disparities.[38]

The NNA decided to lobby a number of NCNC ministers who were made members of the federal government. In a move that would disappoint the UPGA, Azikiwe and the NCNC again went into a coalition that enabled the NNA to constitute a federal government.[39] As far as the NPC was concerned, this was a moment of victory: they won in the North; their man was still in power in the West; Awolowo, the main opposition force, was in jail; the AG had no means to raise substantial money since it was out of power; the census figure was now in use; and the NPC controlled the federal government. However, this was a limited reading of the political landscape: the Yoruba in the West were dissatisfied with the political events; their intelligentsia was still strongly pro-AG; and the use of violence was accepted as an option. The election into the Western House of Assembly was to reveal the grave dangers in the political system.

The regional election in the West in October 1965 reopened all the wounds of the previous year. The AG and its allies were confident that they would win the election, thereby forcing the NPC to change its strategy in the West. Should the AG win, it would mean that the UPGA controlled power all over the South.

In anticipation of this, it was expected that Awolowo would be released from prison to head the UPGA. Perhaps, a political reconciliation was possible. The Akintola regime was at the height of its unpopularity, and his party knew well that it could retain power by fraud. Campaigns were violent, and the level of fraud was unprecedented. The hope for any reconciliation was dashed when the Akintola group declared success in the election, and its NPC ally accepted the results. Three months of violence followed, and both the regional and federal governments not only lost the moral authority to govern but lacked the means to curb the insurrections in the West.

The army struck on January 15, 1966. The army had not been an objective observer in the political crises.[40] It was also divided by various issues relating to promotion, recruitment, and quotas, as in whether recruitment should be based on courage or education. The North, with a limited number of educated people, supported the criterion of courage, while the South wanted more educated people in the force. To what extent should the army reflect regionalism? The AG advocated a system that would be based on merit, but the federal government followed a quota system that would allow the North to have 50 percent of the army be northerners. How the army itself would have resolved all these issues may never be known, but it is clear that the various crises in the nation's politics further politicized the army. By 1964 some members of the public were already speculating that there would be a coup.

The leaders of the 1966 coup were apparently angry with the politicians and their collaborators, as they prepared to kill as many of them as possible. As Major Chukwuma Kaduna Nzeogwu admitted, they wanted to be ruthless in the elimination of leaders of political parties and trade unions and in dismantling the federal system. For his revolution to work, Nzeogwu declared that all the "bigwigs" must die.[41] In a speech that has become one of the most quoted in the country's modern history, he declared:

> Our enemies are the political profiteers, swindlers, the men in high and low places that seek bribes and demand 10 per cent, those that seek to keep the country permanently divided so that they can remain in office as Ministers and VIPs of waste, the tribalists, the nepotists.[42]

This laudable aim could have rallied the younger generation of Nigerians in search of change behind the coupists. The coup also had some connections with radicalism that were opposed to regionalism. But the coup's execution did not eliminate all the "bigwigs." Rather, the two prominent northern leaders (the sardauna and Prime Minister Balewa), Chief Akintola, the finance minister Chief Okotie-Eboh, and a number of northern officers were killed.

Notable Igbo politicians were not killed. As six of the seven majors that planned the coup were Igbo, the coup immediately acquired an ethnic interpretation: the Igbo officers were accused of killing others in order to attain an Igbo domination. The situation was further complicated as the control of federal power went to an Igbo general, Major-General Aguiyi-Ironsi, who was, however, not party to the coup. A deluge followed, from which the country is yet to fully recover. Among the major post-1966 events were the breakup of the big regions into twelve, the declaration of secession in the East, a civil war from 1967 to 1970, prolonged military rule, a short-lived Second Republic from 1979 to 1983, and another round of military rule that lasted until 1998.[43]

Economic changes and planning occurred in this rough political age, and the outcome was predictable: a mediocre performance and the alienation of the majority of the articulate members of the public. This conclusion should not mean that the process should be dismissed altogether or that the mediocre performance is not worthy of analysis. To start with, it is hard to understand modern Nigeria without focusing on the important theme of development that has shaped many of the events and the reactions of the people to their government. From the point of view of the majority of the population, the test of politics lies in economic management. Even if a politician was not corrupt and not regionally oriented, that would not be enough to celebrate his achievements if "progress" did not come from his actions. A corrupt politician who could lobby for a road or a hospital was preferred to a clean one who had nothing to show for access to power. Second, the deficiency of the politicians did not necessarily translate to the deficiency of a planning elite. Here is one of the contradictions during the period. Although not free of corruption, there was a bureaucracy that could create an alliance with scholars and others to formulate elegant economic plans, advise on economic matters, and evaluate the feasibility of projects. From the preambles of all the plans, it is clear that there were planners and economists who believed that development would come, that economic changes were possible, and that the standard of living would improve in spite of the political mess. While the danger of political instability was recognized, the belief was that communities and lower-level tiers of government would continue to perform their economic functions. The bureaucracy, some also believed, could act as the stabilizing factor, creating the conditions for development even at a time of political chaos. In the mid-1970s, a few years after the civil war, leading government officials and economists were able to conclude that the economy was able to withstand political crises and that the economic trends concealed political problems. There was a recognition of some of the variables: the country is big, languages and ethnicity are rather diverse, the people are politically conscious, and there is a great expectation that the primary goal of the government is to uplift the people's lives. In periods of political chaos, or bad government, the expectation is that a new one will come to restore order and set the country on the right economic path.

In both its politics and economy, it is already clear that Nigeria never learns: the clear message is always that the past is of limited relevance, that the country can always begin again. However, it is abundantly clear that the past has too many lessons for Nigeria, as it continues to seek solutions to issues of development and democracy.

3

The Economy, 1945–1960

In the past 15 years Nigeria has experienced a remarkable transformation, economic, social and political. The leisurely pace of the prewar economy has accelerated, living standards generally have improved, educational facilities have expanded, and the people are participating in government in increasing measure. Yet this is only a start. (IBRD, 1955)[1]

The patterns of the Nigerian economy were laid in the first half of the twentieth century. As the country moved to the second half, it began to focus more on development and the modernization of the traditional sectors, but within an economic framework established in the previous years. By the 1950s important changes could be noted, as the opening quotation suggests, and great confidence was being expressed that more positive, even rapid, transformations would occur in the following years.

The economic features that emerged during the colonial period were retained for most of the twentieth century. Nigeria was integrated into an international system, as colonial rule altered traditional economies to create what can be called a "new economy" based on the production of cash crops and dependence on external markets.

The Nigerian economy was expanded and altered in the first half of the century, but not necessarily by abandoning the traditional economies but by adapting them to meet the demands of the export-import trade. The production of agricultural items and the extraction of minerals were the two component parts of the new economy. The goal was to connect Nigeria to an international system as a supplier of raw materials and a market for finished products.

The dominant sector of the economy was agriculture. Indigenous and colonial economies were both dependent on agriculture. In indigenous agriculture, the objective was on production for local needs, mainly crops for human consumption. Food production in all the major staples such as yam, cassava, millet, and corn continued during the colonial period, and the country was self-sufficient. Indeed, in areas not suitable to the major export crops, the emphasis remained on the production of food crops, or, as an alternative, the farmers migrated to other areas to work as tenant farmers or farm laborers.

The scale of production in indigenous agriculture was well beyond the subsistence level, as crops were sold to raise income and stored to prevent starvation. The indigenous economy was also diversified, with many working as hunters, craftsmen, and potters, to mention but a few examples. Markets were many, with transactions in products from within and outside of the country.[2] Such products as salt, natron, kolanuts, cattle, cloth, and metal objects were traded over long distances. Thus, the country had an intricate network of markets, natural transport means such as rivers and the sea, and trade routes that the colonial government inherited. For centuries, the economy had also been linked to regional and international networks through the trans-Saharan and transatlantic trade.

As the country moved to the twentieth century and was managed by forces external to it, the indigenous economy required a better integration in terms of transportation, a common currency, and greater productivity, if it were to serve the needs of the colonial objectives and subsequent modernization projects. The colonial system brought changes that enhanced the participation of Nigerians in international trade and in the consumption of imported items.

A notable step taken to achieve this was the creation of a railway system, new roads, and several measures to achieve an uninterrupted movement of people.[3] To connect the various parts of such a huge country as Nigeria, in order to govern and to tap the resources of the vast countryside in an efficient manner, a network of modern transport facilities was almost a necessity. As the new transport facilities became established, they contributed to the massive expansion of the economy. At a time when roads and lorries were yet to have any significant impact and relying on the Benue and Niger rivers was impossible, the railway was the best option. Thus, railways were the first priority, with construction starting in 1896 and reaching the North in 1906. The eastern lines were completed in 1916, making 1,780 total railway lines in the country. The railways enabled the movement of peanuts, cotton, and cocoa to Lagos. In Lagos, Port Harcourt, Sapele, and Calabar, harbor and wharf facilities were provided to complete the movement of goods between Nigeria and the outside world, notably the United Kingdom, Western Europe, and North America.

However, there was still the need to move the products from the villages to the railway stations. Between 1907 and 1939 about 19,000 miles of roads were built in various parts of the country, although only a small percentage was tarred. The number of cars and lorries increased rapidly, from only two cars in Lagos in 1907, to 31,131 cars and 20,829 lorries in 1960.[4] The mobility of goods and people was further enhanced by the extensive use of lorries from the late 1920s onward. Far more than the railway, the lorry promoted the development of local trade and integrated the rural areas with the cities in a more efficient and effective manner.[5] As it was generally controlled by Nigerians, the lorry business allowed local merchants to develop their businesses and make money, and it enabled greater interregional trade in cattle, kolanuts, foodstuffs, and luxury items.

The society and many of its old practices had to be transformed in order to orient them to an export-import economy. On a gradual basis, slavery was abolished. However, pawnship, a system whereby a person was used as collateral for loans, continued for much longer because of the need for large-scale labor on farms.[6] As many became landless, institutions of dependency were retained in forms such as tenancy and contract farming, domestic work, and pawnship. The most far-reaching change in labor came with the spread of the payments of wages on a daily, weekly, or monthly basis.

The more notable aspect of agriculture, notable because of its connection to an international market, began in the nineteenth century with the production of cocoa, rubber, and palm products. The colonial government did not embark on any major agricultural policy. However, it was concerned that proceeds from agriculture should assist in ensuring that the government was financially stable and politically secure. Balancing the budget rested largely on earnings from exports. Except in the case of cotton, cases of intervention in agriculture were rather minimal until after 1940. The government also treated the farmers as if they were termites that should not be disturbed or exterminated. As much as possible, there was to be no interference in their lives and land-tenure system so that no political crisis would be generated. Foreigners were prevented from acquiring land to establish large plantations and huge investments by banks and entrepreneurships in agriculture were difficult, all in order to preserve the land-tenure system and the essentially small-holding farms. As far as the government was concerned, what was important was not a revolution in agriculture, but the survival of the peasants and their ability to produce food for themselves, sell some to pay tax and to meet basic needs, and to be fully occupied in their farms so that they would not create problems for the administration. The colonial government was able to resist occasional pressure from merchants and investors who wanted to establish large plantations in the country. The leading representatives of the colonial government argued that the Nigerian peasants could deliver the raw materials far more cheaply, that large-scale plantations run by Europeans would add to the cost of colonial administration by way of security and management, and that millions of Nigerians would be ruthlessly exploited as foreign companies competed for the use of their labor and dispossessed them of their land. Governor Hugh Clifford stated the objection of the colonial government to a plantation economy in words that portrayed the government as the defender of poor farmers:

> The agricultural industries in tropical countries which are mainly, or exclusively, in the hands of the native peasantry a) have a firmer root than similar enterprises when owned and managed by Europeans, because they are natural growths, not artificial creations, and are self-supporting, as regards labour, while European plantations can only be maintained by some system of organized immigration or by some form of compulsory labour; b) are incomparably the cheapest instruments for the production of agricultural produce on a large scale that have yet been devised; and c) are capable of a rapidity of expansion and a progressive increase of output that beggar every record of the past, and altogether unparalleled in all the long history of European enterprises in the tropics.[7]

To be antiplantations was not necessarily a way of showing compassion to the peasants. What mattered most was the end result: the supply of raw materials. The option that the Nigerian colonial government adopted was less risky in terms of avoiding violence over land. The traditional land-tenure system would be retained, but changes in the economy would lead to commercialization on the basis of individual ownership by Nigerians. European companies were definitely not excluded from participation in the economy, but they were allowed to make their money through trade, which was actually more lucrative than agricultural production.

A massive expansion in production did occur, as more and more farmers devoted additional time, land, and other resources to cultivation and harvest. Cocoa became established in the Southwest, peanuts and cotton in the North, palm products in the East, and some other products in smaller volumes in various parts of the country.[8] The detailed histories of these crops show the extent to which the farmers were willing to innovate and invest in the hope of greater rewards. In the first thirty years of the twentieth century, the production of export crops increased by sevenfold in volume and fivefold in value, an

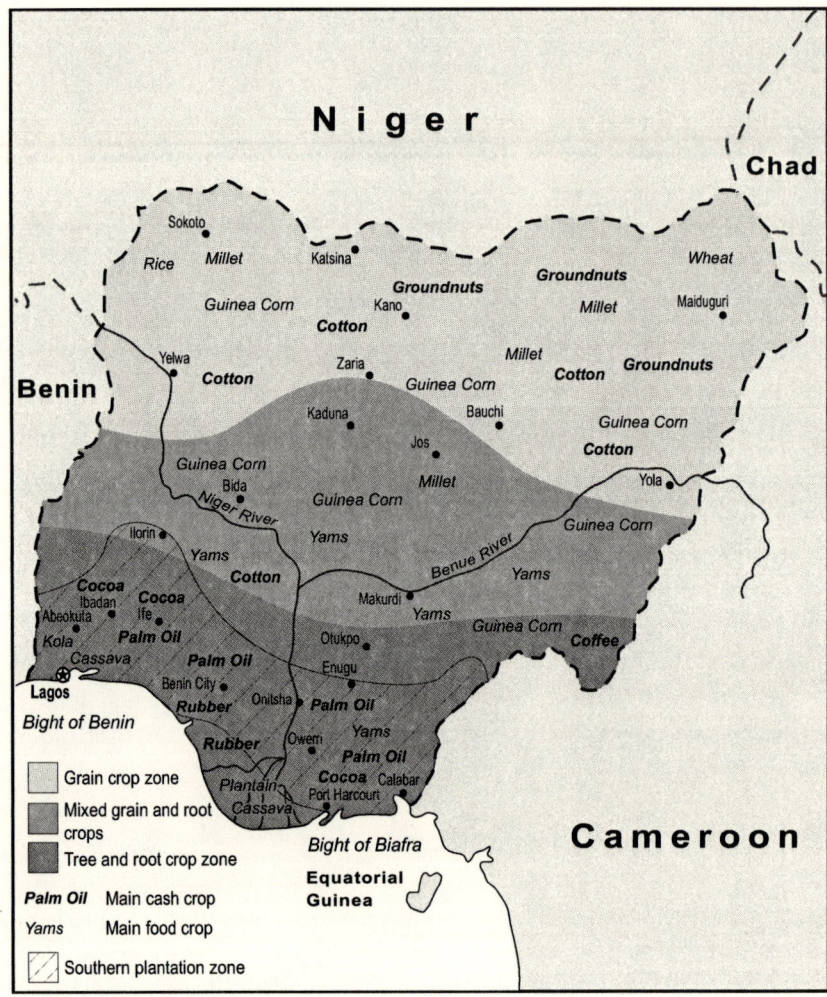

Agricultural Zones and Commodities

increase that owed not to the adoption of new tools but to intensive and extensive farming and use of labor.

In the case of cocoa, a new crop in West Africa, Nigerian farmers went into its cultivation in the last years of the nineteenth century.[9] Cocoa required great care, and a farmer had to wait for seven years for the first harvest. As it flourished in the Southwest, many farmers benefited, making more money than the sales of notable food crops such as yams and corn. The western part of the country became heavily committed to cocoa plantation, and thousands of people came from other parts of the country to work as tenant farmers. At the turn of the twentieth century, Nigeria was a small producer, the market being dominated by Ecuador, the West Indies, and Brazil. By the 1930s Ghana and Nigeria had taken over the lead, contributing almost 45 percent of the total world supply. From a contribution of 1 percent to the total value of exports in 1900, it rose to 16.6 by 1939 and 20 percent by the 1950s. Cocoa became the principal revenue earner for the Western Region, which supplied over 90 percent of the total export. The imports of the West were financed by the proceeds from cocoa, which yielded about one quarter of the public revenues and financed the region's development schemes by almost 72 percent. As various studies have shown, enormous resources of land, labor, and time were devoted to cultivation. As in case of the rush for gold, thousands of farmers took to cocoa planting in the first decade of the century, and the planting of new trees reached their peak in the 1930s. Land devoted to cocoa expanded considerably, as many farmers realized that good harvests could finance their needs and actually enhance their economic and social status better than investments in many other crops. Quantities of production were always on the rise, and prices were good for many years. Labor relations were altered, as enterprising farmers used pawns, hired labor, and even tenants in order to increase production. Struggles for land intensified as ambitious farmers established claims on various plots in order to plant more trees.[10]

When we move to the Northern Region, we come yet again to a case in which one crop, peanuts, had a dominant impact. Peanuts had always been used locally to produce oil, cake, and animal feeds. However, its massive production was associated with exports, which grew in volume within a short period. Between 1911 and 1937 over one million acres of land were devoted to peanuts. During World War II, more lands were brought under cultivation, and the country later became the leading exporter of peanuts.[11] In 1938 the country supplied 9 percent of world exports, rising to 40 percent twenty years later. As with cocoa, the contribution to exports increased over time, from 1 percent of total value of exports in 1900 to 20 percent by 1958. The major areas of production were four provinces, Kano, Borno, Sokoto, and Katsina, with their production generating the bulk of public revenues in export duties.

Oil palm produce came mainly from the South, and more from the Southeast. A multipurpose tree, the palm tree yielded oil, wine, kernels, and fiber. The export of oil and kernels was well established during the nineteenth century, in a way that revealed the intricate connection between trade and politics, and how the drive for profits was one of the primary reasons for the British takeover of Nigeria.[12] In the first half of the twentieth century, the export of palm oil increased fourfold, that of palm kernels from 85,000 tons in 1900 to over 400,000 tons in 1950, and the combined value of palm produce exports increased from £1.3 million in 1900 to £28.7 million in 1950. By 1960, the country had realized £40 million in sales. In the early years of colonial rule, palm produce generated 81.5 percent of the total export value, but this number declined in future years, to about 25 percent after 1940. The leading center of production was in the East: over 80 percent of the farmers there engaged in palm-oil production; the greater percentage of the revenue of the region came from palm-oil export; and about 70 percent of the fund to initiate development projects in the region in the 1950s came from the Oil Palm Produce Marketing Board. In other words, to both the population and the government, palm oil and palm kernels were the basis of survival.

There were other crops as well. Cotton thrived in the North, although most farmers preferred to plant peanuts, which do better in bad soil and need less labor to cultivate and harvest. Rubber was successful in the Delta and Benin provinces (later known as the Mid-West), where it became the mainstay of the economy and attracted the interest of a few foreign firms.

Success in agricultural production, and indeed in other aspects of the colonial economy, owed to the existence of millions of farmers, the encouraging prices offered to producers, and the necessity of earning money in order to pay tax and to buy necessities and luxury goods. The end of the wars of the nineteenth century created more time for thousands of people to work. A number of former warriors took to farming and helped to develop new cocoa farms in the West.[13] Hundreds of others also joined the police and army, and they contributed to the construction of the railway.[14]

Although agriculture brought the largest share of revenues, the rural side and farmers were the least developed technologically. Agricultural technologies were not transformed, as the people continued to use their ancient tools of hoes and machetes. In large areas the colonial economy failed to enhance living standards or even to transform people's lives in more positive ways. Some studies point to a decline in living standards and overall productivity, in spite of cash-crop production.[15] One great danger was the competition for land as successful farmers and entrepreneurs acquired more and more land, thus forcing many others to become tenants and landless.

Next to agriculture was mining. Starting on the aggressive note that has characterized the history of mineral exploration in the country, a foreign company sent a survey party to the tin-producing area of Plateau in 1902. Ignoring local protests, tin mining began two years after. If the evidence of exploitation can be contested in some other aspects of the economy, not so with the mining industry. The colonial government allowed foreign firms excessive control on the mines. The firms sought optimum profits by using minimum technology and maximum labor to obtain tin and other minerals. With hoes, machetes, and baskets, underpaid and unskilled labor searched for tin, wolfram, columbite, gold, and coal in certain parts of the country.[16] Except for coal, which was used to power the railways and was exploited by the government itself, other items were sent abroad, and the workers had little or no share of the profits. Unskilled laborers were attracted by wage incomes, but many discovered that their living standards were no better than what they were used to as farmers. Mining destroyed land and vegetation in some parts of the country, but it made new skills available and the wages received by local workers contributed to the expansion of local trade.[17]

The colonial government was able to generate its revenues in ways associated with the major economic activities outlined above. All the principal methods involved tax on trade and people. The smallest percentage came from collecting tax from foreign companies. Through customs and excise, the government raised revenues from the import-export trade. The most important source was to tax the people, a measure that became widespread after World War I.

A recurrent theme in this analysis, as well as in others that follow, is external trade. In a sense it was the import-export trade that unified the economy: Nigeria with the external world, mediated by transactions in crops and minerals; European firms and farmers, with many locals serving as middlemen; duties from imports and exports financed the government; and taxes from producers and workers added other revenues. Imported items were important, notably consumer goods. It was not just the rank of the growing educated elite that was consuming the imports, even producers in remote villages were imitating the elite and urbanites in purchasing imported textiles, sugar, milk, beverages, and building materials.

The external trade dealt with a limited number of products already mentioned, but the list of imports was longer. A few European companies controlled the most lucrative aspects of it—the international movement and sales of the goods. A dozen or so European firms with the capital and personnel bought almost 95 percent of all the crops. In the war years the United Africa Company acquired the license to purchase 50 percent of peanuts and cocoa and 75 percent of palm kernels. After the war a few Nigerian entrepreneurs entered the business, but control by foreign companies was still above 50 percent. Before 1939 these European firms were served by many Nigerian middlemen. Many among these middlemen operated at a rather small scale, as so-called "pan-buyers," who moved from one village to another to buy small quantities from farmers. Another category of traders, the "scalemen," bought from the pan-buyers. These in turn sold to the "produce buyers" with bigger capital to buy in bulk, store in warehouses, and move goods to the European firms. In a trade marked by competition, prices could fluctuate on a daily basis, and the producers could not even determine ahead of time the prices that would be offered to them.[18]

The "New Economy"

The goal here is not to detail the economic changes prior to 1945[19] but to sketch the main issues and characteristics of the economy, since they constituted what were built upon or reformed during the period under study. The new economy was more exploitative than development oriented. Those who bore the brunt were the farmers. The principal beneficiaries were the colonial governments and the merchants, both foreign and local. To the marginalized groups in a colonial system, notably small-scale producers and the urban landless, the colonial economy laid the foundation of poverty. To the educated elite and local entrepreneurs, the colonial system provided the opportunities for mobility and accumulation.

Adjustments varied from one place to another, even on the basis of social classes. The people also had to adjust to fluctuations in prices and such crises as world wars and the Great Depression. In areas where cash-crop production for export was not common, the people could take to migration, thus creating conditions for the underdevelopment of the rural areas. Where the land could sustain cash crops, enterprising farmers and business-minded people invested in cocoa, peanuts, cotton, and even rubber. Thus productivity expanded in expectation of profits. Where money was made, a substantial portion was used on imported items. Nigerian middlemen were able to expand their businesses by buying farm products and selling to the European firms. Some local merchants actually grew prosperous. Internal trade expanded, as the import-export trade became better integrated. Where the Nigerian merchants could not compete with the European firms, they focused attention on profitable local trade, such as the one in kolanut, salt, cloth, and cattle. To those who were able to deal in export crops in addition to local ones, they were able to make money by being able to advance credit and barter one commodity for another.[20] The successful merchants built impressive houses, raised large families, and invested in the education of their children.

Regional economic disparities began to emerge. The South had more schools than the North, partly because of more intense missionary activities but also because it had more people in wage employment. Combined with money from crops and lorry business, the South had more indicators of progress: houses with pan roofs, storied buildings, schools, and roads of different grades.

The new economy was conditioned by the need to satisfy the goals of the colonial government. This created a narrowly focused economy based primarily on the export of raw materials and some minerals. With this in mind, the government was less motivated to widen the base of the economy. Neither was it preoccupied with using its limited finances for development purposes. Government spending focused on administration (wages and emoluments to civil servants, and the maintenance of the police and army). The budget on social services was generally low. There was also a low percentage of the budget dedicated to "colonial economic development," but this is a misleading label as it referred mainly to railways, harbors, and facilities to promote external trade and not to the welfare of Nigerians. In the first half of the century there were no manufacturing industries of any substance, and the extracted tin was taken abroad to be smelted. A number of local industries declined in importance, but those that catered to the needs of the elite (such as expensive, handwoven textiles) continued to thrive. Local crafts with import substitutes faced stiff competition, such as pottery, soap making, and salt manufacturing. Where imported items were cheap, such as low-quality textiles, they made the goods available to poor consumers. Where some communities had relied on crafts that declined, they either had to move to other occupations or endure sharp falls in income. The big firms that controlled the economy were not interested in industrialization. They could take palm oil to Europe and return with soap. The firms in Nigeria were servicing those abroad, and each calculated the best ways to make profit.

A combination of state control and free enterprise comprised economic policy. The government built the railways and roads, provided electricity and communication facilities, and managed the coal that fueled the railway. The resources came from commercial agriculture, which owed to the local farmers. In other words, the mixed economy depended on the state and farmers, with private investments connecting them. The private investments did not get involved in agricultural production, concentrating mainly on trade. It can be assumed that the mixed economy operated to favor foreign companies. From the point of view of the colonial government, Nigeria was open to British investors. Companies from other countries did compete, as in the case of German ones that took 40 percent of exports between 1900 and 1914. Nigeria was expected to be financially self-sufficient. After 1916 the country balanced its budget and serviced the loans acquired to construct the railways. Through some indirect ways, capital left the country in various forms: as in payments to the British government and companies for services rendered, contributions to World War I, the country's reserve held abroad, and the supply of raw materials.

It was a dependent economy, a pattern that has since been retained. Incorporation into the world economy started in the fifteenth century with the slave trade, later changed to trade in raw materials during the nineteenth century. The emphasis on farm products and minerals meant that no area would escape dependence on the market and Europe. As the core of its economy revolved around the production of primary products, it complemented the British economy, which required raw materials. Either as producers, miners, laborers, migrant workers, or artisans, the majority of Nigerians were pressured to create or consume and to depend on the outside world to generate demands for their products. The world economy penetrated rural Nigeria, bringing with it capitalist relations of production and exchange. Both in its positive and negative changes, Nigeria would not be the same again, as it would be drawn into the volatility of an unstable world economy.[21]

This incorporation has meant that the country would be affected by changes and developments elsewhere. If the industrialized world were prosperous, Nigerians would benefit; if they witnessed a downturn, Nigerians would suffer. The prices Nigerians received and their ability to maintain a decent livelihood would depend in part on the fortunes, or otherwise, of others. Throughout the twentieth century the economy responded to changes in the international system. For instance, in the late 1920s and early 1930s the economy suffered from the Great Depression, when export prices dropped. As world trade slumped in 1929, the value of the export trade reduced by almost 50 percent. Wages, taxes, and prices also fell. The colonial government had to service its debts, pay its officials, and repatriate some profits abroad, all of which meant that the welfare of Nigerians would be secondary. The consequences lasted until the mid-1930s, a great reminder to people that they could be powerless in determining their conditions and future. During World War II demand rose again, and prices increased after the war. For instance, in 1940 the export of 89,000 tons of cocoa brought £1.5 million. Ten years later 100,000 tons fetched £18.9 million, representing a staggering increase of 916 percent. When the volume declined from 100,000 in 1950 to 88,000 in 1955, it was a time of huge price increases that brought £26.1 million. Cocoa prices declined in 1948–49 because of a trade recession in the United States, while the prices increased in the 1950s because of panic buying. Expansion and contraction have both continued to be features of the economy; the country had limited power to control the quantity and prices of its products. The value of export crops was determined in part by demand but also by competition with other countries with similar crops.

Whether in a boom or depression, the colonial system was successful in the cultivation of taste for imported items. The country entered the twentieth century with minimum dependence on imported items. In the South, the area with the greatest interaction with European commodities, the items in use at the beginning of the century were still limited and hardly necessary for day-by-day survival. Notable imports such as gin and clothing were luxury items. However, as colonialism established itself, imported items became many, crucial, and gradually inevitable as in the case of machinery, cars, and a variety of luxury items all needed by a new, educated elite.

Merchant capitalism favored foreigners, and its structure tended to be more monopolistic than competitive. The century opened with a handful of firms controlling the major trade and thus making substantial profits.[22] This trend continued, with cases of companies creating mergers to increase profit margins. A big company emerged in 1919 known as the African and Eastern Trade Corporation (AETC). In 1929 Lever Brothers and AETC combined to create the United African Company (UAC), later acquired by Lever Brothers and the Unilever Group. The UAC became so dominant in the 1930s that it controlled more than 40 percent of the import and export trade, in addition to having the largest number of retail and wholesale stores in the country. Foreign firms also established monopoly control on shipping, banking, mining, and sawmills. A small-but-lucrative corner was also occupied by Indians and Levantines, who served mainly as middlemen. Many Lebanese were to become successful as produce buyers and retailers.[23]

The consequences of foreign domination of the economy included the repatriation of profits outside of the country, the underpayment of Nigerian workers and producers, the failure to develop industries, the low prices of export goods, the attractive prices of imports to the companies, and the emphasis of the economy largely on trade. This transfer of wealth to Europe meant, in part, that the profits generated by economic activities in Nigeria were not used to strengthen local economies.

A point that absorbed the attention of the anticolonial critics was the slow rise of indigenous entrepreneurs. To compete with foreign firms was difficult for Nigerians who lacked the knowledge of business in Europe, access to money, contacts with shipping companies, and the experience to compete. What the enterprising ones did was to collaborate with them, profiting less from direct trade but from internal retails and wholesales. Together with the companies, the local entrepreneurs exploited local farmers and small-scale traders. To scholars of the radical persuasion, the Nigerian entrepreneurs were ruthless profiteers who allowed foreign companies to penetrate the country. Nevertheless, many exhibited great skills as middlemen, taking imports from foreign firms to distribute locally and buying agricultural materials to sell to the big exporters. They sold whatever commodity would bring money, be it cocoa or cassava. Ignoring their methods of profit-making, a few among them have received glowing praises as successful entrepreneurs.[24]

The economic changes affected social classes in different ways. A small percentage of the population made good incomes, were able to live well, and to acquire imported items. The impact on the rural majority who sustained the economy varied greatly. Where opportunities existed to plant and market cocoa and peanuts, a large number benefited to some degree by obtaining more cash than ever before. Local merchants who were well connected with the foreign firms were able to accumulate wealth by acting as their middlemen. In addition, they moved into sectors that the foreign merchants found either less lucrative or too localized, such as road transport, bread making, and retail sales in rural areas. The most successful among them diversified into real estate and transport business, thereby consolidating their businesses.

However, in most other areas, the income of farmers who relied largely on food crops did not keep up with inflation. The status of farmers declined in relation to wage earners. The combined impact of the changes of the period made farming less attractive as an occupation, and by the 1960s many of the younger generation had preferences for some other careers. Food prices continued to soar, caused in part by increases in population and decline in production.

The areas that required considerable improvements were many. As the characterization of the colonial economy reveals, economic development was either slow or considered irrelevant. Many leading officers contradicted the views of the Nigerian educated elite that progress was slow as they saw the consequences of civilization in what they had accomplished, from the most minor policy to major ones such as taxation or the creation of the railways. There were publications that exaggerated the changes, some even calling them an "economic revolution," as in the often-quoted example of Allan McPhee:

> English capital has come in and built the railways and constructed the harbours and cleared the channels; it has also introduced new cultures and improved old ones; it has built roads and towns and established markets; it has introduced banks and a convenient currency; it has exploited minerals. More than this, English government has brought peace and security and abolished slavery. The result is an enormous expansion of trade, in which the natives performed their part and reaped their reward.[25]

Some were even more glowing, often contradicted by official condemnation of the poor and "primitive" and of those labeled the backward elite. McPhee failed to mention that the people paid for the roads and railways; that the communication system moved goods to Europe; that the emphasis was on production for export; that issues of development were taken lightly; that the investments of foreign companies were short-term and calculated for maximum profits; that a so-called philosophy of civilization did not translate to huge public expenditures on education and health; and that few efforts were made to revolutionize agricultural production. The new additions by way of infrastructure and communications were not as many as often portrayed; once the colonial government built the initial railways and dirt roads, there was no need to create more. Some changes began to take place after 1940.

The Economy during World War II

As stated earlier, Nigeria was drawn into World War II mainly to supply resources to assist Britain and its allies. As far as the colonial government was concerned, Nigeria must join all the other colonies to provide the necessary supplies to win the war. In Britain itself, the economy was affected by the war, and policies were initiated to alleviate the sufferings of the British people at the expense of those in the colonies. In Nigeria, it was a period marked by a more direct policy of economic exploitation and interference. Conditions were created during the war that changed various aspects of the economy during and after the war. In the area of state intervention in the economy, World War II represented a major phase in the economic history of Nigeria.

The aims of state intervention were clear, all originally associated with the efforts to win the war and to prevent any likelihood of Germany extending its influence to Nigeria. The possibility of trade leakage to Germany and its allies had to be blocked, by ensuring that exports reached only friendly countries and imports came only from Britain and its allies. A number of European markets were no longer accessible to Nigeria's exports, and the limitation of shipping space and anticipated insecurity on the sea also reduced the opportunities to trade with the United States. The trade in cocoa would be affected, since the supply could be more than what Britain needed. Should the European firms cut down on their purchases in Nigeria, the fear was that the cocoa industry could collapse, and this could in turn create political and social chaos. The British government decided to buy the entire crop, if necessary bearing losses.[26] Foodstuffs and raw materials needed by Britain and its allies had to be supplied, while importers in Africa must recognize the limitation of shipping space and the scarcity of products in Britain. Where imported goods were scarce, local industries had to produce alternatives in part to curb inflation and also to ensure that basic items were available. Indeed, as the volume of imports from European countries was reduced, it became important to think of those alternatives. Where the export of some commodities was necessary but difficult, the government had to find the means to ask the farmers to produce them. If inflation could not be prevented, its rate could be controlled through monetary and economic policies on income, prices, allowances, and wages. All these policies were implemented at different times, but the colonial government hurried to put most of them in place when Italy allied with Germany, and there was the possibility of the German forces making successful advances in Western Europe.

In 1939 legislation was enacted to limit the quantities of goods purchased from countries other than Britain. This affected the importation of textiles and other cheap products from Japan. A much broader policy was to restrict imports in order to conserve foreign exchange. Import restriction was also to punish enemy countries by not buying from them and to ensure that imported goods were necessary to the pursuit of war aims.[27] Some items would be dispensed with, especially those defined as nonessentials, from the colonial government's point of view. If local substitutes were available, then the import would be curtailed, a decision that could have helped the country if more fully pursued. Similarly, a policy of export restriction was implemented on foodstuffs, animal feeds, chemicals, and metals. To the colonial government, the restrictions were necessary in order to prevent diversion of goods to enemy countries, ensure adequate stock in Britain, and to use goods for politics with friendly countries when it became necessary. Policies on exports and imports were also geared toward maximizing the use of scarce shipping space.[28] Changes were tied to new currency regulations to prevent the fall of the British sterling. In 1939 the pound sterling depreciated in value to the American dollar. With other anticipated economic problems, the British government decided to withdraw Nigeria and other countries from the sterling block. Nigeria was free to carry out its own exchange control, but in a way that British sterling and the economy were not threatened. Import control measures ensured that Nigeria would conserve its hard currency by only spending on bare necessities and being careful with capital movements. The results of the currency regulations were to create reserves for Nigeria: the country extended credit to Britain, not only by keeping its reserves there but also by not spending much money during the war.

A policy was also put in place to regulate the prices of export crops. The government decided to fix the prices of all items and to become the sole buyers of some others. With respect to cocoa, the Ministry of Food in London decided to buy all the cocoa in the 1939–40 season. In 1940, the West African Cocoa Board (WACB), controlled by the Colonial Office in London, took over the buying of cocoa. Two years later the same agency (now known as the West African Produce Control Board) added oil and oil seeds to the list of items it purchased. All the exportable oil products (peanuts, palm kernels, and palm oil) were purchased by the Ministry of Food from 1939 to 1942, as there was a market for them. When the Far East fell in 1942, there was further reliance on Nigeria's oil, and farmers were urged to supply more food and cash crops. The various control boards were established to accumulate surplus by underpaying producers. The boards offered Nigerian crops to British buyers at affordable prices. As Nigerians were denied avenues to sell their products at competitive prices, the colonial government established an exploitative monopoly. The revenues accrued by the boards were used to buy low-yielding British stock.

Many control measures were taken that allowed the state to interfere in all major economic spheres. Control measures were announced on produce marketing, food marketing, food prices, and transport. For a company to operate freely and without state interference became difficult indeed. The companies had to apply for licenses and to seek permission of the government to conduct a variety of businesses. A bureaucracy geared toward the maintenance of law and order now acquired control over the economy, and its performance was not always satisfactory. By encroaching upon the economy with so much control, the government opened itself to criticisms and pressure from competing business interests. As far as many Nigerian entrepreneurs were concerned, the government was using its power in favor of expatriate companies.

In view of import restriction, import licensing was introduced. The aim was to use licenses to check the quantities of products that came to the country. Licenses were to be granted when local stocks of essential commodities were low, where an item had to be obtained from areas outside of the United Kingdom, or when it was necessary to trade with countries supportive of British war aims.[29] A new agency was created, the Nigeria Supply Board, charged with the task of coordinating war needs and controlling the prices and quantities of exports and imports.

To start with imports, a primary concern was to conserve foreign exchange and ensure the availability of some essential items. Books, seeds, and medicine were exempted from control; imports of nonessentials were restricted or prohibited altogether; and licenses granted to import in order to monitor the articles as well as the total income being used.[30]

Regarding exports, the focus was on the principal products of cocoa, peanuts, and palm produce. A number of companies would be allowed to buy these products on behalf of the government. The government fixed the price, a low payment to farmers, a middleman's brokerage, and a commission to the firms that exported them. Not only was the price low and fixed, the government would also determine the quantity to purchase.[31] The export of these crops was presented to the farmers as more of a burden to the government than a commercial calculation. Nevertheless, a shrewd price policy ensured that the government did not incur great losses. Prices of cocoa were marked down, with the result that the prices in the world market were considerably higher than what was locally offered and the government was able to amass a huge surplus of close to £4 million between 1939 and 1943. What started as a policy to protect farmers from losses ended in enriching the government.[32] The marketing board chose the buying firms to purchase cocoa, giving each one a quota, and it paid the firm an amount to cover the purchase price of cocoa and profits.

Industrialization would also receive a small boost from a less likely source. In order to conserve shipping space, some companies decided to process bulky raw materials in Nigeria. This opened up opportunities for cottage industries and small manufacturing plants. The companies also realized that there was indeed a market for many products. Some goods were in short supply or imports were totally impossible, thus promoting local manufactures in items such as building materials and furniture. Many Nigerians began to make demands for the establishment of industries, with the belief that they would make it possible to generate wealth to individuals. The creation of industries would become one of the most important new changes after the war.

The Economy in Transition

The Nigerian economy witnessed its greatest expansion after 1945. A substantial increase in public spending, an agricultural boom, and the creation of new industries are some of the reasons for this phenomenal expansion. Many of the restrictions of the war period were lifted, thus generating greater trade and income. The value of total exports rose from £23.7 million in 1946 to £129.8 million in 1955 and to £165.6 in 1960. Similarly, the value of imports rose from £19.8 million in 1946 to £136.1 million in 1955 and to £215.9 million in 1960.[33] The country was confident that money was available for development. A first plan of development was published in 1945, the Colonial Development and Welfare Act of 1945, which identified a number of key sectors to be financed.

The foundations of modern industries were laid. Thanks to the boom in export trade, there was money in circulation to sustain purchase. The number of wage earners had equally increased. Foreign companies realized that they could indeed make sufficient profit by establishing some industries to produce cigarettes, soap, beer, metal drums, and to extract palm oil. Local substitutes were found for items that were too bulky to transport, such as cement and beer. With modern department stores coming onto the scene, outlets did exist to sell the products. The United Africa Company (UAC) founded the Nigerian Breweries in 1949, and a host of new industries by other companies followed in the 1950s. Some were assembly plants of components manufactured abroad, such as Bedford lorries and Raleigh bicycles. No doubt the biggest industrial project at the time was the Sapele sawmill and plywood plant, which employed about three thousand people. Prospecting for minerals was undertaken. Huge deposits of limestone later led in 1961 to the building of a cement company. The biggest prize of them all was petroleum, discovered to be in large quantities in the late 1950s but not fully exploited until after 1967.

Nigerian entrepreneurs witnessed their first major break during this period.[34] It was still difficult for them to compete with the foreigners who controlled over 80 percent of the business; however, they had greater opportunities than before. In the 1950s and beyond, foreign firms gradually appointed more Nigerians to positions of authority, partly in order to deal with the flood of criticism that they practiced a policy of discrimination. The executive positions in charge of major decisions were still retained, in many cases until the 1970s. The control of state power at the regional level enabled Nigerian entrepreneurs to have greater access to contracts and capital. Some were able to move into construction, import-export business, baking, printing, furniture making, and other emerging small businesses that produced soap, textiles, and bottles.

Some business fields were relinquished by foreign firms, either because they were becoming less profitable or they feared that the competition with Nigerians could ruin them. These firms began to withdraw from retail trade and move to wholesale trade and department stores. Those with substantial capital also moved to manufacturing. In the 1950s, when government policy was to encourage the creation of industries, foreign firms found it far more profitable to invest in new import-substitution industries. New industrial centers were beginning to emerge in Kano, Port Harcourt, and Lagos. Among the notable industrial projects of this period included those of food canning, boat building, textiles, cement, cigarettes, soap, margarine, plastics, and oil. As the foreign firms left some businesses, Nigerians found opportunities as their replacements.

Generous conditions to establish industries were provided by all the regional governments in the 1950s. Ignoring the "voice" of radicals and socialists that foreign funding and investments would undermine the country's independence, the regions sought the means to attract foreign investments and to develop local ones at the same time. To the regional leaders and planners, industries would empower the country, reduce dependence, and alleviate poverty. More often than not, the concerns to develop industries were presented at either the expense of agriculture or as an alternative to agriculture. An economy based on agriculture was assumed to lead to poverty, dependence on the West, and a slow economic growth. In presenting this argument and embarking on policies that showed that the argument was sound, the country ultimately devastated its agriculture and failed to develop a credible industrial economy.

Thus, efforts by the regional governments were directed at looking for the means to create industries. Capital was necessary, and the belief before revenues began to come from oil after 1967 was that this would come from the outside and be provided by the government. As the activities of development institutions and government documents revealed, a set of policies had to be formulated to remove the obstacles to industrialization. It was believed, and rightly so, that the managerial and engineering skills to run modern industries were in limited supplies. The universities and technical schools were supposed to correct this. Not many Nigerians had the money to establish industries. Foreign investors had to be invited, and the government had to create businesses and to fund enterprising Nigerians. Indeed, rather than fund people to go into farming, where it was assumed that profits were much smaller and difficult to make, they could be funded to establish industries in order to "modernize" the economy and society.

The central and regional governments announced various incentives in the 1950s in order to promote industries and business incentives. Some of them actually benefited foreigners rather than Nigerians or made it possible for the British to maintain a hold on the economy after their withdrawal in 1960. Some of the development agencies discussed in the next chapter were mandated to promote the creation of new industries and to provide loans to entrepreneurs. In 1952 the central government enacted the Aid to Pioneer Industries Ordinance that relieved companies declared as "pioneers" from paying company tax for between two and three years. A change in income tax law in the same year also allowed the companies to write off their capital investment in fixed assets, in order to enable them to build capital. The Industrial Research Institute was established in 1956 to undertake research on local materials and to fund pilot projects in various industrial areas that could be commercialized.[35]

What, then, was the picture of the industrial sector by 1960? The rough data began to be published only during the 1950s, notably in the *Nigerian National Accounts, 1950–57*, led by a pioneer economist, P. N. C. Okigbo. Taking 1950 as a baseline, the *National Accounts* estimated the contribution of industrial production to the GDP at 2.8 percent. The pattern of the period is more than clear. Regarded primarily as a source of raw materials, the idea was not to generate any massive industrial output. When industries were being created, they were done in a way to reinforce the focus on agriculture. Thus, initial activities were to reduce the cost of freight by reducing the bulk of raw materials exports (for example, rubber processing, peanut crushing, and cotton ginning). Also, as in

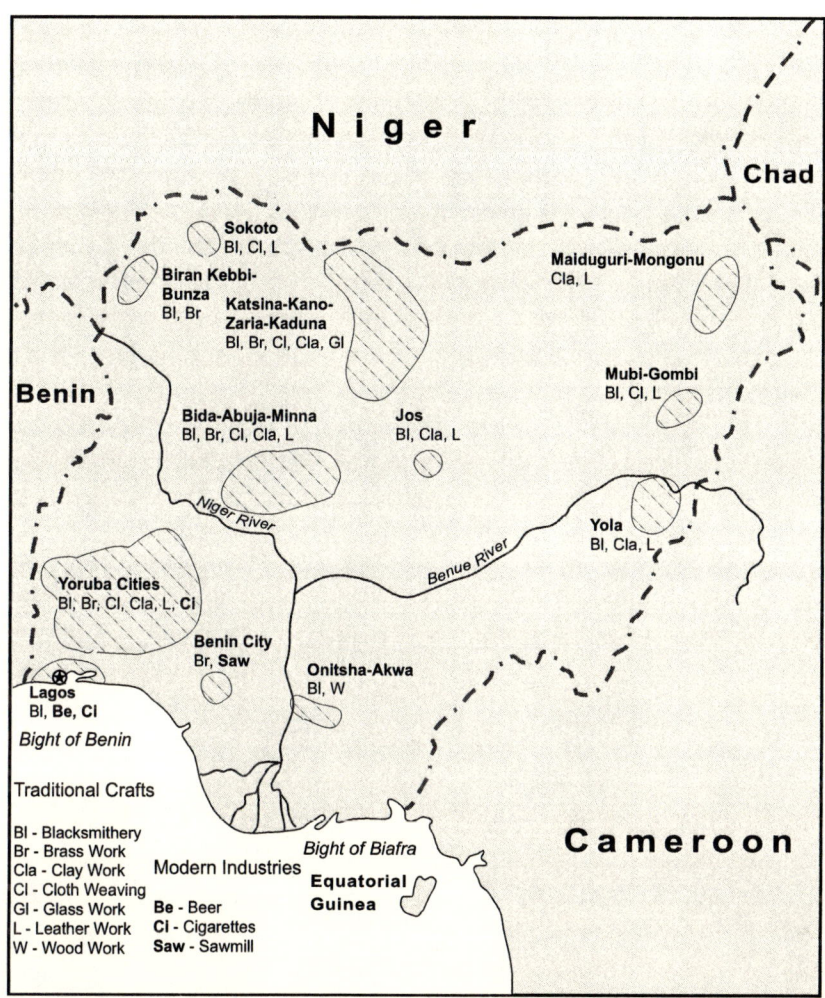

Early Industry in Nigeria

the example of palm products and timber, the materials could also be readied for better processing in Europe. Consumer-oriented companies began to appear after 1940, focusing on leather tanning, sawmilling, and peanut crushing in mills around Kano in the North, rubber processing and palm kernel crushing in the South, and ginneries were established in the North by the British Cotton Growers Association. Other companies were added, notably by the Unilever Group, which produced soft drinks and soap, the Nigerian Breweries produced beer, and the British Tobacco Company produced cigarettes.

The manufacturing sector was not large. A few companies enjoyed "pioneer status," which gave some tax advantages. They were allowed to import the materials and technology they required, and the Nigerian currency could be used in the West African region. However, the companies had to compete with imported items, which ensured that the quality of their product must be high to command respect. The companies were foreign-owned, mainly because the majority of Nigerians lacked the capital to create huge manufacturing operations. The technology, too, was foreign, usually from Britain. However, the Nigerian contributions to this sector were substantial. As many of them were based on the use of local resources, agriculture was connected with manufacturing. Although the number was small (less than 50,000 by 1960), Nigerians supplied the labor. Cheap labor ensured a low-cost production that made it possible to export bulky items.

In spite of the rather extensive and excessive discussion on industries during the period, agriculture remained the bedrock of the economy. Indeed, the expansion in other sectors owed much to the production of export crops to generate external revenues as well as foodstuffs for the country's growing population. The majority of the population survived on agriculture. In the years with available data, the predominant role of agriculture in economy and society is too clear not to see. To take the example of the 1950s, when some data were gathered, two-thirds of the national income came from agriculture: the value of agricultural exports rose from £78.6 million in 1950 to £139.4 million in 1959, when the overall exports for the same period were £88.4 million in 1950 and £160.5 in 1959. Table 1 provides the earnings for the entire decade.

A large percentage of the population (77.7 percent for women and 78.6 for men) were engaged in farming, fishing, and forestry in 1952–53. The transport system as well as extensive marketing profited mainly from agriculture. There was a rise in imported items, indicating an increasing prosperity of the people. The value of imports in 1950 was £61.8 million; in 1954, it rose to £114 million. What sustained the increase were the revenues from the exports of cash crops. The revenues from agriculture also sustained public expenditures on education, health, transport, communication, and other sectors. And, as indicated below, the marketing boards created huge surpluses from the sales of cash crops, and part of the money was used for development purposes.

Good weather and steady incomes made agriculture a reliable revenue earner. Shortages of raw materials in many parts of the Western world instigated a huge demand and better prices. Fat supplies were short, more so after the collapse of the Asian empire, and Britain turned to Nigeria to supply more. The colonial government fixed the prices of exports, and the Ministry of Food in the United Kingdom was the only buyer of oilseeds at a price that would keep production going. An export boom followed, and lasted until the 1950s.[36] Although the farmers continued to be underpaid, they still were able to make

Table 1. Earnings from Agricultural and Domestic Exports

Year	Imports (£m.)	Domestic Exports (£m.)	Agricultural Exports (£m.)	Agric. Percent of Domestic Exports
1950	61.8	88.4	78.6	88.9
1951	84.5	116.6	100.7	86.4
1952	113.2	125.1	110.1	88.0
1953	108.2	120.8	104.2	86.3
1954	114.0	146.2	127.3	87.1
1955	136.1	129.8	108.6	83.7
1956	152.7	132.2	112.7	85.2
1957	152.4	124.1	104.6	84.3
1958	167.0	132.7	115.4	87.0
1959	179.5	160.5	139.4	80.9

Source: H. A. Oluwasanmi, *Agriculture and Nigerian Economic Development* (Ibadan: Oxford Univ. Press, 1966), 225.

profits. New roads were opened in the 1940s and 1950s that allowed more movement of goods and people between the cities and villages.

The land devoted to cash crops, notably cocoa, palm trees, and peanuts, expanded greatly. Agricultural departments were active in distributing insecticides and fungicides in order to increase productivity. More labor went into agriculture, especially into the highly specialized production of cash crops. As before, the major products were cocoa, cotton, peanuts, oil palm products, and rubber. Each of these witnessed some major changes in cultivation and trade. Regarding the oil products, the concerns of the period were on improvement in the quality of oil shipped abroad and on efforts to increase productivity. The production of oil palm products was still in the hands of millions of small-scale farmers in southern Nigeria. The West African Institute for Oil Palm Research in Benin was active in distributing seedlings that could produce high-yield trees, while its officers visited some locations to teach farmers the most effective methods to space new trees. New methods to extract oil from the pericarp began to spread. In the traditional methods of extraction, between 45 and 60 percent of the oil was lost. Hand-presses reduced the loss by almost 20 percent, while the pioneer oil mills were able to extract almost 85 percent. Nevertheless, technology of oil extraction was slow in spreading to many villages, where the women who controlled the industry feared that the use of the new machines would be dominated by men.

Cocoa was still the leading crop in the western part of the country. The industry recovered from the price decline of the war years and the three infections that devastated many trees (capsids, black pods, and swollen shoot) to enter an era of expansion and boom in the 1950s. In the North cotton production increased, and new higher-yield strains were introduced to many farmers. Similarly, rubber and peanut production witnessed expansion.

The public expenditure on agriculture concentrated on research, which included the establishment of agricultural schools to provide staff who would popularize modern agricultural methods, and the establishment of research farms to experiment with new seeds, methods, and technologies. Each crop had a research institute devoted to it: the Cocoa Research Institute at Ibadan, the West African Institute for Oil Palm Research in Benin, and the Central Research Organization in Samaru.

State intervention began at both the central and regional levels. As with many other aspects of the economy, an interventionist orientation began during World War II. In addition, issues of development and welfare were also being discussed. To some colonial officers, development and welfare should be linked by one thing: production. If the farmers produced, resources would be available to improve their conditions. In Britain a group of policy makers argued that the colonies should produce more in order to assist in overcoming the economic crisis of the postwar years. In 1948, a measure was passed to create the Overseas Resources Development Act aimed at generating more production in the colonies (to be sold in the United States) partly in order to pay off war debts. The 1948 act led to the establishment of two agencies, the Overseas Food Corporation and the Colonial Development Corporation (CDC).

It was the CDC that had an impact on Nigerian agriculture. Its task was to invest in agriculture and other aspects of the economy largely ignored by the private sector. The CDC chose to invest in oilseed in Nigeria, leading to the establishment of the West African Groundnut Scheme, also known as the Niger Agricultural Project (NAP). Launched in 1948, the NAP was the country's first major capital-intensive agricultural project. It collapsed five years later, revealing in part the failure to enhance productivity through state intervention.[37] The project was sited in Mokwa, a town located between the two northern emirates of Kontagora and Bida in the Niger province. The choice was based on a belief that a less densely populated area would offer less political resistance to a new project. As the land and area were considered as poor and infected with diseases, NAP hoped to show that a rapid agricultural improvement could also bring about an immediate increase in the standard of living to the people. A scheme that would use modern equipment and cultivate a large expanse of land was embarked upon. The first major problem was to recruit labor. The people in the area either preferred to migrate southward to the cocoa-growing area or to continue work on their small holdings. The project had to rely on forced labor, by requesting the chiefs to send their men to work for what was supposed to be a commercial enterprise. Resentment followed, as the people were unwilling to cooperate. NAP also realized that mechanization was limited to only plowing and ridging, which meant that the machines were actually idle for most of the time. When the peanuts were harvested, the marketing boards bought them at a price that did not justify the cost of production.

At the regional level, the attempt was to increase agricultural production at a number of locations. Loan schemes were established, but the funds were usually directed to nonagricultural activities, even to building personal residential homes. Yet another project was the resettlement schemes. There was a belief that hill farmers would do better by moving to the plains. In the precolonial era some groups chose to live on hills for defensive purposes, and they developed great skills to manage slopes and erosions. During the twentieth century some of these groups began to abandon the hills because they felt more secure, wanted more land to expand agriculture, or preferred the plains for building houses.[38] The colonial government forced some of them to relocate, fearing that the hills offered opportunities for anticolonial protests. Resettlement schemes embarked on from the 1940s onward offered inducements for the hill farmers to move. In 1948 the Shendam Resettlement Scheme embarked on a project to move many groups in the Plateau to the Benue lowlands. In Plateau the Jema'a Scheme resettled a number of Birom; in the Mandara Mountains, the Gwosa Resettlement Schemes began in 1952 and attained a limited success.[39]

Local trade benefited from the agricultural boom. Markets expanded in different parts of the country, and many more people took to trading. Local produce buyers increased in number, and many among them grew prosperous. Nigerians associated the 1950s with prosperity. The number of schoolchildren increased substantially, as either their parents were able to fund them or the regional governments provided free education. In the informal sector activities such as repairs of house utensils, cabinet making, and baking became established. Older crafts such as cloth weaving gained influence.

An era of economic planning began, as the government was prepared to invest in development. A Colonial Development and Welfare Act was embarked upon, leading to the "First Plan" in the country to cover the decade 1945–55.[40] Development was designed to minimize political tension at a time when many were being discharged from the army, workers were becoming more restless, and the nationalists were making a variety of demands.

As the country moved to the 1950s and Nigerians began to control power, an era of underspending by British officers gave way to overspending by Nigerian politicians. Gradually, this culture took root, with a belief that what was needed to solve any problem was to throw money at it. Much money was thrown

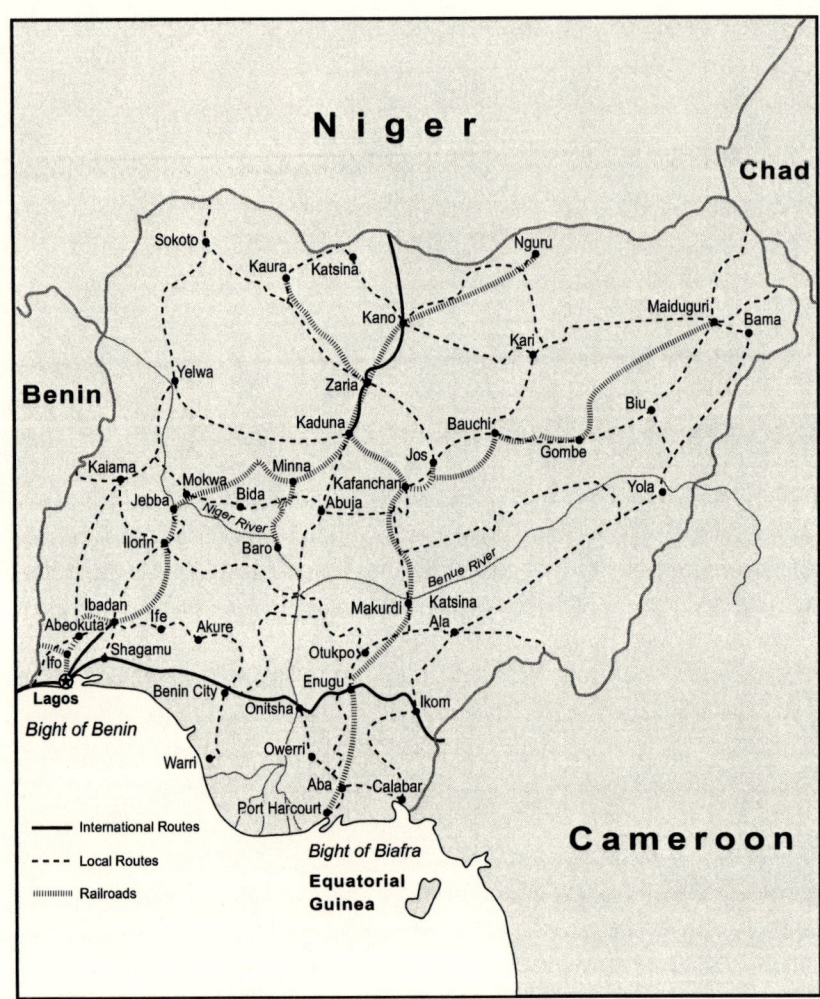

Early Rail and Road Networks

but not always with good results. Corruption on a large scale began to damage the credibility of individuals and that of the country.

Among the areas that received attention in the 1950s were the expansion of the educational system, roads, and hospitals. Space does not allow for a full elaboration, but some important aspects of change can be catalogued here in respect to a number of major sectors. With respect to transport and communication, many things were new and the older roads and railways were maintained. The Niger-Benue river system was improved to provide for better inland waterways. River transport continued to perform rather slowly, compared to roads and railways, although the potentials of the country were now fully known, with intelligent suggestions on how to improve on them.[41] The ports in Lagos, Port Harcourt, Sapele, Warri, Burutu, Calabar, and Degema continued to handle more traffic. One of the major changes was the establishment of the Nigerian Ports Authority in 1954 to manage and improve services. With respect to the railways, the main thing was not to build new lines but to maintain existing coaches and engines. The route mileage was largely unchanged, but the number of passengers continued to record an increase that averaged between five and seven million each year.[42] Road construction was impressive, as both the central and regional governments added new ones and maintained the older ones. The total road mileage in the country almost doubled in a fifteen-year period, from 25,433 miles in 1946 to 41,065 by 1960. Only 5,434 miles were tarred, and the rest were either in gravel or earth. Commercial air transport began in 1946, with small facilities for internal travels and later with two major airports in Lagos and Kano for international flights. The combined impact of air, road, and rail travel contributed to the expansion and efficiency of postal services. Industries, notably mining, oil exploration, public utilities and manufacturing, began to make a slow but impressive contribution to the economy.

A planning effort after 1945 called for more spending, while the adoption of a federal system gave rise to the need to reallocate revenues to the three regions. The sources of revenues did not change for the entire period. The bulk came from customs and excise, which contributed almost 43 percent in 1946 and dramatically increased to 73 percent by 1960. Export duties were raised on palm oil, palm kernels, cocoa, peanuts, hides and skins, and tin, all in order to generate more revenues. Producers were also made to lose some of their profits through the Produce Sales Tax on all the major export crops. Import duties were increased during the same period, in order to make additional revenues from highly demanded products, such as cigarettes, building materials, and alcohol. Where local substitutes were becoming available, such as cigarettes and textiles in the 1950s, an additional levy was imposed on imports just to discourage flooding the market. The various raises on duties were justified by the need to meet the cost of social services.[43] Income tax was also increased in some places, such as Lagos, and regulations were enacted on company tax. Incidence of tax evasion remained high. Between 1946 and 1955 a sum of £36,380,000 also came by way of grants from the Colonial Development and Welfare Act.[44]

If it appears that the country was increasing the size of its income, so too was it spending more. From a total expenditure of £10.6 million in 1946, it increased to £55.3 million in 1950 and £81.7 million in 1960.[45] The federal and regional governments were also acquiring loans, although the total national debt was small. The loans of the regional governments were mainly internal, acquired from the marketing boards. The central government took both internal and external loans. The internal loans were supplied by banks, individuals, cooperative societies, and insurance companies. External loans were obtained from the London money market. By 1960, the interest payment on loans amounted to £2.5 million, a small percentage of total revenue. Nevertheless, the debts represented a major increase over that of the period before the war. Before 1940, public debt was small and mainly spent on building the railways. After 1946, however, the reasons to acquire debts were to accelerate the pace of development in many sectors—agriculture, transport, communications, health, and education. Thus, the federal government acquired £24.8 million in 1946, an amount that increased by £10 million in 1960.[46]

Economic expansion did come during the period, although the evidence of growth did not necessarily translate to a higher standard of living for all Nigerians. Since the national income was very much tied to agriculture, prosperity depended on favorable prices and the ability to distribute the benefits to the majority of the population. As the regional governments took hold, they were rewarding the cities more than the villages, the elite more than the uneducated. Material prosperity was obvious, although the population enjoying it was limited. The educated elite certainly had more opportunities than others.

The pace of growth in sectors such as education and transport was phenomenal. Capital formation among a rising class of entrepreneurs and elites grew at an impressive rate. So also was the volume of national income, which grew because of increases in prices and exports. Although not always reliable, the statistics indicate growth in various sectors. Imports increased, indicating a growing pattern of consumption. Imports increased substantially in value, from a mere £8.6 million in 1937–38 to £215.4 million in 1959–60. The sales of locally manufactured items were on the rise, estimated to be rising at about 15 percent each year. As entrepreneurs, local and foreign, benefited from the increase in public spending and the provision of infrastructure and communication facilities, so too did the level of investments continue to rise. Taking the figures of the major companies alone, their investments increased from £11.7 million in 1954 to £21 million six years later. The contribution of the informal sector is hard to quantify, but growth was visible in various areas as more and more people demanded services and had income to spend.

Increases in productivity were noted in the production of agricultural crops. Indeed, if the population increase was put at 2 percent, that of agricultural productivity was estimated at 30 percent, a trend that could not be sustained in future years. The majority of the population were still farmers, and agriculture contributed more than 60 percent of the national income. Although it was heavily dependent on agriculture, the national economy was still regarded as prosperous and capable of phenomenal growth.[47] Manufacturing industries were growing, recording a 20 percent increase in a space of fifteen years. Water and electricity supply increased about fourfold, as many new towns had services extended to them.

The combined production of all sectors grew, in real terms, at about 4 percent between 1950 and 1960. A rough estimate of the nation's income in 1950–51 was put at £593 million, a figure that recorded a rapid increase six years later, to £812 million.[48] This figure has been contested, for it failed to correctly value the prices of food items. R. O. Ekundare suggests that the figures for the Gross Domestic Product (GDP) reflect a better picture. The GDP actually showed a dramatic increase: at 1957 prices, the GDP was £688.7 million in 1950, increasing to £895.2 million in 1953 and £981.3 in 1960.[49] Using these and other figures, Ekundare also sees an increase in the country's wealth:

> The total gross capital formation in Nigeria was estimated at £36.6 million, of which 45.1 per cent came from the public sector and 54.9 per cent from the private sector. In 1955–6 it increased to £78.3 million, of which the public sector accounted for £45.1, i.e. 57.6 per cent, and the private sector £33.2 million, i.e. 42.4 per cent. Finally, in 1959–60 the total gross capital formation reached the highest value so far of £133.4 million. Of this value the public sector accounted for £88.9 million, i.e. 66.6 per cent, and the private sector 33.4 per cent.[50]

The picture of the "new economy" was clearer to see in the 1950s. In spite of the great changes in transportation and production, living standards were still low. The per capita income in 1952–53 was £21, compared to that of £200 in the West. Table 2 shows the breakdown of the components of the GDP during this period. The total value of all the goods produced amounted to £680 million. Of this, £665 million, almost 98 percent of the gross domestic product represented the income of Nigerians, and the remainder of £15 million represented payments to the nationals of other countries or dividends and interest to foreign countries. Agriculture (farming, forestry, fishing, and animal husbandry) generated two-thirds of the total income. The distribution and transportation sectors and the marketing boards accounted for 15 percent, manufacturing was 2 percent, industries 3 percent, and all the other sources accounted for one-tenth of the total economic output.

Table 2. Gross Domestic Product of Nigeria, 1952–1953

	Million £	% of Total
Agriculture	450.2	66.1
Farm Crops	305.0	44.8
Tree Crops	77.2	11.3
Forest Products	27.3	4.0
Livestock Products	34.4	5.1
Fishing	6.3	.9
Industry	71.2	10.5
Minerals	9.5	1.4
Manufactures and Power	3.9	.6
Building and Civil Engineering	48.3	7.1
Handicraft	9.5	1.4
Services	128.5	18.9
Transport and Distribution*	104.5	15.4
Bank, Insurance, and Other Professions	1.1	.2
Missions	3.0	.4
Domestic Services	3.5	.5
Miscellaneous Services	6.4	.9
Ownership of Building	6.0	.9
Intrahousehold Services	4.0	.6
Government	30.4	4.5
Total	680.3	100.0

*Including operation of marketing boards
Source: IBRD, *The Economic Development of Nigeria* (Baltimore, Md.: Johns Hopkins Univ. Press, 1955), 13.

Table 3. Output and Value of the Principal Export Crops in Selected Years, 1900–1959

Year	Cocoa '000 tons	Cocoa '000 GDP	Palm Oil '000 tons	Palm Oil '000 GDP	Palm Kernels '000 tons	Palm Kernels '000 GDP	Groundnuts '000 tons	Groundnuts '000 GDP	Cotton '000 tons	Cotton '000 GDP	Rubber '000 tons	Rubber '000 GDP
1900	.2	8	45.0	681	85.0	833	.6	3	—	—	1.2	185
1928	49.1	2,420	127.0	3,751	246.0	4,423	103.0	1,848	3.7	348	2.3	255
1938	97.1	1,567	110.0	981	312.0	2,168	180.0	1,306	5.7	297	2.9	136
1940	89.0	1,583	132.7	1,099	236.0	1,500	169.0	1,476	9.0	622	2.9	265
1950	100.0	18,984	173.0	12,072	410.0	16,694	317.0	15,237	12.6	2,957	13.6	2,835
1955	88.0	26,187	182.1	12,151	433.0	19,196	397.0	23,134	33.1	9,380	30.3	5,577
1956	117.0	23,985	185.2	14,866	451.0	20,440	448.0	27,764	27.0	7,113	38.0	6,409
1957	135.0	26,036	166.5	13,801	406.0	17,959	302.0	20,139	25.0	6,337	39.0	7,022
1958	87.6	26,664	170.5	12,660	441.2	20,448	513.1	26,942	33.7	7,848	40.1	7,632
1959	142.8	38,292	183.6	13,812	430.4	25,968	497.2	27,468	36.8	7,296	53.3	10,608

Source: H. A. Oluwasanmi, *Agriculture and Nigerian Economic Development* (Ibadan: Oxford Univ. Press, 1966), 226.

The Marketing Boards

It is necessary to return to the organization of trade, since the postwar marketing also affected many of the economic changes and the means to generate the funds to initiate major economic reforms and execute the development plan formulated during the period. The major policy of the war years was retained: the economic principle was that statutory marketing agencies were necessary for three reasons. The agencies could achieve enduring stability in prices, a fact already demonstrated. There was an assumption that the producers did not mind this stability, a fact not demonstrated since many did not know the extent to which they were underpaid. The agencies could accumulate surplus, another fact that was so glaringly demonstrated that it was actually the main reason for wishing to continue with the policy of state control. The argument that the surplus should be returned to the producers was rejected:

> In one way or another, since the return of a contribution made to those funds by each individual farmer is plainly impracticable and, even if practicable, would be of negligible benefit to the individual, these sums would have to be expended for the benefit of the producing communities. That by itself implies the establishment of representative boards to direct the process.[51]

Of course, it would be hard to explain why a marketing board should be the appropriate agency to keep funds, not to mention why it was the poorest members of the population who would contribute the funds. One thing that was clear was that the promise of development would minimize the opposition by the nationalists. A few years after the war, the nationalists, now in power, went straight to this account, some for the intended purpose of development, and some to line private pockets.

The marketing boards were established during World War II, originally presented as a "humanitarian" scheme to save farmers from financial ruin, but ultimately becoming an avenue for the government to exploit the poor and to build foreign reserves. The boards effectively put in the hands of the government the power to market crops, a power that was shared with a selected number of privileged firms. Marketing boards aimed at maintaining stable prices for export commodities in order to protect the farmers from the unpredictable fluctuations in prices. The boards would build a reserve by underpaying farmers when prices were high, but subsidizing them when prices were low. The funds generated by the marketing boards sustained many of the activities of the regional governments in the 1950s, funded several development programs, and provided opportunities for the first generation of Nigerian politicians to have access to money that they could use to fund political parties and reward political and business associates.

The marketing boards operated at the expense of millions of poor farmers. In its origins, it was essentially a state intervention program in the economy. A government report in 1946 requested the colonial government to use the experience acquired in managing the economy during World War II by adopting a policy that would stabilize the fluctuating prices of export crops. Statutory marketing organizations were to be created to manage the export of all the crops in a way that prices could be determined ahead of time.[52] The boards were expected to make profits, primarily the difference between the price they paid the farmers and the prices at which they sold on the world market, that is, they would deliberately underpay the farmers. The surplus would be invested abroad (thus helping the British economy with available funds) and used for the development of the areas that produced the crops, as well as sponsor research that would modernize agriculture. The boards were expected to spend their money on three major issues. When prices fell, they were expected to "stabilize" prices by paying farmers at the rates determined ahead of harvest. To this extent, they were expected to set aside 70 percent of their reserves. Of the remaining 30 percent, almost 23 percent was to go to the development of the regions that produced the crops and the rest was to be spent on research.[53]

Between 1947 and 1949 marketing boards were created for cocoa, cotton, peanuts, and palm oil. The first was the cocoa board, empowered to "secure the most favorable arrangements for the purchase, grading, export, and marketing of Nigerian cocoa and to assist in the development by all possible means of the cocoa industry of Nigeria for the benefit and prosperity of the producers."[54] These boards negotiated the sales of crops to external buyers and fixed prices to be paid for the products by the buying agencies. When it was possible, as in some years during the 1940s, the board could engage in bulk purchases so that they could sell to one or two external agencies. The boards for palm oil, palm kernels, peanuts, and benniseed (sesame) were able to sign an agreement with the Ministry of Food in the United Kingdom to purchase these items for three years (1949–52). The prices would be fixed ahead of time, around October, so that the farmers would know what they would receive long before harvest. The Ministry of Food paid far below the market prices, a practice that led to the termination of the bulk-buying agreement in 1954.

At their creation, they inherited a huge sum of £8,320,096, part of what had been accumulated since the war years. After the war the prices of commodities were constantly high, but the boards kept paying lower than the international prices. There were some years when the marketing boards accumulated well over 100 percent. For instance, in 1953 the boards realized on the sales of cocoa £73 million but paid only £28 million to the farmers. These surpluses were mainly kept in British banks, where they were used to finance British economic recovery.

The boards were able to continue with this practice and actually acquired so much excess funds because of the economic boom of the postwar years and the high prices of raw materials. The boards used price fixing to accumulate huge reserves. Prices were arrived at by conditions in the world market, domestic transport cost, and the margins of profits to be made by the produce buyers, the middlemen between the farmers and the boards. In years without contracts for bulk buying with a government agency in Britain, the boards relied on the Nigerian Produce Marketing Company, based in the United Kingdom, to sell on the open market and to organize shipping. When the country adopted a federal system in the early 1950s, the previous single commodity boards were replaced by four regional marketing boards and a federal agency known as the Central Marketing Board.[55] The regional boards purchased the crops in their regions, but all depended on the Central Marketing Board to ship and sell abroad. The regional boards were empowered to commit funds to research and development.

The boards enjoyed monopoly powers. They fixed prices and were the only ones who could buy and sell abroad. Where the products were consumed locally, as in the case of peanuts, the boards had to pay competitive prices, lest the farmers sold to local consumers. In the case of cocoa, there was no local use for the product, and a farmer had to wait for five to seven years before harvesting from a new tree. The fact that the farmers had no use for the products other than to sell them meant that the boards could manipulate the prices to accumulate more reserves. From the point of view of the marketing boards, price fixing was to stabilize the incomes of farmers by protecting them from fluctuations. The marketing boards argued that they could offer advantages to the producers, irrespective of whether the world market prices were high or low:

> In some seasons when world prices are high, the price paid to the producer will be less than the average realization on overseas sales. The boards will, on such occasions, show a "surplus." There will, however, be other seasons in which the average world price is below the price paid to producers. On these occasions the boards will make a "loss," which will be financed from the "surpluses" accrued in years of high world prices. The intention is that "profits" will be utilized primarily to maintain the maximum possible stability in the price paid to the producer.[56]

By imposing prices well ahead of the buying season, the problem of fluctuations was removed.

As in the war years, the boards also appointed and determined the number of buying agents, as well as the profits they were able to make. The boards determined the remuneration to the buying agents, which covered the costs of buying the crops, the marketing and management costs, as well as profit. The business was certainly lucrative, although it is difficult to determine by how much. Certainly, it involved very little risk, since a predetermined amount was paid, and the agent could find the means to save expenses on the marketing functions.

An agent required a license to operate, thus allowing the board to control who had a license. As before, the European firms were the most favored. A buying agent was allowed to buy a minimum of 250 tons, initially with its own money, which was as high as £5,000 in a buying season. To receive a license, a firm must provide evidence that it had at least over £5,000, storage facilities, labor, and adequate resources to transport the products to the port cities. The conditions and the required capital made it difficult for Nigerians to participate as agents. The situation changed after 1954 as more and more Nigerians were able to participate in this lucrative trade. With Nigerians in control of regional governments, pioneer politicians found ways to channel capital to local entrepreneurs, including offering Nigerian entrepreneurs advanced payments for goods and even contracts. The new Nigerian banks awarded credit to businessmen, and the emerging cooperative banks also trusted them with credit.

The buying agents used middlemen who went from one village to the next to buy the products. The middlemen did not usually pay the prices set by the marketing boards, as they too had to make profits after selling to the big buying agents. The competition among middlemen was fierce, and each resorted to various ways to undermine the others. The most common method was to advance credit to the farmer and to obtain their products much later, thereby buying far below the market rate.

To some analysts, the marketing boards were rather exploitative of farmers, by withholding their incomes because the government wanted to keep foreign reserves or to fight future inflation.[57] Some even regarded the activities of the marketing boards as an attempt to collect more tax from the farmers. The marketing boards collected far more surpluses than necessary to maintain price stabilization. Indeed, cases of spending surplus funds on subsidy were few. To take the example of cocoa, which was originally used to centralize marketing, for the entire life of the Nigerian Cocoa Marketing Board (1947–54) prices were only subsidized once, in 1948–49, when it paid £1.6 million. Its successor, the Western Region Marketing Board, subsidized prices only twice between 1954 and 1960. In other years the boards acquired huge surpluses. The combined aggregate operations of all the marketing boards showed surpluses. No adequate mechanisms were put in place to return the greater percentage of the surplus to those who generated it. Faced with the criticism that the marketing boards were not spending money on subsidies, the government began to emphasize the point that their mission was to finance economic development. Even then, this was a half-truth. Between 1949 and 1953 a large part of the surplus, almost 70 percent, was kept as investment securities in Britain. The remaining 30 percent was distributed as grants to production development boards and some spent on the repair and construction of roads and other development-related projects. The justification for keeping the money abroad was based on the lack of investment opportunities in Nigeria, no doubt a rationalization for capital flight to contribute to the maintenance of the British economy. As Oluwasanmi wondered, how could investment opportunities not exist "in a country where the long period growth in the incomes of peasant producers is dependent on the investment of their savings, forced or otherwise, in agricultural research and extension, in farm machines, in land resettlement, in improved methods of cultivation, in higher-yielding seed varieties, in better roads and in plants processing raw agricultural products into finished industrial goods."[58]

In spite of these criticisms and even the attack on the boards by the nationalists, the regional governments presided over by Nigerians did not change the functions of the marketing boards. The regional governments were quick to turn them into fiscal agencies that would raise money for the government to spend, without having to increase taxes or collect levies. Thus, the farmers became the backbone of the economy. From the funds of the marketing boards, the regional governments were able to create a number of development institutions that were responsible for various projects.

How did the pioneer nationalists and politicians justify the surpluses and the activities of the marketing boards? They gave the same reasons as the British did. The lead one was that the boards existed because of the farmers. Marketing in the pre–World War II era was usually contrasted with the operations of the marketing boards. The argument was that before 1940, the farmers never knew the worth of their products and prices fluctuated from year to year, thus making it impossible for them to invest, raise credit, or even have a budget. With the boards, not only were the farmers sure of what they would receive, they were also certain that there would be buyers.

With respect to the surplus, the Nigerian leaders and government did not deny that the boards did accumulate but argued that the ability to create and use development funds was good politics and good economy. The constitutional changes of 1953 not only led to the creation of regional marketing boards but also allowed them to control the surplus. Rather than invest abroad, regional leaders were now spending most of the money locally. But like the colonial government, the Nigerian-controlled regions did not necessarily give the money back to the farmers: some went as loans to estate companies, start-up funds to create local banks, and loans to promising entrepreneurs. In the North, the Northern Regional Marketing Board spent most of its surplus on investments and loans in the country, spending over £11 million as loans to the federal and northern regional governments and contributing funds to Nigeria development stocks, Kaduna Textiles, Limited; Bank of the North, Limited; and the Nigerian Produce Marketing Company, Limited.[59] In the East, investments were concentrated on securities abroad, the establishment of the African Continental Bank, and the Nigerian Cement Company. In the West, £33 million was disbursed as investment in a new bank (the National Bank of Nigeria Limited), savings bonds, and the Nigerian Produce Marketing Company. The rest of the funds went as loans to the federal and regional governments, and three public corporations. Thus, in all the regions, the funds of the marketing boards were very much connected with issues of economic planning and the creation of development agencies, both of which form the last segment of this chapter.

Economic Planning and Development Institutions

Many of the economic changes were generated through the routine process of administration and through conscious planning. In 1945 a ten-year plan for development and welfare was announced for the country. The plan was later revised in the 1950s. To implement the plan and other economic programs, a number of development agencies were also created in the 1940s and 1950s. Here, the reasons that led to the plan and describe the development institutions will be analyzed. Two examples of these agencies will be developed more fully in the following chapter. As new creations with the primary responsibility of bringing about development, politicians, civil servants, and many members of the public attached great importance to them. They served to represent the first major opportunity to think critically about various aspects of the economy and to document solutions to a number of problems. As power was transferred to Nigerians, the agencies also began to serve a major political purpose: they provided avenues for members of the political class to divert public money to private purses, and to benefit the areas from whence they came with amenities and infrastructures.

Political opportunism and corruption were, however, secondary to the reasons that led to the creation of a planning document and the agencies. There was a political motive in the 1940s. A level of development and prosperity was found necessary in order to curtail radical nationalism. To prevent the possibility of massive uprising, it was believed that the standard of living had to be enhanced. During World War II and beyond, a number of British officers were discussing issues of economic growth and how some economic sectors could be developed in order to generate funds for social services. Although some of the officers adopted a "humanitarian language," it was not as if they divorced the economic prosperity of Nigeria from that of the economic gains that would accrue to British companies.[60]

But there were genuine economic reasons as well. There was the need to diversify the economy by developing nonagricultural sectors. The regional governments in the 1950s gave considerable attention to this by laying the foundation of many manufacturing and industrial enterprises. Increasingly, the federal and regional governments came to the conclusion that they had to fund the establishment of industries and added to the efforts of private companies to generate more capital. There was also the assumption that the productivity of Nigerians had to be increased, partly in order to increase per capita income. If private investments were limited, the argument was that only the government could accelerate the pace of capital accumulation and increase the overall output of the general population.

There was also the ideology of state intervention in the economy. If growth would not come through the activities of private individuals, the belief was that the state could intervene to bring this about through a conscious planning effort. To the politicians of the 1950s the private sector was not developed enough to generate the level of growth that the people were looking forward to. Neither was there a fully functioning free market that would adequately allocate resources to all the important and productive sectors of the economy. Rather than wait for a so-called free enterprise mechanism to remove the obstacles to growth, the government would initiate important changes.

As the economy was regarded as "too traditional," the belief was that it would require the strong hands of the government to remove all the obstacles that tradition posed in the way of modernization. Among the areas targeted for government intervention were the land-tenure system (in order to make land available to investors and for public use); the provision of infrastructure, notably roads, communications, power; the supply of educated human power; and the control of labor in a way to make more people productive.

Increasingly, the Nigerian government came to accept three major economic functions. First, it would possess, use, and manage resources. In other words, the state would become an entrepreneur. In the 1950s and beyond, the various governments created agencies of entrepreneurship. The creation of each one was greeted with jubilation and promises. However, in most cases, the state ultimately failed as an entrepreneur. Second, the state would allocate the nation's resources to various economic and social projects. This allocation would be done through a planning exercise. After 1945, planning had become one of the principal economic functions of the government. The document is generally elegant in language, with some portions so technical that only trained experts could interpret them. Third, the state would have to generate the wealth to increase investments. This could be by way of building schools (to provide skilled labor) and infrastructure. As these schools and roads were visible and could be built rapidly, many efforts were directed at them in order to score quick political points.

To move to the specifics, the idea about planning began during World War II, when extensive discussions were held by officials in London and in various British colonies, about the need to promote social services and development in all the colonies. The ideas were subsequently published in a 1940 parliamentary paper that enunciated a new policy on development and welfare.[61] Funds were to be allocated for a host of projects that could promote the social and welfare life of the colonial subjects. The British government would fund some of these projects, in part because of a belief that most colonies dependent on agriculture lacked the money to embark upon development projects. All the British colonies were promised funding for ten years to the tune of £5 million each year and an identical amount to develop research. Nigeria and other colonies were mandated to submit plans to spend the money, as long as they conformed to a broad guideline, which stipulated the commitment of the fund to creating more knowledge on available raw materials, improving communications, generating more production of exports, and the creation of new schools, hospitals, clinics, and dispensaries. Although the language of the plan presented it as rendering assistance to the colonies, the development program did not sacrifice the economic interests of Britain. The step to actualize it in Nigeria was taken in 1945 with the inauguration of a ten-year plan to cover 1946 to 1956. A budget of £55 million was allocated to various social and economic projects over a ten-year period, representing a mere £1.16 per person of the total population. Of this amount, it was expected that £23 million would come from the United Kingdom and the rest from local revenues and loans from various sources. Altogether, the fund was not big enough to generate dramatic economic changes. Even some parliamentarians in Britain were skeptical of the result: "this is not planning, if the Ten-Year Plan were carried out overnight the improvement in the condition of the mass of Nigerians would be barely perceptible."[62] They were to be proved right.

The plan was formulated by colonial officers and approved by the Colonial Office in London. Essentially, each department compiled its needs, which is why the plan touched on virtually all subjects: health, education, rural and feeder roads, cottage industries, security matters, and others. The departments solicited inputs from provincial and district levels, thus making some of the projects relevant to local communities. The plan did not reflect the ongoing nationalism necessary to involve Nigerian leaders, and it was far from being a democratic document. However, it was not arrived at without some documentation and consultation, within the political system of the colonial era. A few professional officers and administrators at the local level prepared a proposal. In some cases they even spoke with kings, chiefs, and local elite to determine the priorities. The recommendations were then forwarded to the resident, the British officer in charge of a province who reviewed and sent them to the lieutenant governor, the head of a group of provinces. A final evaluation was conducted before forwarding the document to the governor in Lagos.

The preceding detail of plan formulation is presented to show that consultations did take place among the officials, but not necessarily within any democratic framework or with any level of economic sophistication. Each district and province knew what it wanted. However, none could set targets for the entire country. The officers had an idea of the cost of each project as well as the projects and project designs with which the governor and the Colonial Office would be comfortable. However, they had no data on national income, population, and other important aggregates to attempt any target setting or forecast. The objectives of the plan were clear enough, but not the targets. The emphasis was not to meet certain production outputs, but to organize expenditure on some key projects in welfare, research, and social services.

In allocating the funds, the assumption was that conditions had to be created for the country to attain an economic takeoff. Thus, the plan aimed to improve and expand the infrastructure. The thinking was that roads and communications would lead to increased private investments and productivity. The private sector would be left alone, and the government would take charge of energy, roads, and utilities. Research was considered of vital importance, especially in agriculture. Again, the thinking was that if crop yields could be increased, this would translate into greater productivity. Expenditure was committed to a small host of welfare social services: new dispensaries, clinics, and schools. This was to enable the people to see the activities of government in their areas and also to improve the quality of life.

The need to raise money for the plan and also to execute various projects led to the establishment of various agencies that were development oriented in nature. The office of development secretary was created, ranking below that of the country's financial secretary. Development officers were appointed in 1948 to oversee plan execution. Some agencies were to acquire money and others to spend it. All the agencies survived the colonial period, even if their names were later changed to something else. To initiate the agencies that raised money, legislation was passed in 1946 to create two loan boards: the Development Loan Ordinance No. 3 and the Nigeria (Ten-Year Plan) Local Loan Ordinance No. 10. Ordinance No. 3 empowered the governor to raise a loan of £8 million outside of the country, and the second ordinance gave him the power to raise £1 million within the country. Both loans would constitute a charge on the country's assets and revenue.

The governor was also empowered to create the Loan Development Board (LDB), with funds to be allocated to it by the Nigerian Legislative Council. The LDB was to award loans or grants to cooperative societies or any other agency deemed fit by the governor-in-council. Such loans or grants were to be used for a wide variety of development-oriented projects, such as the establishment of processing plants and cottage industries; the development of plantations, crafts, and industries; the construction of public utilities and public works; or indeed any project that the governor considered appropriate.[63] Regional development committees were established to consider the proposals submitted to the loan boards. In addition, there was a host of established government departments that either suggested new projects or implemented approved ones. For example, the public works departments handled the planning and building of roads and bridges. In some instances the multiplicity of planning agencies at the regional and federal levels were uncoordinated, and little means were available to check overlaps or even coordinate the various efforts.

The execution of the plan raised problems that were solved in part by creating new offices and later by revising the plan. There was no data to determine the number of people to be provided with amenities, or to estimate the output and cost of each project in relation to the population. Between 1948 and 1952, efforts were made to gather data on various subjects. The Office of Statistics was created in 1948, a commission was appointed in 1950 to determine the estimates of national income, another commission was established in 1951 to determine how to share the country's revenues among the regions and the central government, and a head count was carried out in 1952. Not only did the government come up with a realization that an enormous amount of data was necessary for planning, it decided to make changes to the plans in the 1950s.

The final revision during the colonial period came in 1956 in response to the suggestions made by the International Bank for Reconstruction and Development (IBRD), based in New York, which sent a delegation in 1953 to review the country's economy and the resources available for development and to identify the sectors that deserved immediate attention for planning purposes.[64] Another impetus was the adoption of a federal system that made it necessary to transfer some responsibility from the central government to the regional governments and also to divide some central programs into smaller regional ones. Two forces combined to create new ideas and orientation for the economy: "Americanization" and "regionalism."

The American influence was represented by the IBRD, but it was more than this. American global influence was on the rise, as well as its vigorous ambition to spread capitalism and its liberal democracy. The IBRD, in the spirit of "Americanization," wanted a non-Communist path to development: the use of infrastructure and agriculture to promote a free market. To the IBRD, for Nigeria to develop, it required funds and manpower, in addition to having roads, schools, and public works.

With the aid of the recommendations of the IBRD, the plan document was revised and extended to 1960. However, like the previous plan, the revised one was also about expenditures, but it ranked its priorities much more clearly: transport received the maximum funding of 38.7 percent, while the others received less than 10 percent (education 7.2 percent, primary production 5.7 percent, electricity 5.3 percent, and irrigation 5.6 percent).

The IBRD also called for a smaller number of development boards so that activities could be better coordinated. In response, the government established a Federal Loans Board, the Western Region Finance Corporation, and three development corporations, one in each of the regions. A coordinating agency was established, the National Economic Council (NEC), which provided a forum for the representatives of all the regions to meet twice a year to discuss economic plans and coordinate their activities.[65] The NEC created yet another official arm, the Joint Planning Committee, to consider and discuss a variety of new projects. In 1958 the federal government established the Ministry of Economic Development, which later became an elaborate agency with various units for different aspects of economic development. In the same year, a Central Bank was created to serve the entire country.

The data gathering efforts of the late 1940s intensified in the 1950s. The Food and Agricultural Organization (FAO), an agency of the United Nations, carried out a census of agriculture. The federal government commissioned a national income series, and another on higher education. Among other major development-related studies were those on iron and steel, roads, and electricity supply. All of these turned out to be very useful and influenced the decisions to establish new universities, farm settlements, and construct a dam.

Two new agencies were created in 1949, and both functioned with varying degrees of efficiency in the 1950s. What originally gave rise to the new agencies was the decentralization of the loan board in 1949, partly to reflect the emerging political moves to federalism. The new agencies were the Regional Production Development Board (RPDB) and the Regional Loan Board. The Regional Loan Boards would carry out the task originally assigned to the LDB. In the case of the RPDB, it would be funded by the marketing boards with the profits accrued from selling the country's export crops at prices lower than their market worth. The RPDB was a development agency, with the task of sponsoring research, building and improving roads, creating new industries, and contributing to greater agricultural productivity.[66]

The agencies were assigned the responsibility of carrying out the execution of some of the projects outlined in the ten-year plan. The plan was originally to be implemented and coordinated by a central unit in Lagos. However, after 1947, with the country opting for a regional structure, it became difficult to implement some of the schemes. Political changes thus dictated the need to revise the documents. As the regions were empowered to conduct their business, it became necessary to decentralize many activities. The ten-year plan was revised in 1951, with another one that would last until 1956. Projects were assigned to various regions for implementation. Many of the economic thinking and projects were left to these various agencies. In the next chapter, I examine some of these agencies in order to expand the narrative on the economic discourse and agenda during the 1950s, an era when Nigerians were passionate and hopeful about economic transformation and the possibility of an immediate prosperity.

4
"Separate Economies": Regionalism and Development Institutions

The political changes and constitutional reforms of the period affected the economy. The decentralization of power to the regions in the 1950s put the country on different economic and political paths. While the federal government in the center continued to pursue its own programs, the regions, too, embarked upon theirs. The division of the country into three regions, and the extensive power granted to each, encouraged the initiative to formulate and implement separate plans and to produce "three economies," rather than a unified "national economy." Each regional plan was without reference to the plans in other regions or even to any economic targets set by the federal government. In 1955 the National Economic Council (NEC) was established to discuss concerns common to the entire country. However, by the time the representatives of the regions converged in Lagos, they already had all their plans in place. Discussions were productive, but the various plans were not revised and those who controlled power at the regional level did not have to abide by the recommendations made by the NEC.[1]

Most of the regional programs revolved around the activities of two major boards, the production boards and the development boards. The regional governments concentrated most of their development programs in the hands of the boards, by diverting funds to them from the government and the marketing boards. Whereas the other regional agencies and the government could use their own funds for "nondevelopment" purposes, the boards could not. The funds of the boards grew in the 1950s, as they were charged with the responsibility of initiating and implementing various economic projects. For instance, in 1953 the Northern Regional Production Development Board had over £3 million allocated for expenditures and another £1 million unallocated, compared with an estimated expenditure by the regional government of £6 million and an estimated expenditure of £5 million by all the native administrations.[2]

Whereas the Colonial Office had supervisory power over the plans of the 1940s, and most decisions were taken by British officials, the activities of the regional boards were dominated by Nigerians, notably the emerging men of power in the new political parties and senior bureaucrats in the civil service. Drawing again from the Northern Region, the membership of the board comprised influential figures such as the sardauna Ahmadu Bello, the first premier of the region, and Alhaji Tafawa Balewa, the country's first prime minister. The major decisions were taken by the members of these boards, relying on ideas and technical advice by both Nigerian planners and foreign experts. In addition to empowering Nigerians by being in control, many discussed issues of great priority to their people, notably the establishment of new schools and the need to mechanize agriculture. It also provided opportunities for members of the political class to reward one another with contracts and such privileges as good wages and fringe benefits.

The Regional Production Development Boards (RPDBs) were constituted under Section 40 of the Nigeria Oil Palm Produce Marketing Board of 1949. The members were drawn from the executive and legislative branches, and the Oil Palm Representative Committee, an agency originally created to undertake research on palm products.[3] On December 13, 1951, the RPDB ordinance was enacted for the whole country, which specified their compositions and functions.[4] One significant change in the 1951 ordinance was that the board could obtain grants from previous boards in its region, that is, the Cocoa Marketing Board in the West, the Groundnut Marketing Board in the North, and the Oil Palm Produce Marketing Board in the East. These previous boards set aside 22.5 percent of their surplus funds for development and allocated to all the Regional Production Development Boards in proportion to the amount of cocoa, palm oil, and palm kernels produced in the regions. They also transferred their liabilities to the new boards, although they continued to finance them for a period of five years. Thus, in the West, the Cocoa Marketing Board committed £1,000,000 to the Western Region Production Board.[5] The revised 1950 ordinance also made it possible for the first time for the production boards to borrow money from other boards. In addition, they could enter into contracts with the government of Nigeria or with any authority constituted or established by or under any written law or any duly incorporated body for the purpose of participating actively in any scheme or venture which might be initiated or controlled by the government of Nigeria or any such authority or incorporated body. This last power was used by all the boards to justify the recruitment of expatriates, travel overseas on economic missions, and invitations to foreign companies for purposes of joint investments. The major functions of the regional production boards were listed as:

i. the development of the producing industries in respect of which funds accrue to the Board by grants from the Marketing Boards or otherwise; or
ii. the economic benefit or prosperity of the producers; or
iii. the economic benefit or prosperity of the areas of production, including the training of Nigerians in commerce and technical trades; or
iv. the preliminary investigation of any schemes within the provisions of i to iii above.[6]

In all the above, the primary goal was on development, the first time that any board in the country would be so defined. The production boards had the power to make loans to be used only for development purposes. The general policy of the boards was to improve the economy by practicable methods, "having due regard to the special interests of the producers."[7] The justification for making agriculture the pillar of development was stated thus:

In a country which owing to its poverty in mineral resources must remain predominantly agricultural, but which is still very backward agriculturally, the broad lines on which this policy must be implemented can be simply stated: improvement of agricultural production on a field scale while raising, or at least maintaining, the level of soil fertility; establishment of processing industries; and improvement of communications in order to facilitate distribution of local foodstuffs and movement of export crops.[8]

While not dismissing the role of industries, the boards must show interest in all those activities that were dependent on primary products, for instance, processing foods.

Each board had its own members, appointed for a three-year period. The members were drawn from political parties, the educated elite, and civil servants. Schemes had to be approved by the heads of the regions, originally the lieutenant governor but, later, the premiers. In the early years of the board, projects and ideas were proposed by administrative officers and communities, but in later years, members of the board itself, relying on senior technocrats, formulated the programs they wanted.⁹ Reports were issued to elected members who, as in the case of the political representatives in the Western House of Assembly and Western House of Chiefs, could read the reports and ask questions.

As each board operated independently, I now want to turn to some examples of what they discussed and accomplished during the 1950s. The details are extensive, as this is the first major attempt to study the archives of these boards and connect their activities to Nigeria's economic history.

Western Region

The Western Region Development Production Board was established in 1950, reconstituted in 1951, and continued to exist until the end of June 1955, when it was replaced by another board with a similar name.¹⁰ The new changes were mainly administrative: the composition of the board was altered to include representation from the Ministries of Finance, Development and Agriculture, and Natural Resources; the board's affairs were made subject to the approval of the minister of development; and the governor-in-council and the minister were empowered to give the board directions of a general character. The new board acquired all the existing assets, rights, undertakings, and liabilities of the old board, and it continued with the old programs.¹¹

The membership of the board was constituted in 1950, 1952, and 1955. In 1954 the chairman became a fulltime executive, replacing the office of development secretary. In the same year, it was considered necessary to create four management committees, one for each specific project, in order to have more time for discussions and policies.¹² There were significant policy changes, too, from 1956 to 1960, which affected funding and transferred some functions to mainstream departments. Between 1950 and 1955, funds were made available to the board from the surpluses of the marketing board. From 1956 onward, the funds of the marketing board accrued to the regional government, which, in turn, allocated money to the board. A sum of £4.5 million was allocated by the regional government to the board in 1956. The board also transferred its responsibilities on roads and scholarships to other government agencies in order to focus more on agriculture and industries.¹³

The headquarters of the administration of the board was at Ibadan, the capital of the Western Region. The administration evolved gradually, starting with temporary offices, later to expand to have its own huge building, committees, and seven units in charge of agriculture, new projects, engineering, accounts, personnel, industries, and medical, each with its own bureaucracy. From a total expenditure of £26,141 in its first year, 1949–50, to £267,243 in the third, and a total of £387,953 for the 1949–52 period, the board boasted of an expansion and generated public confidence that its money was well spent.[14] In its fifth year of operation, the board highlighted both its mission and accomplishments, in a way that reveals the region's development agenda and the methods implemented to attain it:

i. To improve the Region's agricultural programme by improving and extending the crops which are already the main back-bone of the Region's economy and also by encouraging new crops. The reason we wanted to encourage new crops is because until now, the livelihood of the Western Region has depended upon cocoa (all of which is exported) so that we were completely dependent upon the price of cocoa for our standard of living. By encouraging new crops, we hope to make the economy of the Region less dependent on cocoa. Then a fall in the price of cocoa would not affect the people of the Region so much. There might even be an increase in the prices of the other crops which would enable us to keep the same standard of living.

ii. The Board recognised that for many years to come the agriculture of the Region would be the most important feature of its economy but at the same time it is well known that higher profits arise more from the processing of the crops and by the setting up of industries. For instance, England is a country which is much smaller than Nigeria. It has no big crops like cocoa, palms, bananas or cotton, yet it is a wealthy country because for hundreds of years it has purchased these raw materials from other parts of the world and turned them into such things as chocolate, soap, oils and cloth in the many factories in England. For this reason, the Board decided from the beginning that we should set up factories in the Western Region either to make use of the raw materials of the Region and make them into goods which are necessary all the world over or else to buy cheaper raw materials from outside and make them into goods used here. The result of this would be to increase the money we would get for selling to countries overseas and to reduce the money we would have to pay for goods purchased from abroad by the people of the Western region.

iii. One of the quick results of developing our agriculture and setting up factories would be to cut down unemployment in the Region. We can say straightaway that the Board has considerably helped the Government in its efforts to do this. Altogether we employ about 7,000 people at present, of whom all but 31 are Nigerians. We actively encourage our own people to play an increasing part in the management of our affairs. In 1951, Senior staff numbered thirty, all of whom were expatriates. Now in 1956 our Senior staff number fifty-four, of whom twenty-three are Nigerians. Of a total of seven Heads of Departments and Sectional Heads, four are Nigerians and three expatriates.

iv. For the Western Region of Nigeria to take its rightful place in the modern world, one of our main problems was to train Nigerians to become experienced in all trades and professions. This could be done partly by scholarships, some of which would mean sending some young men overseas, while a lot more could be accomplished by training staff in our plantations, factories and offices. Our record for employment of Nigerians in senior posts is a proud one. We have laid the foundation for making this possible in other parts of the Region by collaborating with the Government in granting scholarships. It is worth noting that before 1935 no scholarships were ever awarded to Westerners by previous Nigerian Government and between 1936 and 1952 a total of only five scholarships were granted to Westerners, but from 1952 to 1956 when the present Government took office, in four years 1,027 scholarships were granted. Of these, this Board awarded 262, of which 239 were for outside Nigeria. The total cost for the Board for these awards will be about £400,000.

v. The Western Region Government realises that it is not sufficient to set up factories and plantations and grant scholarships. The best way to encourage the development of our Region is to make it possible for people to move freely so that they too can extend trade and so make the life of the people more prosperous. For this reason, both the Government and the Western Region Production Board have spent a lot of money on the tarring of the main roads in the Region and on building feeder roads which would make travelling from the main roads to the smaller towns and villages easier. Altogether we have spent £1,366,000 and most of the programmes are complete. In the meantime, our brother Board, The Western Region Finance Corporation, which was set up to assist in the development of the Region, has granted loans to many who were prepared to provide transport vehicles. As a result, the road system in the Western Region is the finest in Nigeria and travelling these days to almost any part of the Region is much easier than it has ever been before.

vi. The Western Region Production Development Board, like the Government, has realised how important it is that the people should enjoy good housing and health. In our plantations, we are building villages and fine houses for the workmen and staff and all our employees whether they be daily paid labourers or permanent staff enjoy free medical attention as do their wives and children. Our Region was the first to increase the minimum wage rate and the Board is glad to report that we accepted and implemented the Government's minimum wage from the very beginning.[15]

Although in its conception, the emphasis was to be on agriculture, there was a diversification in later years to industries, education, and infrastructure, as the board increasingly passed under the control of Nigerian (Yoruba) politicians. By 1955 there were several major agricultural schemes (the Apoje plantation at Ijebu, which had grown to almost twelve thousand acres; the Ikpoba Rubber Processing Factory at Benin; and the Lafia Fruit Canning Factory at Ibadan) and many minor ones on agriculture, education, and road building. By the end of 1960 the board had developed over eight thousand acres of major crops (rubber, oil palms, cocoa, citrus, coffee, cashews, and pineapples) on which it had spent over £2 million.

The first and the most extensive agricultural scheme embarked on was the Ijebu Farming Project located at Apoje, thirty-five square miles of farmland to the east of the Osun River. The project was to offer assistance to farmers in developing plantations. One of the objectives of the production board was to establish large-scale plantations of the major crops. The plantations were expected to make a profit and thus to attract investors from within and outside Nigeria to acquire them, to foster new industries from which the farmers could profit, to become the reservoir of improved planting materials to farmers who wanted to extend or to create new plantations, and to demonstrate efficient farm management and suitable techniques to arouse the interest of local farmers in modern methods. At the Apoje project, plantations of oil palms, citrus, and other crops were established. By mid-1952 about 700 acres of forest were felled for palms, citrus, and *awusa* nuts (*tetracarpidium conophorum*), and another sixty acres were prepared for cocoa. A soil survey completed in 1952 revealed that of the 13,000 acres about 3,500, that is, 27 percent, were good for cocoa, 3,000 for citrus, and the remaining 5,000 for oil palms, rubber, coconuts, and *awusa*. Rice, maize, and cassava were intercropped to supply food items.

There was some collaboration with the Agriculture Department, from where good seeds and advice on nurseries were obtained, and with the West African Institute for Oil Palm Research at Benin, also for seeds. The crops were successful, in spite of troubles from rodents, late planting, and failure of rains. Of all the crops, *awusa* was a new addition to the list of crops to be cultivated by the board. In 1950 the colonial secretary advised the Nigerian government to embark on a commercial cultivation of this indigenous vine whose fruit could be extracted for its oil as a substitute for the linseed oil used in the paint industry.[16]

The Apoje project was able to bring changes in other aspects of the economy. It provided jobs for about five hundred people, many of whom were attracted from the Eastern and Northern Regions because of the favorable contract wages. Model houses were built for the hired farmers and other staff, and new roads were built to link the farms with the towns. New schools, piped water supply, playgrounds, and recreation halls were provided as well, to retain the staff at the plantation. By 1956 the large sum of £600,000 had been spent at Apoje out of an estimate of £1,800,000. Four years later over £100,000 had been added, with increases in the number of acres. The regional government, in collaboration with the board, designed Apoje as the biggest plantation in the country. In the short run, it was a big dream; in the long run, a failure.

Not too far away from the Apoje plantation was the Upper Ogun project, comprising both a ranch and a settlement. The Upper Ogun, mostly a savanna, was different from the rest of the region, which is forestland. The board wanted to turn the savanna to advantage by experimenting with ranching and mechanized farming. Mechanized farming was an abysmal failure, and by 1954 the board had decided to concentrate on a cattle ranch.[17] In 1955 the board imported from Sierra Leone and Belgian Congo breeds that could withstand the tsetse fly. While the ranch survived until 1960, little or nothing came out of it in later years.

The third largest agricultural venture of the board, the four-thousand-acre Urhonigbe Rubber Plantation, was established in 1952 to demonstrate the correct methods of planting and harvesting rubber, to supply very good planting material to farmers, and to invest money within the region.[18] Planting of new rubber seeds was done between 1952 and 1955, with additional expenses on new roads, offices, and houses. As in the Apoje project, many laborers had to be recruited, numbering over one thousand in the busy seasons. Good-quality latex was obtained from the first set of trees in 1957–58. The board's projection to realize £400,000 each year did not materialize in the 1950s.

There were smaller agricultural plantations at Eruwa, Eleiyele, Ibokun, and Oba/Akure. As part of creating an efficient plantation system, the board devised a partnership scheme to provide technical and financial assistance to farmers in order to create model plantations. In 1950, the board proposed a scheme to assist individuals, communities, and cooperative societies in establishing small plantations.[19] The board was to provide capital, planting material, technical skill, and management, while the applicants would provide the land and labor. The board was to recover its expenditure out of the profits of the plantation, although the applicants were expected to repay outstanding capital expenditure and to take over the management of the plantation at the earliest possible date.

The first assistance was offered in 1951 at Asejire, where fifteen farmers combined to form a cooperative farming society to develop plantations in partnership with the board. The board collaborated with the Agriculture Department and the Oil Palm Research Station to render assistance to the Asejire farmers by way of propaganda, a soil survey, and providing palm seeds for the initial fifty-three acres. Asejire was a success story: the farmers were able to intercrop the land with maize and cassava to plant foodcrops. Twenty-two acres were added a year later, again with outstanding results.

Other farmers emulated the Asejire experiment by forming cooperative societies, while hundreds of others applied in their individual capacity.[20] By 1953 the applications for assistance had reached a very high level, as more and more people began to think that the board had lots of money to distribute to interested farmers or to imaginative and clever people who had evidence that they would use the money for farming purposes. By this date, too, the board was yet to realize much from its collaborative ventures. After a visit to many of the projects, a board member criticized the board's partnership scheme and concluded in the same year that "a scheme may be grand and admirable on paper but quite unrealistic in execution." Evidence of fraud, or at least mismanagement, was becoming clearer as each partnership became "a source of prodigious waste of the public fund." There was a strong warning that unless the board reexamined its policy, "money which would have been used to better purpose for the benefit of the people generally would have been scandalously frittered away on uneconomic and unproductive projects or in furthering the exclusive economic interests of a chosen or lucky few out of the teeming millions of people who populate the Western Region."[21] Except for the Apoje project, every other one was consuming money on "a scale outrageously out of all proportion to the results likely to be obtained."[22]

The board did not, however, decide to terminate its partnership projects. Rather than collaborating with individuals, it developed projects with local governments and cooperative societies in order to benefit the entire community. It would also insist on viable projects that would generate profit to the board, its collaborator and the community. What the board decided in 1953 was a policy on partnership with divisional native authorities and registered cooperative societies.[23] In 1955 the regional government accepted the policy of the board to establish plantations in every division of the region in cooperation and often in partnership with the local authorities. Beginning in 1956, the open letter by the board to all councils laid out the procedures for partnership. Where the venture was a partnership, the native authority was to supply the land, the value of which was assessed and treated as their contribution to the scheme. The board would supply the necessary funds and technical direction, the value of which would represent the board's share of the capital. When a plantation came into bearing, the proceeds of the crops were to be used first to repay the partners the money they committed by way of capital and thereafter, the board and the council would share the annual profit on a 50–50 basis. Alternatively, the board could lease land on a long-term-basis contract from councils at economic rent. Should the council receive an annual rent, the board would retain the entire profit.[24]

The partnership with councils encouraged the flow of resources to a number of organized communities and groups. One of two huge schemes was the rubber project at Urhonigbe, which entitled the native authority to £400 per annum. The community requested an advance payment for five years to build a water supply.[25] At Araromi, where a small rubber plantation was established in 1956, the community also collected rent, which it used to tar a road. By 1960 over a dozen partnerships had been established in different parts of the region.[26] Every major partnership translated into rents for communities, and also to the construction of roads to plantations. There was a positive response on the part of the communities who spent their proceeds to develop their areas. A new market or an expansion of the older market took place to derive additional benefits from the new roads, and the influx of farm workers.

The benefits that accrued notwithstanding, there were problems with the schemes which official documentation failed to talk about. The need by communities to surrender land was a big source of trouble. There was the fear that once land was released for government use, the owner would never be able to reclaim it. It is true that the board paid rents, but these went not to the individuals who were dispossessed of their land but to the councils. Next was profit sharing by the participants in cooperative enterprises. Again, for profits to accrue to participating councils they had to be able to use their labor well, monitor sales, prevent corruption, all difficult to achieve, and they had to wait for years for proceeds.

Industries

Although agriculture was to be the main concern of the board, the regional government embarked upon the creation of industries in order to make profit and provide job opportunities. While some initial efforts were made in 1952, with a decision to erect a canning factory to use the citrus from its plantations, the most ambitious industrial plan was the one approved for the 1955–60 period, following the report of an economic mission by the key members of the government led by the premier, Awolowo, to many parts of the world to attract investors.[27] The 1955–60 industrial plan made two major points:

i. that the government would welcome investment of capital from abroad and
ii. that the industries of the region should be broadly divided into
   (a) those which could be carried out by private individuals without assistance;[28]
   (b) those which could be carried out by private individuals with assistance by way of loans possibly from the Government via the Finance Corporation;
   (c) those, which because of their size and importance, must be established in conjuction with a Government agency,[29] of which the Board is the one who would take a direct financial interest.

The board was interested in plastic, cement, tires and tubes, iron and steel, textiles, housing, industrial estates, matches, tanning, boots, and shoes, all of which became the principal areas of attention from 1950 to 1960. On plastic, the board entered a partnership with the United Africa Company and the Yorkshire Copper Works Limited[30] to erect a plastic factory at Ibadan. The major product was to be polythene tubes to replace water pipes made of galvanized steel and copper with plastic water hose pipe and conduit.[31] The goal was to save money by avoiding the importation of steel and copper pipes. The project began in the 1950s, and its products became available in the 1960s.

On cement, the result of investigations conducted up until 1956 was that there were no vast deposits of limestone, as previously believed, but of kaolin, which had limited value in the world market. To satisfy the great demand for cement, the board enlisted the support of Associated Portland Cement Manufacturers Limited, a well-known cement company, to find places with huge deposits of limestone. Abeokuta province became the main center of investigation, with results that proved positive after many months of geological investigation. A successful cement factory was later established in Abeokuta.

The availability of rubber in the region—more than 95 percent of the country's rubber came from here—promoted a rubber plantation and an interest in the tire and tube industry. The board commissioned a U.S. company, the Dayton Rubber Company of Ohio, to investigate the viability of a tire industry. It proved profitable, and a private entrepreneur eventually established a successful tire industry.

As part of its diversification projects, two crops received attention: oil palm and rubber. While the price of rubber was up in the 1950s, performance in the region was poor because of the poor quality of trees and the poor methods of producing rubber sheets. The board set out to improve the quality of yields by establishing an enterprise at Ikpoba, with a plan to spend £3 million to grow rubber, process it, and make rubber products.

Ikpoba was in the rubber-producing area of Benin province. Work on the factory began in 1953, and production started in 1955. To make latex available, the board contacted local farmers to form cooperative societies to supply the factory. By the late 1950s, the company was able to process rubber, but its trading results were generally unsatisfactory because of the inadequate supply of good latex and because of processing difficulties associated with the lack of some spare parts or machinery.[32]

The board commissioned foreign companies from different European countries and the United States to look into the possibility of establishing an iron and steel fabrication plant, a tannery, and factories to produce textiles, matches, boots, and shoes. While several of these looked good on paper, only small beginnings were made in the 1950s.[33]

The most successful of the industrial projects was the Lafia Fruit Canning Factory at Ibadan, also the first to be established.[34] The factory was to export tinned pineapples, oranges, and grapefruits to Europe. Built at a cost of £450,000, the canning factory was the most modern in the region, located close to the railway station in order to transport the products by road or rail to the port in Lagos. The problem of Lafia was not the quality of its equipment or product, but how to ensure a regular supply of fruits and later of machinery. Farmers were advised to plant citrus, although supply was not enough to keep the factory in full operation. By mid-1950, it intended to produce over one million tins of fruit but was only able to make 300,000. To find sufficient fruits, the board gave out loans of £20,000 and subsidized planting materials to the cost of £14,000 by 1956. The performance in the early years was impressive indeed: its fine products were easily exportable; it provided initial training in modern manufacturing; and the need to provide suitable accommodation to its distinguished visitors and to members of the board and the House of Assembly all led to the establishment of the Lafia Rest House, which became a pioneer of modern hotels in the city of Ibadan.

Industrial projects after 1955 involved the consolidation of previous efforts. An executive post of new projects and industrial manager was created in 1956.

Traditional craft worker in a modern economy. Photo by A. Olusegun Fayemi.

A London office was established to maintain continuous contacts with organizations with whom the board was dealing, to conduct the recruitment of staff, and to assist the board in overseas business. Pioneer oil and rice mills were rented to tenants.[35]

Quaranic education still survives alongside Western education. Photo by A. Olusegun Fayemi.

Housing and Infrastructure

To provide houses for an increasing number of city dwellers, mainly civil servants, the government made a special loan to the board in the amount of £500,000, and the board put up an equal amount to establish the Housing Trust. The board was to build a number of houses to be sold to the people who would then repay in monthly installments. Related to this was the establishment of an industrial estate to make it easier for entrepreneurs to build factories and offices. Both were successful projects, with new residential estates in Ibadan and Lagos, and an industrial estate in Ikeja.

Regarding roads, by 1956 the board had spent £1,220,000 on tarring and construction of 284 miles. The major intercity roads included the Abeokuta-Asha, Ibadan-Akanran, Jiga-Ilaro, Akure-Ado-Ekiti, and Owo-Ikare. A large number of feeder roads were constructed, in addition to "cocoa roads" in some areas.

The boards experienced two major problems in the 1950s. The first was a chronic staff shortage. The aim of the board to "Nigerianize" was ongoing, but many senior posts were filled by expatriates. Providing suitable accommodation to these staff was difficult, especially most of the junior ones had to live in uncomfortable conditions. The other was that "development money" was consumed by the need to take care of staff problems. Large sums had to be spent on providing accommodation to staff, cars for the senior staff, and building roads to connect inaccessible places—money that ate the development fund itself. In spite of these problems, the records of the boards were so impressive that many westerners now regard this era as the "golden period" in the modern transformation of their region.

Eastern Region

In the Eastern Region, development activities revolved around two agencies: the Eastern Regional Production Development Board and the Eastern Regional Development Board. In addition, the provincial and native authorities and a number of entrepreneurs implemented and augmented various schemes.

The regulations for the operations of the Eastern Regional Production Development Board (ERPDB) were contained in the Nigerian Oil Palm Produce Marketing Ordinance (No. 12 of 1949), later revised in 1954. The ERPDB comprised eight to twelve members drawn from official and nonofficial members of the Eastern House of Assembly and the Representative Committee of the Nigerian Oil Palm Produce Marketing Board. Its chairman was appointed by the chief commissioner of the region. The first set of members, appointed in mid-July 1949, were two colonial administrators—the regional development secretary, who was the chairman of the board, and the regional deputy director of agriculture. The other eight members were Nigerians, two appointed by the Nigerian Oil Palm Representative Committee and six appointed by the Eastern House of Assembly.[36] An amendment to the ordinance in 1951 added another person to be appointed by the Advisory Committee of the Nigeria Cocoa Marketing Board.[37] The ERPDB held all its meetings at Enugu, the regional capital, an average of three times a year. The committees of the ERPDB also met from time to time, in addition to having its own civil service.

The ERPDB ceased to exist on February 1, 1955, and all its rights, properties, interests, obligations, and liabilities were vested in and assumed by the Eastern Regional Development Board (ERDB), following the terms and provisions of the Law of Eastern Nigeria No. 12 of 1954. While the functions remained essentially the same, the composition of the board was changed. It was made up only of Nigerians, notably the members of the NCNC.[38] To avoid confusion, both the ERPDB and its successor are referred to as the Eastern Board (EB) in the analysis that follows.

The function of the EB was to "to dispose of funds made available by the Oil Palm Produce Marketing Board for the development of the palm produce industry and for the benefit and prosperity of the producers and the areas of production."[39] The detailed guidelines were:

i. Regional Boards are proposed in harmony with the present constitutional arrangements and to ensure that within the limits laid down by the legislation each Region will have freedom to dispose of its funds according to its own judgment of the needs of the Region. It is clear, however, that some schemes, particularly those directly affecting palm produce production, will be of interest to both Regions and it is intended and hoped that there will be a free interchange of information and proposals for the mutual benefit of the Boards and the Regions.

ii. It is not intended that the Boards should spend money on purposes of general welfare, such as the provision of dispensaries, schools, hospitals, etc. The cost of the expansion of Government and Native Administration services of that kind is a proper charge on the revenues of the Government and the Native Administrations. On the other hand if the Boards are restricted by the legislation to spending the funds available to them solely on the development of the palm produce industry they might be unduly hampered. Perhaps the best indication of the kind of object on which funds might properly be expended is conveyed by the phrase "for the development of the industry and the benefit and prosperity of the producers and the areas of production." In the opinion of the Government, as long as the objects of expenditure are economic and are designed to promote economic well-being and development in the main belts of production, it would be imprudent to restrict unduly the latitude of the Boards.

iii. It is proper to mention that improvement in quality must be a major issue for these Boards since it is doubtful whether with the resumption of production in the East Indies, Nigerian palm oil can maintain its position in the world's markets unless there is an improvement in methods of production and extraction and in quality.[40]

The obligation of the EB, therefore, was to use the funds at its disposal to develop the oil palm produce industry and to enhance the prosperity of the producers and their areas of production. At its preliminary meetings, the EB decided to broaden the agenda in a way that all the parts of the region would be affected by its programs:

In considering how best to fulfil this statutory obligation, the Board thought that it would be unrealistic and impossible to attempt to set in isolation the palm produce areas of the Eastern Region from those parts of the Region primarily concerned with the production of food crops, as the latter are both complementary and vital to the main oil palm areas whose populations, for the most part, have to import their food. In addition, areas of oil palm are spread in varying degrees of density throughout the Region. For these reasons the Board decided that it was fully justified in regarding the whole of the Eastern Region as a producing area within the meaning of the Ordinance and in planning the expenditure of the funds at its disposal accordingly.[41]

It was not that the EB wanted to disregard the dominant position of the palm produce industry in the economy of the region and the relationship between the prices of oil palm products and the people's standard of living. However, the EB was worried about the dangers of the dependence on one industry and considered that measures to develop new agricultural products, providing alternative sources of wealth, would be of great benefit to many people. The EB, therefore, decided that "while its principal policy must be to improve the quantity and quality of palm products, it should also be one of the main aims of the board to use all means in its power to plan a more balanced economy by introducing wherever possible alternative cash crops."[42]

In addition, the EB recognized the need to grow more food. Indeed, this had become urgent because of the growing population, a rising standard of living, and the concentration by farmers on the production of cash crops to the detriment of food crops. The EB decided to use parts of its funds on food production, to be achieved by bringing new areas of land into cultivation, improved methods of land use, and the careful use of artificial manure. In summary, the EB would allocate its resources in accordance to three broad principles:

i. The principal function of the Board should be to undertake, either directly or through agencies, schemes of production on a large scale throughout the Region, using wherever possible plantation methods, for the following purposes:
   (a) The improvement in quantity and quality of oil palm products.
   (b) The introduction of new cash crops (such as cashew, cocoa and coffee).
   (c) The improvement of quantity and quality of food crops.
ii. The Boards' funds should not be used to provide social services normally a charge on regional or local Government revenues though the Board would, wherever possible, provide adequate social services for employees on its own projects.
iii. The Board would concentrate on schemes which are commercially sound and which are planned and managed on commercial lines.[43]

Realizing that it had to spend money on roads to be able to reach its areas of operations, and responding to intense demands in 1950 and 1951 for assistance in road construction and maintenance, the EB decided in 1951 to include road-building projects:

- to construct roads to the Board's projects;
- to construct roads into undeveloped areas where in the view of the Board there were possibilities of agricultural, industrial or other economic development;
- to construct roads and/or bridges where in the view of the Board those roads or bridges would be of direct benefit to the industry or to the producer; and
- to maintain only those roads which served the limited purpose of access to the Board's estates or other projects.[44]

The details of the schemes funded by the EB were planned and implemented on the basis of the aforementioned guidelines. The oil palm industry received priority attention. Central to the development of the industry was the establishment of more oil mills. Since 1940 the government had been concerned with the improvement of the quality of palm produce to enable Nigeria to compete with other world producers, and especially those using modern methods of production. The answer was to introduce improved methods of production.

Large plantations controlled by a few people with capital were almost impossible to establish because the government originally discouraged the alienation of land to European firms and because of the nature of the industry, palm farms were scattered over large, densely populated areas and owned by thousands of farmers and clans. To retain the system of individual holdings, and at the same time to introduce modern and efficient methods, the "pioneer oil mill" was designed and became the major innovation of the post-1940 era. An oil mill is a cottage industry with small machines to process palm oil and to crack the kernels.

The first oil mill in the country was installed at Amuro in the East and began operation in 1946.[45] This became successful and generated a lot of demand. Twenty-seven mills were ordered, with eighteen to be installed in the East. By 1950 six mills had been built at Amansi, Amuro, Umuchina, Ahoada, Azumini, and Akpabuyo, and seven more were under construction. The EB inherited the rights, obligations, and loans on the mills amounting to £81,000 from the Nigerian Local Development Board (NLDB), which ceased to exist in 1949. Although the NLDB and EB built the mills, the intention was to hand them over to private Nigerian enterprises. In the 1940s, the policy was to let the Department

A major modern market center, Onitsha. Photo by A. Olusegun Fayemi.

of Commerce and Industries operate the mills to allow Nigerians to gain experience and to seek capital. As a result of this policy, the mill was designed as a small economic unit, with the cost of the machinery and installation kept within a range of £5,500, an outlay considered within the reach of enterprising Nigerians. True to its promise, the Department of Commerce and Industries sold the Amansi mill to the Ibez Trading Company of Onitsha in 1948, and in 1950 negotiations were concluded by the EB to hand over the Amuro mill to the Okigwi Industrial Company while it also approved loans to build two mills for two private companies at Mbawsi and Ndizuogu.

The goal during the 1950s was to expand the program of mill installations in order to improve quality and to ensure a safe market and good prices. There was an assurance of a steady demand for palm oil and kernel in the United Kingdom, which encouraged the EB to consider spending on mills and to propose that new mills be run on a commercial basis.[46] In 1950, the EB decided to take over all the existing mills owned by the NLDB, ratified the order of fifty new mills of the type purchased in the 1940s, and ordered two new ones of double capacity. It decided to invite the Department of Commerce and Industries to manage the new mills, while at the same time arranging to terminate the contract and to take over as soon as possible. In the same year, it decided not to sell the mills to private individuals for some years, anticipating that there could be unforeseen difficulties and that an individual with one mill might incur considerable losses. By keeping and owning many mills, the EB would be able to offset losses on some against the profits made by others. After an experimental stage and assurance that a mill was suitable for private enterprise, the EB would reconsider its position. However, the EB would not discourage any individual from erecting a mill.

By the end of 1950 the EB had one mill in each of the nine divisions: Okigwi, Orlu, Owerri, Aba, Ikot Ekpene, Ahoada, Calabar, Opobo, and Onitsha. The operations of the mills proved to the EB that the innovation would not destroy the palm-oil economy, in spite of the people's opposition to it on this ground. For purposes of expansion, the EB had in every division a mill to train the staff to be employed in other new mills. Leaseholders of mill sites knew from the experience of the existing ones for what they were leasing their lands. The local population, too, was gradually beginning to understand how the mill worked and its advantages. In 1951 the EB successfully constructed and brought into operation thirty-two mills. By March 1952 the EB had a total of forty-six mills in operation, distributed over the region: Aba had eight; Ahoada, seven; Ikot Ekpene, three; Owerri, four; Orlu, nine; Okigwi, six; Onitsha, four; Eket, one; Calabar, two; and Opobo, two. The mills employed 1,084 daily paid workers, 210 junior staff, and 16 senior staff, in addition to a construction staff of 155.[47] In 1951 and 1952, several of the mills made efforts to produce the highest grade of oil, although the difficulty was in obtaining the best fruits from farmers. Available production figures by the mills showed progress. To take two of the early figures, the fruits milled in 1951 were 7.5 million tons, rising to 14.2 million tons a year later.[48]

In 1952 administrative steps were taken to enhance the performance of the mills. Mechanics were to be trained well in advance to avoid shortage. To achieve efficiency and economic management and maintenance of the mills, the headquarters at Aba were to be extended by two new stores and a new office wing. An underground petrol tank and oil stores were built at Aba to meet demands for petrol, oils, and lubricants. A mechanical workshop to repair machines and assemble new ones was under construction, and plans were concluded to train the staff to work the place. To cut down unnecessary traveling and to improve the supervision of the mills, many new suboffices and accommodations were built in 1952: two houses and one suboffice at Ikot Ekpene to cover the Ikot Ekpene, Eket, and Opobo mills; one house in Calabar to cover both management and construction of mills on the far side of the Oron Ferry; two houses and one suboffice at Orlu to cover the Orlu Okigwi mills and another one at Owerri to cover the Owerri-Onitsha mills.

The mill was a small factory, the first of its type in many of these places. It had a small administration, with a minimum of two clerks for each mill. There were mill mechanics and maintenance mechanics to install and repair the mills.

While it was never difficult to recruit clerks, getting well-trained mechanics was always a problem because of the lack of technical schools to produce people with knowledge in mill operations. Unskilled labor worked mainly to separate fiber and kernels from the cracked mixture rather than using power-driven nut-fiber separators that were not more efficient or economical than manual labor. With the exception of the Calabar mills, which had only a senior staff, all the other groups had two senior officers responsible for management, maintenance, and construction of additional mills. The senior officers were all responsible to management and wrote an annual report on each mill.

By January 1955 there were seventy mills in production, five at the stage of completion, and twelve approved for building. There was in general a lot of disappointment with performance, as some mill owners incurred losses. For the mills to work on an economic basis, they required adequate fruit intake and an excellent extracting rate, which would depend on the quality of fruits milled. While the number of mills increased, the average intake of fruits declined as more and more bad fruits were rejected. In general, while the number of mills increased by fourteen units, the average intake of fruits decreased by almost 20 percent.

There was a keen competitor to the mill: the handpresses operated manually. The operating cost of a handpress was lower, and its operators could therefore offer better prices for fruits. The EB was worried about this competition, especially as it feared that it might affect the long-term success of the mills and negate the objectives of improving the quality of palm oil and of making profits. The EB's solution was to seek the support and cooperation of local communities, but this met with problems. By mid-June 1955 the objective was not fulfilled, and it was proposed to transfer the mills from areas considered unprofitable sites to others where more cooperation and support were expected.[49]

Where distance to the mill was not a disadvantage, it became useful to producers who improved their methods of production and enhanced the quality of their products. In the Calabar and Owerri provinces, there was an initial opposition to the erection of mills. At Owerri, women in two villages united to resist the erection of a mill because it would take away income from them. Villages that opposed the mills showed this by not supplying fruits to mill owners. Officials reported signs, toward the end of 1952, that there would be a change of attitude and that the mills would become popular. At Owerri where there was a resistance, many people changed their minds a year later by competing for the erection of a mill because they realized that faster oil processing freed them to do other things.[50]

Apart from the oil mills, the EB also embarked on a project of creating oil estates to increase production. There were to be two categories of estates. The first, the large estates, would be established in so-called underpopulated areas. In 1950 the EB planned to begin an estate of some 10,000 acres in the Calabar division, in a location between the Calabar and Kwa rivers. The EB entered into discussions with the Colonial Development Corporation (West Africa) Limited, which it invited to participate in the scheme as joint partners and to manage the scheme. To open up the area, the EB allocated a sum of £31,125 for half of the cost to construct a road from Calabar to Arochuku, with a plan to spend more money in the future. In the following year the EB set aside a sum of £300,000, half of the estimated cost, for what became known as the Calaro Oil Palm Estate. In March 1951 an investigating mission of the Colonial Development Corporation (West Africa) arrived in Nigeria to join representatives of the Agriculture Department and the EB to investigate the area allocated for the project. The mission was satisfied as to the suitability of the place. The negotiation between the EB and the Colonial Development Corporation was long and frustrating. In 1950 the EB informed the corporation of its terms:

i. the Board to take a lease of the land, when selected, from the owners;
ii. a Company to be formed by the Board and the Colonial Development Corporation jointly, the objective of which would be to operate the scheme on the land;
iii. the Board to sub-lease the land to the Company;
iv. the Colonial Development Corporation to take up 51 per cent of the shares in the Company and the Board to take 49 per cent of the shares;
v. the Directorate of the Company to consist of six Directors, three to be appointed by the Colonial Development Corporation, and three by the Board, the Chairman to be a Colonial Development Corporation nominee and to have a casting vote.[51]

The corporation refused to commit itself until August 1951, when a negotiation meeting was held in London to devise fresh proposals that would be satisfactory to both parties. The corporation demanded a pilot scheme of a thousand acres, the inclusion in the contract of all the oil palm holdings of the EB, and the involvement of two other companies as a third interest. As the representatives of the EB found the conditions unacceptable, it was decided to terminate the negotiations and search for a more suitable partner.

In the process of negotiating with another partner, the Colonial Development Corporation changed its mind and accepted collaboration on terms earlier proposed by the EB. In January 1952 the chairman of the EB traveled to London, where it was agreed to establish a syndicate to finalize the plans for the formation of a company, registered in Nigeria, to develop a plantation of about ten thousand acres of mixed rubber and oil palms. The land chosen for the project was on the edge of the Oban Forest Reserve. In 1952, the EB applied to the governor to "de-reserve" Oban so that the EB could acquire part of it. The operation of the Calaro Estate began in February 1954 and continued very well in the first year. Because of the undulating nature of the place, clearing was difficult, but the company was able to plant forty acres and to anticipate a further forty in 1955.[52]

The second category of oil palm estates was the small ones. While the large ones were the ideal, the small ones of about a thousand acres each were good for maintaining production at a high quality. The sizes were small enough to obtain land even in heavily populated areas, and, if a cluster of them could be established within a radius of thirty miles, it would be possible to reduce overhead cost. The EB believed that one great advantage would be that the villages, as an aspect of community development, would copy the small plantations, and a plantation system would then replace a "palm bush" system. The EB decided to establish in the Afikpo division of the Ogoja province the first of such plantations, and it allocated funds for one in 1950.[53] By 1952 it had four such plantations in its plans: the Kwa Falls Estate, Ikun, Uturu, and Ishiagu Oil Palm Plantations.

The Kwa Falls plantation, located some thirty-four miles to the north of Calabar, was acquired by the EB from the Calabar-Mamfe Road Planning Authority in November 1950. The estate was 3,000 acres of which 650 acres were used by the Agriculture Department for its experiments in swamp-rice growing and another 655 acres planted with oil palms before its transfer to the EB. An estate manager was appointed for Kwa Falls in June 1951 with a responsibility to develop on plantation lines 1,695 acres and to transform an existing 655 acres of a farm resettlement scheme to the plantation. In the first year of his appointment the manager was able to clear 352 acres of land for planting, establish a new nursery with about thirty thousand seedlings, sufficient to cover five hundred acres of new area, and to fell all wild palms. A temporary office and store were opened in 1951, and in the following year work began on the oil mill and the manager's house. By 1954 a total of 1,963 acres had been planted and a total tonnage of 36.52 tons of fruits harvested. Kwa became a success story.

The Ikun estate at Afikpo ran into an initial difficulty, because the land for the plantation was the subject of a most bitter conflict between the Okon and Ikun villages. Both villages disputed their boundaries, and the case had to reach the Supreme Court, which ruled in favor of Ikun. Up until 1952 the EB could not do anything because of the land dispute, and it did not have the staff to conduct its own separate investigation on the matter.[54] The Uturu project was also a failure. Located in the Okigwi division of the Owerri province, the project was to develop a twelve-hundred-acre plantation. Obtaining sufficient land became the handicap. The people of Uturu were willing to release only 483 acres, too small for a plantation. All attempts to persuade the people to lease more land were unsuccessful.[55]

At Ishiagu, Afikpo division, the response was very positive. The people here invited the EB to inspect the land to be leased for the plantation. The land was inspected in 1952 and found to be satisfactory, and a decision was made to choose the place and to abandon Uturu provided there was a place to bore for water.[56]

A pilot project was started in 1954 with a grant of £5,000 to rehabilitate the oil palm grove. This grant was used to pay subsidies to villages and individuals who undertook rehabilitation projects, at a sum of £5 per acre on the basis of: 30 percent per acre on completion of felling and clearing of old palms; 30 percent per acre on completion of planting with improved palms; and 10 percent per acre for four years thereafter for satisfactory maintenance. At the end of the planting season in 1954, 97.5 acres had been rehabilitated in twenty-one villages, involving seventy-nine owners, fifty-eight plots, and a sum of £292. The project was abandoned in later years, not because of a lack of interest by farmers, but the inability of the EB to follow up on performance.

In pursuit of its diversification policy the EB sought expert advice on cocoa, coconut, and rice production. In 1950 it allocated funds for temporary investigation of these products. It believed that a cashew-nut industry should be developed, especially in the eroded sandy areas of the Onitsha and Owerri provinces, which the people had abandoned because of soil infertility. Expert opinion in 1950 was that cashew orchards could help to arrest erosion, restore fertility to the soil, and become another valuable cash crop. The EB decided to establish an orchard of about six thousand acres, including a processing plant, and thus encourage the surrounding villages to establish smaller orchards as village industries.[57]

In 1951 the EB established the Sanata Coffee Estate, a cashew-nut scheme and a coconut plantation at Bonny.[58] The cashew industry was intended to reactivate production on lands that were so infertile that nothing else would grow on them. There were to be economic gains as well: the cashew fruit would become popular locally; the shell of the nut contained about 30 percent phenol, which was worth in 1952 £300 per ton; and cashews were the only natural source of phenol. The kernel was in high demand in the baking and confectionary trades in the United Kingdom and the United States. The EB believed that the economic returns would justify the investment and bring wealth to people who had no other use for their land.[59] The aim was to establish many small, model cashew plantations of a size adequate to pay for the overhead charges of processing the nuts and of issuing seeds to farmers and at the same time encourage and assist surrounding villages in planting cashews and processing the fruits in the EB factories.

A manager for the cashew industry was appointed in 1951, and negotiations were concluded to lease a site of about 1,300 acres in the three villages of Akama, Oyofo, and Neke, all in the Udi Division of the Onitsha province, and to begin planting in 1952. There was also a plan to lease additional land in the Okigwi, Awka, and Awgu divisions in order to expand cashew cultivation by 1953.[60] By 1952 a lot of interest had been generated in the new industry, especially in the Enugu-Okigwi-Awka area. By this date, too, the nucleus of the industry had been established: sites were chosen and surveyed for planting, accommodation and storage facilities were prepared, a tractor driver was trained, and buying agents were appointed in the areas marked for cashew growing. Initial problems were the high cost of hiring labor and transport. A visit by a cashew expert from Britain encouraged more enthusiasm and a proposal was made to establish a mill for the extraction of the pericarp liquid and the preparation of cashew kernels for export. By 1954 three cashew plantations had been successfully established at Ajali, Oji, and Mbala. Experiments were conducted on processing the kernels for local consumption, and the three-year-old trees at Ajali were already yielding their first fruits.[61]

Coffee was not as popular as cashew, although the EB encouraged the industry. A large amount of arabica coffee of high quality was planted by the farmers in the uplands of the Bamenda province in the village of Sanata located close to the international boundary with Cameroon. While the coffee enjoyed a high price, there was no facility for first-rate processing. The EB established a plantation at Sanata to serve as a model for local farmers and a factory to process coffee from the plantation and the local farmers. In January 1952 the EB received the rights to possess 1,200 acres for a coffee plantation plus another 5,200 acres of grazing land surrounding the plantation. A coffee manager was appointed in 1952, who started to plan for the erection of houses and stores and to prepare an area to plant coffee. The Sanata Coffee Estate became one of the most promising of all the projects. The first harvest in 1955 was insignificant, but expectations were that higher yields would follow in later years. The Sanata Coffee Estate also started experimenting on the roasting and grinding of beans.

The coconut industry was designed to strengthen the economy of the creek areas. The difficulty of reaching these areas was an obstacle to an early start of the venture. However, the beginning of the boat industry at Opobo improved the penetration of the creek area. In 1952 the EB was able to allocate funds to establish a small coconut plantation at Bonny. A manager was appointed for the scheme to negotiate a lease and to start the production of copra.[62] An area of twelve hundred acres was leased in 1953. Work was slow because of the difficult access to the place, labor shortages, and the swampy condition of the terrain. In 1954 four hundred acres were discovered to be useless. Of the remaining acres, 145 were planted with good result.[63]

Developing a rubber industry at Oban by taking proper care of the trees and improving the processing methods was another plan. The EB sought a business venture with an overseas rubber company, and, with help from the Colonial Office, it was able to interest Kuala Muda Rubber Estates, Limited. The representatives of Kuala visited the region in January and February 1952 and approved the Oban site for the project. After a series of meetings the partners ratified three proposals:

i. The formation in Nigeria of a Company for the purpose of establishing a rubber plantation in the Oban area of Calabar Division, with the Kuala Muda Rubber Estates, Limited, and their associates and the Eastern Regional Production Development Board as the principal shareholders, subscribing 51 per cent and 49 per cent respectively of the capital requirements estimated at £800,000.
ii. Management by the Kuala Muda Rubber Estates, Limited, or their associates.
iii. The Board of Directors of the Company to consist of three nominees of the Kuala Muda Rubber Estates, Limited, and their associates, and three of the Eastern Regional Production Development Board. The Chairman of the Board of Directors to be nominated by the Kuala Muda Rubber Estates, Limited, and their associates who shall have the casting vote.[64]

This became the second company to be formed by the EB, with the goal of establishing many others. It was intended that Nigerian investors would be encouraged to participate, and, with this end in mind, arrangements would be made for the EB to dispose of all or part of its capital investments to Nigerians. With respect to rubber, the anticipated objectives to be achieved were:

i. A large tract of land at present unproductive will be converted into an area of great economic value;
ii. Villages, even at some considerable distance away, can be encouraged to plant rubber thereby increasing their wealth and improving their standard of living;

iii. Income to the Board will be assured;
iv. The surrounding villages will not be able to provide all the necessary labour force with the result that the regular employment will be available for people from the over-populated Ibibio and Ibo areas;
v. Improved types of trees, which are not available in Nigeria, will be introduced.[65]

In March 1952 an agreement to lease twelve thousand acres was reached with the people of Oban, with the aim of subletting this plantation to the company. Work began on this project with the appointment of a project manager. By the end of 1954 twenty thousand acres of land had been planted with rubber; a total of six thousand acres had already been felled and avenued.[66]

With respect to increasing the quantity and quality of foodstuffs, the EB made plans for a cattle ranch, a fertilizer scheme, a project to produce concentrates for livestock, and rice mills. There was a plan for a cattle ranch, to provide beef in order to correct the shortage of animal protein, the chief deficiency in the people's diet. The price of meat was always on the increase. The greatest problem in increasing supply was the tsetse fly, and those areas free of it (the highlands of Bamenda and Mamfe) were cut off from the other parts of the country by rivers and mountains. The EB thought that it was possible to establish a ranch at Obudu, an area of about twenty thousand acres in the Ogoja province. The proposal was to build up a stock of some four thousand herd of cattle and flocks of sheep and herds of pig. There would have to be a road to link Obudu with the highlands of Bamenda and Mamfe in order to have an expansive cattle industry and another road to link up with the foot of the Obudu plateau. In 1950 the EB provided funds for the latter road.[67] In 1951 the project began with the selection of a site at Obudu, at a height of some 3,500 feet above sea level on a plateau that was cut off from the rest of the region. The difficulties of opening up the place were reported in heroic words:

> The Board's Cattle Ranch ... was started on the 1st of January, 1951, when the Manager (Mr. V. E. Hughes-Jones) and his wife trekked the twenty-six miles from road-head to the foot of the plateau and then, after a climb of about 3,000 feet ... built grass huts and shelters for themselves, their small staff and the cattle. The task facing them, of building up a stock of some 4,000 head of cattle and large flocks of sheep and goats in an area some 221 miles from the nearest stores whence all building materials, the necessities of life and machinery have to be transported 194 miles by lorry and then twenty-seven miles by head-load, would have killed the enthusiasm of most; but within three months a camp had been

established, staff recruited, eighty-two head of cattle and fifty sheep bought and a shop, managed by Mrs. Hughes-Jones, opened for the benefit of the staff from which members could obtain stores essential to their well-being.[68]

Meeting challenges became the daily routine of the ranch. It had difficulties attracting senior staff because of its location. While laborers could be drawn locally, herdsmen could not be retained for long because they had to return to their families in northern Nigeria and elsewhere. Those who remained had to rely on the manager's wife for medical attention and supplies of basic needs as there were neither a dispensary nor a market close to the ranch. Constructing permanent houses was difficult because there was no road to transport the materials. Attempts to make use of a large number of carriers was met with frustration, as the people found the journey rather tough. The timber used for construction had to be brought by head load. Buying cattle for a new ranch was not easy either. The most desired cattle were from N'gaoundere and Banyo in the French Cameroons, and could only be obtained after a long period of waiting and paperwork.

In spite of all these problems the ranch was able to forge ahead. It had 267 cattle in March 1952 and more than 500 one year later. The grazing land was excellent, and the animals did well, although many cases of death and sickness were reported. Many temporary sheds were completed, and the manager's house and a rest house were begun. The employees began to experiment with sheep, both local and imported, and the initial death of several of the animals did not discourage the staff. They were able to acquire horses and, later, a truck and tractor that simplified the work. By 1954 the major road to Obudu was about to be completed, and the herd of cattle had increased to 1,500; butter production continued to rise, but there was no regular slaughter for beef supply.[69] In later years, the ranch became a success and a tourist attraction.

The EB hoped to be able to influence a great many villages by encouraging the farmers to try new crops, establishing small plantations scattered as widely as possible, and encouraging the villages surrounding the plantations to plant the same crops with selected seeds from its plantations. Each of its plantations was to contain the best processing machinery available, and it was hoped that the surrounding villages would sell their crops to the board for processing. In this arrangement, the best seeds would be available to farmers and processing machines brought closer to them so that the highest grade of the processed crops would be available for sale.

The EB embarked on a fertilizer scheme in 1951. The need to increase farm yields was the driving motive behind this scheme. Experiments conducted in

1950–51 proved that in parts of Onitsha, Owerri, and Calabar provinces a judicious use of fertilizer increased yields by 75 percent.[70] In July 1951 the fertilizer manager began his duties with Aba as his headquarters. He selected a number of local sites on which to build stores to sell fertilizers. The EB signed a contract with Costains (West Africa), Limited to build a central store at Aba, where the fertilizers would be mixed and distributed to the smaller stores. The central store was a large building, comprising a mixing plant, a garage for six lorries, and the manager's house. To reach all parts of the region there was a need for a large number of substores located in many areas. For 1951 and 1952 preference was for areas where experiments had concluded that the application of fertilizers increased yields. Hence, Nnewi, Aguata, Awkuzu, Abatete, and Awka in the Onitsha province were the first to be considered. Later, other towns were added, and eleven of such substores were completed in 1952. A substore had a capacity for twenty-four tons, and as a prefabricated building it could easily be erected and dismantled.

The first consignment of one thousand tons of fertilizer arrived in August 1951. To popularize the scheme, it was decided to set the selling price below the cost price. Since the yields of foodstuffs were expected to increase, the subsidy was justified by the EB. In addition, it was decided to establish more demonstration plots at Aba and close to all the substores to convince the farmers as to the potential of fertilizer applications. Posters and pamphlets were also prepared to enlighten farmers on the advantages of fertilizers. Response by farmers to the fertilizer scheme was not too encouraging, and by the fifth year the expectation was that the board would be able to sell only five hundred tons per annum.[71] While the use of fertilizer was initially unpopular, the EB was optimistic that people would change their minds:

> The introduction of artificial fertilizers to any country is a very long-term proceeding. Substantial sales cannot be anticipated under a period of ten to twenty years. It is an interesting fact that in Turkey with a population of twelve million it was only during the third decade that substantial sales of over 10,000 tons per annum were obtained.[72]

A related project was the provision of concentrates for livestock. In 1950 and 1951 the EB made a grant of £2,400 to the Agriculture Department to build stores at the three government farms in Abak, Umudike, and Nkwelle to keep animals and ground feeding stuffs for pigs, sheep, goats, cattle, and poultry. When the demand for concentrates became necessary in the Ogoja province, the EB made another grant of £800 to build a store at the Abakaliki Government Farm. By 1952 the stores for Umudike and Nkwelle were already completed. In addition to supplying the government farms with the concentrates, limited quantities were sold to farmers. Three years later, the sales of concentrates had improved a little, with a total of eighty-two tons sold at Umudike, Abak, Abakaliki, and Nkwelle.

The fourth of the four plans to boost food production was the building of rice mills. Since the propaganda of the war years to grow more rice, production increased from the less than one hundred acres in 1940 to sixty thousand acres in 1952. The hulling of rice by hand was time-consuming and laborious. To further the development of the industry and to simplify hulling, the Agriculture Department established four mills. The EB wanted to complement the activities of the Agriculture Department by setting up mills to encourage more rice cultivation. It made a grant of £5,000 to the Agriculture Department in 1951 to establish three mills in "marginal areas."[73] A major success was recorded at Abakaliki, which became a thriving rice market. While the Agriculture Department kept to the proposal of establishing new mills in marginal areas, the major trouble was that the mills could not work full-time because of insufficient rice paddy to feed them.[74] The department continued to operate the mills but had a plan to sell them when rice growing became established.

With the transfer of the responsibility of the Nigerian Cocoa Marketing Board on development to the regional production development boards, the EB had to take over a number of uncompleted schemes. In collaboration with the Agriculture Department, the EB became involved in cocoa survey, improvement of cocoa quality, and long-term rehabilitation and planting of new cocoa. In 1952 the EB began to anticipate a proposal to bring cocoa production to the Ogoja and Owerri provinces, where the soil and the climate were suitable. In the following year, a cocoa estate was established at Ikom, and one hundred acres were planted by the end of December 1954.[75]

The EB spent money on other projects that were not necessarily labeled as "development," but which nevertheless pumped money into the economy and increased the physical assets of the region. Its members and staff received salaries and allowances. It built many houses for its staff all over the region, where major projects were located, and it built impressive central offices at Enugu and a block of apartments containing six quarters for its senior staff. It spent money on publicity, including a film, *Invitation to Wealth,* to advertise the advantages of Pioneer Oil Mills. The number of its staff expanded rapidly, absorbing a new generation of elite, recruiting hundreds of unskilled workers, and paying many of them a wage income for the first time. In 1952 it had 3,161 laborers, 357 junior staff, and 44 senior staff.

The program on infrastructures was impressive, if it is borne in mind that the EB was concerned with providing facilities to make accessible the places where its projects were located. It embarked upon a boat industry at Opobo and spent money on new roads. In the boat industry, its aim was to provide transport facilities to the creek areas in the hope that the people there would produce rice, coconuts, copra, and fiber. The EB decided to spend money on two barges and train suitable people to become quartermasters and artisans to construct more crafts.[76] As with most of its ventures, it was assumed that some of the trained artisans would later establish boat-building industries of their own at Opobo and in other parts of the creek areas. The boatyard was opened in November 1954, immediately becoming popular for the production of powered craft for passengers and goods transport.[77]

Between 1950 and 1952 the EB granted funds for five roads, all having to do with its development projects. These were: the Owutu-Unwana and the Kpogrikpo-Unwana in the Ogoja province; the Nwaniba Road end and the Atimbo-Ikang Road, Calabar province; and cocoa roads in the Bende division of Owerri province. Each road was important to the economic program of the EB. Unwana, located on the Cross River, was a major produce evacuation center. The deterioration of the road became so bad that lorries could no longer use it, and the EB had to award a grant of £6,000 to repair it. A grant of £4,000 was provided to strengthen the Nwaniba road end so that it could withstand the weight of palm-oil drums. In the case of Bende, where the large sum of £16,000 was granted, the reason was to build four new roads to evacuate cocoa, and, in the case of the Atimbo-Ikang Road, it was to have concrete bridges that could support lorries evacuating palm produce.[78]

The EB also spent a lot of money on some major roads. One was the Calabar-Arochuku Road, chosen so as to open up the large area of fertile land around the bend of the Cross River and to link the Calaro Oil Palm Estate with the Calabar port. Work on the road began in 1950 and was completed in 1956, with an expenditure of over £200,000. Another major road was the Obudu-Plateau Road to connect to a ranch that was contracted to the firm of Dolcino and Micheletti. This project took three years to complete not because of shortage of funds but of labor and the difficult terrain. There were many other miscellaneous roads that received grants between 1953 and 1955. These included the Uyo-Nwaniba Road in the Uyo division, the Amawon-Okproenyi-Nkalunta Road in the Bende division, the access road to the Ikom Coco Estate, the Azia Road at Onitsha, and the Calabar-Ikang, Okundi-Irruan, Okigwi-Ndiawa, and Owutu-Unwana-Kpogrikpo roads.[79]

The EB became interested in the improvement and expansion of the Onitsha market, the biggest trading center on the lower Niger and perhaps in West

Africa. In 1952 this thriving market consisted of about 2600 stalls. Located on the edge of the River Niger, it benefited from the East-West trunk road in addition to the river communication. The EB and several government agencies complained about the ramshackle nature of the market stalls and wanted to modernize it. The native authority hired a British company, Messrs. R. Travers Morgan, to study the market. The company suggested an improvement of the site and the stalls for a sum of £500,000. The NA sought the loan from the EB, which was interested in the market, which, in turn, would contribute to development, in addition to earning the EB 3 percent interest on its money. On January 3, 1952, the EB agreed to finance the project to the tune of £500,000, free of interest in the early years and at 3 percent in later years. Two other conditions ensured that the EB would recover its money:

i. Repayment of the capital sums and of interest shall be secured as a first charge on the revenues of the Onitsha Town Native Authority.
ii. The Board shall have access through its agents to the accounts of the Onitsha Town Native Authority relating to the reconstruction of the market and the revenue of the Authority and shall also have the right through its agents to inspect the constructional works.[80]

The conditions were accepted by the Onitsha Town Native Authority, which received the loan and commenced work on the reconstruction of the Onitsha market in late 1954.[81]

Finally, the EB decided in 1954 to invest £500,000 in the Nigerian Cement Company located at Nkalagu, forty miles from Enugu. Other principal shareholders included the Government of Nigeria, the Government of the Eastern Region, two foreign companies (Tunnel Portland Cement Company, Limited, and F. L. Smidth and Company, Limited). This became a successful industry.

In financing its programs, the EB relied on funds from the Nigerian Marketing Boards, which made grants to regional boards in due proportion to the value of produce purchased in a region. The EB obtained funds from the Nigerian Oil Palm Produce Marketing Board and, as a major center of palm production, the East received a huge proportion of the allocation, over £1 million each year. When the Nigerian Cocoa Marketing Board divested its development powers and made grants to the regional bodies, the East received £172,522 for the 1947–50 seasons and £93,482 for the 1950–51 season, sums based on 3.69 percent of the total purchases. In addition to this fund, the EB was guaranteed by the Nigerian Oil Palm Produce Marketing Board a sum of about £400,000 per year until 1956. The financial capability of the EB was strengthened every year with interest on its savings and investments, and grants from the Nigerian Oil Palm Produce Marketing

Board, the Nigerian Cocoa Marketing Board, and the Nigerian Groundnut Marketing Board. Its total assets in January 1955 were put at £5,334,507.[82]

Loan Programs

The administration of a loan program was vested in the Eastern Regional Development Board (ERDB) under Ordinance No. 14 of 1949, as a joint successor, with three other boards for the rest of the country, to the Nigerian Local Development Board (NLDB), which was closed on March 31, 1949.[83] The EB's initial fund was a sum of £355,514 received from the assets taken over from the NLBD and a direct grant from the central government. The acquired assets consisted of all loans made by the NLDB to bodies in the Eastern Region and the total value of advances made by the NLDB to the Department of Commerce and Industries for the building of the Pioneer Oil Mills. The majority of EB's funds were held by the accountant-general in a deposit account which earned interest at the rate of 1.5 percent per annum, from which funds were withdrawn to meet expenses.[84] After the payment of grants previously approved by the NLDB, the EB was left with £209,000. In general the assets of the EB did not increase because it had to issue loans and grants and wait for many years to recoup its money. During the period under consideration, the focus was to spend and spend, and then to recover gradually.

Like the NLDB, the EB was to foster the economic development of the region "by making grants for a variety of purposes."[85] The EB could assist an individual or group of persons engaged in development schemes of public works, industries, and local crafts; assist in schemes of land settlement and agricultural and forestry development; and provide aid to any experimental body interested in the potentials of any product. The chief commissioner could instruct the EB to advance a loan to assist any scheme that could contribute to development.

The EB considered all applications in the light of its objectives. If members thought a proposal that fell outside of its power could assist development, it could be referred to the chief commissioner for a decision. Because the applications to it were many and its funds limited, the EB established a priority list that placed as frontline projects those on food supplies and road transport (except for the purchase of lorries, whose number in the region was considered adequate). On food supplies, applicants who intended to use the money to produce food rich in protein were favored because these were believed to be in short supply. On transport, those who wanted money to build motor repair trade were most favored because the EB believed that the facility for maintenance in the region was very poor.

Traditional commerce alongside modern advertising. Photo by A. Olusegun Fayemi.

Whether a project was a priority or not, the EB scrutinized all applications and requested technical information from officers in the Agriculture and the Commerce and Industries Departments. If the scheme was already in existence, the EB sought information on past receipts, expenditures, and estimates of future income. Finally, to preserve its funds, security was demanded, except in a few cases. All loans and grants must be approved by the chief commissioner, and loans exceeding £10,000 and all outright grants must be approved by the Standing Committee on Finance of the Regional Assembly.

The activities of the EB in its early years revolved around completing the applications already considered by the NLDB. It inherited a number of loans granted to several organizations and individuals.[86] In 1950 the EB made two outright grants. The first was a sum of £3,186 to the Calabar-Mamfe Road Area Planning Authority, being the last installment of a grant of £17,044 previously approved by the NLDB. The second grant of £1,000 was to the Veterinary Department to finance an experimental scheme on cattle grazing. In addition to these old ventures, the EB approved a number of new loans in 1950. Preference was given to the native authorities, small-scale indigenous enterprises, and those with records of performance. Justifying approval for applications by individuals usually took a long time, time to allow the members to discuss the proposal and to assess the possible risk involved. Not only were many applications rejected, the amount applied for was usually scaled down to be able to spread available money to many people and to minimize risk.[87] In all, there were twelve beneficiaries at the beginning,[88] but the number increased in subsequent years to over fifty. By 1955 loans of £404,072 had been approved and £379,592 paid out.[89]

The number of applications continued to increase from year to year at a rate that alarmed the EB. Neither did it have sufficient funds to meet the demands of the applicants nor even the time to scrutinize the applications. By mid-1951, the amount of money left to be disbursed was £60,510,[90] hardly enough to meet the demands of individual applicants. Late in the 1950s, the EB began to revise its priorities in order to reduce the number of applications. Not only would it require security on loans, it would give assistance to established ventures or those in which applicants had invested a substantial capital. In addition, it gave reasons why it would preclude:

i. rice farming and small sawyers businesses. Necessary development of these industries should be possible without the Board's assistance since low capital was required for their development, while quick and comparatively high profits could be made.
ii. assistance for the purchase of palm oil hand presses, kernel crackers, motor lorries and buses, or for the establishment of building or contracting and wholesale or retail trading businesses because there was no shortage of private capital for any of these purposes.
iii. assistance for furniture making, tailoring or baking because these businesses could not be considered of major importance to the region and they were already adequately represented.
iv. assistance for poultry and pig keeping because disquieting reports were received on the success of businesses to which the Board had already given assistance. It was considered that greater skill and knowledge was required in the management of such businesses than had hitherto been thought necessary, and that before further assistance was given to them more must be known about the eventual success of existing investments.[91]

Encouragement of the arts or development of social services were ruled out because, as the EB argued in 1951, these would not contribute to the wealth of the region.

The EB also had to worry about the control of its loan advances to ensure that they were used for the purpose for which an application was approved. The EB exercised the right to inspect businesses, to issue instructions on how a business should be run, and to demand an early repayment if it was not satisfied with the performance of a business. However, supervision and inspections were limited because the EB had no staff to embark on them.

If determining whether people used the loans for the purpose for which they applied is difficult to ascertain, there is information on debt recovery. Many repaid their loans. Bad debts were limited to a few cases: the Ibez Trading Company did not settle its debt of £1,365 15.6d, and the interest-free loan of £750 made to the Ikot Ekpene Cooperative Raffia Marketing Society could not be recovered.[92] Delay in payment was, however, rampant, as individual debtors were slow in remitting their installment payments.[93]

The loans office of the EB began as a small one. In 1950 it had no staff of its own and relied on the facilities of the regional secretariat and the advice of the district officers and technical departments. It, however, desired a separate office and staff of its own to scrutinize the applications.[94] To cope with a large number of applicants it decided in 1950 to have a committee of four screen all applications. So too did it decide to expand its staff and recruit a full-time accountant.[95]

To evaluate the achievements of the loan program, the main issue is that through the EB about a hundred individuals and a dozen government agencies, especially the local administrations, were able to obtain loans. As the fund of the EB was limited, it ran out of influence very quickly when the money it could offer became small. In the early 1950s the EB was unable to evaluate the success of its loan program:

> It is not yet possible to assess the success or otherwise of the Board's activities as most of the advances made are repayable over a period as long as ten years. Owing to the shortage of staff the Board has not been able to follow up its advances with after visits, and it was therefore a minority of probable failures to which its attention had been drawn shortly before the end of the year, rather than to the far larger number of businesses which by the promptitude of the repayments appear to be running successfully. The available evidence suggests that the failures are due not so much to inherent weaknesses in the schemes themselves, but to a lack of supervision by the owners of the business, the employment of unqualified managers, the dissipation of the loan on purposes entirely foreign to the business, and in partnership disagreements left unresolved.[96]

Through an analysis of those who obtained the loans, the elite and those with connections to political parties were privileged. Those who could not read or write could not apply for a loan. A great deal of documentation was required by the applicant. Either because many were incapable of supplying the documents or did not want to divulge such things as their income and business practices, they failed to qualify for loans. Farmers and the urban poor did not receive much help. Responding to criticism in 1952 for ignoring farmers, the board defended itself:

> It has been suggested, in more than one quarter, that the Board might have done more to achieve its purpose, particularly in the agricultural field, if less emphasis were laid on the necessity for securing any loans made. Nigeria is a predominantly agricultural country and it has been the Board's experience in the Eastern Region that sound agricultural proposals do not lack support or security of some sort. The Board, has, moreover, a clear duty to consider the preservation of its funds, which are public funds, and although if it is to fulfil its purpose, it must be prepared to take normal commercial risks, it must whenever the opportunity offers (and other things are equal) take steps to secure them against loss.[97]

The total number of applications was unusually high. The rejection rate was equally high, over 60 percent did not move beyond preliminary consideration by the office of the District Officer who had to send them to the EB, either because they failed to provide adequate information or they proposed schemes which did not fall within the EB's terms of reference. Having met all the conditions for a loan, an applicant had to provide security. Native authorities and departments did not have problems with this, since they could secure loans with their property and revenues. What an individual could use as security was always a big issue, as many did not have what the EB found acceptable. Many resorted to the use of land as security. However, except for plots in the cities, land was generally not acceptable as security.[98] To have land was not enough: the applicant had to register it and obtain a title, while the value of the land must be determined by the EB.[99] The need to obtain a title was to further encourage the interest in deeds of registration by those who needed them to raise money or to make exclusive claims.[100] The loan program enabled emerging entrepreneurs to benefit from the services of the EB. As small as the loans were in some cases, without Nigerians themselves in control, there would have been nothing whatsoever.

Northern Nigeria

The Northern Regional Production Development Board was created by the Regional Development Boards Ordinance No. 14 of 1949 and by Section 38 of the Groundnut Marketing Ordinance. The composition of the board and the staff were similar to those of other regions. The initial fund of £1,710,900 was

Children at play in a communal village. Photo by A. Olusegun Fayemi.

received from the Groundnut Marketing Board to be spent on the "development of the producing industries concerned and for the benefit and prosperity of the producers and the areas of production."[101] Late in 1949, the Northern Board (NB) decided on four major schemes to be implemented in the 1950s:

i. schemes to increase the quantity and quality of various crops: fertilizer scheme, Sokoto rice scheme, and creating a pool of agricultural equipment;
ii. Land Settlement Schemes: land settlement at Kontagora; the Shendam resettlement scheme, and the Jema'a resettlement scheme;
iii. Development of water resources: purchase of windmill pumps and dam scrapers and purchase of Persian wheels and animal-drawn pumps;
iv. Development of large-scale engineering works: creating a pool of heavy mechanical equipment, improving of groundnut evacuation roads, and the improvement of the Shendam-Kurgwi road.[102]

The policy was permanent for most of the years, by concentrating mainly on the production of food, water, and communications, the three vital sectors, which the Northern Region believed would bring about development.

Schemes to Increase the Quantity and Quality of Various Crops

The aim was to increase the output of cash and food crops. The strategy was to increase the yield per acre of food crops and to open up the land for food crops where export crops did not do well. To increase yield, a sum of £350,000 was allocated to fertilizer. In 1950 one thousand tons of superphosphate were obtained and distributed in Kano, Adamawa, Sokoto, Katsina, Bauchi, and Borno. By the end of the year, 32,000 farmers had received a bag each for use on peanut and corn farms.[103] In the years that followed, more fertilizers were imported, although many farmers refused to use them for fear that they would contaminate their crops.

At Sokoto, a rice project was established in 1950, in the swampy river valleys of the Sokoto and Rima rivers.[104] Here, as in many other parts of the country, rice was becoming a main item of diet. The project was to increase the acreage under rice. The board would supply the capital equipment, while the native authority would bear the recurrent costs for plowing an ultimate area of 150,000 acres per annum. The board allocated £136,000 for the purchase of tractors, mechanical equipment, and the erection of workshops over a period of three years. By the end of 1950, it was also decided to buy heavy equipment to "breakup" the land. To assist other places with modern farm equipment, the board created a pool of equipment to be issued on loan to native authorities. By the end of 1950 many orders had been placed while some, valued at £25,000, had been received. By 1955, the project was completed with offices, equipment, workshops, and over 25,000 acres planted with rice. Profit was recorded after 1953, but it was not always so when salaries were added to the expenditure.

In 1951 the board allocated £82,430, over a five-year period, to the eradication of the riverine tsetse fly in the adjoining areas of Kano, Katsina, and Zaria provinces, as a practical solution to a major requirement of the population and a pilot project for a general preparation of the tsetse-ridden areas for progressive farming.[105] Known as the KKZ Scheme, it was to control human and cattle trypanosomiasis, provide safe grazing, and increase dry-season cultivation on the riverine land freed from tsetse fly. By the end of 1953 a lot of clearing had been done, but the population was slow to respond by refusing to change their cultivation habits.[106] Rather than abandon the project, the board decided to embark upon agricultural resettlement of the area and to undertake a number of "consolidation" works such as improving animal health, and extending mixed farming and irrigation.

The control of the tsetse fly became much more elaborate after 1952, with the creation of several campaigns and small units in different locations.[107] A large sum was spent to stop the advance of more flies to Zaria in 1952 and 1953, and streams were cleared among the Tiv in 1953 and 1954 in order to reduce the areas for the flies to breed. In Kano, Katsina, and Zaria provinces greater attention was paid to clearing the major rivers and their tributaries.

As with the farmers who were resettled (discussed later), an attempt was also made to bring Fulani nomads into settlements, to teach them the value of

A thriving fishing economy near a rural village. Photo by A. Olusegun Fayemi.

quality in animals, and to provide a supply of cattle. One of these experiments was at Agangara in the Sokoto province, where a small dam was constructed in 1951 to provide water.

Among the other major measures embarked upon were the eradication of weeds with chemicals, the distribution of peanut cake to feed stock and of improved peanut seeds to farmers, the purchase of breeding cattle, and a campaign on mixed farming. A production division was established within the KKZ Scheme in April 1952, with a core of officers to supervise agricultural projects.[108]

Land Settlement Scheme

The aim was to encourage migration to those areas with sparse population. In such areas, the land was fertile, and the idea of the land settlement was to move farmers from over-farmed areas into fertile, uninhabited areas, in order to raise people's standards of living, to improve agriculture methods, and to increase the quantity of crops grown. Three such settlements were established at Kontagora, Shendam, and Jema'a.

The Kontagora Settlement, located at the village of Tungar Maidubu, was designed as an experiment in social and economic planning, thus concentrating the efforts of all departments in a concerted endeavor. In 1950 many Hausa and their families were resettled in a new village, each family with a small house, a granary, a shelter for cattle, a farm of twenty-three acres, and a garden of about half an acre. Money was also set aside to recruit labor to build the settlement, to establish a center for the training of plow teams of oxen and a farming equipment maintenance and repair depot. The number of settlers doubled in 1952, and by January 1953 the number was a total of 182 families. By 1955 there were over four hundred plow oxen, a market, a dispensary, and a fishpond.

The Shendam Scheme sought to "canalize" the southward movement of farmers from the hilly northern areas of the Shendam division to the fertile plains lying between the Shemanker and Wase rivers and as far south as the River Benue. In addition, it was to open up new areas of fertile land in order to improve the material and physical conditions of the local population. The project began in 1948 and was inherited by the board. In 1950 the board allocated £8,000 to the Shendam native authority to construct small dams for surface water, subsidiary roads, storage facilities and to purchase some tractors and equipment.[109] By 1953, the Shendam had become the biggest of all the settlements, with many types of equipment, settlers, and big farms.[110]

The object of the Jema'a Resettlement Scheme was to settle farmers from the barren High Plateau on the fertile regions of the land adjacent to the Jos-Wamba road, an area large enough for five thousand people. In the first year a sum of £800 was spent to construct roads, to provide two wells, and to clear land.[111] By the end of 1953 over £6,000 had been spent and sixty-three settlers established.

Two additional settlements were created in 1952. One was at Gwoza, designed to control the agricultural settlement of the "pagan population" of the northern spurs of the Cameroon chain around Gwoza in Borno province, who, because of population pressure on the hills, were moving to the plains. The board was concerned that the Gwoza people would abandon their highly developed terrace-farming practices for haphazard shifting cultivation. An area south and west of Gwoza at the foot of the hills was chosen as a site, a settlement officer was appointed, a new dirt road was constructed to reach the place, and the first settlers were moved there early in 1953.[112] The second new settlement was at Koza in Katsina province, where the first twelve settlers moved in 1952 to grow millet and guinea corn.

The board and the regional government believed that the concept of resettlement was good. In the fifth year of its implementation, the board took a number of photographs of the resettled farmers and their families, all with contented faces, to show to the world how successful the scheme had been and how the farmers' lives were transformed from poverty—"under-nourished," poor, and sick—and from the fear of the open plains to a happy one: "now they are well fed, comparatively prosperous, greatly improved in health, and facing a future in which, through their own efforts, they can live a secure and contented life."[113] This became the repeated story during the decade.

It is true that the resettlement scheme did spend a lot of money on new roads and houses, and that it devoted time to modern agricultural methods. It is also true that several of the farmers showed a keen interest in the project:

they moved to new houses, had land to farm, obtained free seeds and advice, and benefited from social services such as a dispensary and adult education classes. However, there were problems, mainly associated with the inability to consult with the settlers on virtually all aspects of the scheme.[114] Many did not like the layout—a village square and farms grouped around it. The board responded by changing the design to a grid pattern common to the region.[115] As each settler was entitled to a two-bedroom house, there was grumbling that this was too small for a large family. A number of settlers left, after complaining of one problem or another, while some simply used the cover of darkness to disappear. Not everybody or every group responded enthusiastically to the idea. For instance, persuading the Birom to move to Jama'a was difficult.[116] Finally, while there was production and control of tsetse fly, the resettlements were not as economically viable as anticipated. They did not become models to other farmers, and they did not transfer experience of lasting value to the farmers.

Water Resources

The primary aim of developing water resources was to improve agriculture. The conclusion of the board was that the fertility of much of the land could be increased, if farmyard manure was used as fertilizer and there was sufficient water for irrigation purposes. Farmyard manure depended on water being available for cattle in the dry season. The board imported many windmill pumps and erected them over wells in Sokoto, Katsina, Kano, Borno, Adamawa, and Bauchi provinces for drawing water for cattle; also acquired were animal-drawn water pumps and large and small Persian wheels.[117] The board established a dam-building unit and hired a dam builder to construct earth dams in areas where the water table was low. On the plains, the Raba Irrigation Scheme began in July 1952 to irrigate the River Niger. Initial reports on this irrigation project were very favorable indeed,[118] and it actually became an important aspect of farming in future years.

Development of Large-scale Engineering Works

To be able to transport an increasing quantity of export crops, the board decided to improve the road network. The main roads from the larger peanut centers were to be expanded to carry heavy lorries. In addition, the board was interested in terracing and building reservoirs. The board created a pool of heavy mechanical equipment for road making and construction of reservoirs to be loaned to the native authorities. Also a pool of agricultural equipment such as tractors, plows, disc harrows, and cultivators was created.

The board took over the maintenance of peanut evacuation roads. It also spent money on some major roads, such as the improvement of the Shendam-Kurgwi Road.[119] A boat building industry was embarked on at Makurdi, on the River Benue, and two boats were built by 1953. There was a program to construct over two thousand new feeder roads in areas with export crops. Progress on the roads was generally unsatisfactory because of inadequate technical staff and equipment. One great success was the Zamfara Valley Road in the Sokoto province to open up an area rich in cotton and peanuts.

By the mid-1950s the pool of equipment had become one of the most expensive projects of the northern board. The pool had heavy machines for agriculture and road construction, but the pool also experienced financial losses and had problems with maintenance and repairs. However, the native authorities were able to borrow equipment from the pool. For most of the 1950s the northern board was interested in over a dozen other small projects, created either by the needs or the recommendations of board members. Among these miscellaneous activities were the aerial survey and air photographing of development areas and the new settlements, the killing of thousands of baboons that destroyed crops, experiments on corn storage, and the creation of a palm tree plantation in the Kabba province.

On industry, there was no success in developing a button manufacturing industry nor of shea butter extraction, but work progressed satisfactorily on peanut-oil mills and meat canning. In general, progress on the mills was slow. Of the six mills purchased by the Department of Commerce and Industries and transferred to the board, four were in-store, while one was in operation at Funtua and the other at Kaura Namoda. One early difficulty was the low oil extraction, which upset the viability of the project; if there was too much oil in the cake, it lowered its value as animal foodstuff. Three oil palm mills at Ayangba, Alade, and Ola, all in the Igala divison, originally sponsored by the Northern Region Development (Loans) Board were inherited by the Northern Board. The meat-canning industry was located at Kano, and was successful enough to attract the attention of more investors.

An Assessment: Achievements and Limitations of Regional Boards

The boards in different parts of the country were active in attempts to promote a variety of development-oriented projects, mainly in agriculture and industries. All the regional boards invested almost £7 million in agriculture during the 1950s. As already indicated above, and as tables 4–6 show, each region placed emphasis on different aspects of agriculture. In the North, the emphases covered land settlement, irrigation, and production. In the East, pioneer oil mills

Table 4. Agricultural Investments by Regional Boards: Western Region

Project	Expenditure to March 31, 1959 £	Expenditure to March 31, 1960 £
Ijebu Farming Project	1,414,525	1,680,916
Urhonigbe Rubber Estate	405,012	506,223
Upper Ogun Estate	142,729	171,527
Araromi Rubber Estate	592,888	691,959
Ibokun Cocoa Plantation	50,901	58,548
Oda-Akure Cocoa Plantation	196,788	262,285
Partnership Projects	685,805	787,992
Ikenne Plantation	2,045	71,911
Lomiro/Araromi Oil Palm Plantations	133,503	167,439
Eruwa Pineapple Plantation	16,166	12,183
Eleiyele Citrus Nursery	10,188	12,266
Total	3,650,550	4,423,249

Source: *Annual Reports of the Western Regional Production Development Board*

Table 5. Agricultural Investments by Regional Boards: Eastern Region

Project	Expenditure to March 31, 1959 £	Expenditure to March 31, 1960 £
Bonny Coconut Estate	128,335	139,268
Calaro Oil Palm Estate	270,517	312,463
Cashew-Nut Industry	199,448	209,362
Ikom Cocoa Estate	121,554	140,842
Kwa Falls Oil Palm Estate	178,020	183,124
Elele Estate	95	7,169
Abia Cocoa Estate	—	4,519
Umuahia Cocoa Estate	—	2,117
Miscellaneous	19,487	19,487
Total	917,465	1,018,241

Source: *Annual Reports of the Eastern Regional Development Board.*

and rubber cultivation were paramount. In the West, the expansion of cocoa plantations, palm oil, and fruits were the priorities.

There were other development projects in addition to the major ones mentioned above. Many of these activities did not fall under the two aforementioned boards but were executed by the native authorities and provincial governments with funds from the Colonial Development and Welfare Board and

Table 6. Agricultural Investments by Regional Boards: Northern Region

Project	Expenditure to March 31, 1959 £	Expenditure to March 31, 1960 £
Agricultural Land Settlement	238,442	242,937
Agricultural Production Development	1,153,023	1,231,785
Irrigation and Water Development	65,346	73,744
Forest and Veterinary	89,283	102,235
Total	1,546,094	1,650,701

Source: *Annual Reports of the Northern Regional Production Development Board.*

regular public sources. To consider only those activities associated with economic planning, the priority projects included road construction and maintenance, rural water supplies, and agricultural and village development. On the development of rural water projects, rural water supplies inspectors were appointed in different areas to check the quality of drinking water. Wells were popular and many communities voluntarily built new ones. Urban water supply, too, received priority consideration, although progress was slow in many places. The supply of electricity was not as fast as the population expected. Modern medical facilities began to spread to various towns and villages. Several new maternity centers and clinics were opened, and new places to treat leprosy were also established.

The establishment of the boards was a significant milestone in the economic development of Nigeria. The boards were committed to developing the agricultural industry and to increasing the prosperity of farm workers. Some required the introduction of fertilizers and new technologies. In the Eastern Region, for example, the most difficult and expensive project was the oil mill designed to improve the quality and quantity of palm products so that they would attract good prices in the world market. This was even conceived as a temporary measure. The ideal, which was never actualized, was to take away the farms from individual farmers and to substitute village plantations, containing the best available oil palm stock, for the existing wild palm bush. The mills consumed the bulk of the funds but did not make quick profits as originally anticipated. There were several limitations and problems. The initial opposition to the mills has been mentioned. When the mills became popular, individuals with resources desired to own them. The EB refused to hand off because it did not want personal interests to hinder its goal of using the mills to improve the quality of oil. The ambitious individuals fought back by misrepresenting the intention of the EB to mean a takeover of production and people's resources. Up until 1952 the EB was declaring losses on the mills and found it difficult to fulfill its aim of plowing back a portion of its net profits into the area served by the mills. The losses on the mills were described as "considerable" in 1955, although the EB could not rethink the whole idea because it had been conceived as the EB's most central development focus. When a mill incurred a loss, the EB blamed it on the villages where the mill was located for not processing sufficient fruits. Many of the mills began operation at a period when fruits were insufficient to allow full production. Once the mill personnel were engaged, they were not laid off in slack periods, with salary thus contributing to operational costs.[120] Another project that brought huge losses was the boatyard, and a sum of £20,000 had to be provided, in 1955, to cover the deterioration in the stocks of logs. Both the mill and some other projects were still geared toward an export-oriented economy, thus promoting cash crops at the expense of food supply.

Community participation tended to be small, and many projects were conceived without discussion with the people. A step was taken in 1952 to involve local communities by creating advisory committees, composed of representatives from the EB and local communities to discuss problems and to advise on how profits were to be spent.[121] There were cases where development projects led to competition among towns and communities. In the East for instance, communities fought over the location of mills.[122] In some others, people disagreed over whether or not to give up their land for government projects. It took one year to obtain land at Akama in the East for the cashew project.[123] Where the emphasis was on cash crops, development schemes favored areas with products to sell.

A number of the industrial projects did not take off or were unsuccessful. For example, the oil and rice mills in the Western Region were unsuccessful. Some new industries could not even get raw materials in sufficient quantities, as in the examples of the Lafia Fruit Canning Factory and the Ikpoba Rubber Processing Factory. As the boards put their hands in many projects, they began to record limited successes. They all initially tried to focus their schemes: for instance, the North started with food, water, and communication, described as a "trinity of basic needs,"[124] but it later became diverted to many other projects such as road construction and building staff houses. They were often beset with the problem of shortage of skilled manpower.

Changes were expected to come in ways defined by a tiny elite or bureaucrats. The most common objectives were to create or extend plantations, provide more food, increase production, increase the number of producers, make farming more attractive, provide reasonable amenities and infrastructure, create a comprehensive scheme of land utilization, provide funds, and create model farms. Many of these goals were laudable, even if they only existed on paper.

The boards provided opportunities for a first generation of Nigerian politicians and planners to exercise leadership. There was a lot of enthusiasm for the development projects, mainly social, but how the bill of ever-expanding social services would be met increasingly became a problem. The reports of the various boards boasted that they improved the people's standards of living, health, and happiness, even if many of the projects did not demonstrate success.

The elite in power and members of the bureaucracy certainly benefited from the development institutions. A regime of experts was created, especially in the Western Region, with some describing themselves as "planners" and a host of technocrats in agriculture, cooperative societies, and health services. As an employer, the boards had to pay salaries and provide some benefits to their staff. More and more Nigerians struggled to attain senior positions on these boards. Originally, they were jealous and critical of the European staff. In 1953, the West complained that:

> Well-qualified and experienced European field officers on fat salaries and with most attractive conditions of service are maintained in the field on idle jobs or assignments which could have been more economically and advantageously entrusted to junior Nigerian Agricultural Assistants. Unaccountably large sums of money are being spent by European field officers on hardly necessary and profitable preliminary investigations, negotiations and propaganda which are best handled by the natives. Only organisations with large and inexhaustible funds can afford to spend money on the scale and at the rate the Board is spending money on its agricultural projects or partnership schemes.[125]

As it turned out, this kind of criticism was to pave way for the appointments of Nigerians who regarded development as a dual role of developing the Self and the Nation at the same time.

The boards provided opportunities for the new regional governments administered by Nigerians to distribute power to key politicians. The membership of the boards was dominated by the politicians who had one eye on service and another on contracts. Those who served on the boards received sitting allowances, emoluments, and some privileges. In 1955 the West took a step further to make the positions of the chairman and deputy chairman full-time,[126] with generous salaries and allowances. When four committees were created in the same year, it enabled prominent businessmen and scholars who identified with the action group to gain more access to the board. To the clever politicians, civil servants, and those well connected with them, some of the boards' projects were sources of making fast money. The West began to complain in 1953 of "prodigious waste of public fund" in unproductive and uneconomic projects,[127] the desire of some individuals to become plantation owners at all cost by making use of public funds and diverting money meant for agriculture to other enterprises that would turn them into rich landlords. The combination of the pursuits of self-interest and regional planning goals was to continue during the First Republic and for many years thereafter.

5
The Economy, 1960–1965

Production methods are still primitive, the great majority of the population is illiterate and standards of nutrition, housing and medical care are low. The people of Nigeria are anxious to live better and hence produce more goods, in greater variety; they want to become better educated; they show a growing willingness to modify those social institutions which hold back economic progress and to accept methods of social, economic and political organization which elsewhere have proved conducive to such progress.
—IBRD, 1955[1]

Colonial Legacy

As the opening remark written in the last decade of colonial rule shows, Nigeria inherited a precarious economy at independence in 1960. The economy was dependent on revenues from export crops, with agriculture contributing about 64 percent of the Gross Domestic Product (GDP). The prices of these crops were determined by the buyers, and the revenues were subject to price fluctuations in the international market. The industrial sector was relatively young. The government believed that, without attracting foreign funds and companies, the pace could only grow slowly. The number of members of the middle class with good incomes was small, a reflection of the low number of educated and skilled people. The per capita income was low, physical and social infrastructures were grossly inadequate, and industry was still in its infancy, contributing merely 3.6 percent of the GDP. The national income was put at naira (N)2,244.6 million, and the income per capita was N56. New roads had been constructed, but the total, tarred and untarred, of 41,065 miles cannot be described as adequate for a country the size of Nigeria. Educational enrollment was expanding, but the number of schools was grossly inadequate. In 1953 only twenty thousand students were enrolled in secondary schools and four hundred in the university. With 209 hospitals and 425 doctors, the country lagged far behind in the provision of medical services.[2]

Political independence did not necessarily lead to economic independence. The country needed to halt the transfer of wealth abroad, to develop its technology, to create a capital-goods sector, and to produce consumer goods. For the duration of the First Republic, foreign companies controlled the banking, insurance, and manufacturing sectors. A number of well-placed Nigerians regarded their role as that of servicing and protecting external interests in various functions as middlemen, contract agents, and partners in joint ventures. Influential members in the federal cabinet assured foreign investors of risk-free enterprises and provided them with various incentives. Indeed, the major plan document of the era was drawn by outsiders who placed much hope on raising substantial external funds to generate investments. The expectation of investments from abroad was based on an ages-long assumption, formulated in the hey days of colonial rule, that "without foreign investment, neither public nor private endeavor can achieve the rate of growth that the Nigerian people desire."[3]

There were other aspects that revealed the limitations of independence. A number of colonial officers were still around and influential in various capacities. The Nigerian currency still depended on British sterling to attain some level of international respect. The new leadership was not imbued with the economic nationalism to fight dependence and to risk the political consequences.

As in previous years, the country relied on export crops. To show how vulnerable the economy was, the price of cocoa—a major source of revenue and foreign exchange—fell by almost 66 percent from 1962 to 1966. This created both an economic and political crisis. Between 1960 and 1965, the terms of trade and balance of trade were negative, from -92.4 in 1960 to -14.3 in 1965.

The country inherited an ideology of mixed economy. This was a brand of capitalism based on a combination of state control and private enterprise. The Nigerian government would control the major aspects of the economy, provide the infrastructure, and create favorable laws, while the individuals would control the means of production, distribution, and exchange. In the early years of independence, this arrangement put more pressure on the government, as there were not very many Nigerians with the huge capital needed to set up industries. The private sector was hostage to the government, who allocated the contracts to a select few. This excessive reliance on the government meant that the private sector could not operate independently of the public, as ideology in a mixed economy assumed. The control of many key sectors of the economy by outsiders was yet another problem, which altered the balance between government and private enterprises. The government served essentially as an agency to award contracts to private enterprises, but it lacked the capacity to manage the economic enterprises that it established.

Independence and Change

By and large, the regional and federal governments continued with the economic programs and philosophy of the 1950s. The economic objectives at independence were clear: the country would seek the means to transform its economy at a rapid rate, from a "backward" to a "developed" one. To attain this, it would expand its educational and social services, revise the plan document of the 1950s, and pump more money into the economy.

It is important to understand the economy from the point of view of the government and its leading civil servants, since they initiated and implemented the major policies. Whether they meant it or not, they knew that the objective of all their actions was to raise living standards. In specific terms, this would translate into jobs for the majority of the population, access to cheap food, clean water, hospitals, good homes and schools, and the opportunity to take part in civic and political activities.

The majority of the population, too, agreed with this specific catalogue. However, the politics that led to the transfer of power had created an exaggerated expectation about what the government could do. From the 1940s onward, aspiring politicians promised "milk and honey," often speaking as if it was even unnecessary for the people to work in order to live. Once there was a political kingdom, to borrow from the famous statement of Kwame Nkrumah of Ghana, an economic kingdom would follow. As far as many were concerned, they had been led to believe that the government was a provider, and it was expected to solve all problems and to create abundant opportunities for all. Even those who wanted to create their own businesses expected the government to fund them. The pioneer leaders did not popularize the ideal of a linkage between the people's work in their various individual and collective capacities with development.

Education was regarded as crucial to economic transformation: skilled human power was required in virtually all sectors; and it would enhance the capability to generate wealth. The needs were easy to identify. Elementary schools were needed to reduce the high rate of illiteracy and to create a pool of farmers and crafts workers who could apply educational knowledge to their day-to-day work. Indeed, some aspects of technical education were added to the school curriculum just to show that one could be educated and, at the same time, work in traditional occupations. However, the greatest areas of need were associated with higher education: engineers, doctors, teachers, lawyers, and so forth. Whether in the private or public sector, experienced well-trained workers were in short supply. A policy of "Nigerianization"—the replacement of foreigners by Nigerians—created hundreds of vacancies. These vacancies actually enhanced the worth of education. Within a limited period, many could rise in their positions and in virtually all occupations. This quick rise turned education and independence into a golden opportunity for the elite.

The government was more than ready to establish schools; it could easily be done and used as evidence of progress and achievement. To the people, it was the best opportunity to obtain diplomas and wage employment. Educational facilities were expanded in the 1950s, thanks to the priority devoted to it by all the regional governments. In the mid-1950s "less than one person in ten of school age and over can read and write."[4] The programs of the regional governments changed this, especially in the South where the number of children in schools increased almost fourfold. The concern in the early 1960s was for the schools to produce qualified people to replace Europeans in administration and management positions. In addition, for Nigerians to control their economies, they also required educated people. Thus, education was connected to development in various ways. Four new universities were established in Lagos, Ile-Ife, Nsukka, and Zaria, and they all grew rapidly within the decade.

Given the large percentage of Nigerians in agriculture, the government could not ignore this sector. As stated below, they had to take a number of measures. Among the problems of the period was the limited information on various aspects of the country's resources. New research institutes and the universities began to investigate various issues in order to improve productivity or to alert the government to potential resources. Can the livestock industry thrive in the South? To what use can the river system be put? What industries can best use local materials? What could be done to stop or slow down soil depletion? Why do crops have low yields? These and other questions were actually encouraging, as they were posed in the framework of a country with untapped resources.

There was a desire to change the economic structure, by making it less dependent on agriculture and external forces. The "magical solution" was regarded as industrialization. If Nigeria could become like one of the advanced countries, it was believed that the role of agriculture would gradually decline, and that industrialization would lead to social changes. Indeed, when many Nigerians talked about an economic revolution, they only meant one thing: industrialization.

One area where success was attained was in the maintenance and building of infrastructure and communications.[5] Almost 40 percent of the capital expenditures by various ministries and parastatals were devoted to one construction or another. The existing airways and railways were maintained. New roads were added and the Kainji Dam was built to generate electricity. Other aspects of construction were equally impressive, especially with respect to public and private buildings.

In spite of these objectives the standard of living did not increase, and the optimism of the 1950s began to give way to doubts and cynicism. Thus the economic history of the First Republic revolved around promises and actions, projections, and failures. As if the country was doomed to continue with these contradictory trends, oil revenues began to increase after 1967, but at a time of civil war and political instability, thereby providing an environment unsuited to rapid economic transformation.

Agriculture

Agriculture remained the mainstay of the economy, but, seven years after independence, oil began to make its impact, pushing agriculture to a second position. However, for the duration of the First Republic, agriculture was the most important aspect of the economy, accounting for 65 percent of the national income. It provided employment for the majority of the population, close to 70 percent in the 1960s. Agriculture was the major source of revenues and foreign exchange and of funds to develop industries, infrastructures, and other important aspects of the economy. The marketing boards continued to generate revenues from the farmers, collecting between 30 and 47 percent as surpluses from the product prices. The economy rested heavily on agriculture, although the sector was being ignored, and it was manifesting many signs of backwardness in production methods.

By 1960 three types of agriculture were inherited.[6] The first was the ancient one of small-scale farming based on the use of indigenous technologies and shifting cultivation—an exhausted land was temporarily abandoned to allow for self-regeneration.[7] In the North, livestock production was an integral part of agriculture, although in general all over the country, crop husbandry and animal husbandry were hardly integrated.[8] Land in use could be for food and crops, and land out of use could be under temporary fallow or part of a forest reserve.

In the South, the concentration was on tree crops and tubers (notably yam, cassava, palm produce, kola nuts, citrus fruits, and cocoa). In the North, sorghum, rice, peanuts, cotton, and millet were the most common crops. The censuses in the 1950s indicated that almost 90 percent of the surface area was not at all in use for tree or food crops, which meant that land was available for agriculture. In traditional farming, small patches were cultivated using a few tools, with the result that yields tended to be small. Farm sizes (the average in the South was 2.5 acres and in the North 4.4 acres) were small because of reliance on the family as the source of labor, the use of hoes, machetes, axes, and knives instead of machines, and the land-tenure system, which was egalitarian in its distribution. The land-tenure system in areas where land was not already commercialized ensured the access of all to land, thus providing the opportunities to farm and build. Those interested in cash crops had land to plant, even if small, thus ensuring access to the market economy. In spite of the smallholding farms, the farmers, who numbered in millions, actually sustained the country's exports and produced over 90 percent of the food crops.

After 1945 all the plans and programs to change agriculture revolved mainly around how so-called traditional agriculture and its practices would be modernized. The assumption in the 1960s was that "traditional" agriculture operated at a subsistence level and that "primitive farmers" needed new knowledge and tools in order to increase their productivity and to generate surplus for the markets. Among the notable ideas for the transformation of traditional agriculture were the need for new production techniques, tools, the injection of capital, the spread and adoption of fertilizers, availability of better-yielding seeds, the expansion of land under cultivation, an increase in the number of farmers knowledgeable enough to use the results of research generated by experts, and changes in farm organization to expand the unit of production beyond family size to new, large-scale cooperatives, collective farms, or the Israeli kibbutz. Experiments were conducted on mixed farming and green manuring, both of which led to limited successes. One major problem was the increasing pressure to alter the land-tenure system, as a few people were able to acquire more land at the expense of others. This trend would continue in future years, leading to a tiny minority of absent landlords based in cities who were acquiring large expanses of land. Traditional farming was equally undermined by population pressure in various parts of the country. The allocation to each person was considerably reduced, especially in areas with high-population density, as in the East. Small farm holdings tended to discourage commercialization or innovations that were considered expensive relative to productivity. In situations where collateral was needed to raise capital, small farm holdings prevented the holders from accessing capital. As the land available to families was reduced, the old system of shifting cultivation became difficult to sustain. Excessive use of land or the short duration of the fallow reduced soil fertility. Where land holdings were small, attempts to mechanize agriculture always ran into problems.

If the land-tenure system was changing, so too was the use of labor on farms. As more and more young men and women went to school, the number of hands for farm work was reduced. As many former students tended to seek employment in cities, the villages lost a productive segment of the population. Many women were also diverting their labor to other activities, especially to trading in urban locations. One other source of additional labor, the use of friends and village associates for cooperative farming, was also being threatened. Either because village loyalty was breaking down or because people chose to work for money, asking for free help on the farm was becoming an anachronistic arrangement. Other than the problems associated with land, many farmers saw their problems differently: to them, they needed access to credit, which was generally unavailable except through traditional sources. The majority of them, especially in the South, would rather use their "surplus" money to send their children to school than to invest in agriculture, which yielded less returns.

The second was farming geared toward cash-crop production, an orientation established by the colonial government. By the 1950s the country had become the world's leading producer of peanuts and palm oil, and the second leading producer of cocoa. The three products formed the basis of agricultural exports and revenues in the early 1960s. The farmers produced the majority of export crops that brought substantial revenues to the government. The regional governments believed that the use of fertilizers and tractors would enhance productivity and bring more revenues. While the shortage of food was seen as a problem, a number of policy makers still believed that greater investments in cash-crop-oriented farming was necessary. However, it was becoming untenable to sustain the distinction between so-called subsistence farming and cash crops, and to target one and leave the other. Such a distinction was not only unrealistic but ignored the "logic" of investments undertaken by the farmers. To start with, the farmers maximized the use of their land by intercropping, or mixed farming, which meant that they planted both food and tree crops in the same area. What this means is that their investments in both were not necessarily separated. More important, since they sold food crops to the market as well, they did not necessarily make the distinction that the government made between those crops that would bring money and those that were purely subsistence. All brought money, at different times during the year. Thus, it was not as easy as some officials believed, to simply target the cultivation of cocoa or peanuts, as a farmer could not be compelled to concentrate on one crop at any particular time. What was certain is that since the tree crops yielded more money than the food crops, they would devote more land to them.

The third was plantation agriculture, mainly established by the government in the 1950s and 1960s. The idea behind plantations was that a bigger, collective farm organization was better than the family-oriented ones based on small plots. Agriculture experts believed that plantations were better than traditional farms in generating massive production of cash crops, adopting new production techniques, maximizing the efficiency of labor, raising capital, and even selling their products at competitive prices.[9] Although the colonial government had rejected the idea of plantation agriculture, Nigerian planners believed in them. In both the East and West, cocoa, rubber, and oil palm plantations were created in the 1950s. In the East, the Eastern Region Development Corporation spent about £1 million to establish cashew, cocoa, coconut, and oil palm plantations. In the West, the Western Nigeria Development Corporation spent about £4.2 million to establish cocoa, rubber, palm oil, coffee, citrus, and cashew plantations. These plantations were retained in the 1960s, justified on the grounds that the government could use its money to generate better harvests, to spread new technology (for example, the mechanical extraction of oil), and to modernize agriculture.

Small in number and scattered in different parts of the country, they were no more than new experiments in modern agriculture. Their contribution to overall agricultural output was meager, although the focus was on how to use new technologies and seeds that would yield more crops. Economic planners placed much hope on plantation agriculture during the 1960s. Both the Western and Eastern Regions embarked upon ambitious farm settlement schemes to lure young educated people into farming. On paper, this was one of the most ambitious plans to revolutionize agriculture and halt a growing rural-urban drift.[10]

To take the example of the West where the idea of farm settlements began in 1960, a settlement would have fifty settlers and at least 1,500 acres of land, that is, ten times the size of traditional peasant holdings. The focus would be on young people with at least a primary education, and the goal was to encourage them to see modern farming as a respectable occupation. Where a young person had had no prior experience with farming, he could attend a two-year program in a farm institute created by the government. Each settler was expected to cultivate thirty acres on modern lines, a productivity ten times that of the traditional farmer. Machines would be available in a pool, and use would be accessible to all. A budget of ₦5,000 was allocated to each settler. In the early years, the settlers received allowances to sustain them. When the farm became productive, they were supposed to pay back all the initial investments over a

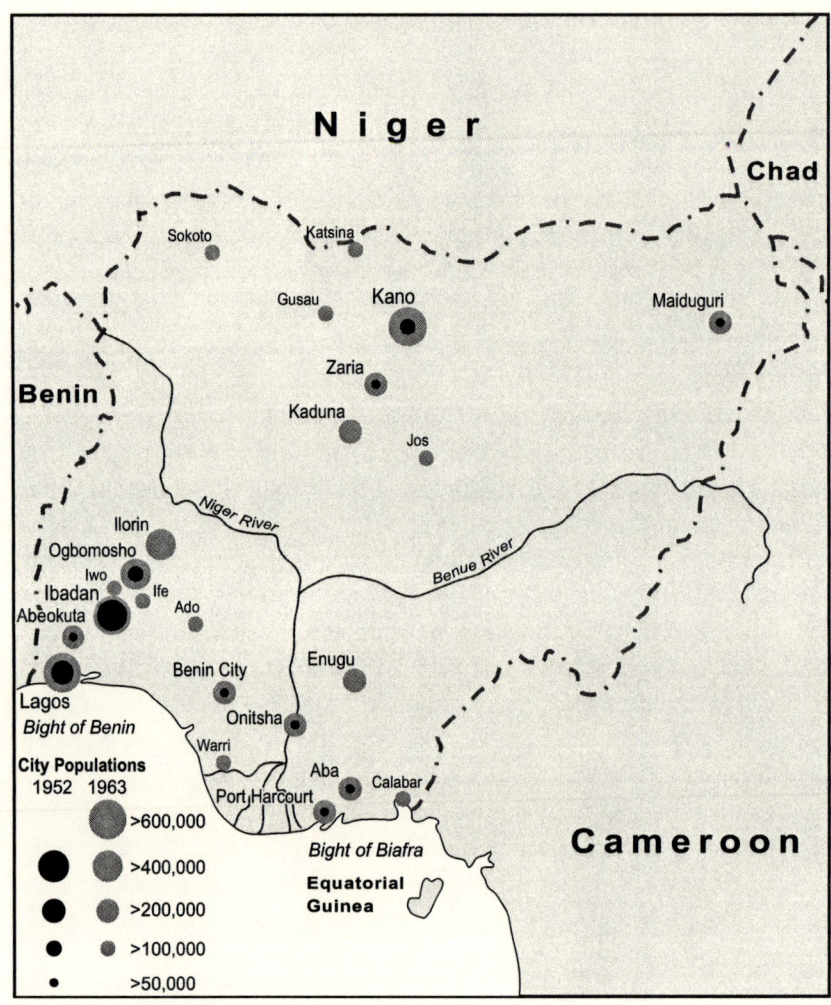

Urbanization in Nigeria, 1952–1963

fifteen-year period. The individual would run his farm, but the use of machinery, storage facilities, and sales of farm products would be on a cooperative basis. The regional government planned to create twenty-seven farm settlements, at a cost of £1 million. By 1961 the Western Region had established thirteen farm settlements. Each farm settlement had modern houses for the farmers, with village amenities to be shared by all. Eleven of the thirteen farm settlements were to specialize in tree crops—cocoa, coffee, rubber, citrus, and palm oil. A settler was expected to cultivate twenty to thirty acres of tree crops and use a small plot for food. The two remaining settlements consisted of arable crops and livestock. Each farmer had seventy acres, divided into two, one half for grain crops (maize, cowpeas, and sorghum) and the other half for grass and legumes for cattle grazing.

Both in the East and West, the schemes ran into problems. They turned out to be rather expensive, without the harvests to justify huge expenditure. Too much of the public resources went to a small number of settlers, about 1,500 in the West. In the East, obtaining land was a problem, as many local communities resisted the government's acquisition of their land. The old-time farmers considered the settlers as "privileged," enjoying free housing and communal facilities. The maintenance cost of farm equipment was rather high, and very often there were no spare parts to repair damaged ones.

In the farm settlements and elsewhere, the problems of mechanized agriculture were manifesting themselves. Not only were the use of tractors and other machines expensive, they were not efficient in doing various aspects of farm work associated with some major food crops such as yam and cassava. Thousands of small-scale landowners found the machines rather cumbersome to use, if they were even available.

There were other projects and initiatives on agricultural education and research, and extension to see the results of new experiments. In all the regions, various proposals were made to improve agricultural technologies, techniques of production, and growing more tree crops (notably cocoa and palm trees). The development boards of the 1950s continued to operate in the 1960s by adding investments to the agricultural sector and promoting policies to improve farm management. The new universities and some existing institutes paid attention to research on various food crops, soils, and tools. The great challenges were to find alternatives to the hoe and machete, and the system of shifting cultivation. The problem was how to introduce the results of research to the farmers.

In spite of the attempts to invest on agriculture, a major phase in its decline began during the 1960s. This decline was manifested in various ways, some visible at the period, some hard to see. As more and more schools were created, many young girls and boys were withdrawn from farming communities. Farm yields were declining, exports falling, prices of food were increasing, and the contribution of agriculture to the national income was decreasing. The value of food imports reached N46.1 million in 1965, a figure that increased dramatically in future years. The average growth rate of agriculture in the 1960s was -0.5 percent. Tables 7 and 8 reveal evidence of decline. Agricultural output declined by 1 percent per annum, due mainly to bad weather and difficulties in transportation. The food production index rose only in 1966 but declined for most of the period.

Writing during the First Republic, H. A. Oluwasanmi, one of the pioneer scholars of agriculture, posed an important question: can a "technologically stagnant agriculture sustain a developing economy in which the industrial urban population is expanding, while the farm population is declining?"[11] He was not alone in expressing this question, and his answer also reflected the commonly held opinion at the time:

> At the present stage of economic development in Nigeria agricultural improvement is central to the expansion of the modern sectors of the economy. Increased food supply will be needed to feed the urban population which is certain to grow as industries expand; manufacturing industries will require an adequate and cheap supply of raw materials while the surplus earnings of an improved agriculture will provide a major source of financing for the imports of capital equipment. Consequently, there must be a drastic revolution in agricultural practices before large numbers of the people can be advantageously diverted from agriculture to non-farm occupations.[12]

This revolution is yet to occur, although the concerns about declining agriculture have been expressed over and over again by scholars, government officials, the media, and the public. Since 1960 all governments and budgets have actually devoted attention to agriculture. Thus, it cannot be argued that there has been no interest to either sustain this sector or revitalize the aspects that have been crumbling. Why, then, has the end result been negative? To start with the most obvious, the pace of technological changes in agriculture has grown rather slowly, such that farm sizes are still small. The representatives of the government can be accused of talking, without walking, with regard to the transformation of agriculture. Less than 10 percent of the budget is generally devoted to agriculture. Even, then, only a small portion of this ever gets to the farmers, as the rest is consumed by bureaucracy and corruption. In other words, even budgetary allocation has not translated to the expansion of farm sizes or greater productivity. In the 1950s and early 1960s the desire was to seek the means to attain rapid industrialization. After 1967 with oil revenues pouring in, this desire continued, with the result that agriculture was relocated to the back burner. Where government became involved, as in resettlement schemes and farm settlements, the projects did not always justify the cost. Many actually became highly unprofitable as the management and workers get wages and benefits far more than the sale of harvests can even sustain, and there were cases of gross mismanagement. Where the government limited itself to assisting the farmers with seeds and fertilizers, the official access to thousands of small-scale farmers was either limited or uncoordinated.

Table 7. Annual Average Yield of Important Food Crops, 1960–1971 (kg per hectare)

Crop	1960–1962	1966–1968	1969–1971
Yam	9,703.62	7,913.72	10,098.49
Cassava	9,025.55	9,308.47	6,525.06
Maize	830.06	872.51	1,000.00
Rice	1,089.82	1,424.66	1,164.71
Cowpea	335.13	172.03	228.43
Millet	587.46	506.06	603.84
Sorghum	852.58	637.83	714.21

Source: S. O. Olayide, *Economic Survey of Nigeria, 1960–75* (Ibadan: Aromolaran, 1976), 28.

Table 8. Earnings from Agricultural Exports, 1960–1974

Year	Value (N million)	% of GDP	% of Total Agriculture
1960	282.5	12.6	19.8
1961	283.0	11.9	19.3
1962	260.0	9.9	16.2
1963	285.9	10.2	17.1
1964	303.9	10.4	18.1
1965	327.3	10.6	19.3
1966	292.5	9.1	16.4
1967	264.5	8.7	15.4
1968	263.7	8.4	15.3
1969	278.7	8.5	16.0
1970	280.5	8.0	15.7
1971	265.2	2.8	7.8
1972	190.1	1.7	5.3
1973	278.4	2.3	8.3
1974	297.8	2.3	9.2

Source: Olayide, *Economic Survey of Nigeria*, 26.

Foreign Trade

The import-export trade sustained the colonial economy. Inherited by the independent country as well, the trade depended on agriculture and was expected to generate the country's economy. The characteristics of the trade remained essentially the same during the First Republic. Britain was the principal trading partner—the bulk of exports went there, and the lion's share of imports was also from there. This was not a mere coincidence. For one thing, this pattern had long been established. For yet another, the colonial government, in its last years, created conditions to ensure favorable trade relations between Nigeria and Britain. The components of exports were still dominated by crops. The level of imports was on the rise. In 1961, the bills reached £222 million, divided as follows: £22.7 million on food; £6.1 million on tobacco and beverages; £2.4 million on "inedible materials"; £13.3 million on lubricants and mineral fuels; £12.5 million on chemicals; £87.5 million on manufactured goods; £50.3 million on transport and machinery; £26.7 million on "miscellaneous manufactures" and transactions.[13]

The balance of payments recorded a deficit, a new development. Before 1959, when the Central Bank of Nigeria was established, the country's membership in the West African Currency Board ensured that the Nigerian pound would be converted to the British sterling, an arrangement that prevented the occurrence of a balance-of-payment crisis. During the 1950s, when a balance of payment surplus occurred, the fiscal arrangement was to increase the domestic supply of money in order to adjust the situation. During the First Republic, the programs to accelerate development created balance of payment deficits that, unlike in the 1950s, could not be financed by reducing domestic money supply. The deficits were corrected by reducing the level of foreign reserves, a policy that forced the government to ultimately impose some restrictions on foreign trade. Among the measures to curtail the deficits in the 1960s were the imposition of import quotas, higher import duties, and foreign exchange regulations.

Intraregional trade within Africa was rather minimal, although it was recognized that this was necessary. Established precolonial trade contacts were not promoted. As each modern country looked toward Europe, they ignored one another. It was not until the mid-1970s that the Economic Community of West African States (ECOWAS) was established to correct the lapses, although this regional organization is yet to accomplish many of its goals.

Industrialization

Since the 1950s the country's politicians and economic planners have regarded industrialization as a top priority. The justification for industrialization has been consistent: it is regarded as the best avenue to generate jobs, wealth, and higher living standards. The degree of industrialization is regarded as the crucial difference between Nigeria and Western countries. One issue has always been in what aspect of industries to emphasize: those relating to agriculture (for example, farm implements, the manufacturing of fertilizers) or highly visible and complex ones, such as iron and steel. The overall philosophy in the 1960s was that investment in industries would yield more than investments in agriculture. Various proposals and ideas were formulated to accelerate the pace of industrialization.

By the 1950s the contribution of industries to the GDP was 1.5 percent. In the 1950s and 1960s a number of import-substituting industries emerged, with the leading ones producing cement, beer, textiles, and cigarettes. A few were geared to an external market, such as the tin mining in Jos and the timber and plywood industry in Sapele. The task in the 1960s was to add to the existing ones.

The regional and federal governments continued with most of the strategies to promote industrialization embarked on in the 1950s. Official statements expressed in annual budgets promised a huge expansion in manufacturing, economic diversification, and the reduction of dependence by producing new local substitutes. In the First National Development Plan, manufacturing received a priority, next to agriculture, with a projected expenditure of 13.4 percent of the total. The objectives were to use incentives to attract foreign investors and to promote local entrepreneurs. Moving against the demands made by socialist-oriented thinkers, the various governments assured that they would not nationalize foreign companies and would pay compensation if private interests were to be expropriated. In addition, various fiscal incentives were offered, including tax holidays, import duty relief, protective tariffs to ensure that profits were accumulated and retained by new industries, and firm assurance that capital and profits could be moved freely out of the country. Public expenditures were committed to building infrastructure and industrial estates to locate new companies. Investment in manufacturing increased substantially after 1960, although the foreign capital as the percentage of the total did not decline until after 1969 (see table 12).

As table 9 shows, the importance of industries continued to rise throughout the First Republic and beyond. The growth rate of manufacturing was impressive, at an average of 15.5 percent between 1960 and 1975. The contribution of manufacturing to the GDP increased at an average of 2 percent per year in the 1960s and an average growth rate of 17.2 percent in the first five years of independence. Relative to the entire economy, manufacturing still contributed a small quota to the GDP (about 6 percent by 1965–66).[14]

The exploitation of petroleum began in small quantities. The resources were discovered in the late 1950s. The quality of the crude is high, it is sulfur free, and the country is accessible to Europe and the United States by sea. By 1961 British Petroleum was producing 46,000 barrels a day, but no one knew that the country would later create a dominance in export. Production increased by 20 percent each year, reaching 600,000 barrels a day by 1967.[15] By the mid-1960s it was clear that the country would grow rich on it. It became part of the calculations in the civil war, as Biafra reckoned that the region would become rich, and the federal side did not want to lose the Niger Delta, the source of the oil.

Table 9. Contribution of Manufacturing Industries to Gross National Product

Year	Total GNP (N million)	Value of Manufacturing and Craft (N million)	% of Manufacturing and Craft in GNP (%)
1960	2,244.6	80.6	3.6
1961	2,373.4	88.2	3.7
1962	2,630.8	93.4	3.6
1963	2,806.4	151.8	5.8
1964	2,914.0	157.8	5.6
1965	3,080.6	164.8	5.6
1966	3,210.0	192.2	6.2
1967	3,051.8	196.0	6.1
1968	3,140.8	231.2	7.6
1969	3,278.2	270.4	8.6
1970	3,485.8	311.0	9.5
1971	9,442.1	475.1	5.0
1972	11,177.9	460.3	4.1
1973	11,993.1	570.1	4.8
1974	13,135.5	626.5	4.8
1975	14,410.7	683.9	4.7

Sources: Olayide, *Economic Survey of Nigeria*, 56; F. A. Olaloku, ed., *Structure of the Nigerian Economy* (Lagos: Macmillan, 1979), 27.

Table 10. Growth Rates of Manufacturing Industries

Year	Growth Rate
1960	Not available
1961	9.4
1962	5.9
1963	62.5
1964	4.0
1965	4.4
1966	17.0
1967	1.7
1968	18.0
1969	17.0
1970	15.0
1971	52.8
1972	3.1
1973	23.9
1974	9.9
1975	9.2

Source: Olayide, *Economic Survey of Nigeria*, 56.

Fixing a flat at the bicycle repair shop. Photo by A. Olusegun Fayemi.

The characteristics that would dominate the manufacturing sectors emerged in the 1960s. First and most important, manufacturing was dominated by light industries using low technology, notably the production of tobacco, beverages, and food. Raw materials were still processed for export. Import-substitution and consumer-oriented products were also prominent. By the early 1970s the production of food, tobacco, and beverages constituted one-third of the manufacturing sector. The production of textiles was next, contributing 17 percent. The dominance of these four products shows that manufacturing was still underdeveloped. Mining and quarrying outperformed the manufacturing sector, growing at a record high rate of 158 percent per annum. This performance owed primarily to oil extraction. The market, however, was able to support the expansion of the light industries, notably consumer products such as sweets and confectionery, soft drinks, singlets, paints, batteries, tires, shoes, and the assembly of radios, sewing machines, and bicycles. A trend to move toward import substitution was taking place, as market forces and the country's needs shaped the orientation of investments.

A second aspect was the weakness of the engineering industries. The manufacturing of equipment and machines for household use, agriculture, and mining was so low that it accounted for only 2.3 percent by the early 1970s. The most prominent engineering industries were in fabricated metal, structural metal products, and metal furniture and fixtures, all of which actually grew in significance in the 1970s.

A third characteristic was the weakness of high technology to produce intermediate products such as industrial chemicals, pesticides, and fertilizers. Consumer-oriented products (detergents and toiletries) accounted for 8.2 percent of the value added in the 1970s.

A fourth characteristic was that of foreign domination. Attempts to increase the number of manufacturing industries involved the participation of foreigners. The strategy actually encouraged foreign control, as the country sought foreign funding. In 1965 foreign private investments reached 61 percent of the total paid-up capital, while Nigerian private investment was a mere 12 percent and that of the Nigerian government 27 percent. Foreign firms fully owned one hundred and ten firms, with paid-up capital estimated at N28 million, compared to fifty-two fully owned Nigerian firms with a capital of N4 million. The importation of various goods reveals dependence on the industrialized countries. The use of imported parts and technology also meant that the value added in local manufacturing was low.

Finally, the demands for manufactured goods continued to be on the rise, thus necessitating huge expenses, both public and private. As the Nigerian consumers preferred imported items, local substitutes were looked upon negatively. Indeed, the importation of various items became a source of balance-of-payment deficits and of inflation, two tendencies that undermined a so-called desire to minimize dependence. In some cases, as in butter and margarine, the locally produced ones were not necessarily cheaper than imported ones, largely because the cost of production was high due to reliance on imported machines and skilled personnel recruited from abroad. Thus, even in its early years, local manufacturing had to compete with well-established foreign industries that had access to the Nigerian market.

The industrial sector experienced great difficulties, some of which have been pointed out. Financial losses on a number of projects were fairly common. In the East, the oil mills did not always receive adequate fruits. In the West, the Ibadan Canning Factory faced difficulties in obtaining regular supplies of pineapples and grapefruits. The rubber-processing factory in Benin sustained losses, again because of inadequate supply of latex.

Entrepreneurship

The process of empowering indigenous entrepreneurs continued. By the end of the First Republic, Nigerians controlled about 30 percent of the overall industrial investment.[16] Both the traditional trading sector and a growing informal sector of various small-scale enterprises actually did flourish, but the skills were not necessarily applied to modern enterprises. Nigerians controlled local trade in food and retail trade in cash crops and imports. The number of Nigerian-owned and lucrative businesses in the import-export sector kept growing.

There were significant problem areas, all connected to the issues of industrialization and entrepreneurship. The pool of skilled people to manage modern businesses was rather small. Business partnership was rather uncommon, as each person tried to create and manage "one-man" operations. Modern business practices did not mean that the "one-man" owner would keep records or that he would invest in operations that would not yield immediate profits.

The business community looked to the government for various benefits. The major sources of money were through government contracts, and the most successful were those that obtained major deals to supply materials or to construct roads and houses. Only a few wanted to venture into manufacturing, and there was little or no interest in large-scale farming. Where large capital was needed or where the waiting period for profits was rather long, the Nigerian entrepreneurs were not very much interested. Consequently, the government had to fill the gap in some enterprises by creating public corporations. Linkages were being established between Nigerian businesses and foreign ones, especially in the area of trade.

In one speech after another, the key members of the government indicated that the private investors would be partners in an impending economic revolution. The government always promised to encourage the development of entrepreneurship and local investment. From the economic plan of the period, as well as the annual budgets, the government would provide infrastructure, sponsor research, create favorable policies, and provide credit. The government rejected the Marxist-oriented suggestion that foreign companies should be expropriated.

Revenue Allocation

The politics of regionalism affected the discussion on how to share the country's revenues, and who should determine and collect income tax.[17] Each region wanted a bigger share of the federally controlled money in order to pursue its own agenda. In the West, where cocoa ensured prosperity, the politics were to obtain autonomy and advocate a policy of "derivation," which was that a region should keep as much as it generated. Less fortunate areas wanted the wealth to be distributed on other bases, such as population. As indicated in chapter 3, there were commissions during the colonial period, and the country had a total of five review panels between 1947 and 1965. Each commission sought a balance between regionalism and integration, but at the same time failed to satisfy all the regions. Both the North and the West supported a principle of derivation and complained that their revenues from peanuts and cocoa were being used to fund the East, which relied on palm products.

The formula agreed on in 1958, following the Raisman Commission, was incorporated into the constitution that applied to the First Republic. The fiscal system stressed the principles of population, development, and the public responsibility of the regional governments. These principles were used to allocate common funds, known as the distributable pool, to the regions on the following basis: the North would get 40 percent; the West, 24 percent; and the East, 31 percent.[18] Although several politicians wanted changes that would divert more funds to their areas, the incorporation of a revenue formula made it difficult for whoever was in power to do whatever he liked. Thus, the North could not use the control of federal power to take more or to punish rival regions. The assurance that federal money would come also gave the regions a greater level of autonomy to determine their budgets.

The 1958 arrangement lasted for seven years and was minimally revised in 1964 in the Binns's Formula (named after K. J. Binns, the sole commissioner), which allocated funds from the distributable pool in the following ratio: 42 percent for the North, 20 percent for the West, and 30 percent for the East. Like the previous one, this formula ensured stability at a time when federal and regional revenues were on the increase (see Table 11). Although each region always wanted more funds, by underplaying a formula of derivation in preference for "principles," the conflicts between the regions over the calculations of different accounts were minimized.

In spite of the political crises of the period, the revenues that accrued to all the governments increased. Except in the 1961–62 fiscal year, when things slowed down, the percentage of increase was actually very high, never lower than 12 percent in the case of the federal government. All the regions also recorded an impressive annual growth rate. Not only did the regions collect their shares of the federal revenues, they also had the power to benefit and expand other sources, notably income taxes, levies, and fees that could amount to as much as 30 percent of their recurrent revenues.

The First National Development Plan

Development planning in the 1960s was shaped by the need to overcome the "backwardness" of the economy inherited in the 1960s. But, in overcoming colonial legacy, the independent nation returned to the idea of the colonial

Table 11. Federal and Regional Recurrent Revenues, 1959–1966

Year	Federal	All Regions	North	West	East	Mid-West*
1959–60	50.24	51.08	17.52	18.68	14.88	—
1960–61	70.09	55.05	17.66	20.55	16.84	—
1961–62	65.79	63.69	21.44	23.18	19.10	—
1962–63	66.86	68.05	23.50	24.46	20.09	—
1963–64	75.57	71.62	25.31	20.36	22.18	3.77
1964–65	85.53	89.60	33.46	20.87	27.03	8.24
1965–66	94.30	95.44	32.59	22.40	30.52	9.93
Total	508.68	494.53	171.45	150.50	150.64	21.94

*The Mid-West was created in 1963.
Source: A. G. Adebayo, *Embattled Federalism: History of Revenue Allocation in Nigeria, 1946–1990*, (New York: Peter Lang, 1993), 221.

era: the use of a plan based on an economic model of free enterprise to bring about change. A plan document was regarded as a crucial instrument to explain how great changes would come about, how the country's abundant resources would be harnessed, and how a new leadership would define the priorities of the new nation. In the laudable words of the plan:

> The basic objective of planning in Nigeria is not merely to accelerate the rate of economic growth and the rate at which the level of living of the population can be raised; it is also to give her an increasing measure of control over her own destiny.... Nigeria should be in a position to generate from a diversified economy, sufficient income and savings of its own to finance a steady rate of growth with no more dependence on external sources for capital or manpower than is usual to obtain through the natural incentives of international commerce.[19]

The confident assumption was that resources were available for rapid economic development. As the first and subsequent plans stated, Nigeria is a huge country (with a land mass of 98,321 hectares), of which almost two-thirds is arable, a large population of approximately 55 million, enormous forest resources and mineral deposits, a long coastline, and a large market. Even external money was seen to be forthcoming, such that the plan even expected almost 50 percent of the expenditure to come from abroad.

The First National Development Plan (FNDP) was drawn to cover a period between 1962 and 1968, although political instability and civil war led to its premature death by 1966. The political context of regionalism also affected the commencement and formulation of the plan. The various regional plans of the 1950s did not terminate in the same year: that of the West in 1959, the North in 1960, and the East in 1962. The National Economic Council (NEC) agreed to extend and terminate all the regional plans by early 1962 so that a national one could be formulated.

The Ministry of Economic Development assumed the task of formulating the plan. Unlike before, ideas and projects did not emanate from the district officers. From then on, planning would be assigned to professionals, mainly economists and civil servants, who would think for the people. The planners who set economic targets would not be the ones to implement them, and reality may be far different from the facts. The planners could stay in Lagos, the federal capital, and simply coordinate the documents submitted by their colleagues in the regional ministries. A top-down approach began, and the plans became both sophisticated and long.

The first one did not owe solely to Nigerians. The regional politicians knew what they wanted, but there were still few Nigerians to formulate the plans. The authors included foreigners, two American economists, and an Indian working for the World Bank. A number of colonial officers were still around, now called "expatriate officials," to advise the new ministry. A few experts were also provided by the World Bank and the Ford Foundation. There was a decision-making structure in place. At the federal level, this included the legislature, the council of ministers, and development agencies (the National Economic Council, the Joint Planning Committee, and the Economic Planning Unit). At the regional level, it comprised the House of Assembly, the Executive Council, the Ministry of Finance, and the Ministry of Economic Development.

How the technocrats and politicians would work together constituted a great challenge. Still more difficult was how the considerations and preferences of the majority of the population would be reflected in a plan document. The technocrats and planners had no way of reaching the populace. One option they had was to collate the manifestoes of the various political parties and their campaign promises. These were mainly exaggerated promises, which did not relate the country's income to the desire of the politicians seeking votes. They could also adopt the manifesto of one political party and turn this into a plan. This was possible at the regional level where one party was in control. At the federal level, however, a coalition government of two political parties was in power. In theory, this should not be a problem, if it is assumed that a coalition meant that a solution had been found to the management of differences and power could be shared. In reality, the two parties in coalition, the NPC and the NCNC, did not have a common economic platform. Indeed, the NCNC often presented itself as socialist oriented, with promises to industrialize the countryside and provide free education. The plan ignored the socialist agenda and the rhetoric.

Far more important than the issue of personnel who drafted the plan is that of the idea of the "nation." Although described as a "national plan," and officially adopted by the federal government as such, it should be borne in mind that the idea of "national" was defined with some restrictions. In some ways, the plan was national: it attempted to talk about the entire country; it carried the approval of the national state; and it did indicate some national targets to be achieved. However, the power of the regions was reflected in various ways, and the regions were also free to disregard the plan and pursue their own agenda. When the plan was being formulated, each region presented a long list of projects, similar to what the district officers and residents did in the 1940s. The projects were similar, but the plan did not attempt to centralize or coordinate them. The intense rivalry among the regions would have made any centralization difficult to propose, not to talk of implementation. On the whole, all the three proposals by the regions and the one by the federal government were to attain modernization and were truly impressive on paper. A coordinated effort would have made development more rational to pursue, but the competition among the regions also led to the formulation of various projects, although not all were well executed. Political decentralization and regional rivalries did affect the plan, making it only national in name and making it hard for a central organization to monitor the performance of the various regional governments.

Without clear political guidance and awareness of the intensity of regional politics, the planners trusted themselves and fell on personal experiences. The economic advisor to the federal government, who was also the chair of the Joint Planning Committee, was an Indian economist sent to Nigeria by the World Bank. He quickly fell on his experience and recommended as a model the Indian Five-Year Plan, which he knew well in his previous capacity as a member of the Indian Planning Commission. The planners submitted to the politicians generalized economic objectives and the functions required by the public. These were accepted without much scrutiny.

As if the political problem was not enough, there was a technical one, a revelation of the underdevelopment of the country. *Planning without Facts* is the title of a book written by one of the plan's architects.[20] It is both appropriate and brilliant, a summary of the inadequacy of the tools to understand and macro manage the economy. The data to determine and set economic targets was lacking. Also lacking was the information to determine individual consumption preferences. If they wanted schools, what current consumption habits were they willing to give up? If the country wanted investment growth, how would it generate it? There was no data to establish all the different options and estimate their consequences. The planners resorted to guesswork and estimates based on limited household data, food prices, and rough population estimates. The planners even had to resort to analogies and comparisons with some other developing countries to estimate growth rate, investment rate, productivity, future levels of consumption, levels of income and expenditure, national savings, population increase, acreages under cultivation, and the possible number of livestock. Nothing was certain; all were either estimates based on the crude figures of the 1950s or intelligent estimates. The costs, too, were mere guesses. With all the problems associated with the lack of or inadequate data, there was no means to test the feasibility of the plan or to relate population increase to certain expenditures.

That data was not available did not mean there could be no vision, even a grandiose vision. Economic planning could acquire the characteristics of a dream: the desire for what was believed to be realistic, not what was possible. Thus, the plan reads like a catalogue of various items worthy of attracting public expenditure. The document captured the optimistic mood of the period: nothing was impossible; transformation was just around the corner. The plan was clear about its objectives:

> The achievement and maintenance of the highest possible rate of increase in the standard of living and the creation of the necessary conditions to this and including public support and awareness of both potentials that exist and the sacrifices that will be required.[21]

To achieve the objectives, emphasis was placed on agriculture, industry, and education. In statistical terms, the plan would achieve a growth rate of 4 percent a year, an investment of 15 percent a year, and a savings ratio of 15 percent. The plan anticipated an economic growth rate of 4 percent, a target savings of 15 percent of the GDP over a fifteen-year period, an annual investment of almost 15 percent. Public expenditures would concentrate on roads (38.7 percent), administration (14.7 percent), education (7.2 percent), agriculture and other primary production (5.7 percent), and water (5.6 percent). Thus, there was indeed an attempt to prioritize, with roads being the preeminent target.

The anticipated planned investment in the public and private sectors was put at N2,366 million. Part of the investment money would go to the preparation and costing of various projects. The construction of roads would consume the most. While the importance of other production inputs such as cement, steel, water, energy, and fertilizers was understood by the planners, they could not set the appropriate target because there was no data, but they anticipated expenditure as well. The country hoped to raise more than 50 percent of the investment money from abroad.

With respect to investment in the private sector, the plan was mainly silent. As in the colonial one, expenditures on the public sector were limited, with the expectation that this would improve private sector investment. It was also assumed that the private sector would generate significant investments to complement those of the public. If public data either did not exist or was difficult to collect, that on the private sector posed even greater challenge. How many entrepreneurs exist? What businesses interest them? What resources are available to them? It was hard to answer these questions and harder still to guess how this sector would add to the national income.

The shortage of staff was a great obstacle in the early years of independence. Engineers, technical experts, doctors, teachers, artisans, and others were few. Even the agency that was to monitor planning had limited staff to do so.[22]

Regionalism and political tension complicated plan implementation. The machinery was clearly worked out in theory. The Ministry of Economic Planning, a federal agency, was to coordinate and supervise. Within the ministry, the Economic Planning Unit was to decide the projects to be submitted to the government for approval; however, the unit lacked the power to determine the recurrent budget, nor could the unit force the regions to do anything.

The approval of a project did not necessarily mean that it would be executed. Progress reports on various aspects of the plan were generally reported as financial allocation. Thus, it was treated as a progress merely to say that a certain amount of money had been committed to buying ten tractors. There was little or no way to know whether the tractors were actually purchased. As the regions competed, they exaggerated levels of financial allocations to hundreds of projects, which gave a very misleading picture of the development that was taking place.

The unstable political circumstances of the period created major problems. As regional representatives spoke glowingly about their regions, the meetings of the National Economic Council became less friendly. The plan became more complicated when the Mid-West Region was carved out of the West in 1963, and a fourth plan had to be added. The members of the opposition parties, notably the Action Group (AG), were opposed to many of the political and economic agenda items of the federal government. As the politicians fought for power, members of the public lost faith in them and in their economic statements, and in the plan.

The plan failed to accomplish many of its stated goals. The greatest problem was finance. This could have been anticipated, even by an amateur economist. All the regions exaggerated the projects they wanted to accomplish, without providing information on how to finance them. The planners, aware of the need to satisfy the politicians, did not contest most of their submissions and included many of their programs in the plan. As the implementation began, the plan was trimmed on a regular basis, because of a lack of funding. Foreign aid did not come as anticipated, thus reducing the projected level of public investments. Midway in the plan's execution, the amount of foreign capital expected was cut to 50 percent, but this was even a miscalculation. The country misread the statements of foreign leaders and politicians who promised to contribute to the development of the new nation. The statements were divorced from the foreign policy calculations of these countries and the desire of their companies to make money from Nigeria, not to give to Nigeria. Not only did the government believe that foreign investments were possible, they equally assumed that progress was impossible without them. Financial capital was regarded as in short supply and the country as lacking in the entrepreneurial talents to design creative opportunities that would generate wealth within a few years. Yet, the data for the 1950s and 1960s clearly showed that a large percentage of the so-called foreign investments were actually the reinvestment of money made in the country by established firms, that what the new companies were bringing was not substantial and not intended to be spent in aiding the projects of the government. It is true that investment was needed to accelerate economic growth, but it is untrue that this would come easily and without strings. When foreign companies invest, they intend to repatriate a large part of the profits to their home base. If the inexperienced Nigerian leaders and planners were banking on foreign capital for development, they were not only to suffer disappointment but also to realize that they had to actually spend more money to attract the capital, they had to offer their markets, and turn their population into consumers. The World Bank and several international financial agencies also warned that the country had to beg for foreign capital and that citizens and foreign investors must be treated alike.

Some changes did come. Investment expenditure was high, especially in the private sector and that of the public averaged almost 20 percent. National income grew at a fluctuating rate of between 3.8 percent in 1963 and 6.7 percent in 1966. The overall average growth rate was 5 percent. The Gross National Product (GNP) increased from N2,244.6 million in 1960 to N3,140.8 in 1968. There were changes in various sectors that reveal either growth or decline. The real per capita income grew slowly, from N48.1 in 1960 to N53.8 in 1965, a mere increase of 2 percent, which shows the limited changes in the standard of living. From a high contribution of 63.4 percent to the GDP, agriculture declined to 55.6 percent by 1966. At an average growth of 2 percent a year, agriculture's growth lagged behind that of the population. But others experienced upward changes. The contribution of mining changed from 0.9 percent in 1960 to 4.8 percent in 1966; manufacturing from 3.6 percent to 6.2 percent; and distribution of goods from 9.1 percent to 14.0 percent. Money supply increased by 6 percent, but there was no corresponding increase in inflation, which stood at 3 percent. Changes were also made in electricity and water supply, construction, communication and transportation.[23] Some of these changes reveal the shifts in the economy that would be consolidated in later years, and the decline in agriculture continued as that of mining grew. As the country invested more in infrastructure, the construction of roads and bridges received attention. The plans of the 1970s and 1980s consolidated and expanded infrastructure and the number of industrial projects financed by the government.[24] Private investments rose, accounting for over 60 percent of the fixed capital formation, although most of this came from external investments. There was a balance-of-payment problem: merchandise trade saw a deficit; the balance on goods and services was in huge deficit; and foreign exchange reserves decreased from N370 million in 1960 to N197 million in 1965.

To close on the economy of the First Republic, it should be remarked that the issues that the leaders were trying to deal with have remained with the country. Nigeria got richer after this era, but this did not translate into a higher standard of living by the close of the century. The economy was neocolonial: it relied on exports for foreign exchange and public finance; it expected foreign capital for its development; its trade, insurance, and banking were dominated by foreign firms; and its capacity was underdeveloped. The colonial legacy remained strong as Britain maintained a great deal of control. The investment of British companies in the country was estimated at over a £1 billion, in such areas as shipping, banking, trade, insurance, and mining. The Shell–BP company dominated oil exploration; the Amalgamated Tin Mining (Nig) Ltd., another British company, dominated the cobalt, tin, and iron mining. The United Africa Company (UAC) and John Holt, two British companies, controlled the major trade and manufacturing.

The economic policies of the government promoted the neocolonial structure. The export of raw materials and the extraction of minerals constituted the main core. Industrialization was based on a strategy of import substitution, but this actually facilitated the imports of tools, equipment, raw materials, and food. Foreign investments were sought not just because there was a belief that internal sources of capital were inadequate but also that the country could not thrive without foreign support. As oil revenues increased substantially, there was no longer the need to look outside, at least in the 1970s; but thus far, dependence remains a problem. In the concluding chapter, a review of the economy between the First Republic and the close of the twentieth century reveals the inability of the country to move beyond a neocolonial and extractive orientation.

Postscript:
Economy and Society after 1965

It was hard to anticipate the direction of the Nigerian economy at the end of the period under study. The country entered a difficult political phase, with much attention on how to keep the country from collapse. The civilians were replaced by the military, which hung on to power for a long time. By and large, the military cannot be described as essentially different from the civilians, but they had the privilege of presiding at a time when huge revenues were acquired from oil. Without doubt, huge oil revenues, generated soon after independence, enabled the Nigerian political class to survive its gross inability to manage the economy and society in a creative and intelligent manner. By their very nature, oil revenues came as easy profits collected from multinational companies.

ECONOMIC TRENDS AND PATTERNS

The first decade of independence closed with a civil war. During the war, various aspects of the economy slowed down.[1] The economy grew at the rate of 0.8 percent between 1965 and 1970, the country lost over N600 million in physical damage, and the component of agriculture to the GDP fell by 5 percent during the war. External countries, such as the United States, Britain, and France, calculated their interest from the point of view of the oil market and not necessarily from the desirability, or otherwise, of the unity of Nigeria. Oil produc-

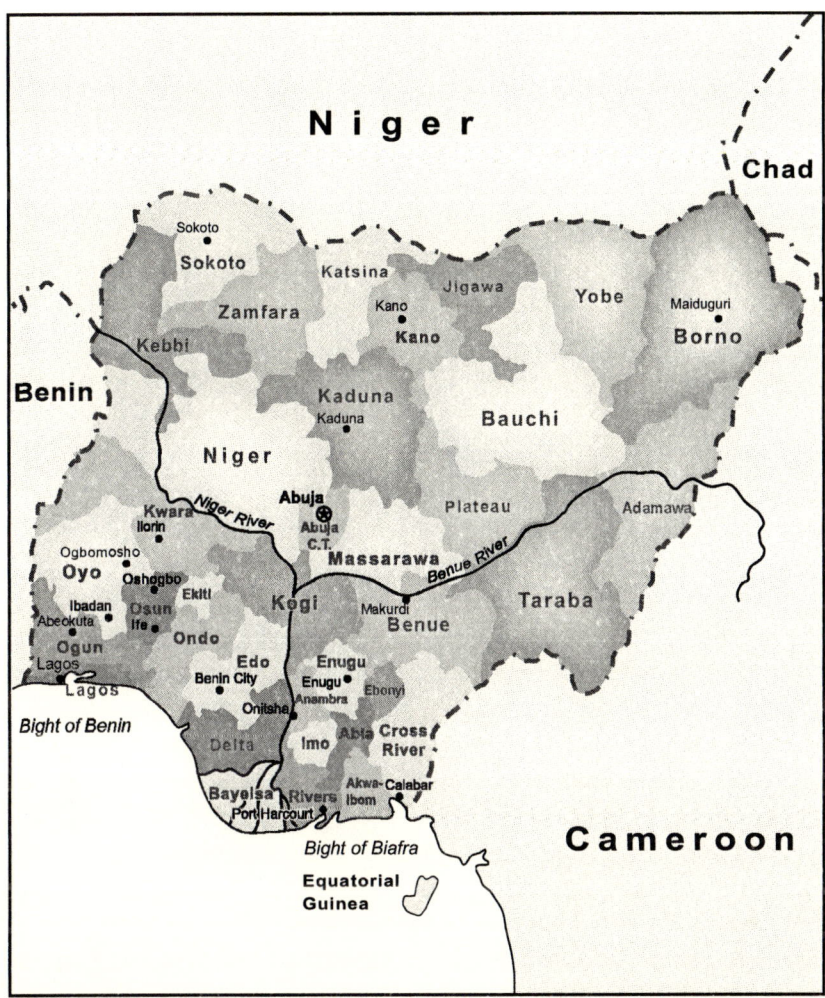

Nigerian States Today

tion was temporarily affected, but the federal forces prevailed in winning control of the oil fields.

The large revenues from oil after 1967 enabled the country to finance the civil war and the massive expansion of the 1970s. Oil and other mining activities contributed about 5 percent to the GDP in 1965 and 1966 but rose significantly to 30 percent by 1970 and 1971. Revenues also increased at a fast pace, from US$33.5 million in 1962 to N262.0 million in 1969. An oil boom occurred in the 1970s, and the country grew to depend solely on oil. From US$14.7 per barrel in early 1973, the price rose to $38.77 a year later, allowing the country to realize a huge sum of $4 billion within a short time. Nigeria's membership in the Organization of Petroleum Exporting Countries (OPEC) certainly paid off, as the country was able to unite with others to negotiate the quantity of production. The substantial wealth from oil brought about economic growth, but reinforced an economy based on dependence on exports and the volatility of commodity prices in the international market.

The 1970s offered an era of prosperity, decline set in the 1980s, and the poverty level increased in the 1990s. As oil revenues accrued to the Nigerian state, interest in agriculture declined. Industrialization received a boom during the war: a restriction on imports encouraged local manufacturing. After the war, oil revenues made possible the expansion of the infrastructure on a grandiose scale. Various efforts were also taken to improve agriculture, although the results were disappointing. Among the measures embarked upon during the period were the cultivation of better varieties of palm trees, the provision of seeds and loans to farmers, and a gigantic program named Operation Feed the Nation, which involved people of various classes in food production.

The country has always regarded formalized plans as inevitable to its development agenda. They could be ignored or projects executed below expectation, but not to have a plan is regarded as a negative comment on the government. The features of the plans are also markedly the same: a partnership will be created between the government and private entrepreneurs to transform the economy; the government will provide the infrastructure; investments will come from within and outside; and the people are expected to increase their productive capacity. There are some major differences. In the colonial plan, the sectors were not integrated, a policy of export of raw materials was crucial, and local industries should merely be working on import substitution. In the first plan of the 1960s the emphasis was on transportation, and the possibility of obtaining external investments to industrialize. In the 1970s the second plan wanted to empower more Nigerians, to develop the oil industry, and to increase the standard of living of the general population. It is fair to conclude that all the plans were not successful in their overall performance. From the left, the criticism is that they are "bourgeois" in orientation. From the liberals, it is because they were hurriedly put together and badly executed. From all critics, the flaws were repeated in all the plans. Both the colonial and first plans have been discussed in previous chapters; in this chapter, those of the 1970s and 1980s are discussed in brief.

The Second National Plan (1970–74) planned for an investment of ₦3,192 billion, the largest in the country's history. This plan was geared toward instigating an economic expansion, as well as rehabilitating the damages caused by the war. The war had generated nationalism to keep the country together, and millions of people endured the suffering of the time. As in the 1950s many now looked for great changes in the immediate future. Written in a most confident language, the second plan envisaged a rise in the GDP from N3.028 billion in 1969 to 1970 to N3.98 billion in 1973, and an annual growth rate of 7 percent. These expectations were met, in spite of occasional decline in agriculture, and the GDP actually increased to N9.4 billion in 1971 and N14.4 billion in 1974–75. The substantial growth came from oil revenues. Indeed, the contribution of agriculture to the GDP further declined, from 51.3 percent in 1970 to 24.7 percent in 1974. The mining sector acquired dominance, rising from a 3.7 percent component of the GDP in 1970 to 45.1 percent in 1974. The sectors that expanded the most from the point of view of growth were physical infrastructure, a massive expenditure on schools, the rehabilitation of some industries, and investment in agriculture, notably food and tree crops.[2]

An indigenization decree of 1972 and 1976 empowered Nigerians to own companies and participate in various joint ventures with foreign partners. A 1972 military decree divided foreign businesses into two groups. Those of small-scale nature were to be solely owned by Nigerians[3] while others, about thirty-three of them, must have 40 percent Nigerian participation. The policy did not seek nationalization, foreign business interests survived, and only a handful of well-connected Nigerians actually benefitted.[4] A revised decree in 1978 raised the equity of Nigerians to 60 percent in fifty-seven businesses, reserved forty types of business only to Nigerians, and in another set of thirty-eight businesses participation by Nigerians was set at 40 percent. The government established agencies to sell stocks and to give Nigerian entrepreneurs loans to buy businesses formerly owned by foreigners or to buy equity participation in them. Indigenization provided entrepreneurs with access to the government to use public money to create their businesses. Indigenization did not bring an end to foreign participation in the economy. Rather, the multinationals moved to the more lucrative oil-drilling business. The huge spending on roads also brought in foreign construction companies.

Inflation set in the 1970s, hugely compounded by very large, across-the-board pay raises to all wage earners. Transport and food costs increased in response. A price-control mechanism was put in place in 1970, but, as demand outstripped supply, it was difficult to enforce government prices. As it became profitable to deal in products such as milk, sugar, beer, and soft drinks, traders hoarded them to maximize profit.

Ten times larger than the second plan was the Third National Plan that covered the period 1975–80. An oil boom in 1973 encouraged the country to become bolder and more confident and to expect an annual growth rate of 9.5 percent. Funding would come from within, and trade and industry would be boosted to generate revenues and to create jobs for millions of people. The Third National Plan envisaged an investment of ₦30 billion, with the public component running as high as ₦20 billion. The GDP was expected to rise from ₦18.05 billion in 1975 and 1976 to ₦26.5 billion by the end of the plan period. A genuine concern was shown to reduce poverty by raising issues of social justice and increasing the allocation to agriculture. The annual growth rate was less than expected, as it averaged only 5 percent. However, the GDP increased from ₦27.3 billion in 1976 to ₦35.2 billion in 1980. In the 1980s the growth rate fluctuated between 1.2 percent and 8 percent, as demand and prices of oil also fluctuated. The expectations that the contributions of manufacturing and agriculture to the GDP would have increased were unmet, and oil continued to gain in dominance. The structural imbalance in the economy continued well into the new millennium.

The Fourth National Plan, 1981–85, was again more ambitious than the preceding ones. Formulated by the civilians of the Second Republic, it placed priorities on transport (17.2 percent of allocation), education (10.7 percent), and agriculture (7.9 percent). The plan was doomed by the fall in oil prices and unbridled corruption.

A period of prolonged economic decline began in the mid-1980s, reaching a point near a total economic collapse in the late 1990s. The signs began to show in the early 1980s, when the country had a debt-service ratio of 34 percent (1984), increasingly fell on its reserves, and also negotiated additional loans from external lending agencies. A policy of austerity measures was announced in 1981, and many businesses experienced great difficulties because of the decline in foreign exchange. Increasing corruption undermined any policy that the government announced, and the public was disenchanted. A military coup occurred at the end of 1983, but the story of economic decline continued. Additional austerity measures were announced, but without bringing any improvement.

In 1985 the military regime announced the Structural Adjustment Program (SAP),[5] justified on the grounds that the economy was in bad shape, that the country needed to respond to the global recession of the early 1980s, and that it had become necessary to break the reliance on only oil revenues. The country's debt was mounting, and the International Monetary Fund (IMF) and the World Bank were insisting on certain conditions before rescheduling debt payment. By agreeing to embark on a SAP, the country was assured new credit lines and the payment of external debts were rescheduled.

Under the SAP, the economy would be more open to market forces; public companies would be privatized; subsidies removed on a few items, notably the sale of refined gas; and the naira devalued by over 50 percent. At its inception in 1985 the government assumed full control of the economy, cut the salaries of public servants by between 2 and 20 percent, the subsidies on petroleum products were cut by 80 percent, imports were surcharged at 30 percent, defense expenditure reduced by 19 percent, certain imports were banned (notably of wheat, rice, vegetable oil, and maize), a package of incentives was offered to exporters, and commodity boards were scrapped. In addition, the various state governments created new taxes and levies on many things, including attendance at school. The government stated these and other measures would rationalize the civil service and make it more efficient, promote appropriate pricing of many essential products, improve international trade, stimulate production for export and local consumption, and positively transform the economy. The government promised that the SAP would last for one year and that the results would be immediate and positive. Neither happened—the SAP lasted until 1994 and brought untold hardship to Nigerians.

The program did not produce the intended results, oil earnings fell, commodity prices declined, foreign debts increased, and the naira was devalued by 69 percent. While a tiny number made huge profits from economic liberalization and joined the government in urging the people to be patient, the ranks of the poor were enlarged. As far as the IMF and the World Bank were concerned, Nigeria would be able to service its debts, even if its people would suffer. The expectation that the SAP would bring foreign investments did not materialize. Outside the lucrative and predictable banking and petroleum sectors, foreigners stayed away. By the 1990s the once-comfortable middle class was devastated as the cost of cars became prohibitive, public transportation became rather expensive, social services were hard to pay for, and food prices reached high levels.[6] The government lacked the fiscal discipline to implement such a rigorous program. As it saved money and made more because of the depreciation of the currency, so too did it waste the money. Budget deficits were high and commonplace, currency printing made the naira unworthy except in large quantities, new agencies were created that actually consumed more money on the public service at a time when people were being laid off, and government shares and some companies were sold at below market rate to reward allies. The economic growth was slow (at an average of 3 percent), inflation rate was high (between 40 and 50 percent), external investments declined, the manufacturing and industrial sectors were damaged, economic diversification did not occur, and the standard of living reached its lowest level during the twentieth century. The structural adjustment program is now remembered in oral discourse as the worst economic policy of the century. An informant described it as "throwing someone who cannot swim into the sea." He was not referring to the country or the rich, but the millions of poor people who were so badly battered that the majority of them lost their survival capabilities.

The Structural Adjustment Program had failed by 1993, when a new military figure, Gen. Sani Abacha, came to power. Like others before him, he also made promises. His policies were not always clear: one day he would promote a strategy of state intervention, and the next day that of the free market. On the one hand, he was calling for overseas investments, even announcing in 1996 the Nigerian Investment Promotion Decree, a package designed to attract investors. On the other hand, he was running an authoritarian regime, which alienated him from the population and the country from the international community. In 1996 he called for privatization, even of the oil industry. A year later his government changed its mind.

The reasons for these unpredictable economic changes were not unconnected with political instability and corruption.[7] Abacha was undermining the economy through a massive network of corrupt officials, allies, and children. Economic calculations were in part based on how best to divert public resources into a few hands, how to privatize in a way that benefited his allies, and how to retain control if those allies provided opportunities to steal public funds. He was unable to fool the members of the public who organized a series of strikes, riots, and other forms of organized activities to protest military rule, the annulment of the 1993 presidential elections, increases in the price of gasoline, and the worsening economic crisis.

As to the magnitude of the economic crisis, there can be no doubt. The GDP growth rate barely reached 2.5 percent, even falling below 1 percent in 1994. The rise in consumer price inflation was staggering, reaching 58 percent in 1993 and 60 percent in the following year. Salaries of state employees, particularly of the teachers, were unpaid for months, while millions of people had no jobs. The oil industry moved from one problem to another, affecting overall production. Rather than attract new investments, those on the ground were resorting to divestment and to moving their capital elsewhere.

The economic policies shifted from excessive state intervention to market reforms, both of which did not work. Early in 1994 the Abacha regime opted for a state-controlled economy, which chose to peg the interest rate at 21 percent, impose duties on some goods, spend on infrastructure, and insist on the use of local raw materials by a number of manufacturing companies. The naira was also pegged at an official rate of N22 to US$1. The trouble was that the Central Bank of Nigeria was unable to supply the foreign exchange needed by investors and individuals. A flourishing "black market" emerged, which actually pushed the exchange rate to N90 for US$1. As traders and manufacturers bought foreign currency from the black market, prices of goods escalated, while those who were able to obtain the dollars from the Central Bank made more profit by selling them locally. As the World Bank and the IMF were not happy with this arrangement, they did not cooperate with debt rescheduling and additional trade credits. The government was able to pay for imports in cash, but debt servicing increased. In 1994 the prices of petroleum products were increased, in part to generate more money but also to satisfy one of the conditions of the IMF. As external pressure increased, the government changed to a policy of economic liberalization in 1995. The naira was devalued, and new regulations provided generous conditions for foreign investors. No policy was successful enough to generate an economic recovery.

In the 1980s and 1990s the rates of inflation and unemployment soared to double digits. Inflation, for instance, increased at the rate of 18 percent per annum. Health facilities and schools approached a state of total collapse. The roads and the railways suffered from disrepair, and Nigeria Airways, the major airline, operated far below expectation. Corruption became endemic such that huge sums of money devoted to development could not be accounted for. Unemployment was endemic, affecting even university graduates who had hitherto expected that their skills would bring them jobs. The people lost confidence in their government, and one political crisis followed another. From the possibility of becoming an economic power, the country closed the twentieth century as one of the poorest in the world. Totalitarian military regimes in the 1980s and 1990s caused great depression among the people.

Nigeria had to deal with the legacy of colonial rule in the 1960s, but the global situation had changed by the 1990s to a post–cold war era. In a so-called global era, investments did not necessarily move around in favor of Nigeria, and the necessary elements to compete in world trade now include advantages of technology and skills. While oil remained important, the country required greater political stability and improved infrastructure to be able to compete in the international system. But as the global setting was changing, Nigeria closed the century with the worst political regime in its history. The consequences to the economy have been disastrous.

Major Economic Sectors

The decline of agriculture is perhaps the most significant aspect of the economic imbalance. In spite of the condemnation of farmers as "primitive" and their technologies as poor, this sector contributed to the expansion of world trade in the nineteenth and the first half of the twentieth centuries; it contributed to the industrialization and the expansion of the economies of Europe; it sustained the revenue system of the colonial administration in Nigeria; and it provided sources of income to the majority of the population. When it was time to serve Nigerians, the sector suffered a retreat and a devastating setback.

From a dominance in the early 1960s, the contribution to the national income fell to 23.4 percent by the 1970s.[8] The decline continued in the 1980s and 1990s to the extent that the country lost its leading position in the production of cocoa, peanuts, and oil palm products. Tragically, it also lost the ability to feed itself. The outcome has been devastating, especially in the countryside. Still largely an agrarian society, agriculture is linked to income, nutrition, employment, and overall standard of living. Oil has saved the government, but diminishing agricultural productivity means that the majority of the poor people have had no where to turn.

It should be pointed out that the massive expansion in agricultural production in the first half of the twentieth century did not benefit from the introduction of new technologies or radical changes in the cultivation system. Since independence, various schemes, some actually ambitious in their definition and scope, have been taken to revitalize agriculture. These include the use of cooperative societies to collectivize farming; government-sponsored mechanization projects; irrigation schemes; and new, mixed farming methods. Many of these projects are part of the public investments stated in the various developments from the 1960s to the 1980s. As stated in all the plans, the government does recognize the role of agriculture, and there is a belief that it could serve as the basis for an industrial takeoff. Although there is always a gap between projected and actual expenditures, all the plans devoted respectable public investment allocation to agriculture (13.6 percent in the first plan; 10.5 percent in the second; 6.3 percent in the third, and 12.4 percent in the fourth). All have yielded very limited positive results.[9]

Farming increasingly lost its respect among a new generation of Nigerian youth who preferred wage employment and city life. In the 1980s the production of food crops declined considerably, and prices of food were so high as to push down the standard of living. The government resorted to large-scale food imports, especially of rice. For instance in 1978, the bill on food imports reached US$1 billion, an amount that increased by 100 percent two years later. Obstacles to agriculture have multiplied since 1960. The alternative and large income from oil means that the government needs not pay urgent and sincere attention to agriculture. As the currency, the naira, acquired strength in the 1970s, it was cheaper to import food, and there was no urgency to promote agricultural exports as before. As agriculture increasingly relied on the importation of farm inputs (such as fertilizer and machinery), the country became more dependent on external markets, more so as the inputs did not necessarily lead to

Women at a meeting discussing local issues. Photo by A. Olusegun Fayemi.

greater domestic production. Farming methods are yet to be revolutionized: the majority still work on fragmented land holdings, have little or no credit to expand their farms; have no access to new technologies; and find it hard to even obtain labor for farm work.

By the time the country was formulating the Third National Plan for the 1975–80 period, the planners were already raising an alarm that the country was heading for a serious crisis. Data revealed gross shortages in major food crops such as maize, sorghum, millet, peanuts, vegetables, and plantain, and the country could only generate 50 percent of its food supply by the mid-1970s. The contribution of agriculture to the GDP had fallen to 34 percent, and cocoa was the only major export crop. The country was even importing those items that it once produced in large quantities: maize, palm oil, and peanuts. Nonfood items, such as rubber, cotton, and timber were also being imported. Also contained in the third plan is an explanation for the shortages and overall decline in the agricultural sector, which apportioned the blame not on the government but on other things, such as the shortage of labor, the land-tenure system, inadequate credit facilities, and poor transportation. As the third plan and the subsequent ones show, drastic measures became necessary to revitalize agriculture. However, state intervention in agriculture proved to be costly, did not lead to any massive increase in food production, and led to the takeover of land from many poor people. As a number of former politicians, military officers, and senior civil servants moved into farming and bought extensive tracts of land, some political tensions have been created between them and those dispossessed of land.[10]

If agriculture declined, the industrial and mining sectors witnessed impressive growth rates in the 1960s and 1970s. The average growth for the period 1966 to 1970 was 12.9 percent, rising to 18.5 percent for the 1970–75 period (see table 9). The rate of investment in manufacturing increased, rising to an unprecedented level in the 1970s.

The success in the nonagricultural sector was due primarily to petroleum. The civil war affected production in 1967 and 1968, but this changed afterward, reaching 540,000 barrels a day in 1969 and later over one million in the 1970s. In 1971 the country joined the Organization of Petroleum Exporting Countries (OPEC), and the oil boom that followed brought substantial money (over $100 billion in the 1970s) to initiate development programs. Many of these projects were hurriedly put together, and their collapse came in the 1980s and 1990s. Some, notably the Ajaokuta Steel Mill, consumed a huge sum, without significant results, in addition to draining huge amounts of foreign exchange since they tend to be import intensive. Three refineries were built between 1965 and 1980, with a total capacity of 445,000 barrels a day, but this is usually unmet because of plant shutdowns and inefficiency. At the same time supplies of refined oil, gas, and kerosene are hardly adequate. New oil companies joined in oil exploration, and the many members of political class became wealthy by being able to collaborate with multinationals, in addition to their control over state resources. The country became assertive in its foreign policy, and the projection that oil revenues would remain substantial and enduring encouraged thinking that the "giant of Africa" had emerged and that industrialization was on the horizon. Even if the expectations were unfulfilled, it is not because oil sources dried up. In the 1980s, the country was able to generate two million barrels a day, bringing in 80 percent of the federal income. Oil also ensured the importance of Nigeria to the international community, bringing to it political and economic leaders from different parts of the world. The multinational companies from Europe and the United States continue to profit from the country's oil.

During the 1960s, in the rush to attract foreign companies, the incentives appeared more generous than necessary. Protective tariffs for companies pro-

Table 12. Investment in Manufacturing and Processing (N million)

Year	Total Investment	Foreign Capital as % of total
1967	70.90	80.0
1968	83.00	81.0
1969	129.20	59.3
1970	116.86	57.3
1971	139.00	65.7
1972	172.87	57.0
1973	173.66	58.4

Source: Central Bank of Nigeria, *Economic and Financial Review* 14 (Mar. 1976): 82.

Table 13. Oil Contribution to Federal Government Revenue, 1961–1977

	Oil Revenue	Total Revenue	Oil Revenue as % of Total Revenue
1961	17.1	223.6	7.6
1962	16.9	238.8	7.1
1963	10.1	249.0	4.1
1964	16.4	277.6	5.9
1965	27.1	321.0	8.4
1966	37.7	339.2	11.1
1967	41.2	300.0	13.7
1968	23.3	299.0	7.8
1969	72.5	435.9	16.6
1970	196.4	758.1	25.9
1971	740.1	1410.9	52.5
1972	576.2	1389.9	41.5
1973	1461.6	2171.3	67.3
1974	4183.8	5177.1	80.8
1975	4611.7	5861.6	78.7
1976	5548.5	7070.3	78.5
1977	5821.5	8251.3	70.6

Source: Akin Iwayemi, "The Military and the Economy," in *Nigerian Government and Politics under Military Rule, 1966–79*, ed. Oyeleye Oyediran, 69.

ducing flour, textiles, and shoes were high. Local industries and public enterprises were promoted even when they were inefficient. Companies resorted to malpractice and corruption to gain tax advantages and to make as much profit as they wanted. Indigenous entrepreneurs benefited from access to public money to enrich themselves. Senior civil servants, through corruption, enhanced their power and enriched themselves by favoring some companies with land allocation, the granting of pioneer licenses, and generous expatriate quotas.

The oil industry is now fully established as the most important aspect of the economy. In the 1970s a massive infusion of capital went into the oil industry, with good results, and into iron and steel, but without much to offer in return. Policy objectives were also clearly stated in the plan document:

i. To promote even development and fair distribution of industries in all the parts of the country;
ii. To ensure a rapid expansion; and diversification of the industrial sector of the economy;
iii. To increase the incomes realized from manufacturing activity;
iv. To create more employment opportunities;
v. To promote the establishment of industries which cater for overseas markets in order to earn foreign exchange;
vi. To continue the programme of import-substitution, as well as raise the level of intermediate and capital goods production;
vii. To initiate schemes designed to promote indigenous manpower development in the industrial sector; and
viii. To raise the proportion of indigenous ownership of industrial investments.[11]

The location of industries favored the coastal cities, no doubt because of the use of the sea to import and export. Industrial employment grew, reaching almost 100,000 by 1970, but still small compared with the overall population. The issue of foreign control and ownership was seen as a concern, although the country always sought foreign investments. Two indigenization decrees in the 1970s increased the participation of Nigerians in the economy and attempted to reduce capital flight. Some industries were reserved only for Nigerians, and equity participation in some others put at between 40 and 60 percent. The indigenization programs did not stop foreigners and multinational companies from exercising control, even when reducing their investments. To take the example of oil, the leading sector, a public company was formed in 1971 to manage the government's share in exploration. Later known as the National Petroleum Corporation (NPC), it controlled an almost 60 percent share of the oil companies. However, the multinational companies and external agencies still had the major control in the exploration for and sales of Nigerian oil. As the country pursued the Structural Adjustment Program in the 1980s and 1990s, the multinational companies benefited from the withdrawal of the government in many businesses.

Manufacturing recorded considerable expansion after the 1970s. Oil revenues created opportunities to expand industrial investments, to generate employment, and to create new firms. The manufacturing of cotton textiles, beer, cement, paint, and roofing sheets succeeded as import-substitution industries. The intervention of the government expanded the list of import substitutes that were locally produced (most notably sugar, paper, and pulp), the promotion of new industries in plastics and petrochemicals, assembly plants, and investments in iron and steel. Oil money also allowed the government to venture into many new areas, such as the assembly of cars, iron, and steel, and the manufacturing of a host of new products such as sugar, fertilizer, and paper. Investments in manufacturing reached a very high magnitude in the 1980s, mainly due to import-substitution industries. Among the notable industries of the period were fertilizer, steel mills, and vehicle-assembly plants.

As clearly stated as the above objectives were, and in spite of the public and private investments, Nigeria can still not be described as an industrialized country. These objectives were repeated over the years, and each government promised a program of economic diversification. Manufacturing has not deteriorated as rapidly as agriculture. Yet, the contribution of manufacturing to the GDP was below 10 percent in the 1960s, 1970s, and 1980s. The sector is dominated by textiles, detergents, food, beverages, textiles, and light assembly, all concentrated in a few parts of the country: Kaduna, Kano, Ibadan, Lagos, Port Harcourt, and Aba. Oil revenues finance an import-dependent manufacturing sector, with the result that the value added to the economy has generally been low. For example, in 1975 it was calculated that for every ₦1 of value added, the country spent almost two-thirds of this (70 kobo) on imports. In cases where construction (for example, of roads) is involved, the sector enables contracts to be inflated in order for officials to collect bribes. The sector has also generated a low rate of employment, in spite of the large amount of money it consumes.

By the 1980s the government had emerged as the leading investor in industries. If foreigners dominated up until the early 1970s, the considerable diversion of oil revenues changed this. In a rapid manner, the government established a monopoly on the following: the manufacturing of fertilizers, yeast and alcohol, machine tools, steel, petroleum refining, petrochemicals, salt, steel plants, pulp and paper, and liquefied natural gas. Expenditures tended to be large, management and efficiency always a problem, the intervention increased the cost of doing business as construction costs became inflated, and final products were not always satisfactory. Since the 1990s, the government has had to embark on privatization, a strategy of selling public companies to private individuals.

Whether produced by the government or private companies, goods are never enough to meet the ever-growing demands. Locally, the cost of manufactured products is high, as the consumers have to virtually pay for the high cost of production and the import of essential machines. Although the capacity to export goods within the region and outside the continent exits, the country is yet to exploit this. For instance, the country should be able to dominate the regional trade in gas, petrochemicals, and fertilizers given its abundant natural resources.

The industrial sector has mainly been dominated by oil. This is actually an understatement, as the entire post-1965 economy of Nigeria revolves largely around the oil industry. From an insignificant producer in the 1960s, the country enjoyed an oil boom in the 1970s and became one of the top ten exporters in the 1980s. In the mid-1990s the country ranked as the eighth leading producer of oil, but the thirtieth in liquefied natural gas since most of this continued to be flared. Revenues from oil became extensive, dependence on oil became so predominant as to make all other sectors inconsequential. Economic growth came; so too did inflation, social inequity, and mass poverty, all arising from the gross mismanagement of the economy. The oil industry is dominated by multinational companies who share the profits from the country. For a long period, abundant natural gas was wastefully flared into open space.

It is important to highlight the constraints to an industrial transformation to show the difference between the dream and reality, and reveal other significant aspects of the modernizing economy. As the planners of the 1940s and 1950s realized, there could be no industrial takeoff without telephones, roads, railways, and adequate port facilities. Huge investments have been made in this area, with visible results in various parts of the country. Financial allocations to transportation were staggering: in the four plans from the 1960s to the 1980s, they amounted to 19 percent, 23 percent, 22 percent, and 15 percent, respectively. New highways and bridges appeared, and older ones were expanded. By 1985 over forty thousand kilometers of roads were tarred.

Similarly, investments were made in the supply of power. Up until 1951 electricity was supplied locally by the Public Works Department and the local governments. The Electricity Corporation of Nigeria (ECN) was formed to manage all existing supplies and to expand services into new areas. As of 1960 only a few places had electricity, the installed capacity for the whole country was 220,000 kilowatts, and the capacity in Lagos and the West was inadequate. After independence, thermal units were expanded, and the big Kainji Dam was completed in 1968, increasing the power capacity by almost 2,000 megawatts.

Nevertheless, the transport, communication, and power systems remain either inadequate or inefficient to support many enterprises and to provide comfort to the people. Although the railways were the "revolution" of the colonial period, and the possibility of waterways exists, the emphasis after independence, especially during military rule, was on the roads. The increase in motor vehicles makes many areas dependent on the use of roads. However, the majority of the roads are of high maintenance, since the quality of initial construction tends to be poor. The erratic supply of electricity and water has meant a huge increase in the cost of running businesses as the companies have to either generate their own supply or create expensive backups. The mastery of technology is still weak, in spite of the extensive importation of tools. Nigerians have acquired the skills of operating machines, but not of producing them. Consequently, each major new enterprise still involves buying from abroad and even using foreign engineers to assemble them. Production cost is always high, because of the scarcity of raw materials, the purchase of imported machines at exorbitant prices, the constant devaluation of the local currency, and inflation. Consequently, products are generally expensive.

The operation of manufacturing industries requires meeting too many regulations set by the government, thus creating the opportunities for civil servants and government officials to control entrepreneurs and even to change policies that could destroy enterprises. In some regions and cities, the regulations can be rather restrictive, or it can be that the number of authorities to negotiate with is too numerous. Where licenses and permits have to be obtained, avenues to receive bribes have been set up as part of the issuing process. The greater the profit to be made from a venture, the more the bribe to offer to start and operate it. Laws on royalties, repatriation of profits, license fees, and the importation of raw materials have changed many times and in ways that have frustrated many genuine investors.

The majority of Nigerian entrepreneurs prefer to trade than to invest in industries. For the greater part of the twentieth century not many people had the substantial capital needed to invest. Trade required a less initial capital outlay and technical skills might not be required. Unlike industries, trade generates immediate returns as commodities can be bought and sold quickly.

Public finance and banking expanded after 1960. The main sources of public finance were associated with exports, from agricultural products to hydrocarbon. The number of banks began to increase from the 1950s onward, as the regional governments created additional ones. The banking industry acquired trust. However, the SAP and the foreign exchange liberalizations of the 1980s and 1990s led to a huge rise in the number of small banks and mortgage companies, all in the hope of making immediate profits and participating in capital flights. By 1995 half of these had collapsed, with many customers, including a few rich people, losing their money.

The politics of how to divide the country's revenues have been intense since 1965. The centralization of power during military rule enabled the federal government to control the bulk of the revenues. Correspondingly, the states have lost power, and the various additions of new states have made them too small and overly dependent on the federal government. The regions were less dependent on the center during the First Republic, when they expected 55 percent of their budgets from the federal government; however, when the figure increased to over 80 percent after the 1980s, dependence increased. Indeed, the majority of the states cannot survive without grants from the center. The center itself cannot survive without trade, originally based on agriculture but later on oil. Careless spending patterns ultimately led the country onto the path of acquiring huge external debts.

The power of the federal government over revenue has led to intense ethnic rivalries. Whenever power is exercised by someone from the North, which happens to be the case for most of the time, the southern politicians complain that resources from the South are being diverted to the North. When population is used to determine the share of the revenues, the North gets more since it has more people. In the last two decades of the century, an attempt was made to distribute equally, while reflecting the population of each area. Other areas of contention remain. To start with, there is a large portion always retained by the federal government. Then, there is the issue of derivation, as oil-producing states in the Southeast always demand more. In the late 1990s the percentage of derivation was increased from 3 to 13, in order to halt a rising tide of violence in oil-producing areas.

Except for a period between the early 1970s and 1980s, Nigeria expected the injection of foreign investments into the manufacturing sector. This has been a source of problems, either because expectations are not met or the returns are less than anticipated. Until the oil boom of the 1970s and the 1972 Indigenization of Industries Decree, the problem was one of a high share of foreign capital. For most of the 1960s over 50 percent of capital in manufacturing belonged to foreign private investments. During the same period, foreign contractors benefited the most from civil engineering works and building. When Nigerian participation increased in the 1970s, the failure to combine in order to create a better pool of capital and skills made the local companies less competitive than the foreign ones.

Economic equity shows an imbalance, as the majority of the population fails to benefit from the economic prosperity of the 1970s and 1980s and substantial oil wealth. The traditional sector has always been the least rewarding. The modern sector has been dominated by the government, the major employer of labor. The salaries and wages of government employees tend to influence the general trend, although salaries in the private sector have generally been higher than in the public. Average per capita income rose in the 1960s and 1970s, from ₦350 in 1960 to ₦520 in 1967. Wages and salaries have been higher in services, mining, and manufacturing and lowest in agriculture and construction, and the rewards of economic growth have generally been reaped by those in paid employment. Although the salaries and wages have been rising since the 1960s, they have generally fallen far behind the rate of inflation. By the 1990s the majority of the country's population was poor. Among the most badly affected have been rural farmers. The per capita income of farmers has been hard to calculate, but all the rough estimates indicate a very low income: in 1963, it was put at N44; and in 1967 between N68 and N144; and in 1975 at N175.[12] Similarly, average annual wages of workers in the informal sector were put between N133 and N325 in the 1970s, well below the poverty line.[13]

Oil wealth added to the inequity and other problems. In some direct ways it contributed to inflation, which made life more difficult for the majority of the population. It has complicated politics as military officers and civilian politicians struggle to gain access to power, primarily because they want to get a share of the oil wealth without having to work. The government has been able to embark on various projects, some desirable, some not, but all enabling the award of contracts to the well connected, who thereby became wealthy. The ranks of the rich have grown, but this has not necessarily translated into greater productivity. As it became easier (if not cheaper) to buy food from abroad than to produce it at home, oil money was used carelessly on food imports. The multinational companies, in collaboration with the successive Nigerian governments, have done little to protect the environment or even to ensure any rapid improvement in the standard of living of those whose land generated the oil. Consequently, the Niger Delta has witnessed many cases of violence and targeted attacks directed at oil companies.[14] The need to control and distribute oil revenues led to an excessive concentration of power in the center, thus effectively undermining the principles of federalism, which were agreed to during the 1950s. The military took control, both for power and money, and reports of missing or stolen money became common.[15] As new states were created, in every decade, regional power and alternative centers of power were undermined. The competition for oil revenues intensified, as the federal government collected and distributed them.

Issues of inequity reveal the deeper problems of underdevelopment. In the final analysis, what counts is the extent to which economic programs over the years have transformed people's lives, moving them away from poverty to the ability to meet their basic needs. There was hope in the 1950s and 1960s that the members of the new political class would initiate far-reaching economic programs to enhance people's lives. Gradually but increasingly, this expectation began to wane, as the struggles for power consumed far more attention than concerns for economic upliftment. For most of the 1950s and 1960s the educated elite were doing well economically, as the majority had good jobs. Indeed, many among them were already thinking of reproducing elitism as they made various suggestions to improve the access of their children to good schools. At the same time, we begin to see evidence of either slow growth or stagnation in the living standards of urban poor and rural dwellers. The capacity of the country and its political class to provide adequate food, houses, and social facilities has also showed clear signs of diminishing. In spite of oil revenues, poor people have actually grown poorer since independence, while revenues from oil and access to power have created a group of millionaires whose estates and cars are clearly visible for all to see.

A focus on economic growth can also obscure the major issues in the structural transformation of the economy. Have productive forces been changing? To what extent has the widening gap in incomes affected political and social relationships? Have there been noticeable changes in the composition of national output? Has the society improved its capacity to use technology? One conclusion is that the modernization of the Nigerian economy has not necessarily brought about structural transformations in all aspects of economic life. By and large, the economy has revealed consistent characteristics over a long period. The country moved from dependence on agriculture to oil with an economic base that has always been narrow. Multinational firms have been able to establish control over the sale of oil. Industrialization has focused more on import substitution. The distribution of the country's wealth is uneven, and there is no solution to underdevelopment.

Economic growth has certainly not translated into economic development. The data on economic growth are clear. The evidence is largely associated with the post-1965 revenues from oil. As the various statistical data from the country's Central Bank show, from a GDP of N9.4 billion from 1970 to 1971, the figure rose to N14.4 billion in 1975, N36.1 billion in 1980, and N41.3 billion in 1982.[16] If the figures were broken down further, they show an average GDP growth of 10 percent between 1973 and 1983. During the same period, per capita income grew at 7 percent per annum, from a sum of N170 in 1973 to N427 in 1980.

However, the features of underdevelopment are clear to see. The plan documents read elegantly, even profoundly in many parts, but none has brought any efficiency to the economy. The majority of the population has always made wages well below the poverty level. Food scarcity and high cost have brought enormous suffering to many homes, with increasing cases of malnutrition and starvation. Quality of life keeps diminishing, and the majority of the population was earning less than US$1 a day at the close of the twentieth century.

Underdevelopment in Retrospect

To bring this book to a close, it is important to unite all the issues that have been discussed in the framework of economic expansion and underdevelopment. Since World War II, Nigeria has been seeking answers to the problems of underdevelopment. Indeed, various "development plans" have been formulated to identify all the possible projects that will move the country forward. Only a small percentage of the population is doing well, as wealth inequality continues to be accentuated by access to state power. The poor members of the society hold the belief that a few Nigerians pocketed the money meant for development purposes. In the 1980s the problems began to extend into the middle class and the educated elite, who then found it hard to eat well, to find jobs, and to live a comfortable lifestyle. Alternative ways of survival have led many to migrate to other countries. Those who stay do seek all means to survive, with many taking to crime.

The country is prone to violence and crime, with many cases related to poverty. Some cases of crime involve attempts to defraud foreign investors. Some others are related to drugs, as the country serves as an important link in the chain of international drug traffic. Issues of environmental degradation have compounded the crises. In the cities, there is inadequate housing and social amenities. Slums and joblessness prevail, creating an army of the dispossessed and marginalized. In the countryside, the forest is being rapidly destroyed. In the North, there are occasional problems of drought. In the oil-producing areas, the oil companies are just beginning to pay attention to the problems posed by pollution.

As already shown, economic growth and change have taken place, but underdevelopment persists. The growth since 1970 has owed largely to the oil industry. As agriculture declined, the country has become more and more dependent on imported food, thus wasting its external reserves. Colonial rule forms the major component of this study, as well as what Nigerians inherited and managed during the first five years of independence. The first half of the twentieth century was dominated by British rule. Changes took place in various aspects of society, but the positive impact on the majority of the population was limited. Poverty was endemic in many places. But the foundation of development and "modernization" had been laid: the local forces initiated by Nigerians are always present, and colonial rule broadened the vision and horizon, and added new models and technologies to improve upon. As Nigerians managed their politics and economy, their fortunes changed from the positive to the hopeless. Oil allowed economic growth but no sustainable development. The diversification of the economy is not attained, agriculture is not improved, and the productive capacities are not dramatically enhanced. The Structural Adjustment Program of the 1980s destroyed the middle class and created millions of poor people. By the 1990s Nigeria was on the verge of economic collapse.

Opinions are sharply divided on the explanation of the persistent underdevelopment. On the one hand are those who see the failure in the gross political and economic mismanagement of the period, declining agriculture, escalating external debts, and low productivity. Those who subscribe to this position tend to seek the means to inject more capital into the system, negotiate better deals with the World Bank and the International Monetary Fund, and pursue a strategy of mixed economy. On the other hand there is a growing number of radical scholars, whom underdevelopment generally throws up, and who always question the power structure and dependence on the West. The data on poverty and declining economies tend to dominate the discussion. Here, there is no disagreement, even with liberal-oriented scholars, that the country has not been doing well.[17] It is in the analysis of causes and what to do that radicals disagree with almost all the economic plans and policies of the successive governments. To those who seek foreign investments, the left will say that this actually brings greater dependence and control of the country by multinational forces. A primary condition, as far as the left is concerned, is to seek autonomy from external forces and prevent the domination of power by the powerful.[18]

Nigeria's economy and underdevelopment have inevitably been associated with the international system. During the colonial period and in the 1960s the country depended on the export of raw materials; thereafter on that of oil. The country is dependent on extraction, which has led a number of analysts to describe Nigeria as a "rentier state." The government collects "rents" from oil extractors, foreign companies who use imported technology. There is a consensus among analysts that the country needs to deal with the problems of dependence, if it is to develop. As all the plans and economic policies show, too many failed attempts have been made to attain this, including strategies of import substitution, ban on the imports of a number of commodities, indigenization, industrialization, economic diversification, and many more. However, as the political system has remained unstable and corrupt, policies have either been too hard to pursue or have been damaged by fiscal irresponsibility. A largely unproductive political class prefers the easy ways to making money, which include collaboration with multinational companies, access to the "rents" collected from them, and access to power. The rentier state and those who run it have created problems for development. In a characterization that the left will support, William D. Graf concludes that Nigeria demonstrates features with the endemic problems of a rentier state:

It is, first, and almost by definition, *crisis-susceptible* and hence tendentially unstable. Fluctuation in global demand, after-effects of world-wide recessions, technical breakdowns, even labour disputes may reduce the flow of rents and thus undercut national plans, intricate budgets and the entire "development" process.... Second, the rentier state at the periphery of the world capitalist system is locked into, and *dependent upon, North-South trade patterns.* Trade links, for both imports and exports, are overwhelmingly with the advanced capitalist areas of the OECD, between 80 and 90% in each category.... Third, the oil-dominated economy is an enhanced *enclave economy.* Oil production is necessarily a high-technology, capital intensive enterprise which cannot generate either jobs or direct ("forward" and "backward") linkages with the other sectors of the economy.... Fourth, then, the oil economy *perpetuates* and *deepens* patterns of *economic disarticulation* generated in the colonial phase and reinforced by neo-colonial petty commodity production. Oil revenues, as it were, overwhelm and eclipse the other sectors of the dependent economy, so that balanced, autocentric development becomes an even more remote prospect than during the colonial era.[19]

Graf was referring to the period after the 1970s, but many analysts tend to conclude that the foundation of underdevelopment was laid during the period covered by this book. But what about the money generated by the "rents"? Here, many will agree that the political system tends to make it difficult to invest them in a wise manner.

No analysis of underdevelopment and the reasons for the poverty of its people can ignore the declining importance of agriculture. The sector that the majority of the population relies on has become the most backward. Of course, there are other reasons which limit productivity in agriculture and the economy in general: political incompetence and decay, corruption and gross mismanagement of national income, dependence on the outside world, elitism and antidevelopment elements in the culture, the ineffective coordination of resources and human power, and occasional drought in parts of the North. Although information on the output of farm products are usually estimates, production of the eight major food crops (yams, cassava, cocoayams, guinea corn, millet, maize, rice, and beans) has not been showing much increase, especially in the South, for many years. Efficiency in production has been on the decline, while the food crops are inadequate to meet the nutritional needs of the majority of the population. While the country pursues the means to industrialize, it does not do so bearing in mind the need to connect agriculture with manufacturing in a way that the emerging industrial sector will transform agriculture and the rural side. In the early years of independence, the government favored a policy of exports, understandably to raise revenues. When another source of revenues opened up with oil, the government also used the scarcity of foods and agro-related equipment to justify large expenditures on imports from abroad. The elite and millions of others consumed rice and bread more than ever before, thereby creating the need to import. And although there is evidence of public investment in agriculture, import dependence actually undermined agriculture. Foreign companies and local contractors turned the imports into opportunities to make huge profits. A detailed case study on the country's dependence on wheat bread shows not just how the country could not feed itself, but also how food imports became necessary to stabilize politics even if local production was badly affected.[20] Also, an analysis of leading sources of income and profits, both to the government and entrepreneurs, reveals that agriculture has not been the favorite choice for investment since the mid-1960s. When the government turned to oil, investors preferred to trade, both local distributive trade and import-export commerce. The citizens preferred to go to school, in order to benefit from lucrative wage employments.

Agriculture also reveals a number of leading tendencies in the economy and the related issues of development. To start with, agriculture makes clear the dependence of the country on external forces. Up until the 1960s revenues depended on agricultural exports, and the country was unable to control either the prices or the quantities in demand. Since independence, other forms of dependence have been the importation of food, raw materials, ideas, equipment, and chemicals. When the country is not importing rice, it has to be herbicides or fertilizers. In cases where imports are massive, foreign and local companies have turned this to great advantage to make huge profits. Inflation (running to over 15 percent since the 1970s), food shortage, and massive importation all reveal the troubles with agriculture. Millions of small-scale producers have been ignored in the allocation of welfare and social services, exploited in times when the government relied on agriculture for revenues, and pursued by local governments that needed them to pay taxes. Rather than contributing revenues to the government as it did in the first sixty years of the twentieth century, agriculture becomes a "consumer" of funds generated from other sources. As it uses these funds, agriculture is not necessarily transforming the economy but bringing it down, especially with the gross failures of large-scale commercial farming, subsidy programs in the importation of machinery and chemicals, expenditure on twenty research institutes, and other elaborate projects funded by the regional and federal governments. Even the impact of government funding is either hard to evaluate or misdirected; the data on substantial funding and the limited agricultural output do suggest a disconnect. An analysis of the involvement of the government in commercial agriculture shows that little or no profits have been made, that many of the companies are inefficient, that public funds are mismanaged, and that the cost of operations is excessive.

One other source of concern, in addition to declining agriculture, has been the issue of population growth. Here, the intention is not to argue that there is an optimum population for Nigeria or that the current figure of about 100 million is rather large. The issue in focus is that population has been growing faster than economic growth or that the management of economic resources has been inadequate for the needs of the population since 1960. Of course, most of the data on the country's population are unreliable, but small-scale surveys have confirmed that population has always been on the rise. For the entire duration of the period under study, it was not considered an important issue to be addressed, in part because the majority was still rural and could cater for themselves, and in part because there were still jobs for virtually all the educated elite.

Historical trends are hard to establish for the country's population figures. All figures before 1952 were intelligent guess works. The estimates were generally presented as an undercount, but they revealed one that doubled between 1910 and 1952, from 15.9 million to 30 million. Most of the increase occurred in the 1940s attributed to improved nutrition and medical facilities. The rate of increase was put at 2.1, and this again increased in the 1950s and 1960s to 2.5 each year. The majority lived in the rural areas, but the modernization of health, education, and social services occurred mainly in the cities. A few places, notably in the East, were showing tendencies of overpopulation. In the 1950s the population density of some areas in the South was approaching five hundred per square mile, a figure that the land and the farming techniques could hardly sustain. Given the nature of ethnic politics in the country, it was not feasible to move the population around, from overpopulated areas to the sparsely populated, or from places with bad soils to others. The International Bank for Reconstruction and Development (IBRD) warned in the mid-1950s that economic changes must recognize the inevitable fact of an immediate accelerated population increase.

As Nigeria begins this new millennium, it is doing so not necessarily by having to consolidate any enduring and solid economic foundation, but by rebuilding damaged political institutions and economic infrastructures. It has become more than clear that without improving the economic well-being of the majority of the population, political stability will elude the country. In some sectors such as agriculture, the hands of the clock have been turned back by more than 180 degrees. Agriculture has to be revamped if only to make food

Traditional musicians playing in local festivities. Photo by A. Olusegun Fayemi.

available to millions of poor and hungry people and to create opportunities for farmers to produce a variety of cash crops for the local and international markets. Employment opportunities continue to diminish, but an expansion of the manufacturing and the industrial sector will bring major improvements. Not many positive changes will happen in the economic sector until Nigerian politics take a different turn: the country has to stabilize its politics, depoliticize the economy, avoid excessive corruption, manage the available resources with prudence, and execute policies that will benefit the majority of the country's population. The conditions remain favorable: a huge country, a population of over a hundred million people, abundant resources, an integrated chain of local markets, and the existence of producers and entrepreneurs. What remains is a leadership to stabilize the politics and to pursue economic projects that will transform the lives of the millions of poor and suffering people.

Appendix: Statistical Tables on the Nigerian Economy

The various statistics provided in this appendix shed more light on the nature of economic growth and development since 1945. The tables indicate the nature of the "mixed method" research strategy adopted in developing the narrative: a combination of "thick description," narration, interpretation of documents, events, ideas, traditions, movements, and figures. While the tables support some of the issues and conclusions reached in the book, readers can draw other interpretations and conclusions from them.

However, it should be noted that using the data generated during this period offers challenges and serious problems. With respect to Nigeria, Benjamin Disraeli's remark that "there are three kinds of lies: lies, damn lies, and statistics" should be ignored. The government was not interested in using the statistics to cover up or tell lies. For most of the period there were no statistics to use to manipulate the public. The problem was just that data collection was a new enterprise. The government did not keep any credible track of demographic information. The collection was unsophisticated for most of the time. Various regions and departments in the country often failed to harmonize the figures and, when they did, serious rounding up errors occurred such that the total figures can be disconnected from the components.

Those provided below were collected by various government agencies, scholars who worked for government agencies, and new research institutes. The tables can be read at two main levels: some describe society or a particular moment in time, and others provide crude means to relate one economic variable to another.

Table A1. The GDP at Factor Costs by Economic Sector, 1950–1957

Economic Sectors	1950	1951	1952	1953	1954	1955	1956	1957
Primary Sector	913.6	989	1006	1042.8	1099	1138.2	1087.2	1114
Secondary Sector	95.2	105.8	98.8	112.4	140	144.8	149.2	164.4
Mining	15.2	15.2	16.4	15.8	16.2	18	19.2	18.8
Petroleum	0.6	0.8	1.2	1.2	1.2	1.4	1.6	2
Other Mining	14.6	14.4	15.2	14.6	15	16	17.6	16.8
Manufacturing	37.8	38	41.6	42.6	45.4	47.2	53.4	55.2
Crafts Manufacturing	31.6	31.8	32	32.2	32.4	32.8	33	33.4
Ind.	6.2	6.1	9.6	10.4	13	14.4	20.4	21.8
Construction	40.6	51.8	38.8	51.8	75.6	76.6	73	86
Electricity, Gas, Water	1.6	1.8	2	2.2	2.8	3	2.6	4.4
Tertiary Sector	365.4	385.6	481.2	464.4	505.4	523.2	511.8	541.6
Total	1522.4	1639.4	1742.8	1790.4	1946	2006.2	1970.2	2058.4

Source: P. N.C. Okigbo, *Nigerian National Accounts, 1950–57* (Lagos: Federal Ministry of Economic Development, 1961), 21.

Table A2. Sectoral Composition of the GDP, 1960–1982 (percent)

Sector	1960–66	1965–66	1970–71	1970–76	1980	1982
Agriculture, forestry, and fishing	64.0	55.4	43.8	28.1	18.9	19.0
Mining (including oil)	1.2	4.8	12.2	14.2	12.8	8.9
Manufacturing	4.8	7.0	7.6	10.3	7.7	9.0
Distribution	2.7	13.3	12.3	12.3	22.3	23.8
Construction (excluding housing)	4.0	5.2	6.4	11.3	13.3	13.0
Transport and Communications	4.6	4.6	3.2	5.2	4.1	5.5
Electricity and Water	0.3	0.6	0.6	0.9	—	—
General government	3.2	3.1	7.5	9.1	8.0	7.2
Education	2.6	3.1	2.7	3.8	—	—
Health	0.5	0.7	0.9	1.3	—	—
Other services	2.0	2.3	2.8	3.6	—	—
Finance and Insurance	—	—	—	3.1	3.7	4.4
Crude Petroleum	—	—	—	12.9	12.8	8.9
Housing	—	—	—	6.2	5.5	5.8
Services (excluding trade, finance, and government)	—	—	—	41.7	40.4	40.3

Sources: Nigerian Economic Society, *The Nigerian Economy under the Military: Proceedings of the 1980 Annual Conference* (Ibadan: Nigerian Economic Society, 1981), 240; Nigerian Economic Society, *Proceedings of 1984 Annual Conference* (Ibadan: Nigerian Economic Society, 1985), 35.

Table A3. Growth of the GDP, 1960–1982 at 1973–1974 Factor Cost (N million)

Year	GDP	Year	GDP	Year	GDP
1960–61	3892.5	1968–69	4220.7	1976–77	14993
1961–62	3978.3	1969–70	5441.1	1977–78	16285
1962–63	4241.9	1970–71	7332.4	1978–78	17182.20
1963–64	4560.8	1971–72	8135.3	1979–80	18740.4
1964–65	4778.6	1972–73	8566.5	1980	32174
1965–66	5115.9	1973–74	12118	1981	30471
1966–67	5146.6	1974–75	12799	1982	29815
1967–68	4302.3	1975–76	13393		

Sources: Federal Office of Statistics, *National Accounts of Nigeria, 1958–59, 1973–74*, June 1976 (Lagos: Federal Ministry of Economic Development, 1981), 3–10; Federal Ministry of Economic Development, *Guidelines for the Fourth National Development Plan, 1980–85* (Lagos: Federal Ministry of Economic Development, 1984), 15.

Table A4. GDP at 1977–1982 Factor Cost: Percentage Distribution

Sector	1977–78	1978–79	1980	1981	1982
Agriculture	14.6	13.3	12.7	12.7	12.6
Livestock	3.9	3.3	3.5	3.7	4
Forestry	0.9	0.9	0.8	0.9	0.8
Fishing	5.2	5.1	5.2	5.4	6
Crude Petroleum	21.3	23.5	21.5	15.5	13.4
Other Mining & Quarrying	2.6	2.4	2.3	2.3	3.1
Manufacturing	5.9	6	7	8	8
Utilities	0.4	0.4	0.5	0.6	0.7
Constructions	9.5	8.7	9.5	10.5	9.7
Transport	3.5	3.5	3.9	4.6	4.5
Communications	0.2	0.2	0.2	0.2	0.2
Wholesale & Retail Trade	20.5	21.6	21.5	22.7	22.5
Hotels & Restaurants	0.3	0.3	0.3	0.3	0.4
Finance & Insurance	2.5	2.4	2.5	3.2	3.5
Real Estate & Business Service	0.3	0.3	0.3	0.3	0.4
Housing	3.6	3.4	3.4	3.6	3.9
Producer of Govt. Services	4.8	4.7	4.9	5.3	5.6
Total	100	100	100	99.8	99.3

Source: Federal Office of Statistics, *National Accounts of Nigeria* (Lagos: Federal Office of Statistics, 1978), 15.

Table A5. GDP by Activity Type

	1970	1971	1972	1973	1974	75–76	76–77	77–78	78–79	79–80
Agriculture	2576	3034	3093	3123	3531	5730	6426	7474	7854.2	8425.6
Petroleum	490	944	1144	1899	5671					
Other Mining	45	63	76	90	110	4668	6797	7905	6874.3	10903.9
Manufacturing	378	416	511	591	655	1170	1464	1555	2212.9	2746.5
Construction	270	412	529	646	970	2866	3617	4072	3548.4	5568.8
Electricity and Water	37	41	48	52	59	58	72	99	121.7	133.3
Transport & Communication	149	188	238	268	360	674	852	1039	1277.7	1617
General Government	343	377	339	463	766	1353	1492	2216.8	1968	2236.3
Health & Education	194	227	239	256	400					
Other Services	799	950	979	1065	1425	659	733	859.9	980.1	1219.7
GDP at Factor Cost	5281	6651	7188	8453	13947	21327	26956	31992	31120	40436.3
Indirect taxes less subsidies	400	500	480	460	520					
Gross domestic product	5281	7151	7668	8913	14467					
Growth rate of GDP at FC	25.90%	8.10%	17.60%	65%	14.90%	26.40%	18.7	2.70%	29.90%	—
Growth rate of Non-oil GDP	19.10%	5.90%	8.40%	26.30%	30.50%	—	—	—	—	—

Source: T. O. Adeboye, "A General Survey of the Economy," in *Nigeria since Independence: The First 25 Years*, vol. 11, *The Economy*, ed. M. O. Kayode and Y. B. Usman (Ibadan: Heinemann, 1989), 19.

Table A6. Nigeria's Term of Trade, 1949–1960 (1954=100)

1949	73	1953	83	1957	82
1950	79	1954	100	1958	86
1951	87	1955	90	1959	92
1952	86	1956	83	1960	88

Source: *Digest of Statistics* (Lagos: Nigeria, 1955 and 1960).

Table A7. Earnings from Commodity Trade

Year	All exports (£'million)	Cocoa %	Palm Oil %	Palm Kernel %	Groundnut %	Rubber %	Aggregate %
1960	169.7	21.6	8.2	15.5	13.5	8.4	71.6
1961	173.6	19.4	7.6	11.5	18.5	6.3	63.3
1962	168.5	19.8	5.3	10.0	19.2	7.9	62.2
1963	189.7	17.0	4.9	11.0	19.2	6.2	58.3
1964	214.7	18.7	5.0	9.8	16.0	5.7	55.2
1965	268.3	15.9	5.1	9.9	14.1	4.1	49.1
1966	271.0	20.2	4.8	2.9	13.1	2.3	43.3

Sources: Nigeria, *Annual Abstracts of Statistics,* 1961, 1962, 1963, 1964, 1965; S. O. Olayide and Dupe Olatunbosun, *Trends and Prospects of Nigeria's Agricultural Exports* (Ibadan: Ibadan Univ. Press, 1975), 114.

Table A8. Food Imports as Proportion of Total Imports and Per Capita Food Imports, 1961–1983

Year	Total Imports (N million)	Food Imports (N million)	Percentage of Food as Total Imports	Population	Per capita
1961		45.442		52.921	0.86
1962		47.042		54.278	0.87
1963		43.826		55.670	0.79
1964	507.76	41.240	8.12	57.062	0.72
1965	550.79	43.062	8.37	58.489	0.79
1966	513.93	51.576	10.03	59.951	0.86
1967	447.10	42.560	9.52	61.450	0.69
1968	385.16	28.448	7.37	62.986	0.45
1969	497.38	41.726	8.39	63.561	0.65
1970	752.58	57.694	7.67	66.175	0.87
1971	1,075.07	88.254	8.18	88.160	1.29
1972	986.22	95.104	9.64	70.205	1.35
1973	1,220.95	126.260	10.34	72.311	1.75
1974	1,737.38	154.765	8.96	74.480	2.10
1975	3,717.38	298.805	8.01	76.714	3.90
1976	5,132.51	441.846	8.55	79.015	5.59
1977	7,091.70	781.190	10.38	81.380	9.60
1978	8,211.70	1,108.660	12.43	83.830	13.22
1979	6,169.20	1,105.900	16.90	85.970	12.86
1980	9,095.60	1,480.000	15.60	88.549	16.71
1981	12,919.60	2,198.3	17.00	91.206	23.20
1982	9,130.00	2,048.2	15.50	94.624	21.65
1983	6,375.50	1,477.9	14.10	98.309	15.03

Source: Z. A. Bonat, "Agriculture," in *Nigeria since Independence,* ed. Kayode and Usman, 76.

Table A9. Expansion of the Nigerian Road Network, 1962–1980 (in kilometers)

Year	Length of Tarred Roads	Total Length of All Roads
1962	11,053	71,870
1968	15,200	91,210
1969	15,758	90,958
1971	16,122	91,210
1972	18,109	95,374
1976	28,242	113,938
1980	28,632	114,768

Source: Federal Republic of Nigeria, *Fourth National Development Plan, 1980–85* (Lagos: Federal Ministry of Information, 1980), 220.

A10. Tonnage of Non-Oil Cargo Handled by Nigerian Ports, 1961–1982 (millions of tons)

Year	Non-oil Cargo	Year	Non-oil Cargo
		1977	14.7
1961	2.4	1978	32.7
1970	2.7	1979	16.0
1974	7.4	1980	18.4
1975	8.4	1981	21.2
1976	7.2	1982	18.4

Sources: Federal Republic of Nigeria, *Third National Development Plan, 1975–80*, vol. 1 (Lagos: Federal Ministry of Information, 1975), 221 (table 14.8); Central Bank of Nigeria, *Annual Reports and Statements of Accounts*, 1976, 1979, 1980, 1981, 1982, 1983.

Table A11. Performance of the Nigerian Railway Corporation, 1961–1965

Year	Train Miles (in '000)	Gross railing in Ton/Miles ('000,000)	Net Ton/Miles ('000,000)	Total Revenue (£'000)	Total Expenditure (£'000)
1961–62	27,871	3,667	1,412	15,211	16,275
1962–63	7,521	3,651	1,411	14,893	15,883
1963–66	7,304	3,649	1,555	16,288	16,254
1964–65	6,538	2,915	1,221	14,179	17,619

Source: Federal Republic of Nigeria, *Report of the Nigerian Railway Corporation Tribunal of Inquiry Appointed under the Tribunal of Inquiry Decree, 1966, to Inquire into the Affairs of the Nigerian Railway Corporation* (Lagos: Federal Government Printer, 1967), 261.

Table A12. Electricity Demand in Nigeria, 1970–1980

Year	Maximum Demand MW	Maximum % Growth
1970–71	253	—
1971–72	330	30.4
1972–73	390	18.2
1973–74	405	14.1
1974–75	527	18.4
1975–76	629	19.4
1976–77	758	20.5
1977–78	979	29.1
1978–79	1,201	22.6
1979–80	1,392	15.9

Source: Nigerian Electric Power Authority, *Power System Development Plan, 1976* (Lagos, Nigeria: NEPA, 1976), 6.

Table A13. Nigeria Gas Development, 1971–1980 (million cubic meters)

Year	Gas Production	Gas Flared	Gas Utilized
1971	12,980	12,796	184
1972	27,122	16,849	273
1973	20,561	20,258	303
1974	26,623	20,219	404
1975	18,955	18,553	402
1976	22,101	21,469	632
1977	21,445	20,945	500
1978	20,428	20,945	380
1979	30,049	28,671	1,378
1980	24,552	23,482	1,070

Source: NAPETCOR (in-house journal of the Association of Nigerian Oil Workers) 5, no. 2 (1981): 12.

Table A14. Some Indicators of the Growth of Transport and Communication in Nigeria, 1945–1960

Item	1945	1950	1955	1960
Tonnage of Goods Hauled by Railways ('000)	1,425	1,773	2,602	2,803
No. Passengers Carried by Railways ('000)	4,262	5,552	5,451	7,881
Length of Tarred Roads (miles)	705	1,024	2,442	5,434
Total Length of All Roads (miles)	25,433	28,042	35,696	41,065
No. Registered Commercial Vehicles	1,413	2,898	5,830	7,879
No. Private Cars, Including Taxis	702	2,463	5,398	11,615
No. Telephone Instruments in Use	5,800	—	21,000	31,000(a)
No. Telegrams Handled	1,520(b)	1,962	2,234	2,036
No. Postal Articles	22,714(b)	53,612	78,698	100,138

Sources: R. O. Ekundare, *An Economic History of Nigeria, 1860–1960* (London: Methuen, 1973), 262–78; National Economic Council, *Economic Survey of Nigeria*, 1959 (Lagos: Government Printer, 1969), 85.
(a) This figure for 1958
(b) This figure for 1945

Table A15. Sectoral Growth Rates of the Economy, Selected Years 1962–1982

Sector/Activity	1962–63 to 1966–67	1965–66 to 1969–70	1969–70 to 1975–76	1980	1982
Agriculture	2.6	-3.3	1.9	-3.8	-8.7
Mining	40.3	14.9	22.2	-8.0	-3.5
Manufacturing	14.7	4.5	15.5	17.6	-1.3
Power, Water, Transport, and Communication	9.3	-0.9	22.4	11.3	13.3
Other Services	9.7	5.2	13.4	—	—
Finance and Insurance	—	—	—	4.0	8.8
Housing	—	—	—	1.3	-1.8
Wholesale and Retail Trade	—	—	—	0.2	-7.5
Government	—	—	—	3.5	-18.2
Building and Construction	—	—	—	10.0	-4.7

Source: B. Onimode, et al., *Multinational Corporations in Nigeria* (Ibadan: Les Shyraden, 1983), 54.

Table A16. Index of Agricultural Production in Nigeria, 1979–1983 (1975=100)

	1979	1980	1981	1982	1983
1. Agriculture (crops)	73.9	77.7	84.3	85.5	74.3
(a) Staples	64.4	67.9	71.6	73.8	63.5
(b) Other Crops	104.0	109.4	124.1	122.2	108.1
2. Livestock	113.4	117.1	94.2	104.4	99.3
3. Fish	114.8	102.8	104.3	107.5	109.9
4. Forestry	111.9	114.5	114.5	113.4	105.6
Aggregate Index	87.2	89.4	92.4	92.5	83.8

Sources: Central Bank of Nigeria, *Annual Reports and Statements of Accounts,* December 1981 and December 1983.

Table A17. Fiscal Structure under the Nigeria (Constitution) Order in Council, 1960

Revenue Item	Revenue Power	Assignment of Revenue	Distribution Formula
Direct Taxes			
Personal income taxes	Regional governments	Each government	
Company income taxes	Federal government	100% to federal government	
Customs Duties	Federal government		
Motor spirits, diesel oil	Federal government	100% to regions	Distribution for consumption in previous quarter
Tobacco	Federal government	100% to regions	Distribution for consumption in previous quarter
Beer, potable spirits, wine	Federal government	100% to federal government	
Other duties	Federal government	80% to distributable pool account, 70% to federal government	40/95 to North, 31/95 to East, 24/25 to West
Excise Duties			
Tobacco	Federal government		
Sales taxes (produce & petrol)	Regional governments	100% to regions	Distribution for consumption
Export Duties			
Produce, hides, and skins	Federal government	100% to regions	Derivation-purchase for export in previous quarter or previous 12 months
Other Duties	Federal government		
Mining Royalties and Rents	Federal government	90% to distributable pool, 50% to regions	40/95 to North, 31/95 to East, 24/25 to West Derivation

Miscellaneous Revenues
  Stamp duties — Each government
  License fees, including vehicles — Each government
  Crown land leases — Each government
Loan Funds
  Internal — Regional and federal governments
  External — Federal government

Source: P. N. C. Okigbo, *Nigerian Public Finance* (Evanston, Ill.: Northwestern Univ. Press, 1965), 54.

Table A18. The Funding of Agricultural Development Projects

ADPs	Federal Grants (N million)	State Grants (N million)	World Bank Loans ($ million)
Funtua	9.0	8.8	39.0
Gusau	9.0	9.8	30.6
Gombe	7.9	8.2	30.7
Ayangba	9.0	10.6	64.0
Lafia	9.0	8.5	52.6
Bida	10.3	1.0	61.8
Ilorin	9.0	0.2	36.6
Total	63.2	47.1	315.3

Source: Y. A. Abdullahi, "The State and Agrarian Crisis: Rhetoric and Substance of Nigerian Agricultural Development Policy" (conference paper presented at a workshop on the state of the Nigerian economy, Kaduna, October 1983), 17.

Table A19. Crude Oil Production (in barrels)

	Total National Production	Former East Nigeria	Midwestern—production Absolute	%
1960–61	6,642,473	6,642,473	—	—
1961–62	20,935,215	20,935,215	—	—
1962–63	25,042,444	25,042,444	—	—
1963–64	29,590,450	29,590,450	—	—
1964–65	54,981,045	54,701,377	279,668	0.5
1965–66	112,419,457	81,618,574	30,800,883	27.4
1966–67	170,986,833	108,800,370	62,186,463	36.4
1967–68	69,836,980	36,054,213	33,782,767	48.4
1968–69	95,776,053	25,057,181	70,718,872	73.8
1969–70	197,204,418	75,177,883	122,026,535	61.9
1970	395,841,764	164,537,536	231,304,228	58.4

Source: J. O. Abiodun, "Locational Effects of the Civil War on the Nigerian Petroleum Industry," *Geographical Review* 64 (1974): 253.

Table A20. Public Capital Expenditure in the Agricultural Sector, 1962–1985 (N million)

Year	Federal Expenditure	State Expenditure	Total Expenditure
1962–68	10,961	41,562	52,623
1970–80	34,023	93,263	127,286
1975–80	1,112,598	1,188,582	2,301,180
1981–85	5,400,000	3,427,531	8,827,531
Total	6,557,582	4,750,938	11,308,620

Source: Y. A. Abdullahi, "Comments on Press Briefing by Minister of Agriculture," *New Nigerian*, February 18, 1985.

Table A21. Proposed Changes in Revenue Allocation Formula, 1977–1981

Type of Sharing	Governments	Aboyade Technical Committee (rejected)	Okigbo Commission Proposal	Fed. Govt. Proposals on Okigbo Report	Revenue Allocation Act 1981 (nullified)	Second Federal Govt. Proposal	Current Revenue Allocation Act, 1981
Vertical	Federal Government	60.0% Special Grants Account (3.0%)	53.0% Special Fund 7.0% FCT (2.5%)	55.00% Special Fund 7.0% FCT (2.5%) Mineral Prod. Areas 2.0% Ecology 1.0% Equalization Fund 1.5%	58.5% FCT (2.5%) Ecological Problems 1.0% Mineral Prod. Areas 3.5% Ecology 1.0%	55.0% FCT (2.5%)	55.0%
	State Governments		30.0%	30.0%	30.0%	31.5% Mineral Prod. Areas 3.5% Derivation on 2.0% Devlp. of Area 1.5% Ecological Problems 1.0%	30.0% 30.5% Ecological problems 1.0% Mineral Prod Areas 3.5% Devlp. of Area 1.5% Derivation on 2.0%
	Local Governments		10.0%	10.0%	8.0%	10.0%	8.0% 10.0%

Source: *Reports of the Fiscal Commission*, in *Nigeria since Independence*, ed. Kayode and Usman, 198–99.

Table A22. Recurrent Expenditure of Nigerian Federal Government, Selected Years 1959–1983

Function	1959	1961	1965	1969	1975	1979	1981	1983
Administration (NM)	30.3	40.7	65	338.4	1055.4	999.5	2143.8	2567.9
% of total	(41.8)	(42.0)	(41.4)	(60.3)	(62.6)	(41.8)	(42.2)	(48.8)
Economic Services (NM)	6.8	14.2	33.9	22.6	131.8	113.5	484.9	380.0
% of total	(9.4)	(14.7)	(21.6)	(7.9)	(7.8)	(4.8)	(9.60)	(7.20)
Social & Community Services (NM)	23.8	22.3	20.1	12.2	287.5	511	984.9	904.4
% of total	(32.9)	(23.0)	(12.8)	(4.3)	(17.0)	(21.4)	(19.4)	(17.2)
Transfers	11.5	19.7	37.9	79.9	211.2	765.4	1463.9	1426.5
% of total	(15.9)	(20.3)	(24.2)	(27.6)	(12.5)	(32.0)	(28.9)	(27.00)
Total (NM)	72.4	96.9	156.9	287	1685.9	2389.4	5077.5	5278.8

Sources: Okigbo, *Nigerian Public Finance*, 185; Kayode and Usman, *Nigeria since Independence*, 212.

Table A23. Total Federal Government Expenditure at Current Prices, Selected Years 1959–1985

Year	Current Expenditure N million	Current Expenditure % of total exp.	Capital Expenditure N million	Capital Expenditure % of total exp.	Total Expenditure N million
1959	72.4	50.1	72.1	49.9	144.5
1961	96.9	59.1	67	40.9	164
1965	156.9	66.3	79.6	33.7	236.5
1969	287	75.8	91.6	24.2	378.6
1971	492.8	77.1	146.2	22.9	639
1975	1685.9	34.5	3207.7	65.5	4893.6
1979	2389.4	36.2	4219.6	63.8	6609
1981**	5077.5	47.1	5696.9	52.9	10774.4
1983**	5278.8	43.7	6807.3	56.3	12086.1
1985**	5473.1	48.6	5796.4	51.4	11269.5

Source: Okigbo, *Nigerian Public Finance*, 183–84.
**Budget estimates only

Table A24. Nigerian Federal Government Revenue from Crude Petroleum, 1961–1985 (N million)

Year	Oil Revenue	Total Current Revenue	Oil Revenue as % of Total Revenue
1961	17.1	223.6	7.6
1962	16.9	238.8	7.1
1963	10.1	249.0	4.1
1964	16.4	277.6	5.9
1965	27.1	321.0	8.4
1966	37.7	339.2	11.1
1967	41.2	300.0	13.7
1968	23.3	299.9	7.8
1969	72.5	435.9	16.6
1970	166.4	633.2	26.3
1971	510.2	1169.0	43.6
1972	764.3	1404.8	54.4
1973	1016.0	1695.3	59.9
1974	3726.7	4537.0	82.1
1975	4271.5	5514.7	77.5
1976	5365.2	6765.9	79.3
1977	6080.6	8080.6	75.2
1978	4654.1	7371.1	63.1
1979	8880.9	10913.1	81.4
1980+	9918.6	11859.8	83.6
1981*	9194.4	12377.5	74.3
1982*	5161.3	11630.4	44.4
1983*+	5550.3	93006.8	59.6
1984*	7797.0	11331.7	68.8
1985*	7445.8	11277.7	66.0

Source: Federal Ministry of Finance, *Federal Government Annual Estimates* (Lagos: Federal Government Printer, 1985), 111–19.
*budgetary estimates
+(nine-month period)

Table A25. Revenue of Nigerian Federal Government, Selected Years 1959–1985 (N million)

Type of Source	1959	1961	1965	1969	1971	1975	1979	1981*	1983*	1985**
Direct Taxes	(11.10)	(15.20)	(21.20)	(44.00)	(451.20)	(2990.20)	(5753.70)	(6862.50)	(3831.70)	(4561.20)
Company Income Tax	7.9	9.5	13.0	28.40	67.50	261.90	575.10	508.20	561.50	600.50
Petroleum Profit	na	na	0.7	4.30	383.10	2707.50	5164.1	6325.8	3247.7	3936.4
Personal Income Tax	3.2	3.5	4.9	1.60	0.20	15.90	2.90	12.00	4.50	9.70
Others	na	2.2	2.6	9.70	0.30	4.90	11.60	16.50	18.00	14.50
Indirect Taxes	(29.20)	(160.10)	(234.20)	(261.00)	(491.00)	(760.60)	(1143.90)	(2325.80)	(2136.20)	(1830.40)
Import Duties	50.2	120.3	169.6	151.60	284.80	629.30	870.60	1748.60	1271.80	1044.30
Export Duties	2.1	27	31.5	37.50	37.70	5.80	0.20	0.10	0.00	13.00
Excise Duties	3.9	12.8	33.1	71.90	168.50	125.50	273.10	577.10	864.40	773.10
Non-tax Revenue	(19.60)	(48.40)	(65.60)	(72.80)	(226.60)	(1763.80)	(4014.90)	(2790.60)	(3338.90)	(4886.10)
Interest & Repayment	6.2	10.5	14.7	20.70	36.6	162.70	274.60	522.00	975.50	1301.30
Mining (rents, etc.)	1.4	8.6	25.6	23.60	127	1564.00	3716.70	2238.00	2303.30	3513.60
Miscellaneous	12	29.3	25.3	28.50	63	37.00	23.60	30.00	60.00	71.20
Total	86.9	223.7	321	377.80	1168.7	5514.60	23.60	30.00	60.00	71.20

Source: Kayode and Usman, *Nigeria since Independence*, 206.
*Provisional figures
**Budget estimates

Table A26. Federal Government Oil Revenues and Total Current Revenues, 1969–1976

	Federal Revenue from Oil (N millions)	Total Federal Revenue (N millions)	Oil Revenue (% of total)
1969	33.4	378.4	8.8
1970	166.4	633.2	26.3
1971	510.2	1169.0	43.6
1972	764.3	1404.8	54.4
1973	1016.0	1695.3	59.9
1974	3726.7	4537.0	82.1
1975	4271.5	5514.7	77.5
1976	5365.2	6765.9	79.3

Source: Central Bank of Nigeria, *Annual Reports and Statements of Accounts* (Lagos: Central Bank of Nigeria, 1970–76).

Table A27. Gross Manufacturing Contribution, 1959–1960 (£'000)

	1959	1960
Bakeries	19.0	316.0
Oil Mining	363.6	2,610.0
Margarine	2.5	18.2
Beer and Soft Drinks	275.9	2,800.0
Tobacco	1,395.8	2,190.0
Textiles	4.5	613.0
Rubber Processing	19.5	1,378.0
Tanning	5.6	40.5
Saw Milling	498.7	1,800.0
Cement	0.0	1,160.0
Total	3,129.3	15,650.0

Source: *First National Development Plan, 1962–68* (Lagos: Federal Ministry of Economic Development, 1962), 9.

Table A28. Foreign Investments in the Economy, 1975–1981

	Paid-up Capital + Liabilities + Reserves	Investment in Fixed Assets (book value)
1975	2287.5	1869.2
1976	2333.8	1858.2
1977	2531.4	2201.7
1978	2863.2	2557.0
1979	3153.1	2595.8
1980	3620.1	2656.5
1981	3757.9	2537.0

Source: Central Bank of Nigeria, *Economic and Financial Review* 2, no. 3 (Sept. 1983): 21–23.

Table A29. Foreign Private Capital Outflows and Unremitted Profits, 1975–1981

	Foreign Capital as % of Total	Foreign Private Capital Outflows	Unremitted Profits	Changes in Foreign Share Capital (N million)
1975	56.6	-282.0	147.6	+30.2
1976	59.4	-474.8	167.7	+63.5
1977	57.1	-519.7	210.4	+35.4
1978	53.5	-332.9	192.9	+17.2
1979	24.3	-414.1	165.6	+79.0
1980	20.7	-319.4	104.5	+50.5
1981	17.2	-447.1	159.5	+41.6

Source: Central Bank of Nigeria, *Economic and Financial Review* 2, no. 3 (Sept. 1983): 21–33.

Table A30. Foreign Private Investment as Percent of Total

Year	Total Foreign	Mining and Quarries	Manufacturing & Process	Agriculture, Forest & Fishing	Transport & Communication	Building & Construction	Trading & Business	Misc.
1975	56.6	37.6	52.7	63.6	40.0	61.3	73.5	62.3
1976	59.4	39.2	56.7	69.7	43.1	64.6	75.3	62.7
1977	57.1	49.8	54.0	64.8	38.8	60.5	72.4	55.1
1978	53.5	40.9	50.1	63.4	35.9	50.9	69.2	43.9
1979	24.3	66.5	27.0	37.0	36.3	33.7	7.7	52.7
1980	20.7	63.9	32.2	37.0	38.1	42.9	8.8	8.4
1981	17.2	64.5	30.5	38.6	20.4	43.0	3.8	22.0

Source: Central Bank of Nigeria, *Annual Reports and Statements of Accounts*, 1983.

Table A31. Sectoral Composition of Planned and Actual Expenditures in the 1962–1968 Development Plan (percent)

Sector	Planned Expenditures (%)	Actual Expenditure (%)
Primary Production	13.6	10.8
Trade and Industry	13.4	12.6
Electricity	15.1	6.8
Transport	21.3	29.4
Communications	4.4	1.5
Water Supplies	3.6	4.7
Education	10.3	9.9
Health	2.5	2.1
Town and Country Planning	6.2	4.3
Administration	9.6	17.9

Source: *First National Development Plan*, 1962–68.

Notes

ARCHIVAL ABBREVIATIONS

Agbor Dist	Agbor District Papers
Ben Prof	Benin Provincial Papers
CMS	Church Missionary Society Papers
COL	Colonial Office, London
CSE	Chief Secretary, Enugu, Papers
CSO	Chief Secretary's Office
CSSP	Records of the Holy Ghost Fathers
NAE	Nigerian National Archives, Enugu
NAI	Nigerian National Archives, Ibadan
NAK	Nigerian National Archives, Kaduna
OG Prof	Ogoja Provincial Papers
Oyo Prof	Oyo Provincial Papers
PRO	Public Records Office, London
SNP	Secretary to the Northern Province Papers

1. Economy and Politics in a Colonial Society

1. See Sir Alan Burns, *History of Nigeria,* 5th ed. (London: Allen and Unwin, 1955); Joyce Cary, *Britain and West Africa* (London: Longman, 1946); and A. A. Cook, *British Enterprise in Nigeria* (Philadelphia.: Univ. of Pennsylvania Press, 1943).

2. See J. C. Anene, *The International Boundaries of Nigeria, 1885–1960* (London: Longman, 1970); and T. N. Tamuno, *The Evolution of the Nigerian State: The Southern Phase 1898–1914* (London: Longman, 1972).

3. This warning was recorded by a European visitor to his court. See H. Clapperton, *Journal of a Second Expedition into the Interior of Africa* (London: Murray, 1829), 199.

4. A large body of literature exists on the issues of Anglo-Nigerian trade in the fifteenth to the nineteenth centuries. See A. W. Lawrence, *Trade Castles and Forts of West Africa* (Stanford, Calif.: Stanford Univ. Press, 1963); K. Onwuka Dike, *Trade and Politics in the Niger Delta* (London: Oxford Univ. Press, 1959); Daniel P. Mannix, with Malcolm Cowley, *Black Cargoes: A History of the Atlantic Slave Trade, 1518–1865* (New York: Viking, 1962); and G. I. Jones, *The Trading States of the Oil Rivers* (London: Oxford Univ. Press, 1963).

5. R. S. Smith, "The Lagos Consulate, 1851–1861: An Outline," *Journal of African History* 15 (1974): 393–416. For a more elaborate discussion, see R. S. Smith, *The Lagos Consulate, 1851–1861* (London: Macmillan, 1978), 1–90.

6. See J. D. Hargreaves, *Prelude to the Partition of West Africa* (London: Macmillan, 1963), 145–301.

7. For the idea of race during the nineteenth century, see Philip D. Curtin, *The Image of Africa* (Madison: Univ. of Wisconsin Press, 1964).

8. See E. A. Ayandele, *The Missionary Impact on Modern Nigeria, 1842–1914: A Political and Social Analysis* (London: Longman, 1966), 1–71.

9. See Jean Herskovits Kopytoff, *A Preface to Modern Nigeria: The "Sierra Leonians" in Yoruba, 1830–1890* (Madison: Univ. of Wisconsin Press, 1965).

10. See S. E. Crowe, *The Berlin West African Conference, 1884–85* (Westport, Conn.: Negro Universities Press, 1970).

11. On his so-called glorious career, see J. E. Flint, *Sir John Goldie and the Making of Nigeria* (London: Oxford Univ. Press, 1960).

12. Robinson to Lang, September 14, 1887. CMS G3/A3/1887/109.

13. For details, see J. C. Anene, *Southern Nigeria in Transition, 1884–1906: Theory and Practice in a Colonial Dependency* (Cambridge, U.K.: Cambridge Univ. Press, 1965).

14. See Sir Charles Orr, *The Making of Northern Nigeria*, 2d ed. (London: Frank Cass, 1965).

15. For some major episodes of conquest, see O. Ikime, *The Fall of Nigeria: The British Conquest* (London: Heinemann, 1977).

16. For the events leading to the amalgamation, see Lord Lugard, *Report by Sir F. D. Lugard on the Amalgamation of Northern and Southern Administration, 1912–19* (1919). PRO, Cmd 468.

17. See Don C. Ohadike, *The Ekumeku Movement: Western Igbo Resistance to the British Conquest of Nigeria, 1883–1914* (Athens: Ohio Univ. Press, 1991).

18. See I. F. Nicolson, *The Administration of Nigeria, 1900–1960: Men, Methods, and Myths* (Oxford, U.K.: Clarendon, 1969); S. O. Okafor, *Indirect Rule: The Development of Central Legislature in Nigeria* (Walton/Thames, U.K.: Nelson, 1981); and I. M. Okonjo, *British Administration in Nigeria, 1900–1950: A Nigerian View* (New York: Nok, 1974).

19. On the caliphate and its subsequent transition to an indirect rule system, see S. Abubakar, *The Lamibe of Fombina: A Political History of Adamawa, 1809–1901* (Zaria: Ahmadu Bello Univ. Press, 1977); R. A. Adeleye, *Power and Diplomacy in Northern Nigeria: The Sokoto Caliphate and Its Enemies 1804–1906* (London: Longman, 1971); A. M. Fika, *The Kano Civil War and British Overule, 1882–1940* (Ibadan: Oxford Univ. Press, 1978); and M. Last, *The Sokoto Caliphate* (London: Longman, 1967).

20. See Lord Hailey, *Native Administration in the British African Territories,* part 3, *West Africa: Nigeria, the Gold Coast, Sierra Leone, Gambia* (London: HMSO, 1950–53); and A. E. Afigbo, "Herbert Richmond Palmer and Indirect Rule in Eastern Nigeria, 1915–1928," *Journal of the Historical Society of Nigeria* 3 (1965): 295–312.

21. See M. Crowder and O. Ikime, eds., *West African Chiefs: Their Changing Status under Colonial Rule and Independence* (Ile-Ife: Univ. of Ife Press, 1970).

22. See A. E. Afigbo, *The Warrant Chiefs: Indirect Rule in Southeastern Nigeria, 1891–1929* (London: Longman, 1972); and H. A. Gailey, *The Road to Aba: A Study of British Administrative Policy in Eastern Nigeria* (London: Univ. of London Press, 1971).

23. See J. A. Atanda, *The New Oyo Empire: Indirect Rule and Change in Western Nigeria, 1894–1934* (London: Longman, 1973), 1–172.

24. See P. A. Igbafe, *Benin under British Administration: The Impact of Colonial Rule on an African Kingdom, 1897–1938* (London: Longman, 1979)

25. See John H. Harris, *Dawn in Darkest Africa* (London: Frank Cass, 1968).

26. On his contribution, see Margery Perham, *Lugard: The Years of Authority, 1898–1945* (London: Collins, 1960).

27. F. D. Lugard, *The Rise of Our East African Empire* (London: Blackwood, 1893), 381–82.

28. CSSP, "Nigeria Meridionale 1920–37," Eugene Groetz, report of March 31, 1922. PRO.

29. Margery Perham, "The British Problem in Africa," *Foreign Affairs* (July 1951): 2.

30. See Sir Frederick D. Lugard, *Political Memoranda,* 1906, section on taxation. This document was revised and reprinted years later as *Revision of Instructions to Political Officers on Subjects Chiefly Political and Administrative* (London: HMSO, 1919).

31. See Don Ohadike, "Exploitation of Labor" in *Britain and Nigeria: Exploitation or Development?* ed. Toyin Falola (London: Zed, 1987), 142–63.

32. See J. F. Ade Ajayi, *Christian Missions in Nigeria 1841–1871: The Making of an Educated Elite* (London: Longman, 1965).

33. See Hilda Kuper, ed., *Urbanization and Migration in West Africa* (Berkeley: Univ. of California Press, 1965).

34. R. M. Prothero, "Migratory Labour from North-Western Nigeria," *Africa* 27, no. 1 (1957): 251–61.

35. See S. O. Osoba, "The Phenomenon of Labour Migration in the Era of British Colonial Rule," *Journal of the Historical Society of Nigeria* 44 (June 1969): 515–38.

36. See A. Fajana, *Education in Nigeria, 1842–1939: An Historical Analysis* (Lagos: Longman, 1978), 1–213.

37. See O. Adewoye, *The Legal Profession in Nigeria, 1865–1962* (Lagos: Longman, 1977).

38. See Michael Crowder, *Revolt in Bussa* (London: Faber and Faber, 1973); and J. A. Atanda, "The Iseyin-Okeiho Rising of 1916: an example of Socio-political Conflict in Colonial Africa," *Journal of the Historical Society of Nigeria* 4, no. 4 (June 1969): 497–514.

39. See N. E. Mba, *Nigerian Women Mobilized: Women's Political Activity in Southern Nigeria, 1900–1965* (Berkeley, Calif.: Institute of International Studies, 1982).

40. See G. O. Olusanya, *The West African Students Union and the Politics of Decolonization, 1925–1958* (Ibadan: Daystar, 1982).

41. See P. D. Cole, *Modern and Traditional Elites in the Politics of Lagos* (Cambridge, U.K.: Cambridge Univ. Press, 1975).

42. Qtd. in E. A. Ayandele, *The Educated Elite in Nigerian Society* (Ibadan: Ibadan Univ. Press, 1974), 74.

43. See O. E. Ejimofor, *British Colonial Objectives and Policies in Nigeria: The Roots of Conflict* (Onitsha: Africana-Fep, 1987).

44. Qtd. in E. A. Ayandele, *The Missionary Impact on Modern Nigeria, 1842–1914: A Political and Social Analysis* (London: Longman, 1966), 149.

45. See O. Ikime, *Niger Delta Rivalry: Itsekiri-Urhobo Relations and the European Presence, 1884–1936* (London: Longman, 1969).

46. See James P. Hubbard, *Education under Colonial Rule: A History of Katsina College, 1921–1942* (Lanham, N.Y.: Univ. Press of America, 2000).

47. See D. Killingray and Richard Rathbone, eds., *Africa and the Second World War* (London: Macmillan, 1986).

48. See Falola, "Cassava Starch for Export in Nigeria during the Second World War," *African Economic History* 18 (1989): 73–98.

49. See O. N. Njoku, "Contributions to War Efforts," in *Britain and Nigeria*, ed. Falola, 164–85.

50. Official testimonies of their impressive role can be found *The Colonial Empire* (1939–47). PRO, Cmd 7167.

51. Sultan of Sokoto, qtd. in *West Africa*, April 6, 1940.

52. *West Africa*, June 29, 1940.

53. Nigeria, *The Constitution of the National Council of Nigeria and the Cameroons* (Lagos: NCNC, 1945), 1.

54. See Falola, "'Salt Is Gold': The Management of Salt Scarcity in Nigeria during World War II," *Canadian Journal of African Studies* 24, no. 3 (1992): 412–36.

55. For details, see the section about trade in M. Perham, ed., *Mining, Commerce and Finance in Nigeria* (London: Faber and Faber, 1948); and P. T. Bauer, *West African Trade* (London: Routledge and Kegan Paul, 1954).

56. See *Nigeria: Ten Year Educational Plan, 1942* (Lagos: Government Printer, 1942).

57. Qtd. in J. A. Atanda, *The New Oyo Empire*, 205.

58. See Afigbo, *The Warrant Chiefs*.

59. R. Cudjoe, "Some Reminiscences of a Senior Interpreter," *Nigeria Field* 6, no. 6 (1953): 159.

60. J. S. Coleman, *Nigeria: Background to Nationalism* (Berkeley: Univ. of Calif. Press, 1963), 302.

61. Qtd. in G. O. Olusanya, *The Second World War and Politics in Nigeria* (Lagos: Evans Brothers, 1973), 158.

62. Okoye, qtd. in Olusanya, *The Second World War*, 123.

63. See L. Franklin Blitz, ed., *The Politics and Administration of Nigerian Government* (London: Sweet and Maxwell, 1965); and Okoi Arikpo, *The Development of Modern Nigeria* (Baltimore, Md.: Penguin, 1967).

64. See *Political and Constitutional Future of Nigeria*, Sessional Paper no. 4 of 1945, NAI.

65. See G. O. Olusanya, *The Evolution of the Nigerian Civil Service, 1861–1960: The Problems of Nigerianization* (Lagos: Univ. of Lagos Press, 1975).

66. See I. I. Ekanem, *The 1963 Census: A Critical Appraisal* (Benin: Ethiope, 1973).

2. The Political Context of Economic Reforms and Modernization

1. Kalu Ezera, *Constitutional Developments in Nigeria* (Cambridge, U.K.: Cambridge Univ. Press, 1960), 76–84; and Obafemi Awolowo, *Path to Nigeria Freedom* (London: Faber and Faber, 1947), 124–34.

2. See Nigeria, *Proceedings of the General Conference on Review of the Constitution, January 1950* (Lagos: Government Printer, 1950).

3. Nigeria, *House of Representatives Debates, 2d session*, vol. 2 (March 19–April 1, 1953), 989.

4. See *Report by the Conference on the Nigerian Constitution Held in London in July and August 1953* (London: HMSO, 1953), PRO, Cmd 8934; and *Report by the Resumed Conference on the Nigerian Constitution Held in Lagos in January and February 1954* (Lagos: Government Printer, 1954), PRO.

5. See *Report by the Conference on the Nigerian Constitution held in London in May and June 1957* (London: HMSO, 1957), PRO, Cmd 207; *Report by the Ad Hoc Meeting on the Nigerian Constitutional Conference held in Lagos in February 1958* (Lagos: Government Printer, 1958); *Report of the Resumed Nigerian Constitutional Conference held in London in September and October 1958* (London: HMSO, 1958), PRO, Cmd 569; and *Report of the Ad Hoc Committee of the Conference on the Nigerian Constitution Lagos, April 1959* (Lagos: Government Printer, 1959).

6. See Nigeria, *Administrative and Financial Procedure under the New Constitution: Financial Relations between the Government of Nigeria and the Native Administration* (Lagos: Government Printer, 1947).

7. See Nigeria, *Report of the Fiscal Commission on Revenue Allocation* (Lagos: Government Printer, 1951).

8. See Nigeria, *Report of the Fiscal Commission* (London: HMSO, 1957), PRO, Cmd 481.

9. For their ideas and the leading figures of this era, see Rina Okonkwo, *Heroes of West African Nationalism* (Enugu: Delta, 1985); Falola, *Nationalism and African Intellectuals* (Rochester, N.Y.: Rochester Univ. Press, 2001).

10. See George Shepperson, "Notes on Negro American Influences on the Emergence of African Nationalism," *Journal of African History* 1, no. 2 (1960): 299–312; George Padmore, *Pan Africanism or Communism? The Coming Struggle for Africa* (London: Dobson, 1953); and W. E. B. Du Bois, *The World and Africa: An Enquiry into the Part which Africa Has Played in World History* (New York: International, 1965).

11. See James Bertin Webster, *The African Churches among the Yoruba, 1888–1922* (Oxford, U.K.: Oxford Univ. Press, 1964).

12. Qtd. in Coleman, *Nigeria*, 193.

13. This incident is well reported in P. D. Cole, *Modern and Traditional Elites in the Politics of Lagos* (Cambridge, U.K.: Cambridge Univ. Press, 1973).

14. Nnamdi Azikiwe, *West African Pilot*, October 20, 1938.

15. See F. E. O. Schwarz Jr., *Nigeria: The Tribes, the Nations, or the Race* (Cambridge, Mass.: MIT Univ. Press, 1965), 1–86.

16. The leading figure in NEPU was Alhaji Aminu Kano. An impressive biography on him is by Alan Feinstein, *African Revolutionary: The Life and Times of Nigeria's Aminu Kano* (Boulder, Colo.: Lynne Rienner, 1987).

17. See N. Azikiwe, *My Odyssey: An Autobiography* (London: C. Hurst, 1970).

18. For details on Awolowo, see Falola et al., ed., *Obafemi Awolowo: The End of an Era?* (Ile-Ife: Obafemi Awolowo Univ. Press, 1988).

19. For details on this party, see B. J. Dudley, *Parties and Politics in Northern Nigeria* (London: Frank Cass, 1968), 116–49.

20. See C. S. Whitaker Jr., *The Politics of Tradition: Continuity and Change in Northern Nigeria, 1946–1966* (Princeton, N.J.: Princeton Univ. Press, 1970).

21. For an impressive biography on him, see John N. Paden, *Ahmadu Bello, Sardauna of Sokoto: Values and Leadership in Nigeria* (Bungay, England: Richard Clay and Hudahuda, 1986).

22. On the premier and additional information on the politics of the period, see Trevor Clark, *A Right Honourable Gentleman: The Life and Times of Alhaji Sir Abubakar Tafawa Balewa* (Zaria: Hudahuda, 1991).

23. *Gaskiya Ta Fi Kobo,* qtd. in Coleman, *Nigeria,* 362.

24. Qtd. in Kenneth W. J. Post and Michael Vickers, *Structure and Conflict in Nigeria, 1960–65* (Madison: Univ. of Wisconsin Press, 1963), 221.

25. Richard L. Sklar, "Contradictions in the Nigerian Political System," *Journal of Modern African Studies* 8, no. 2 (1965): 201–13.

26. Qtd. in Sklar, *Nigerian Political Parties,* 128n88.

27. Sir Ahmadu Bello, *My Life: The Autobiography of Alhaji Sir Ahmadu Bello, Sardauna of Sokoto* (Cambridge, U.K.: Cambridge Univ. Press, 1962), 111.

28. Memo by the Northern Delegation to the Ad Hoc Constitutional Conference, 1966, NAK, SNP178.

29. Sklar, "Nigerian Politics: The Ordeal of Chief Awolowo, 1960–65," in *Politics in Africa: 7 Cases,* ed. Gwendolen M. Carter (New York: Harcourt, Brace and World, 1966), 119–65.

30. See B. J. Dudley, *Instability and Political Order* (Ibadan: Univ. of Ibadan Press, 1974), 1–182.

31. See the case study of Alhaji Adegoke Adekbu in Kenneth W. J. Post and George D. Jenkins, *The Price of Liberty: Personality and Politics in Colonial Nigeria* (Cambridge, U.K.: Cambridge Univ. Press, 1973).

32. Post and Vickers, *Structure and Conflict in Nigeria,* 31–49.

33. S. A. Aluko, "How Many Nigerians?" *Journal of Modern African Studies* 3, no. 3 (1965): 371–92.

34. The most impressive study on this remains Remi Anifowose, *Violence and Politics in Nigeria: The Tiv and Yoruba Experience* (New York: Nok, 1982).

35. Sklar, "Nigerian Politics," 119–65.

36. Like Awolowo, Akintola was a remarkable figure of the time and he also had a law degree. Akintola was a veteran politician, starting as a member of the NYM and the editor of its newspaper, the *Daily Service.* He was the legal adviser to the Egbe Omo Oduduwa, a foundation member of the AG. He became the deputy leader of the party in 1955, a member of the federal parliament, and minister from 1957 to 1959. When Awolowo became the leader of opposition in 1959, Akintola replaced him as the premier. On Akintola and his rise to power, see Akinjide Osuntokun, *Chief S. Ladoke Akintola: His Life and Times* (London: Frank Cass, 1984).

37. See R. Cohen, *Labour and Politics in Nigeria* (London: Heinemann, 1974).

38. Douglas G. Anglin, "Brinkmanship in Nigeria: The Federal Election of 1964–65," *International Journal* 30 (Spring 1965): 187.

39. For the details of this election and the complicated politics that followed, see John P. Mackintosh, *Nigerian Government and Politics* (Evanston, Ill.: Northwestern Univ. Press, 1966), 545–609.

40. On the military during this time, including their involvement in politics, see S. K. Panter-Brick, ed., *Nigerian Politics and Military Rule: Prelude to Civil War* (London: Athlone, 1970); A. H. M. Kirk-Greene, *Crisis and Conflict in Nigeria: A Documentary Sourcebook, 1966–1970*, vols. 1 and 2 (London: Oxford Univ. Press, 1971); and N. J. Miners, *The Nigerian Military, 1956–66* (London: Methuen, 1971).

41. R. Luckham, *The Nigerian Military: A Sociological Analysis of Authority and Revolt, 1960–70* (Cambridge, U.K.: Cambridge Univ. Press, 1971), 43.

42. Major Chukwuma Nzeogwu, Proclamation, January 1966. Qtd. in Schwarz, *Nigeria* (Cambridge, Mass.: MIT Univ. Press, 1968), 196.

43. For an overview history of this period, see Falola, *The History of Nigeria* (Westport, Conn.: Greenwood, 1999).

3. The Economy, 1945–1960

1. International Bank for Reconstruction and Development (IBRD), *The Economic Development of Nigeria* (Baltimore, Md.: IBRD and Johns Hopkins Univ. Press, 1955), 3.

2. U. I. Ukwu. "The Development of Trade and Marketing in Iboland," *Journal of the Historical Society of Nigeria* 3, no. 4 (1967): 647–63. On the broad outline of indigenous economies, see A. G. Hopkins, *An Economic History of West Africa* (London: Longman, 1973); Stephen Baier, *An Economic History of Central Niger* (Oxford, U.K.: Clarendon, 1980); and Toyin Falola and Ann O'Hear, eds., *Studies in the Nineteenth-Century Economic History of Nigeria* (Madison: University of Wisconsin African Studies Program, 1998).

3. See A. McPhee, *The Economic Revolution in British West Africa* (London: Routledge, 1926); R. J. Gavin and Wale Oyemakinde, "Economic Development in Nigeria since 1800," in *Groundwork of Nigerian History*, ed. Obaro Ikime (Ibadan: Heinemann, 1980), 482–517.

4. Nigeria, *Digest of Statistics,* July 1961.

5. For the development of this form of transport, see Gilbert Walker, *Traffic and Transport in Nigeria,* Colonial Research Studies series no. 27 (London: HMSO, 1959).

6. See Falola and Paul Lovejoy, *Pawnship in Africa: Debt Bondage in Historical Perspective* (Boulder, Colo.: Westview, 1994).

7. Sir Hugh Clifford, *Address to the Nigerian Council, 29 December 1920* (Lagos: Government Printer, 1920), 186.

8. See S. S. Berry, *Cocoa, Custom, and Socio-Economic Change in Rural Western Nigeria* (Oxford, U.K.: Oxford Univ. Press, 1975); J. S. Hogendorn, *Nigerian Groundnut Exports: Origins and Early Development* (Zaria: Ahmadu Bello Univ. Press, 1978).

9. G. B. Masefield, *A Short History of Agriculture in the Colonies* (Oxford, U.K.: Oxford Univ. Press, 1950), 54–55.

10. Berry, *Cocoa, Custom, and Socio-Economic Change in Rural Western Nigeria,* 90–125; Band R. Galleti, K. Baldwin, and I. Dina, *Nigerian Cocoa Farmers* (Oxford, U.K.: Oxford Univ. Press, 1956).

11. Hogendorn, *Nigerian Groundnut Exports,* 36–57.

12. See K. O. Dike, *Trade and Politics in the Niger Delta* (London: Oxford Univ. Press, 1956).

13. I. B. Akinyele, *The Outlines of Ibadan History* (Lagos: self-published, 1946), 88–95.

14. See Wale Oyemakinde, "A History of Indigenous Labour on the Nigerian Railway, 1895–1945," Ph.D. diss., University of Ibadan, 1970.

15. See Polly Hill, *Rural Hausa: A Village and a Setting* (Cambridge, U.K.: Cambridge Univ. Press, 1972).

16. See M. Perham, ed., *Mining, Commerce and Finance in Nigeria* (London: Faber and Faber, 1948).

17. For a detailed analysis of the tin industry in Nigeria, see Bill Freund, *Capital and Labour in the Nigerian Tin Mines* (London: Longman, 1981).

18. On the problems in the marketing of export crops, see *Report of the Commission on the Marketing of West African Cocoa* (London: HMSO, 1938), PRO.

19. For details of the economy in the first four decades of colonial rule, R. O. Ekundare, *An Economic History of Nigeria* (London: Methuen, 1973); Gerald K. Helleiner, *Peasant Agriculture, Government, and Economic Growth in Nigeria* (Homewood, Ill.: Richard D. Irwin, 1966); K. M. Buchanan and J. C. Pugh, *Land and People in Nigeria* (London: Univ. of London Press, 1955); and Falola, ed., *Britain and Nigeria: Exploitation or Development?* (London: Zed, 1987).

20. See the example of how the Dantata family of Kano acquired fortune in trade in peanuts and other products in Hogendorn, *Nigerian Groundnut Exports*, 92–116.

21. See R. Shenton, *Studies in the Development of Capitalism in Northern Nigeria* (Toronto: Univ. of Toronto Press, 1986).

22. These were the African Association, Miller Brothers, the Company of African Merchants, and the Niger Company.

23. Falola, "Lebanese Traders in Colonial Southwestern Nigeria," *African Affairs* 89 (Oct. 1990): 523–53.

24. F. I. Ekejiuba, "Omu Okwei, The Merchant Queen of Osomari: A Biographical Sketch," *Journal of the Historical Society of Nigeria* 3 (1967): 633–46.

25. Allan McPhee, *The Economic Revolution in British West Africa*, 104.

26. *Report on Cocoa Control in West Africa, 1939–43* (London: HMSO, 1944), COL.

27. For an elaboration of the official policy, see "Import and Export Restrictions, 1939: Secret Import Restrictions in Emergency," August 29, 1939, NAI, CSO 18/19.

28. "Vegetable Oil and Oilseeds," August, 29, 1939, NAI, CSO 26/36414.

29. "Import and Export Restrictions, 1939: Secret Import Restrictions in Emergency," August 29, 1939, NAI, CSO 18/19.

30. "Control of Imports," Secret Circular Dispatch to Officer Administering (Colonial) Governments (OAGS) for Secretary of State, Malcolm MacDonald, August 23, 1939, NAI, Department of Commerce and Industries, 1/1//4032, vol. 1.

31. "Distribution of Markets for the Sale and Purchase of Produce for Export," confidential, SWP to CSG, November 30, 1940, NAI, CSO 26/37453.

32. *Report on the Cocoa Control in West Africa*, 6.

33. R. O. Ekundare, *An Economic History of Nigeria*, 225–26.

34. See P. Kilby, *Industrialisation in an Open Economy, Nigeria 1945–1966* (Cambridge: Cambridge Univ. Press, 1969), 1–112.

35. For the details of these and other incentives, see Nigeria, *Setting up an Industrial Enterprise in Nigeria* (Lagos: Federal Department of Commerce and Industries, 1955); and Nigeria, *The Role of the Federal Government in Promoting Industrial Development in Nigeria*, Sessional Paper no. 3 of 1958 (Lagos: Government Printer, 1958).

36. Helleiner, *Peasant Agriculture, Government, and Economic Growth in Nigeria*, 160–64.

37. For a detailed history of the project, see K. D. S. Baldwin, *The Niger Agricultural Project* (Oxford, U.K.: Basil Blackwell, 1957).

38. R. M. Netting, *Hill Farmers of Nigeria: Cultural Ecology of the Kofyar of the Jos Plateau* (Seattle: Univ. of Washington Press, 1968), 17–29.

39. In later years, the increasing devastation of agriculture and the expansion of wage labor made possible by oil revenues instigated the movement of people far more than the resettlement schemes accomplished.

40. This is a subject of extensive study in Falola, *Development Planning and Decolonization in Nigeria* (Gainesville: Univ. Press of Florida, 1996).

41. Nigeria, *Statement of Policy for the Niger and Benue Rivers*, Sessional Paper no. 3, 1959 (Lagos: Government Printer, 1959).

42. For valuable statistical information on the railway, see Nigerian Railway Corporation, Report and Accounts (various years).

43. Nigeria, *Colonial Annual Report, 1953* (Lagos: Government Printer, 1954), 21–22.

44. Nigeria, *Report of the Accountant-General, 1950* (Lagos: Government Printer, 1951). This report was updated in subsequent years.

45. See Nigeria, *Nigerian Handbook of Commerce and Industry* (Lagos: Government Printer, 1960); and *Annual Abstract of Statistics* (Lagos: Government Printer, 1963); also Ekundare, *An Economic History of Nigeria*, 234.

46. See Nigeria, *Annual Abstract of Statistics*, 1963.

47. For an optimistic account, see Nigeria, *First National Development Plan, 1962–1968* (Lagos: Government Printer, 1962), 6–13.

48. See United Africa Company, *Statistical and Economic Review* (September 1957).

49. R. O. Ekundare, *An Economic History of Nigeria*, 251–52.

50. Ibid., 252.

51. See *Statement of the Policy Proposed for the Future Marketing of Nigerian Oil, Oil Seeds, and Cotton*, Sessional Paper no. 18, 1948 (Lagos: Government Printer, 1948), 8. NAI.

52. See *Statement on Future Marketing of West African Cocoa*, 1946, PRO, Cmd 6959.

53. See *First Annual Report of the Nigerian Government Marketing Board*, NAI.

54. *Statement of the Policy Proposed for the Future Marketing of Nigerian Oil, Oil Seeds, and Cotton*, 8, NAI.

55. This agency was abolished in 1958 and replaced by the Nigerian Produce Marketing Board Company, which performed essentially the same functions.

56. See *Statement on Future Marketing of West African Cocoa* (London: HMSO, 1946), PRO, Cmd 6950.

57. P. T. Bauer, *West African Trade* (Cambridge, U.K.: Cambridge Univ. Press, 1954), 283–318.

58. H. O. Oluwasanmi, *Agriculture and Nigerian Economic Development* (Ibadan: Oxford Univ. Press, 1966), 179.

59. Northern Nigeria, *Northern Regional Marketing Board, Annual Report, 1959–60* (Zaria: Government Printer, 1961), 57.

60. *Economic Development in the United Kingdom Dependencies* (London: Central Office of Information, 1956), PRO.

61. *Statement of Policy on Colonial Development and Welfare* (London: HMSO, 1940, PRO, Cmd 6715.

62. Qtd. in W. F, Stolper, *Planning without Facts: Lessons in Resource Allocation from Nigeria's Development* (Cambridge, Mass.: Harvard Univ. Press, 1966), 37.

63. Nigeria, *Colonial Annual Reports, 1946,* 64.

64. IBRD, *The Economic Development of Nigeria,* see the preface.

65. One major project that came out of the National Economic Council was a valuable book of documents on various aspects of the Nigerian economy, *The Economic Survey of Nigeria* (Lagos: National Economic Council, 1959).

66. The next chapter is devoted to a detailed analysis of two of the important agencies created during this period.

4. "Separate Economies": Regionalism and Development Institutions

1. Nigeria, *First National Development Plan, 1962–1968* (Lagos: Federal Ministry of Economic Development, 1962), 6–7.

2. Northern Nigeria, *Fourth Annual Report of the Northern Regional Production Development Board 1950–52* (Zaria: Government Printer, 1953), 25.

3. Ibid., 13. This comprised the development secretary as chairman, the director of agriculture, and four to eight unofficial members of the House of Assembly.

4. Ibid.

> The membership will be: (a) a chairman, (b) an official, and (c) a member of the Agricultural Department engaged on cocoa duties, all appointed by the Lieutenant-Governor; (d) Not less than four nor more than eight members appointed by the Lt. Governor of whom at least half shall be members of the Western House of Assembly; (e) Two members of the Oil Palm Representative Committee appointed by that Committee; and (f) Two members of the Cocoa Marketing Advisory Committee appointed by that Committee.

5. Western Nigeria, *Annual Report of the Western Region Production Development Board, 1951–52* (Ibadan: Public Relations Department, 1952), 2.

6. Ibid.

7. Ibid., 3.

8. Ibid.

9. Agbor District Papers, NAI, Agbor Dist. AG 639/B.

10. The new board acquired a modified title of the Western Region Production Development Board, the only change being the substitution of "regional" for "region."

11. *Annual Report of the Western Regional Production Development Board, 1955–56* (Ibadan: Public Relations Department, 1956), 6, NAI, AR 8/PC 7.

12. These were for the Lafia Fruit Canning Factory, Ibadan; Rubber Processing Factory, Ikpoba, Benin; Ijebu Farming Project, Apoje; and other agricultural schemes.

13. *Annual Report of the Western Regional Production Development Board, 1956* (Ibadan: Public Relations Department, 1957), NAI.

14. *Annual Report of the Western Region Production Development Board, 1951–52* (Ibadan: Public Relations Department, 1952) 1, NAI.

15. Oyo Provincial Papers, NAI, Oyo Prof 1/4670.

16. The interest of the Colonial Office was to find a substitute to linseed, which was in short supply in Britain in the late 1940s and early 1950s. *Annual Report of the Western Region Production Development Board, 1951–52*, 6.

17. Western Nigeria, *Western Region Production Development Board Annual Report, April 1952 to March 1953* (Ibadan: Public Relations Department, 1953).

18. Ibid.

19. Western Nigeria, *Annual Report of the Western Region Production Development Board for 1950–51* (Ibadan: Public Relations Department, 1951).

20. Western Nigeria, *Third Annual Report of the Western Region Production Development Board, 1951–52* (Ibadan: Public Relations Department, 1953).

21. Western Nigeria, *Western Region Production Development Board: New Policy for Partnership* (Ibadan: Public Relations Department, 1953), 7.

22. Ibid.

23. Western Nigeria, *Western Region Production Development Board: New Policy for Partnership Schemes* (Ibadan: Public Relations Department, 1953).

24. Correspondence from the Office of the Chairman, WRPDB, to all councils in the Western Region, April 28, 1956; encl. in NAI, Oyo Prof 1/4670.

25. Ibid.

26. For details see Oyo Provincial Papers, NAI, Oyo Prof 1/4670, 36.

27. Correspondence from the Office of the Chairman, WRPDB, to all councils in the Western Region, April 28, 1956, NAI, Oyo Prof 1/4670.

28. These include industries for biscuits, fiber, furniture making, glass, bricks and tiles, and garment manufacture. Interested individuals were advised to approach the Regional Finance Corporation for assistance.

29. These included industries for cement, textiles, tires and tubes, iron and steel, tanning, leather boots and shoes, paper, and matches.

30. This was a British company with over one hundred years' experience in water piping.

31. The use of plastic for piping was new to many countries in the 1950s, and the Western Region thought that it would be better than copper and steel pipes because plastics were more flexible and could withstand heavy use.

32. *Annual Report of the Western Regional Board, 1955–56*, NAI.

33. For details on these various projects, see Oyo Provincial Papers, NAI, Oyo Prof 1/4670.

34. The idea occurred in 1949, following the outbreak of swollen shoot disease that destroyed many cocoa farms in Ibadan. To help, the farmers were advised to shift to citrus, with a promise that the government would buy the fruits.

35. *Annual Report of the Western Regional Production Development Board, 1955–56*, 33, NAI.

36. *First Annual Report of the Eastern Regional Production Development Board, 1949–50* (Enugu: Government Printer, 1950), 2, NAE.

37. The first members listed here were not permanent throughout the period. Some were replaced in 1952 and 1954.

38. E. O. Eyo became the chairman, P. N. Motomby-Woleta the deputy chair, and the other members were J. E. Eyo, U. Ibeagi, J. H. E. Nwuke, M. E. Oji, S. E. Onukogu, and J. N. Wachuku, all prominent politicians.

39. *Statement of the Policy Proposed for the Future Marketing of Nigerian Oils, Oil Seeds, and Cotton*, Sessional Paper no. 18, 1948, NAI.

40. Ibid.

41. *First Annual Report of the Eastern Regional Production Development Board*, 3, NAE.

42. Ibid.

43. Ibid.

44. *Third Annual Report of the Eastern Regional Production Development Board, 1951–52*, 5, NAE.

45. The design and testing of the first prototypes of oil mills were done by the Engineering Department of the United Africa Company, which studied the problem of developing a small power unit to meet local demands and a design that could resist poor maintenance. The first oil mill was offered to the Nigerian government by the UAC as a gift. For details on the invention of the machine, see *Statistical and Economic Review*, March 7, 1951.

46. *First Annual Report of the Eastern Regional Production Development Board*, 4, NAE.

47. *Third Annual Report of the Eastern Regional Production Development Board*, part 1, 15, NAE.

48. Ibid., 17.

49. Ibid., 8.

50. *Third Annual Report of the Eastern Regional Production Development Board*, part 1, 8, NAE.

51. Ibid., 20.

52. *Eastern Regional Production Development Board: Report to the Premier* (Enugu: Government Printer, 1955), 6.

53. *First Annual Report of the Eastern Regional Production Development Board*, 4, NAE.

54. *Second Annual Report of the Eastern Regional Production Development Board, 1950–51*, 5, NAE.

55. *Third Annual Report of the Eastern Regional Production Development Board*, 24, NAE.

56. Ibid.

57. *First Annual Report of the Eastern Regional Production Development Board*, 6, NAE.

58. *Second Annual Report of the Eastern Regional Production Development Board, 1950–51*, 3, NAE.

59. *Third Annual Report of the Eastern Regional Production Development Board*, part 1, 25–26, NAE.

60. Ibid., 26.

61. *Eastern Regional Production Development Board: Report to the Premier*, 6.

62. Ibid., 30.

63. Ibid., 6.

64. *Third Annual Report of the Eastern Regional Production Development Board*, 31.

65. Ibid., 32.

66. *Eastern Regional Production Development Board: Report to the Premier*, 9.

67. *Third Annual Report of the Eastern Regional Production Development Board*, 6.

68. Ibid., 32.

69. *Eastern Regional Production Development Board: Report to the Premier.*

70. Lt-Governor Sir James Pyke-Nott, *Address to the Eastern House of Assembly, 12 February 1952,* NAE.

71. *Eastern Regional Production Development Board: Report to the Premier,* 7.

72. Ibid.

73. These were areas considered unattractive to private capital but where the facility of a mill would encourage more rice production.

74. The marginal areas were Bende, Itu, Calabar, and Obudu, where the quantity of rice hulled in tons were 17.9; 8.5; 0.9; and 46.4, respectively.

75. *Eastern Regional Production Development Board: Report to the Premier.*

76. This was a small craft, flat-bottomed, spoon-bow wooden boat, forty-six feet long "with a nine feet seven inches beam, three feet six inches molded depth and with an eight inches unloaded and twenty-one inches loaded draught." It had a tiller steering and powered with a fifteen-horse-power diesel engine. Ibid., 117.

77. *Eastern Regional Production Development Board: Report to the Premier,* 7.

78. *Third Annual Report of the Eastern Regional Production Development Board,* part 1, 58, NAE.

79. *Eastern Regional Production Development Board: Report to the Premier,* 11–12.

80. *Third Annual Report of the Eastern Regional Production Development Board,* 53, NAE.

81. *Eastern Regional Production Development Board: Report to the Premier,* 11.

82. Eastern Region, *Financial Report and Accounts for the Period 1st April, 1954 to 31st January, 1955* (Enugu: Government Printer, 1955), 29.

83. *First Annual Report of the Eastern Regional Development Board 1949–50,* 1, NAE.

84. Eastern Regional Development Board: Audit Report on the Accounts for the Year ended 31st March, 1950, NAE.

85. *First Annual Report of the Eastern Regional Development Board, 1949–50,* 2, NAE.

86. Ibid., 3.

87. *Minutes of the Sixth Meeting of the Eastern Region Development Board, 1950,* NAE, OG Prof 2/1/2955.

88. These were:

(i) The Local Authority, Enugu which received £12,000 to assist it in the laying out of a new residential estate in the town. Enugu's population was on the increase, with shortage of decent accommodations.

(ii) United Ex-Servicemen's Motor Repair and Training Workshop, Aba. This was a small business of mechanical repairs and general motor established by four ex-servicemen from their savings. It received £300 to improve its buildings and buy equipment.

(iii) The Calabar-Mamfe Road Area Planning Authority. Two loans were granted to supplement expenses on the establishment of the Bamenda-Calabar Cross-River Settlement Scheme. In the process of clearing 2,000 acres to establish palm plantations, so much timber became available and the Authority received £5,150 to establish a sawmill and furniture shop. Another loan of £1,200 was awarded to purchase agricultural lime processing equipment.

(iv) Industry and Service Agency, Buguma. This was an agricultural and trading business growing staple crops. A loan of £400 was granted to improve its farms and farm buildings.

(v) Mr. E. U. O. Moody of Abak. Moody was an ex-serviceman. With three other ex-servicemen he began a piggery in 1949. When his associates lost interest, he bought them out. He took a loan of £200 to complete new buildings and start a poultry.

(vi) Mr. A. A. Geh of Bamenda, a school headmaster and part-time farmer with a dairy herd of cows and a piggery. He received £200 to improve the dairy and repair his piggery buildings.

(vii) Mr. J. V. Clinton of Calabar. Clinton established a sea-fishing business. He had a loan of £600 to buy a launch, nets and other fishing equipment.

(viii) Iheneme and Sons Plantations, Aba. This was a partnership of small plantations at Aba and Port Harcourt, growing rubber, coffee, oil palms, kola and coconut and running a small poultry in addition. They received a loan of £500 to install new equipment.

(ix) Nwachuku Sawmills Limited, Port Harcourt. This was a partnership running a sawmill business in Port Harcourt, supplying timber on a contract basis to different government departments and private individuals. They obtained £1000 to purchase equipment and improve their buildings.

(x) Onitsha Town Native Authority. A loan of £5,000 was granted to survey the site of the Onitsha Market with a view to rebuilding it.

(xi) E. M. W. Epelle of Opobo. Epelle was a retired civil servant, inspired by the demonstrations of the Fisheries Section of the Commerce and Industries to start an off-shore sea-fishing business at Opobo. He obtained a loan of £400 to start the business.

(xii) Galega, Fon of Bali. The Fon of Bali, a member of the Eastern House of Assembly, was a farmer in the Bamenda Province of the Cameroons. He received a loan of £200 to improve his piggery. (Ibid.)

89. *Sixth Annual Report of the Eastern Regional Development Board, 1954–55* (Enugu: Government Printer, 1955).

90. Ibid., 2.

91. *Second Annual Report of the Eastern Regional Production Development Board, 1950–51*, 3, NAE.

92. *Third Annual Report of the Eastern Regional Production Development Board*, 6, NAE.

93. *Fourth Annual Report of the Eastern Regional Production Development Board, 1952–53*, 7, NAE.

94. *Minutes of the Sixth Meeting, Eastern Regional Development Board, 1950*, NAE, OG Prof 2/1/2955.

95. Ibid.

96. *Third Annual Report of the Eastern Regional Production Development Board*, 5.

97. Ibid., 4.

98. Deeds submitted by Land Officers for Registration, Eastern Regional Production Development Board, NAE, CSE 1/85/11188.

99. Ibid. The preference of the Eastern Regional Production Development Board was for land in areas where it had high value and cases that were certain that there would be no one to contest the ownership of the land with the applicant.

100. Deeds of Registration of Land, Eastern Regional Production Development Board 1951, NAE, CSE 1/85/11188.

101. See Section 43 (1) of the Nigeria Groundnut Marketing Ordinance, 1949, NAE.

102. Northern Nigeria, *Annual Report and Accounts of the Northern Regional Production Development Board, 1949–50* (Kaduna: Government Printer, 1950).

103. Northern Nigeria, *Northern Regional Production Development Scheme, Annual Report, 1950–55* (Zaria: Government Printer, 1955), 2.

104. Northern Nigeria, *Annual Report of the Northern Regional Production Development Board, 1949–50* (Kaduna: Government Printer, 1950).

105. Northern Nigeria, *Northern Regional Production Development Scheme, Report for 1951* (Zaria: Government Printer, 1952).

106. Northern Nigeria, *Northern Regional Production Development Scheme, Report for 1953* (Zaria: Government Printer, 1954).

107. Northern Nigeria, *Third Annual Report of the Northern Regional Production Development Board, 1951–52* (Kaduna: Government Printer, 1953), 10–11.

108. Northern Nigeria, *Third Annual Report of the Northern Regional Production Development Board, 1951–52.*

109. Northern Nigeria, *Annual Report and Accounts of the Northern Regional Production Development Board, 1950–51* (Kaduna: Government Printer, 1951), 11–12.

110. Northern Nigeria, *Fourth Annual Report of the Northern Regional Production Development Board, 1952–53* (Zaria: Gaskiya, 1953).

111. Northern Nigeria, *Annual Report and Accounts of the Northern Regional Production Development Board, 1950–51,* 12.

112. Northern Nigeria, *Fourth Annual Report of the Northern Regional Production Development Board, 1952–53.*

113. Ibid.

114. Oral interviews with author and O. Rasaki, Zaria, 1992, and O. Dantata, Zaria, 1992.

115. Northern Nigeria, *Fourth Annual Report of the Northern Regional Production Development Board, 1952–53.*

116. Ibid.

117. Northern Nigeria, *Northern Regional Production Development Scheme, Annual Report, 1950–55.*

118. Northern Nigeria, *Fourth Annual Report of the Northern Regional Production Development Scheme* (Zaria: Government Printer, 1953), 20.

119. This road connected an area to the south of the High Plateau, where benniseed, sunflower, and food crops were grown, with the High Plateau itself, where these crops were marketed.

120. *Third Annual Report of the Eastern Regional Production Development Board,* part 1, 19, NAE.

121. Ibid., 1.

122. Ibid., 12.
123. Ibid., 26.
124. Northern Nigeria, *Annual Report and Accounts of the Northern Regional Production Development Board, 1950–51*, 2.
125. *New Policy for Partnership Schemes*, 8, NAK.
126. Oyo Province Papers, NAI, Oyo Prof 1/4670.
127. *New Policy for Partnership Schemes, 1953*, NAK.

5. The Economy, 1960–1965

1. IBRD, *The Economic Development of Nigeria*, 3.
2. For important components of the GDP and other data, see, S. O. Olayide, *Economic Survey of Nigeria, 1960–75* (Ibadan: Aromolaran, 1976), 1–13.
3. M. Perham, *Native Administration in Nigeria* (London: Oxford Univ. Press, 1937), 28.
4. IBRD, *The Economic Development of Nigeria*, 11.
5. A fertile area of research is the historical analysis of the construction industry in Nigeria.
6. On the details of traditional and modern farming methods, see Helleiner, *Peasant Agriculture, Government, and Economic Growth in Nigeria*, 118–92.
7. A farmer could have about four plots, using each one in turn. He would work at a location for some years, usually three or four, abandon it for another location, and return when he thought that the land's fertility had been restored.
8. Space does not permit any elaborate discussion of the livestock industry. On information about livestock production in the first half of the twentieth century, see the important but always ignored Thomas Shaw and Gilbert Colville, *Report of Nigerian Livestock Mission* (London: HMSO, 1950).
9. For the various arguments in support of plantation agriculture, see V. D. Wickizer, "Plantation Crops in Tropical Agriculture," *Tropical Agriculture* (July 1958): 167–78.
10. H. A. Oluwasanmi, *Agriculture and Nigerian Economic Development* (Ibadan: Oxford Univ. Press, 1966), 191.
11. Ibid., 5.
12. Ibid.
13. Nigeria, *Trade Summary, December 1961* (Lagos: Government Printer, 1962).
14. See P. Kilby, *Industrialisation in an Open Economy, Nigeria 1945–1966* (Cambridge, U.K.: Cambridge Univ. Press, 1969).
15. For an account of the early history of petroleum exploration, see Peter O. Olayiwola, *Petroleum and Structural Change in a Developing Country: The Case of Nigeria* (New York: Praeger, 1987).
16. E. O. Akeredolu-Ale, "Private Foreign Investment," in *Nigeria: Economy and Society*, ed. G. Williams (London: Rex Collins, 1976), 106.
17. For details, see A. G. Adebayo, *Embattled Federalism: History of Revenue Allocation in Nigeria, 1946–1990* (New York: Peter Lang, 1993).
18. The Southern Cameroons was given 5 percent. See Jeremy Raisman and R. C. Trees, *Report of the Fiscal Commission* (London: HMSO, 1958), 13, para. 10.

19. Nigeria, *First National Development Plan, 1962–68* (Lagos: Federal Ministry of Economic Development, 1962), 3.

20. W. F. Stolper, *Planning without Facts: Lessons in Resource Allocation from Nigeria's Development* (Cambridge, Mass.: Harvard Univ. Press, 1966).

21. Nigeria, *First National Development Plan, 1962–68*, 4.

22. E. Dean, *Plan Implementation in Nigeria, 1962–1966* (Ibadan: Oxford Univ. Press, 1972), 208–9.

23. For their contribution to the GDP, see Olayide, *Economic Survey of Nigeria*, 1–13.

24. On these plans and official characterization of the economy during this period, see the Federal Republic of Nigeria, *Second National Development Plan, 1970–1974* (Lagos: Federal Ministry of Information, 1970); the Federal Republic of Nigeria, *Third National Development Plan, 1975–1980* (Lagos: Federal Ministry of Information, 1975); Federal Republic of Nigeria, *Fourth National Development Plan, 1980–1985* (Lagos: Federal Ministry of Information, 1980).

Postscript: Economy and Society after 1965

1. An appendix with a list of tables follows this chapter. Due to the focus of this book, an extensive narrative cannot be offered on the various tables. However, they do summarize the trends of the economy after 1960. A future project will be devoted solely to the post-independence economy.

2. Federal Republic of Nigeria, *Third National Development Plan, 1975–1980*, 5–15.

3. These included the local transport system, advertising, and bottling.

4. Thomas J. Biersteker, "Indigenisation in Nigeria: Renationalization or Denationalization?" in *Nigerian Foreign Policy: Alternative Perceptions and Projections*, ed. Timothy M. Shaw and Olajide Aluko (London: Macmillan, 1983), 125–46.

5. See Adebayo Olukoshi, ed., *The Politics of Structural Adjustment in Nigeria* (London: James Currey, 1993).

6. Falola and Akanmu Adebayo, *The Culture and Politics of Money Among the Yoruba* (New Brunswick, N.J.: Transaction, 2000), chapters 12 and 13.

7. Peter Lewis, "From Prebendalism to Predation: The Political Economy of Decline in Nigeria," *Journal of Modern African Studies* 34, no. 1 (1996): 79–103.

8. Olayide, *Economic Survey of Nigeria*, 13.

9. Michael Watts, ed., *State, Oil, and Agriculture in Nigeria* (Berkeley: Institute of International Studies, University of California, 1987).

10. For some important studies on declining agriculture, see Ade S. Olomola and A. C. Nwosu, eds., *Perspectives on Food Security in Nigeria* (Lagos: Nigerian Rural Sociological Association, 1993); and Eno Blankson Ikpe, *Food and Society in Nigeria: A History of Food Customs, Food Economy and Cultural Change, 1900–1989* (Stuttgart, Ger.: Steiner, 1994). For a contrary argument that agriculture did not perform as poorly as often presented, see Tom Forrest, *Politics and Economic Development in Nigeria*, chapter 9.

11. Nigeria, *Second National Development Plan, 1970–74: Programme of Post-War Reconstruction and Development* (Lagos: Federal Ministry of Information, 1970), 14.

12. J. C. Wells, *Agricultural Policy and Economic Growth in Nigeria* (Ibadan: Oxford Univ. Press, 1974), 53. For various calculations of farmers' incomes, see essays on rural poverty in O. Teriba, ed., *Poverty in Nigeria* (Ibadan: Nigerian Economic Society, 1975).

13. See results of two surveys in University of Ife, *Small-scale Industries in Mid-Western State, Kwara State, and Lagos State* (Ile-Ife: Industrial Research Unit, 1972); and University of Nigeria, *Small-scale Industries in South-Eastern and Benue-Plateau States* (Nsukka: Industrial Research Unit, 1973).

14. The most celebrated case is the protest by the Ogoni to protect their environment and obtain better shares of the oil revenues. This led to the execution of Ken Saro Wiwa, a writer, in 1994.

15. Kayode Soremekun, "Oil and the Democratic Imperative in Nigeria," in *Governance and Democratisation in Nigeria*, ed. Dele Olowu, Kayode Soremekun, and Adebayo Williams (Ibadan: Spectrum, 1995), 97–109.

16. Central Bank of Nigeria, *Annual Reports and Statements of Accounts* (Lagos: Central Bank, 1970–82).

17. See Edwin Madunagu, *Nigeria: The Economy and the People* (London: New Beacon, 1983); and Yusufu Bala Usman, *For the Liberation of Nigeria* (London: New Beacon, 1979).

18. Okwudiba Nnoli, ed., *Path to Nigerian Development* (Dakar, Senegal: Codesria Book Series, 1981); and Okwudiba Nnoli, ed., *Dead-end to Nigerian Development: An Investigation on the Social, Economic and Political Crisis in Nigeria* (Dakar: Senegal: Codesria Book Series, 1993).

19. William D. Graf, *The Nigerian State: Political Economy, State Class, and Political System in the Post-Colonial Era* (London: James Currey, 1988), 220–21.

20. Gunilla Andrae and Björn Beckman, *The Wheat Trap: Bread and Underdevelopment in Nigeria* (London: Zed, 1985).

Selected Bibliography

Primary Sources

Archives

Agbor District Papers. Nigerian National Archives. Ibadan, Nigeria (hereafter NAI).
Annual Reports of the Eastern Regional Development Board. 1949–1960. Nigerian National Archives. Enugu, Nigeria (hereafter NAE).
Annual Reports of the Eastern Regional Production Development Board. 1949–55. NAE.
Annual Report of the Nigerian Government Marketing Board. NAI.
Annual Reports of the Northern Regional Production Development Board. 1950–1960. Nigerian National Archives, Kaduna (hereafter NAK).
Annual Reports of the Western Regional Production Development Board. 1951–60. NAI.
Benin Provincial Papers. NAI. NAE.
Chief Secretary, Enugu, Papers. NAE.
Chief Secretary's Office Papers. NAI.
Church Missionary Society Papers. Birmingham University Library. London, England, and NAI.
Colonial Development Advisory Committee Papers. PRO.
The Colonial Empire. 1939–1947. PRO.
Commission on the Marketing of West African Cocoa Reports. PRO.
CSSP [Records of the Holy Ghost Fathers]. Public Records Office. London, England (hereafter PRO).
Department of Commerce and Industries Papers. NAI.
Oyo Provincial Papers. NAI.
Report on Cocoa Control in West Africa, 1939–43. London: HMSO, 1944. Colonial Office, London (hereafter COL).

Reports by the Conference on the Nigerian Constitution. 1953–1958. PRO.
Secretary to the Northern Province Papers. NAK.
Sessional Papers. 1945–1948. NAI.
Sessional Papers. 1948. NAE.
Walker, Gilbert. *Traffic and Transport in Nigeria*. Colonial Research Studies Series, no. 27. London: HMSO, 1959. PRO.
Zaria Province Papers. NAK.

Newspapers and Periodicals

African Echo, Lagos. 1949.
Daily Times, Lagos. 1948–60.
Digest of Statistics. 1955–80.
Napetcor. 1975–85.
Nigeria Trade Journal. 1955–65.
Nigeria Year Book. 1953–60.
Nigerian Mercantile Guardian, Lagos. 1950–51.
Nigerian Statesman. 1950–60.
West Africa, London. 1940–85.
West African Pilot. 1945–60.

Nigerian Official Publications: Federal and Regional Governments

Adebo Report. *First Report of the Wages and Salaries Review Commission*. Lagos: Federal Government of Nigeria, 1970.
Central Bank of Nigeria. *Twenty Years of Banking in Nigeria*. Lagos: Central Bank, 1979.
———. Annual Reports and Statements of Accounts. Lagos: Central Bank, 1970–76.
Federal Ministry of Finance. *Federal Government Annual Estimates*. Lagos: Federal Government Printer, 1985.
Federal Office of Statistics. *National Accounts of Nigeria. 1958–1976*. Lagos: Federal Office of Statistics, 1958–77.
———. *National Accounts of Nigeria*. Lagos: Federal Office of Statistics, 1978.
Nigeria. *Administrative and Financial Procedure under the New Constitution: Financial Relations between the Government of Nigeria and the Native Administration*. Lagos: Government Printer, 1947.
———. *Annual Abstracts of Statistics*. Lagos: Government Printer, 1961–65.
———. *The Attack on Inflation: Government Views on the First Report of the Anti-Inflation Task Force, 1975*. Lagos: Federal Ministry of Information, 1975.
———. *Colonial Annual Reports*. Lagos: Government Printer, 1947; 1954.
———. *The Constitution of the National Council of Nigeria and the Cameroons*. Lagos: National Council of Nigeria and the Cameroons (NCNC), 1945.
———. *The First and Second Reports of the Wages and Salaries Review Commission, 1970–71*. Lagos: Federal Ministry of Information, 1971.
———. *First National Development Plan, 1962–1968*. Lagos: Federal Ministry of Economic Development, 1962.

———. *Fourth National Development Plan 1980–1985.* Lagos: Federal Ministry of Information, 1980.

———. *National Conference on Rehabilitation and Reconstruction, 1970.* Ibadan: NISER, 1971.

———. *Nigeria: Ten Year Educational Plan, 1942.* Lagos: Government Printer, 1942.

———. *The Nigerian Enterprises Promotion Decrees, 1972 and 1976.* Lagos: Federal Ministry of Information, 1976.

———. *Nigerian Handbook of Commerce and Industry.* Lagos: Government Printer, 1960.

———. *Proceedings of the General Conference on Review of the Constitution, January 1950.* Lagos: Government Printer, 1950.

———. *Report of the Accountant-General, 1950.* Lagos: Government Printer, 1951.

———. *Report of the Fiscal Commission on Revenue Allocation.* Lagos: Government Printer, 1951.

———. *Report of the Fiscal Commission,* Cmd 481. London: HMSO, 1957.

———. *Report of the Industrial Enterprises Panel, 1976.* Lagos: Federal Ministry of Information, 1976.

———. *Report of the Nigerian Railway Corporation Tribunal of Inquiry Appointed under the Tribunal of Inquiry Decree, 1966, to Inquire into the Affairs of the Nigerian Railway Corporation.* Lagos: Government Printer, 1967.

———. *The Role of the Federal Government in Promoting Industrial Development in Nigeria.* Sessional Paper No. 3 of 1958. Lagos: Government Printer, 1958.

———. *Second National Development Plan 1970–74: Programme of Post-War Reconstruction and Development.* Lagos: Federal Ministry of Information, 1970.

———. *Setting Up an Industrial Enterprise in Nigeria.* Lagos: Federal Department of Commerce and Industries, 1955.

———. *Statement of Policy for the Niger and Benue Rivers.* Sessional Paper No. 3, 1959. Lagos: Government Printer, 1959.

———. *Third National Development Plan, 1975–1980.* Vol 1. Lagos: Federal Ministry of Information, 1975.

———. *Trade Summary, December 1961.* Lagos: Government Printer, 1962.

Nigerian Economic Society. *The Nigerian Economy under Military Rule.* Ibadan: National Economic Society, 1980.

Northern Nigeria. *Annual Report of the Northern Regional Production Development Board.* 1949–50. Kaduna: Government Printer, 1950.

———. *Fourth Annual Report of the Northern Regional Production Development Board.* 1950–52. Zaria: Government Printer, 1953.

———. *Northern Regional Marketing Board, Annual Report.* 1959–60. Zaria: Government Printer, 1961.

———. *Northern Regional Production Development Scheme, Annual Report.* 1950–55. Zaria: Government Printer, 1955.

———. *Northern Regional Production Development Scheme, Report for 1951.* Zaria: Government Printer, 1952.

———. *Northern Regional Production Development Scheme, Report for 1953.* Zaria: Government Printer, 1954.

———. *Third Annual Report of the Northern Regional Production Development Board, 1951–52.* Kaduna: Government Printer, 1953.

Northern Regional Government. *Report on the Kano Disturbances: 16th, 17th, and 19th May 1953.* Lagos: Government Printer, 1953.

Western Nigeria. *Annual Report of the Western Region Production Development Board, 1951–52.* Ibadan: Public Relations Department, 1952.

———. *Third Annual Report of the Western Region Production Development Board, 1951–52.* Ibadan: Public Relations Department, 1953.

———. *Western Region Production Development Board Annual Report April 1952 to March 1953.* Ibadan: Public Relations Department, 1953.

———. *Western Region Production Development Board: New Policy for Partnership Schemes.* Ibadan: Public Relations Department, 1953.

Oral Interviews (dates refer to the final interview session in a series)

Adepoju, S. F. (bookshop manager). Ile-Ife, August 1, 1992.
Adeyemi, O. (contractor). Zaria, July 15, 1992.
Agbakoba, O. L. (contractor). Epe, August 3, 1991.
Dantata, O. (trader). Zaria, August 23, 1992.
Elere, A. E. (Native Administration staff). December 12, 1992.
Ichaver, M. (ex-serviceman). July 8, 1992.
Johnson, K. (civil servant). Uyo, August 13, 1991.
Labinjo, M. (civil servant). Kaduna, August 14, 1992.
Olabiyi, A. (local historian). Ikare, January 12, 1993.
Rasaki, O. (entrepreneur). Zaria, August 29, 1992.
Tarr, O. (teacher). Zaria, July 23, 1991.
Zaccheus, S. (community leader). August 14, 1992.

United Nations Documents

United Nations. *Community Development and National Development.* New York: United Nations, 1963.

———. *Economic Development and Planning in Asia and the Far East.* New York: United Nations, 1961.

———. *Economic Development of Under-developed Countries.* New York: United Nations, 1949–50.

———. *Economic Survey of Africa since 1950.* New York: United Nations, 1959.

———. *Enlargement of the Exchange Economy of Tropical Africa.* New York: United Nations, 1954.

———. *Measures for the Economic Development of Under-developed Countries.* New York: United Nations, 1951.

———. *Measures for the Economic Development of Under-developed Countries.* New York: United Nations, 1954.

———. *Report of the First National Conference on International Economic and Social Development.* New York: United Nations, 1952.

———. *Review of Economic Conditions in Africa.* New York: United Nations, 1951.

———. *Technical Assistance Administration: Formulation and Economic Appraisal of Development Projects.* New York: United Nations, 1951.
———. *World Economic Report for 1948.* New York: United Nations, 1949.
United States Bureau of Foreign Commerce. *Investments in Nigeria: Basic Information for U.S. Businessmen.* Washington, D.C.: U.S. Government Printing Office, 1957.

SECONDARY SOURCES

Abba, A., et al. *The Nigerian Economic Crisis: Causes and Solutions.* Zaria: Academic Staff Union of Universities, 1988.
Abbot, G. C. "British Colonial Aid Policy during the 1930s." *Canadian Journal of History* 5 (1970): 73–89.
———. "A Re-examination of the 1929 Colonial Development Act." *Economic History Review* 24 (1971): 68–81.
Abdullahi, Y. A. "Comments on Press Briefing by Minister of Agriculture." *New Nigerian,* February 18, 1985.
———. "The State and Agrarian Crisis: Rhetoric and Substance of Nigerian Agricultural Development Policy." Conference paper presented at a workshop on the state of the Nigerian economy. Kaduna, Nigeria. October 1983.
Abique, M. *The Development of African Economic Underdevelopment.* Ikeja: Afrografika, 1977.
Abernethy, David B. *The Political Dilemma of Popular Education: An African Case.* Stanford, Calif.: Stanford Univ. Press, 1969.
Aboyade, O. *Foundations of an African Economy: A Study of Investment and Growth in Nigeria.* New York: Praeger, 1972.
———. *Issues in the Development of Tropical Africa.* Ibadan: Ibadan Univ. Press, 1976.
Abubakar, S. *The Lamibe of Fombina: A Political History of Adamawa, 1809–1901.* Zaria: Ahmadu Bello Univ. Press, 1977.
Achebe, C., et. al. *Beyond Hunger in Africa.* Nairobi, Kenya: Heinemann and James Currey, 1990.
Adamolekun, Ladipo. *Public Administration: A Nigerian and Comparative Perspective.* London: Longman, 1982.
Adebayo, A. G. *Embattled Federalism: History of Revenue Allocation in Nigeria, 1946–1990.* New York: Peter Lang, 1993.
Adeboye, T. O. "A General Survey of the Economy." In *Nigeria since Independence.* Vol. 2. *The Economy,* ed. M. O. Kayode and Y. B. Usman, 4–47. Ibadan: Heinemann, 1989.
Adedeji, A. "Economic Planning in Theory and Practice." *Nigerian Journal of Economic and Social Studies* 4, no. 1 (1962): 7–15.
———, ed. *The Indigenization of African Economies.* London: Hutchinson Univ. Library, 1981.
Adejugbe, Michael. "The Myths and Realities of Nigeria's Business Indigenization." *Development and Change* 15 (1984): 577–92.
Adejumobi, S., and A. Momoh, eds. *The Political Economy of Nigeria under Military Rule: 1984–1993.* Harare, Zimbabwe: HAPES, 1995.
Adekanye, J. *Nigeria in Search of a Stable Civil-Military Rule, 1966–79.* Boulder, Colo.: Westview, 1981.

Adeleye, R. A. *Power and Diplomacy in Northern Nigeria: The Sokoto Caliphate and Its Enemies, 1804–1906.* London: Longman, 1971.
Adelman, I. "On the State of Development Economics." *Journal of Development Economics* 1, no. 1 (1974): 3–5.
Adeniji, Kola. "Government Regulation of Business in Nigeria: A Case Study of Regulatory Administration in a Mixed Economy." *Quarterly Journal of Administration* (July 1978): 409–29.
Adeogun, A. A. "Strikes, the Law and the Institutionalization of Labour Protest in Nigeria." *Indian Journal of Industrial Relations* 16, no. 1 (1980): 1–23.
Adewoye, O. *The Legal Profession in Nigeria, 1865–1962.* Lagos: Longman, 1977.
Ady, P. "Britain and Overseas Development." In *The British Economy, 1945–50,* ed. G. D. N. Worswick and P. H. Ady, 547–69. Oxford, U.K.: Clarendon, 1952.
Afigbo, A. E. "Herbert Richmond Palmer and Indirect Rule in Eastern Nigeria, 1915–1928." *Journal of the Historical Society of Nigeria* 3 (1965): 295–312.
———. *The Warrant Chiefs: Indirect Rule in Southeastern Nigeria, 1891–1929.* London: Longman, 1972.
Aina, S. "Bureaucratic Corruption in Nigeria: The Continuing Search for Causes and Cures." *International Review of Administrative Science* 1 (1982): 70–76.
Ajaegbu, Hyacinth. *Urban and Rural Development in Nigeria.* London: Heinemann, 1976.
Ajayi, J. F. Ade. *Christian Missions in Nigeria 1841–1871: The Making of an Educated Elite.* London: Longman, 1965.
———, and Bashir Ikara, eds. *Evolution of Political Culture in Nigeria: Proceedings of a National Seminar Organized by the Kaduna State Council for the Arts and Culture.* Ibadan: Ibadan Univ. Press, 1985.
Ake, C. *A Political Economy of Africa.* London: Longman, 1981.
———. *Social Science as Imperialism: A Theory of Political Development.* Ibadan: Ibadan Univ. Press, 1979.
———, ed. *Political Economy of Nigeria.* Lagos: Longman, 1985.
Akeredolu-Ale, E. O. *The Underdevelopment of Indigenous Entrepreneurship in Nigeria.* Ibadan: Ibadan Univ. Press, 1975.
Akingbade, Tunde. *Nigeria: On the Trail of the Environment.* Lagos: Desktop Publishing, 1991.
Akinjogbin, I. A., and S. O. Osoba, eds. *Topics on Nigerian Economic and Social History.* Ile-Ife: Univ. of Ife Press, 1980.
Akinyele, I. B. *The Outlines of Ibadan History.* Lagos: self-published, 1946.
Alder, J. H. "The Economic Development of Nigeria; Comment." *Journal of Political Economy* 64, no. 5 (1956): 435–41.
Allan, Keith. "Nation, Tribalism and National Language." *Cahiers d'Études Africaines* 18, no. 3 (1978): 397–415.
Aluko, S. A. *Federal Election Crisis 1964: An Analysis.* Onitsha: Etudo, 1965.
———. "How Many Nigerians?" *Journal of Modern African Studies* 3, no. 3 (1965): 371–92.
Amin, Samir. *Imperialism and Unequal Development.* New York: Monthly Review, 1977.
———. *Neo-colonialism in West Africa.* London: Penguin, 1973.
Anababa, W. *The Trade Union Movement in Nigeria.* London: C. Hurst, 1969.
Andrae Gunilla, and Björn Beckman. *The Wheat Trap: Bread and Underdevelopment in Nigeria.* London: Zed, 1986.

Anene, J. C. *The International Boundaries of Nigeria, 1885–1960*. London: Longman, 1970.
———. *Southern Nigeria in Transition, 1884–1906: Theory and Practice in a Colonial Dependency*. Cambridge, U.K.: Cambridge Univ. Press, 1965.
Anglin, Douglas G. "Brinkmanship in Nigeria." *International Journal* 30, no. 2 (1965): 173–88.
Anifowose, R. *Violence and Politics in Nigeria: The Tiv and Yoruba Experience*. New York: Nok, 1982.
Anjorin, A. O. "The Background to the Amalgamation of Nigeria in 1914." ODU: *A Journal of African Studies* 3, no. 2 (1967): 72–86.
Anyawu, K. C. "Bases of Political Instability in Nigeria." *Journal of Black Studies* 13 (1982): 101–17.
Apter, David E. *The Politics of Modernization*. Chicago: Univ. of Chicago Press, 1965.
Arikpo, O. *The Development of Modern Nigeria*. Baltimore, Md.: Penguin, 1967.
Atanda, J. A. "The Iseyin-Okeiho Rising of 1916: An Example of Socio-political Conflict in Colonial Africa." *Journal of the Historical Society of Nigeria* 4, no. 4 (June 1969): 497–514.
———. *The New Oyo Empire: Indirect Rule and Change in Western Nigeria, 1894–1934*. London: Longman, 1979.
Awa, Eme O. *Federal Government in Nigeria*. Los Angeles: Univ. of California Press, 1964.
Awolowo, O. *Awo: The Autobiography of Chief Obafemi Awolowo*. Cambridge, U.K.: Cambridge Univ. Press, 1960.
———. *Path to Nigerian Freedom*. London: Faber and Faber, 1947.
———. *The People's Republic*. Ibadan: Oxford Univ. Press, 1968.
———. *The Strategy and Tactics of the People's Republic of Nigeria*. London: Macmillan, 1970.
———. *Thoughts on the Nigerian Constitution*. Ibadan: Oxford Univ. Press, 1966.
Ayandele, E. A. *The Educated Elite in Nigerian Society*. Ibadan: Ibadan Univ. Press, 1974.
———. *The Missionary Impact on Modern Nigeria, 1842–1914: A Political and Social Analysis*. London: Longman, 1966.
Ayida, A. A. *Economic Survey of Nigeria, 1960–1975*. Ibadan: Ibadan Univ. Press, 1976.
Ayo, E. J. *Development Planning in Nigeria*. Ibadan: Ibadan Univ. Press, 1988.
Ayoade, J. A. A. "Federalism and Wage Politics in Nigeria." *Journal of Commonwealth and Comparative Politics* 13, no. 3 (1986): 282–89.
Ayorinde, J. A. *History of Cocoa in Nigeria*. Ibadan: Ministry of Agriculture and Natural Resources, 1957.
Azikiwe, N. *The Economic Reconstruction of Nigeria*. Lagos: African Book, 1948.
———. "Essentials for Nigerian Survival." *Foreign Affairs* 43, no. 3 (1965): 447–61.
———. *My Odyssey : An Autobiography*. London: C. Hurst, 1970.
———. *Renascent Africa*. Reprint. London: Cass, 1937.
———. *Political Blueprint for Nigeria*. Lagos: African Book, 1945.
———. *Zik: A Selection of the Speeches of Dr. Nnamdi Azikiwe*. London: Cambridge Univ. Press, 1961.
Bach, Daniel C. "Managing a Plural Society: The Boomerang Effects of Nigerian Federalism." *Journal of Commonwealth and Comparative Politics* 27, no. 2 (1989): 218–45.
Baier, Stephen. *An Economic History of Central Niger*. Oxford, U.K.: Clarendon, 1980.
Bailey, A. E. "Development Plans in Nigeria: Rapid Advance with Government Aid." *Electrical Review* 8 (1960): 53–55.

———. "Report on the Electricity Corporation of Nigeria." *Electrical Review* 1 (1960): 53–55.
Baker, Pauline H. "The Politics of Nigerian Military Rule." *African Report* (Feb.1971): 18–21.
Balabkins, Nicholas. *Indigenization and Economic Development: The Nigerian Experience*. Greenwich, Conn.: Jai, 1982.
Baldwin, K. D. S. *The Niger Agricultural Project: An Experiment in African Development*. Oxford, U.K.: Basil Blackwell, 1957.
Balewa, Sir Abubakar Tafawa. *Nigeria Speaks: Speeches Made between 1957 and 1964*. Ed. Sam Epelle. Lagos: Univ. of Lagos Press, 1966.
Balogun, J. O. *The Existence of Virtual Monopoly in the British Colony of Nigeria*. Lagos: self-published, 1944.
Balogun, Ola. *The Tragic Years: Nigeria in Crisis 1966–1970*. Benin City: Ethiope, 1973.
Bamisaiye, A. "Ethnic Politics as an Instrument of Unequal Socio-Economic Development in Nigeria's First Republic." *African Notes* 6, no. 2 (1971): 94–106.
Baran, P. A. *The Political Economy of Growth*. New York: Monthly Review, 1976.
Barbour, Kenneth M. *Planning for Nigeria*. Ibadan; Ibadan Univ. Press, 1972.
Bates, R. H. *Beyond the Miracle of the Market: The Political Economy of Agrarian Development in Kenya*. Cambridge, U.K.: Cambridge Univ. Press, 1989.
Batten, T. R. *Problems of African Development*. Part 1: *Land and Labour*. Oxford, U.K.: Oxford Univ. Press, 1954.
Bauer, P. T. *Dissent on Development*. London: Weidenfeld and Nicolson, 1971.
———. "The Economic Development of Nigeria." *Journal of Political Economy* 63, no. 5 (1955): 398–411.
———. *West African Trade: A Study of Competition, Oligopoly, and Monopoly in a Changing Economy*. Cambridge, U.K.: Cambridge Univ. Press, 1954.
Beer, C. E. F. *The Politics of Peasant Groups in Western Nigeria*. Ibadan: Ibadan Univ. Press, 1976.
Belasco, Bernard. *The Entrepreneur as Culture Hero: Preadaptations for Nigerian Development*. New York: Praeger, 1980.
Bello, Alhaji Sir Ahmadu. *My Life: The Autobiography of Alhaji Sir Ahmadu Bello, Sardauna of Sokoto*. Cambridge, U.K.: Cambridge Univ. Press, 1962.
Bello, Sule. "Some Remarks on the Development of Raw Material Production in the Colony of Kano, c. 1912–1919." In *Studies in the History of Kano*, ed. B. M. Bakindo, 171–85. Ibadan: Heinemann, 1983.
Benham, F. *Economic Aid to Underdeveloped Countries*. London: Oxford Univ. Press, 1964.
Bernstein, H., ed. *Underdevelopment and Development: The Third World Today*. Harmondsworth, U. K.: Penguin, 1973.
Berry, S. F. *Cocoa, Custom and Socio-Economic Change in Rural Western Nigeria*. Oxford, U.K.: Oxford Univ. Press, 1975.
Bienen, H. *Political Conflict and Economic Change in Nigeria*. London: Frank Cass, 1985.
———, and V. P. Diejomah, eds. *The Political Economy of Income Distribution in Nigeria*. New York: Holmes and Meier, 1981.
Biersteker, Thomas J. "Indigenisation in Nigeria: Renationalization or Denationalization?" In *Nigerian Foreign Policy: Alternative Perceptions and Projections*, ed. Timothy M. Shaw and Olajide Aluko, 125–46. London: Macmillan, 1983.

———. *Multinationals, the State, and Control of the Nigerian Economy.* Princeton, N.J.: Princeton Univ. Press, 1987.

Blitz, L. Franklin. *The Politics and Administration of Nigerian Government.* London: Sweet and Maxwell, 1965.

Blitzer, C. R., P. B. Clark, and L. Taylor, eds. *Economy-wide Models and Development Planning.* Washington, D.C.: World Bank, 1975.

Bonat, Z. A. "Agriculture." In *Nigeria since Independence,* ed. Kayode and Usman, 48–85.

Bourdillon, B. H. *Economic Development of Nigeria.* Lagos: Government Printer, 1939.

Bower, P. A. *The Balance of Payments of Nigeria in 1936.* Oxford, U.K.: Basil Blackwell, 1949.

Bretton, Henry L. *Power and Stability in Nigeria.* New York: Praeger, 1962.

Brown, Charles V. *Government and Banking in Western Nigeria.* Ibadan: Oxford Univ. Press, 1964.

Buchanan M., and J. C. Pugh. *Land and People in Nigeria.* London: Univ. of London Press, 1955.

Burns, Sir Allan. *History of Nigeria.* 5th ed. London: Allen and Unwin, 1955.

Caine, Sir Sidney. "Colonial Development: A British Contribution to World Progress." *Progress* 46, no. 256 (1957): 82.

Cairncross, A. "The Postwar Years, 1945–77." In *Africa Today,* ed. C. G. Haines, 420–30. Baltimore, Md.: Johns Hopkins Univ. Press, 1955.

Callaway, Helen. *Gender, Culture, and Empire: European Women in Colonial Nigeria.* London: Macmillan, 1987.

Campbell, J. G. *Observations on Some Topics in Nigeria during the Administration of His Excellency Sir Frederick Lugard G.C.M.G.* Lagos: self-published, 1918.

Carland, J. M. *The Colonial Office and Nigeria, 1898–1914.* Stanford, Calif.: Hoover Institute Press, 1985.

Carney, D. E. *Government and Economy in British West Africa.* New York: Bookman, 1961.

Carr, E. H. *The Soviet Impact on the Western World.* London: Macmillan, 1946.

Cary, Joyce. *Britain and West Africa.* London: Longman, 1946.

Cèsaire, A. *Discourse on Colonialism.* New York: Monthly Review, 1972.

Charle, E. G. "An Appraisal of British Imperial Policy with Respect to the Extraction of Mineral Resources in Nigeria." *Nigerian Journal of Economic and Social Studies* 6, no. 1 (1964): 13–24.

Chukunta, N. K. Onuoha. "Education and National Integration in Africa: A Case Study of Nigeria." *African Studies Review* 21, no. 2 (1978): 67–75.

Chukwuemeka, N. *Industrialization of Nigeria.* New York: William-Fredrick, 1952.

Clapperton, H. *Journal of a Second Expedition into the Interior of Africa.* London: Murray, 1829.

Clark, Trevor. *A Right Honourable Gentleman: The Life and Times of Alhaji Tafawa Balewa.* Zaria: Hudahuda, 1991.

Clifford, Sir Hugh. *Address to the Nigerian Council, 29 December 1920.* Lagos: Government Printer, 1920.

Cohen, R. *Labour and Politics in Nigeria, 1945–71.* London: Heinemann, 1974.

———. "Michael Imoudu and the Nigerian Labour Movement." *Race and Class* 3 (Spring 1977): 345–62.

Cohon, J. L. *Multiobjective Programming and Planning.* New York: Academic, 1978.

Cole, P. D. *Modern and Traditional Elites in the Politics of Lagos.* Cambridge, U.K.: Cambridge Univ. Press, 1975.
Coleman, J. S. *Nigeria: Background to Nationalism.* Berkeley: Univ. of California Press, 1963.
Collins, H. "Economic Problems in British West Africa." In *The New West Africa,* ed. B. Davidson and A. Ademola, 79–94. London: George Allen and Unwin, 1963.
Collins, Paul. "The Political Economy of Indigenization: The Case of the Nigerian Enterprises Promotion Decree." *African Review* 4 (1976): 491–503.
Cook, A. A. *British Enterprise in Nigeria.* Philadelphia: Univ. of Pennsylvania Press, 1943.
Coupland, R. *The Empire in These Days.* London: Macmillan, 1935.
Crowder, M. *Revolt in Bussa.* London: Faber and Faber, 1973.
———. *West Africa under Colonial Rule.* London: Hutchinson, 1968.
———, and O. Ikime, eds. *West African Chiefs: Their Changing Status under Colonial Rule and Independence.* Ile-Ife: Univ. of Ife Press, 1970.
Crowe, S. E. *The Berlin West African Conference, 1884–85.* Westport, Conn.: Negro Universities Press, 1970.
Cudjoe, R. "Some Reminiscences of a Senior Interpreter." *Nigeria Field,* no. 6 (1953): 158–60.
Curtin, P. D. *The Image of Africa.* Madison: Univ. of Wisconsin Press, 1965.
Davidson, B. *The Black Man's Burden: Africa and the Curse of the Nation-State.* London: James Currey, 1992.
Dean, E. R. *Plan Implementation in Nigeria, 1962–1966.* Ibadan: Oxford Univ. Press, 1972.
———. "Planning Nigeria's Development: A Study of Alternative Techniques." Ibadan, NISER Research Project no. 3 (1965): 18–28.
Diaku, I. "A Capital Surplus Illusion: The Nigerian Case Revisited." *Nigerian Journal of Economic and Social Studies* 14, no. 1 (1972): 47–62.
Diamond, Larry. *Class, Ethnicity, and Democracy in Nigeria: The Failure of the First Republic.* Syracuse, N.Y.: Syracuse Univ. Press, 1988.
Diamond, L., J. L. Linz, and S. M. Lipset, eds. *Democracy in Developing Countries: Africa.* Boulder, Colo.: Lynne Rienner, 1988.
Dike, K. O. *Trade and Politics in the Niger Delta.* London: Oxford Univ. Press, 1956.
Dosser, D. "The Formation of Development Plans in British Colonies." *Economic Journal* 69, no. 274 (1959): 255–66.
DuBois, W. E. B. *The World and Africa: An Enquiry into the Part which Africa Has Played in World History.* New York: International, 1965.
Dudley, Billy, J. *Instability and Political Order: Politics and Crisis in Nigeria.* Ibadan: Ibadan Univ. Press, 1973.
———. *An Introduction to Nigerian Government and Politics.* Bloomington: Indiana Univ. Press, 1982.
———. *Parties and Politics in Northern Nigeria.* London: Frank Cass, 1968.
Economic Commission for Africa. *Comprehensive Planning in Africa.* Addis Ababa, Ethiopia: Economic Commission for Africa (ECA), 1962.
Edokpayi, S. I. "The Impact of the Oil Industry on the Economy of Nigeria." *Nigerian Journal of Economic and Social Studies* 4, no. 1 (1962): 77–83.
Edozien, G. C. "The Impact of Direct Foreign Investment on an Underdeveloped Economy: the Nigerian Case, 1924–64." Ph.D. diss., University of Michigan, 1966.

Eicher, C. K., and C. Liedholm, eds. *Growth and Development of the Nigerian Economy.* East Lansing: Michigan State Univ. Press, 1970.

Ejimofor, O. E. *British Colonial Objectives and Policies in Nigeria: The Roots of Conflict.* Onitsha: Africana-Fep, 1987.

Ekanem, I. I. *The 1963 Census: A Critical Appraisal.* Benin: Ethiope, 1973.

Ekejiuba, F. I. "Omu Okwei, The Merchant Queen of Osomari: A Biographical Sketch." *Journal of the Historical Society of Nigeria* 3 (1967): 633–46.

Ekundare, R. O. *An Economic History of Nigeria, 1860–1960.* London: Methuen, 1973.

Enahoro, Chief Anthony. *Fugitive Offender: The Story of a Political Prisoner.* London: Cassell, 1965.

Ergas, Z., ed. *The African State in Transition.* London: Macmillan, 1987.

Ezera, Kalu. *Constitutional Developments in Nigeria.* Rev. ed. Cambridge, U.K.: Cambridge Univ. Press, 1960.

Fajana, A. *Education in Nigeria, 1842–1939: An Historical Analysis.* Lagos: Longman, 1978.

Falola, Toyin, ed. *Britain and Nigeria: Exploitation or Development?.* London: Zed, 1987.

———. "Cassava Starch for Export in Nigeria during the Second World War." *Journal of African Economic History*, no.18 (1988): 73–98.

———. *Development Planning and Decolonization in Nigeria.* Gainesville: Univ. Press of Florida, 1996.

———. *The History of Nigeria.* Westport, Conn.: Greenwood, 1999.

———. "The Lebanese in West Africa." In *People and Empire in Africa*, ed. J. F. Ade Ajayi and J. D. Y. Peel, 121–41. London: Longman, 1992.

———. "Lebanese Traders in Colonial Southwestern Nigeria." *African Affairs* 89 (1990): 523–53.

———. *Nationalism and African Intellectuals.* Rochester, N.Y.: Rochester Univ. Press, 2001.

———. "'An Ounce Is Good Enough': The Gold Industry in Colonial Southwestern Nigeria." *African Economic History*, no. 20 (1992): 27–50.

———. "'Salt Is Gold': The Management of Salt Scarcity in Nigeria during World War II." *Canadian Journal of African Studies* 24, no. 3 (1992): 412–36.

———, and Ann O'Hear, eds. *Studies in the Nineteenth-Century Economic History of Nigeria.* Madison: University of Wisconsin African Studies Program, 1988.

———, and Paul Lovejoy, eds. *Pawnship in Africa: Debt Bondage in Historical Perspective.* Boulder, Colo.: Westview, 1994.

———, et al., eds. *Obafemi Awolowo: The End of an Era?* Ile-Ife: Obafemi Awolowo Univ. Press, 1970.

Fapohunda, O. J. *The Informal Sector of Lagos: An Inquiry into Urban Poverty and Employment.* Ibadan: University Press Ltd., 1985.

Feinstein, Alan. *African Revolutionary: The Life and Times of Nigeria's Aminu Kano.* Boulder, Colo.: Lynne Rienner, 1987.

Fieldhouse, D. K. "The Economic Exploitation of Africa: Some British and French Comparisons." In *France and Britain in Africa*, ed. P. Gifford and William R. Louis, 593–662. New Haven, Conn.: Yale Univ. Press, 1971.

Fika, A. M. *The Kano Civil War and British Overule, 1882–1940.* Ibadan: Oxford Univ. Press, 1978.

Filani, M. "Nigeria: The Need to Modify Centre-Down Development Planning." In *Development from Above or Below?* ed. W. B. Stohr and D. R. Taylor, 36–47. New York: Wiley, 1981.
Flint, J. E. *Sir John Goldie and the Making of Nigeria*. London: Oxford Univ. Press, 1960.
Folarin, A. *A Short Historical Review of the Life of the Egbas from 1829 to 1930*. Abeokuta: self-published, 1931.
Forrest, Tom. *The Advance of African Capital: The Growth of Nigerian Private Enterprise*. Charlottesville: Univ. Press of Virginia, 1994.
———. *Politics and Economic Development in Nigeria*. Boulder, Colo.: Westview, 1995.
Fortes, M. "The Impact of the War on British West Africa." *International Affairs* 31, no. 2 (1945): 218.
Frank, A. G. *Capitalism and Underdevelopment in Latin America*. New York: Monthly Review, 1967.
Frankel, H. *Capital Investment in Africa*. London: Oxford Univ. Press, 1938.
Freund, B. *Capital and Labour in the Nigerian Tin Mines*. London: Longman, 1981.
Gailey, H. A. *The Road to Aba: A Study of British Administrative Policy in Eastern Nigeria*. London: Longman, 1973.
Galbraith, J. K. *Economic Development in Perspective*. Cambridge, Mass.: Harvard Univ. Press, 1964.
Galleti R., K. Baldwin, and I. Dina. *Nigerian Cocoa Farmers*. Oxford: Oxford Univ. Press, 1956.
Gavin, R. J., and Wale Oyemakinde. "Economic Development in Nigeria since 1800." In *Groundwork of Nigerian History*, ed. Ikime Obaro, 482–517. Ibadan: Heinemann, 1980.
Ghai, D. P., ed. *Economic Independence in Africa*. Nairobi, Kenya: East African Literature Bureau, 1973.
Godfrey, F. "The Mining Industry in Nigeria." *Journal of the Royal African Society* 38 (1938–39): 247–59.
Goreux, L. M. *Interdependence in Planning*. Baltimore, Md.: Johns Hopkins Univ. Press, 1977.
Goulet, D. *The Cruel Choice: A New Concept in the Theory of Development*. New York: Atheneum, 1971.
Grace, J. J. "Tin Mining on the Plateau Before 1920." In *Studies in the History of Plateau State*, ed. E. Isichei, 111–127. London, Macmillan, 1982.
Graf, William D. *The Nigerian State: Political Economy, State Class, and Political System in the Post-Colonial Era*. London: James Currey, 1988.
Greaves, Ida. *Colonial Monetary Conditions*. London: HMSO, 1953.
Green, R. H. "Four African Development Plans: Ghana, Kenya, and Tanzania." *Journal of Modern African Studies* 3 (1965): 249–79.
Gutkind, P. C. W., and P. Waterman. *African Social Studies: A Radical Reader*. New York: Monthly Review, 1977.
Hagin, E. R., ed. *Planning Economic Development*. Homewood, Ill.: R. D. Irwin, 1963.
Hailey, Lord. *An African Survey*. London: Oxford Univ. Press, 1956.
———. *Native Administration in the British African Territories*. Part 3. *West Africa: Nigeria, the Gold Coast, Sierra Leone, Gambia*. London: HMSO, 1950–53.
Hancock, W. K. *Survey of British Commonwealth Affairs*. Vol. 2. London: Oxford Univ. Press, 1962.
———. *Wealth of Colonies*. Cambridge, U.K.: Cambridge Univ. Press, 1950.
———, and M. M. Gowing. *British War Economy*. . London: HMSO, 1949.

Haney, L. H. *History of Economic Thought*. London: Macmillan, 1949.
Hargreaves, J. D. *Prelude to the Partition of West Africa*. London: Macmillan, 1963.
Harris, John H. *Dawn in Darkest Africa*. London: Frank Cass, 1968.
Hazlewood, A. "Sterling Balances and the Colonial Currency System. A Note." *Economic Journal* 62, no. 248 (1952): 942–45.
Helleiner, G. K. "The Fiscal Role of the Marketing Boards in Nigerian Economic Development 1947–1961." *Nigerian Journal of Economic and Social Studies* 73, no. 295 (1964): 582–610.
———. *International Trade and Economic Development*. London: Penguin, 1972.
———. *Peasant Agriculture, Government, and Economic Growth in Nigeria*. Homewood, Ill.: Richard D. Irwin, 1966.
Heussler, Robert. *The British in Northern Nigeria*. London: Oxford Univ. Press, 1968.
Higgins, B. *Economic Development: Principles, Problems, and Policies*. New York: Norton, 1959.
Hill, Polly. *Development Economics on Trial: The Anthropological Case for a Prosecution*. Cambridge, U.K.: Cambridge Univ. Press, 1986.
———. *Rural Hausa: A Village and a Setting*. Cambridge, U.K.: Cambridge Univ. Press, 1972.
Hinden, R. *Empire and After: A Study of British Imperial Attitudes*. London: Essential, 1949.
Hirschman, A. O. *The Strategy of Economic Development*. New Haven, Conn.: Yale Univ. Press, 1958.
Hodder, B. W. *Economic Development in the Tropics*. London: Methuen, 1968.
Hodgkin, Thomas. *Nationalism in Colonial Africa*. London: Frederick Muller, 1956.
Hoggendorn, J. S. *Nigerian Groundnut Exports: Origins and Early Development*. Zaria and Ibadan: Ahmadu Bello Univ. Press and Oxford Univ. Press, 1978.
Holland, S., ed. *Beyond Capitalist Planning*. Oxford, U.K.: Basil Blackwell, 1979.
Hopkins, A. G. "Clio-Antics: A Horoscope for African Economic History." *African Studies Since 1945. A Tribute to Basil Davidson*, ed. C. Fyfe, 31–48. London: Longman, 1976.
———. *An Economic History of West Africa*. London: Longman, 1973.
———. "Some Economic Aspects of Political Movements in Nigeria and in the Gold Coast, 1918–1939." *Journal of African History* 7, no. 1 (1966): 133–52.
Hubbard, James P. *Education under Colonial Rule: A History of Katsina College, 1921–1942*. Lanham, N.Y.: Univ. Press of America, 2000.
Igbafe, P. A. *Benin under British Administration: The Impact of Colonial Rule on an African Kingdom, 1897–1938*. London: Longman, 1979.
Ikejiani, O., ed. *Nigerian Education*. London: Longman, 1964.
Ikime, O. *The Fall of Nigeria: The British Conquest*. London: Heinemann, 1977.
———. *Niger Delta Rivalry: Itsekiri-Urhobo Relations and the European Presence, 1884–1936*. London: Longman, 1969.
Ikoku, S. G. *Nigeria for Nigerians: A Study of Contemporary Nigerian Politics from a Socialist Point of View*. Lagos: self-published, 1963.
Ikpe, Blankson Eno. *Food and Society in Nigeria: A History of Food Customs, Food Economy and Cultural Change 1900–1989*. Stuttgart, Germ.: Steiner, 1994.
Ikpuk, John Smith. *Militarisation of Politics and Neo-Colonialism: The Nigerian Experience, 1966–90*. London: Janus, 1995.

Imoagene, Oshomha, ed. *The Nigerian Class Structure*. Ibadan: Evans, 1989.
International Bank for Reconstruction and Development. *The Economic Development of Nigeria*. Baltimore: IBRD and Johns Hopkins Univ. Press, 1955.
Iwayemi, Akin. "The Military and the Economy." In *Nigerian Government and Politics under Military Rule, 1966–79*, ed. Oyeleye Oydiran. London: Frank Case, 1978.
Jalee, P. *The Pillage of the Third World*. New York: Monthly Review, 1970.
Jones, A. C. *Labour's Colonial Policy*. London: Fabian, 1947.
Jones, G. I. *The Trading States of the Oil Rivers*. London: Oxford Univ. Press, 1963.
Joseph, Richard A. "Affluence and Underdevelopment: The Nigerian Experience." *Journal of Modern African Studies* 16, no. 2 (1978): 221–39.
———. *Democracy and Prebendal Politics in Nigeria*. Cambridge, U.K.: Cambridge Univ. Press, 1987.
July, Robert W. *The Origins of Modern African Thought*. New York: Praeger, 1967.
Kayode, M. O., and O. Teriba, eds. *Industrialization in Nigeria*. Ibadan: Ibadan Univ. Press, 1977.
Kayode, M. O., and Y. B. Usman, eds. *Nigeria since Independence: The First 25 Years*. Vol. 11. *The Economy*. Ibadan: Heinemann, 1989.
Keynes, J. M. *The General Theory of Employment, Interest and Money*. London: Macmillan, 1936.
Kilby, P. *Industrialisation in an Open Economy: Nigeria, 1945–1966*. Cambridge, U.K.: Cambridge Univ. Press, 1969.
Killingray, D., and Richard Rathbone, eds. *Africa and the Second World War*. London: Macmillan, 1986.
Kirk-Greene, A. H. M. *Crisis and Conflict in Nigeria: A Documentary Sourcebook, 1966–1970*. 2 vols. London: Oxford Univ. Press, 1971.
Knowles, L. C. A. *The Economic Development of the British Overseas Empires*. Vol. 1. London: Routledge, 1924.
Koehn, Peter. "Competitive Transition to Civilian Rule: Nigeria's First and Second Experiments." *Journal of Modern African Politics* 27, no. 3 (1989): 401–30.
Kopytoff, Jean Herskovits. *A Preface to Modern Nigeria: The "Sierra Leonians" in Yoruba, 1830–1890*. Madison: Univ. of Wisconsin Press, 1965.
Kukah, Matthew Hassan. *Religion, Politics and Power in Northern Nigeria*. Ibadan: Spectrum, 1993.
Kupah, Hilda. *Urbanization and Migration in West Africa*. Berkeley: Univ. of California Press, 1965.
Landauer, C. *The Theory of National Economic Planning*. Berkeley: Univ. of California Press, 1947.
Langley, J. A. *Pan Africanism and Nationalism in West Africa 1900–1945*. Oxford, U.K.: Clarendon, 1973.
Last, Murray. *The Sokoto Caliphate*. London: Longman, 1967.
Lawal, Bayo. "Sharing Profits with Subjects: The Colonial Fiscal Policy." In *Britain and Nigeria*, ed. Falola, 186–222.
Lawrence, A. W. *Trade Castles and Forts of West Africa*. Stanford, Calif.: Stanford Univ. Press, 1963.

Lee, J. M. *Colonial Development and Good Government*. Oxford, U.K.: Clarendon, 1967.

———, and M. Petter. *The Colonial Office: War and Development Policy*. London: Maurice Temple Smith, 1982.

Leibenstein, H. *Economic Backwardness and Economic Growth*. New York: Wiley, 1957.

Lewis, Peter. "From Prebendalism to Predation: The Political Economy of Decline in Nigeria." *Journal of Modern African Studies* 34, no. 1 (1996): 79–103.

Lewis, W. A. "On Assessing a Development Plan." *Economic Bulletin of the Economic Society of Ghana* (June–July 1952): 21–32.

———. *Development Planning: The Essentials of Economic Policy*. London: Allen and Unwin, 1966.

———. "Economic Development with Unlimited Supplies of Labour." *Manchester School* 20 (May 1954): 139–92.

———. *The Principles of Economic Planning*. Washington, D.C.: Public Affairs, 1951.

———. *The Theory of Economic Growth*. London: Allen and Unwin, 1961.

———, ed. *Tropical Development 1880–1913*. London: Oxford Univ. Press, 1956.

Little, I. M. D. *Aid to Africa*. Oxford, U.K.: Pergamon, 1964.

Loynes, J. B. *The West African Currency Board, 1912–62*. London: West African Currency Board, 1962.

Luckhan, R. *The Nigerian Military: A Sociological Analysis of Authority and Revolt, 1960–67*. Cambridge, U.K.: Cambridge Univ. Press, 1971.

Lugard, F. D. *The Dual Mandate in British Tropical Africa*. London: Frank Cass, 1922; repr. 1965.

———. *The Rise of Our East African Empire*. London: Blackwood, 1893.

Lynn, Martin. *Commerce and Economic Change in West Africa: The Palm Oil Trade in the Nineteenth Century*. Cambridge, U.K.: Cambridge Univ. Press, 1997.

Mabogunje, A. L. *The Development Process: A Spatial Perspective*. London: Hutchinson, 1980.

Mackintosh, John P. *Nigerian Government and Politics*. Evanston, Ill.: Northwestern Univ. Press, 1966.

———. "Politics in Nigeria: The Action Group Crisis of 1962." *Political Studies* 11, no. 2 (June 1963): 126–55.

Macmillan, W. W. *The Road to Self-Rule: A Study in Colonial Evolution*. London: Faber and Faber, 1959.

———. *Warning from the West Indies*. Rev. ed. Harmondsworth, U.K.: Penguin, 1949.

Madunagu, Edwin. *Nigeria: The Economy and the People*. London: New Beacon, 1983.

Mannix, Daniel P., and Malcolm Cowley. *Black Cargoes: A History of the Atlantic Slave Trade, 1518–1865*. New York: Viking, 1962.

Maseful, G. B. *A Short History of Agriculture in the Colonies*. Oxford, U.K.: Oxford Univ. Press, 1950.

Mba, N. E. *Nigerian Women Mobilized: Women's Political Activity in Southern Nigeria, 1900–1965*. Berkeley, Calif.: Institute of International Studies, 1982.

Mbadiwe, K. O. *British and Axis Aims in Africa*. New York: Wendell Malliet, 1942.

McClelland, D. C. *The Achieving Society*. Princeton, N.J.: Van Nostrand, 1961.

McLean, W. H. "Economic and Social Development in the Colonies." *Journal of the Royal African Society* 35, no. 139 (1936): 191–201.

McPhee, Allan. *The Economic Revolution in British West Africa*. London: Routledge, 1926.

Mehta, S. C. *Development Planning in an African Economy: The Experience of Nigeria*. Delhi, India: Kalinga, 1990.

Meier, G. M., ed. *Leading Issues in Development Economics: Selected Materials and Commentary*. New York: Oxford Univ. Press, 1964.

———, and D. Seers, eds. *Pioneers in Development*. New York: Oxford Univ. Press, 1984.

Mellamby, K. *The Birth of Nigeria's University*. London: Methuen, 1958.

Melson, R. *Nigeria: Modernization and the Politics of Communalism*. East Lansing: Michigan State Univ. Press, 1971.

Meredith, D. "The British Government and Colonial Economic Policy, 1919–1939." *Economic History Review* 28, no. 3 (1975): 484–98.

Meyer, F. V. *Britain's Colonies in World Trade*. London: Oxford Univ. Press, 1948.

Mikesell, R. F., and Allen, R. L. "Economic Policies toward Less Developed Countries." In *Leading Issues in Developing Economics: Selected Materials and Commentary*, ed. G. M. Meier, 113–28. New York: Oxford Univ. Press, 1964.

Miners, N. J. *The Nigerian Army, 1956–1966*. London: Methuen, 1971.

Morgan, D. J. *British Aid-5: Colonial Development*. London: Overseas Development Institute, 1964.

Mortimore, M. *Adapting to Drought: Farmers, Famines and Desertification in West Africa*. Cambridge, U.K.: Cambridge Univ. Press, 1989.

Myint, H. *Economic Theory and the Underdeveloped Countries*. London: Oxford Univ. Press, 1971.

———. *The Economics of Developing Countries*. London: Hutchinson, 1967.

Netting, Robert M. *Hill Farmers of Nigeria: Cultural Ecology of the Kofyar of the Jos Plateau*. Seattle: Univ. of Washington Press, 1968.

Newlyn, W. T., and D. C. Rowan. *Money and Banking in British Colonial Africa*. Oxford, U.K.: Clarendon, 1954.

Nicolson, I. F. *The Administration of Nigeria, 1900 to 1960: Men, Methods, and Myths*. Oxford, U.K.: Clarendon, 1969.

Niculescu, B. *Colonial Planning: A Comparative Study*. London: George Allen and Unwin, 1958.

Nigerian Economic Society. *The Nigerian Economy under the Military: Proceedings of the 1984 Annual Conference*. Ibadan: Nigerian Economic Society, 1985.

———. *Proceedings of the 1980 Annual Conference*. Ibadan: Nigerian Economic Society, 1981.

Njoku, O. N. "Contributions to War Efforts." In *Britain and Nigeria*, ed. Falola, 164–81.

Njoku, R. A. *Commerce and Industry in Nigeria*. Lagos: Government Printer, 1955.

Nnoli, O. *Ethnic Politics in Nigeria*. Enugu: Fourth Dimension, 1978.

———. *Ethnicity and Development in Nigeria*. Aldershot, U.K.: Avebury, 1995.

———, ed. *Path to Nigerian Development*. Dakar, Senegal: Codesria, 1981.

Nugent, J. B., and P. A. Yotopoulos. "What Has Orthodox Development Economics Learned from Recent Experience?" *World Development* 7 (1979): 541–54.

Nwabueze, B .O. *Constitutional Developments in Nigeria*. Rev. ed. Cambridge, U.K.: Cambridge Univ. Press, 1964.

———. *A Constitutional History of Nigeria*. London: Longman, 1982.

Nwankwo, G. O. *The Nigerian Financial System*. London: Macmillan, 1980.

Nzimiro, I. *The Nigerian Civil War: A Study in Class Conflict*. Enugu: Fourth Dimension, 1979.

O'Connell, Father J. O. "Some Social and Political Reflections of the Plan." *Nigerian Journal of Economic and Social Studies* 4, no. 2 (1962): 131–40.
Odetola, T. O. *Military Politics in Nigeria*. New Brunswick, N.J.: Transaction, 1978.
Odumosu, F. O. "Credit Facilities for Farmers and Traders in Nigeria." Masters thesis, Trinity College, Dublin, 1962.
Odumosu, Oluwole I. *The Nigerian Constitution: History and Development*. London: Sweet and Maxwell, 1963.
Ofonagoro, W. I. *Trade and Imperialism in Southern Nigeria, 1881–1929*. New York: Nok, 1979.
Ogunsheye, A. "Nigerian Nationalism, 1919–1952." In *Nigerian Year Book, 1953*. Lagos: *Daily Times*, 1953.
Ohadike, Don C. *The Ekumeku Movement: Western Igbo Resistance to the British Conquest of Nigeria, 1883–1914*. Athens: Ohio Univ. Press, 1991.
———. "Exploitation of Labour." In *Britain and Nigeria*, ed. Falola, 142–63.
Ojike, O. *My Africa*. New York: John Day, 1946.
Okafor, S. O. *Indirect Rule: The Development of Central Legislature in Nigeria*. Walton/Thames, U.K.: Nelson, 1981.
Okigbo, P. N. C. *National Development Planning in Nigeria, 1900–92*. London: James Currey, 1989.
———. *Nigerian National Accounts, 1950–57*. Lagos: Federal Ministry of Economic Development, 1961.
———. *Nigerian Public Finance*. Evanston, Ill.: Northwestern Univ. Press, 1965.
Okongwu, Chu. *The Nigerian Economy: Anatomy of a Traumatised Economy with Some Proposals for Stabilisation*. Enugu: Fourth Dimension, 1986.
Okonjo, I. M. *British Administration in Nigeria, 1900–1950: A Nigerian View*. New York: Nok, 1974.
Okonkwo, Rina. *Heroes of West African Nationalism*. Enugu: Delta, 1958.
Okoye, M. *A Letter to Dr. Nnamdi Azikiwe*. Enugu: Fourth Dimension, 1979.
Olaloku, F. A., ed. *Structure of the Nigerian Economy*. Lagos: Macmillan, 1979.
Olayide, S. O. *Economic Survey of Nigeria, 1960–75*. Ibadan: Aromolaran, 1976.
———, and Dupe Olatunbosun. *Trends and Prospects of Nigeria's Agricultural Exports*. Ibadan: Ibadan Univ. Press, 1975.
———, and S. Olajuwon. *Food and Nutrition Crisis in Nigeria*. Ibadan: Ibadan Univ. Press, 1982.
Olayiwola, Peter O. *Petroleum and Structural Change in a Developing Country: The Case of Nigeria*. New York: Praeger, 1987.
Olomola, Ade S., and A. C. Nwosu, eds. *Perspectives on Food Security in Nigeria*. Lagos: Nigerian Rural Sociological Association, 1993.
Olorunsola, Victor A. *Soldiers and Power: The Development Performance of the Nigerian Military*. Stanford, Calif.: Hoover Institution, 1977.
Olukoshi, Adebayo, O. *Crisis and Adjustment in the Nigerian Economy*. Lagos: JAD, 1991.
———, ed. *The Politics of Structural Adjustment in Nigeria*. London: James Currey, 1993.
Olusanya, G. O. *The Evolution of the Nigerian Civil Service, 1861–1960: The Problems of Nigerianization*. Lagos: Univ. of Lagos Press, 1975.
———. *The Second World War and Politics in Nigeria, 1939–1953*. London: Evans, 1973.
———. *The West African Students Union and the Politics of Decolonization, 1925–1958*. Ibadan: Daystar, 1982.

———. "The Zikist Movement: A Study of Political Radicalism." *Journal of Modern African Studies* 4, no. 3 (1966): 323–33.
Oluwansanmi, H. A. *Agriculture and Nigerian Economic Development*. Ibadan: Oxford Univ. Press, 1966.
Oni, O., and Bade Onimode. *Economic Development in Nigeria: The Socialist Alternative*. Ibadan: Nigerian Academy of Arts, Sciences, and Technology, 1975.
Onimode, B. *Imperialism and Underdevelopment in Nigeria: The Dialectics of Mass Poverty*. London: Macmillan and Zed, 1983.
———. *A Political Economy of the African Crisis*. London: Zed, 1988.
———, et al. *Multinational Corporations in Nigeria*. Ibadan: Les Shyraden, 1983.
Onitiri, H. M. A. "Nigeria's Balance of Payments and Economic Policy, 1946–1960." Ph.D. diss., University of London, 1963.
Onukaogu, G. U. "Conditions Affecting the Administration of Technical Assistance Programs in Nigeria." Ph.D. diss. University of Indiana, 1955.
Orr, Sir Charles. *The Making of Northern Nigeria*. 2d ed. London: Frank Cass, 1965.
Osaghae, Eghosa E. *Crippled Giant: Nigeria Since Independence*. London: Hurst, 1998.
Osoba, S. O. "The Colonial Antecedents and Contemporary Development of Nigeria's Foreign Policy: A Study in the History of Social, Economic and Political Conflict." Ph.D. diss., Moscow State University, Moscow, Russia, 1967.
———. "The Phenomenon of Labour Migration in the Era of British Colonial Rule." *Journal of the Historical Society of Nigeria* 4, no. 4 (June 1969): 515–38.
Osuntokun, Jide. *Chief S. Ladoke Akintola: His Life and Times*. London: Frank Cass, 1984.
———. "Post–First World War Economic and Administrative Problems in Nigeria and the Response of the Clifford Administration." *Journal of the Historical Society of Nigeria* 7, no. 1 (1973): 35–48.
Otite, O. *Ethnic Pluralism and Ethnicity in Nigeria*. Ibadan: Shaneson, 1990.
Oyediran, Oyeleye, ed. *Nigerian Government and Politics under Military Rule, 1966–79*. London: Frank Cass, 1978.
Oyejide, T. A. *Tariff Policy and Industrialization in Nigeria*. Ibadan: Ibadan Univ. Press, 1975.
Oyemakinde, Wale. "A History of Indigenous Labour on the Nigerian Railway, 1895–1945." Ph.D. diss., University of Ibadan, 1970.
———. "The Impact of the Great Depression on the Nigerian Railway and Its Workers." *Journal of the Historical Society of Nigeria* 8, no. 4 (1977): 143–60.
Oyenuga, V. A. "Latest Development in Marxist Ideology." Action Group summer school lecture. Lagos, Nigeria, 1956.
Oyovbaire, S. E. *Federalism in Nigeria: A Study of the Development of the Nigerian State*. London: Macmillan, 1985.
Paden, John N. *Ahmadu Bello, Sardauna of Sokoto: Values and Leadership in Nigeria*. Bungay, England: Richard Clay, 1986.
———. *Religion and Political Culture in Kano*. Berkeley: Univ. of California Press, 1973.
Padmore, George. *Pan Africanism or Communism? The Coming Struggle for Africa*. London: Dobson, 1953.
———, and D. Pizer. *How Russia Transformed Her Colonial Empire*. London: Dobson, 1946.
Panter-Brick, S. Keith, ed. *Nigerian Politics and Military Rule: Prelude to Civil War*. London: Athlone, 1970.

———. *Soldiers and Oil: The Political Transformation of Nigeria*. London: Frank Cass, 1978.
Peel, J. D. Y. "Olaju: A Yoruba Concept of Development." *Journal of Development Studies* 14, no. 2 (1978): 135–65.
Perham, Margery. *The Colonial Reckoning*. London: Fontana, 1963.
———. *Lugard: The Years of Authority, 1898–1945*. London: Collins, 1960.
———. *Native Administration in Nigeria*. London: Oxford Univ. Press, 1937.
———. "Restatement of Indirect Rule." *Africa* 7, no. 3 (1934): 321–34.
———, ed. *Mining, Commerce and Finance in Nigeria*. London: Faber and Faber, 1948.
———, ed. *The Native Economies of Nigeria*. London: Faber and Faber, 1946.
Pim, A. W. *The Financial and Economic History of the African Tropical Territories*. Oxford, U.K.: Clarendon, 1940.
———. "Public Finance in Nigeria." In *Mining, Commerce and Finance in Nigeria*, ed. M. Perham, 112–29.
Post, Kenneth W. J. *The Nigerian Federal Elections of 1959*. London: Oxford Univ. Press, 1963.
———, and George D. Jenkins. *The Price of Liberty: Personality and Politics in Colonial Nigeria*. Cambridge: Cambridge Univ. Press, 1973.
———, and Michael Vickers. *Structure and Conflict in Nigeria, 1960–65*. Madison: Univ. of Wisconsin Press, 1963.
Prest, A. R., and I. G. Stewart. *The National Income of Nigeria, 1950–51*. London: HMSO, 1954.
Prothero, R. M. "Migratory Labour from North-Western Nigeria." *Africa* 27, no. 1 (1957): 251–61.
Raisman, Jeremy, and R. C. Trees. *Report of the Fiscal Commission*. London: HMSO, 1958.
Richards, P. *Indigenous Agricultural Revolution: Ecology and Food Production in West Africa*. London: Hutchinson, 1985.
Rimmer, D., ed. *Africa 30 Years On*. London: Royal African Society and James Currey, 1991.
Robinson, R., J. Gallagher, and A. Denny. *Africa and the Victorians*. London: Macmillan, 1961.
Robson, P., and D. A. Lury, eds. *The Economies of Africa*. London: Allen and Unwin, 1969.
Rodney, W. *How Europe Underdeveloped Africa*. Dar-es-Salaam: Tanzania Publishing House, 1972.
Rostow, W. W. *The Stages of Growth: A Non-Communist Manifesto*. Cambridge, U.K.: Cambridge Univ. Press, 1960.
———. *Theorists of Economic Growth from David Hume to the Present: With a Perspective on the Next Century*. New York: Oxford Univ. Press, 1990.
Rothschild, D., and N. Chazan, eds. *The Precarious Balance: State and Society in Africa*. Boulder, Colo.: Westview, 1988.
Royal Empire Society. *The Crucial Problem of Imperial Development*. London: Longmans, 1938.
Saro-Wiwa, Ken. *Genocide in Nigeria: The Ogoni Tragedy*. Port Harcourt: Saros, 1992.
Schatz, S. P. "Achievement and Economic Growth: A Critique." *Quarterly Journal of Economics* 79 (1965): 234–47.
———. "Economic Environment and Private Enterprise in West Africa." Unpublished mimeo, 1964.
———. *Economics, Politics, and Administration in Government Lending: The Regional Loans Boards of Nigeria*. Ibadan: Oxford Univ. Press, 1970.

———. "The Influence of Planning on Development: The Nigerian Experience." *Social Research* 27 (1960): 451–68.
———. *Nigerian Capitalism*. Berkeley: Univ. of California Press, 1977.
———. "Nigeria's First National Development Plan, 1962–68: An Appraisal." *Nigerian Journal of Economic and Social Studies* 5, no. 2 (1963): 221–35.
———. "Obstacles to Nigerian Private Investment." *Nigerian Journal of Economics and Social Statistics* 4, no. 1 (1962): 66–73.
———. "Two Years of Progress of Planning." *West Africa* 2510 (1965): 773–74.
Schumpeter, J. A. *The Theory of Economic Development*. Cambridge, Mass.: Harvard Univ. Press, 1934.
Schwarz, F. E. O., Jr. *Nigeria: The Tribes, the Nations, or the Race*. Cambridge, Mass.: MIT Univ. Press, 1965.
Scitovsky, T. "Two Concepts of External Economies." *Journal of Political Economy* 62 (1954): 143–51.
Seers, D. "What Are We Trying to Measure?" *Journal of Development Studies* 8 (1972): 21–36.
Seidman, A. "Changing Theories of Political Economy." In *African Studies since 1945*, ed. C. Fyfe, 49–65. London: Longman, 1976.
———. *Planning in Subsaharan Africa*. New York: Praeger, 1974.
Shaw, Thomas, and Gilbert Colville. *Report of Nigerian Livestock Mission*. London: HMSO, 1950.
Shenton, R. *Studies in the Development of Capitalism in Northern Nigeria*. Toronto: Univ. of Toronto Press, 1986.
Shepperson, George. "Notes on Negro American Influences on the Emergence of African Nationalism." *Journal of African History* 1, no. 2 (1960): 299–312.
Sklar, Richard L. "Contradictions in the Nigerian Political System." *Journal of Modern African Studies* 8, no. 2 (1965): 201–13.
———. "The Contribution of Tribalism to Nationalism in Western Nigeria." *Journal of Human Relations* 8 (1960): 407–18.
———. *Nigerian Political Parties: Power in an Emergent African Nation*. Princeton, N.J.: Princeton Univ. Press, 1963.
———. "Nigerian Politics: The Ordeal of Chief Awolowo, 1960–65." *Politics in Africa: 7 Cases*, ed. Gwendolen M. Carter, 119–65. New York: Harcourt, Brace and World, 1966.
Smith, A. *The Wealth of Nations*. Vol. 2, book 4. London: J. M. Dent, 1910.
Smith, R. S. *The Lagos Consulate, 1851–1861*. London: Macmillan, 1978.
———. "The Lagos Consulate, 1851–1861: An Outline." *Journal of African History* 15 (1974): 393–416.
Smythe, Hugh H., and Mabel H. Smythe. *The New Nigerian Elite*. Stanford, Calif.: Stanford Univ. Press, 1960.
Soremekun, Kayode. "Oil and the Democratic Imperative in Nigeria." *Governance and Democratisation in Nigeria*, ed. Dele Olowu, Kayode Soremekeun, and Adebayo Williams, 97–109. Ibadan: Spectrum, 1995.
Stewart, F., S. Lall, and S. M. Wangwe, eds. *Alternative Development Strategies in Sub-Saharan Africa*. London: Macmillan, 1992.
Stolper, W. F. "How Bad Is the Plan?" *Nigerian Journal of Economic and Social Studies* 6, no. 3 (1964): 261–73.

———. *Planning without Facts: Lessons in Resource Allocation from Nigeria's Development.* Cambridge, Mass.: Harvard Univ. Press, 1966.
Tamuno, T. N. *The Evolution of the Nigerian State: The Southern Phase, 1898–1914.* London: Longman, 1972.
Taylor, M. J., and N. J. Thrift, eds. *The Geography of Multinationals.* London: Croom Helm, 1981.
Teriba, O., ed. *Poverty in Nigeria.* Ibadan: Nigerian Economic Society, 1975.
Toye, J. *Dilemmas of Development: Reflections on the Counter-Revolution in Development Theory and Policy.* Oxford, U.K.: Blackwell, 1987.
Tseayo, P. *Conflict and Incorporation in Nigeria: The Integration of the Tiv.* Zaria: Gaskiya, 1975.
Udogu, E. Ike. "The Allurement of Ethnonationalism in Nigeria Politics: The Contemporary Debate." *Journal of Asian and African Studies* 29, nos. 3–4 (1994): 159–71.
Ukwu, U. I. "The Development of Trade and Marketing in Iboland." *Journal of the Historical Society of Nigeria* 3, no. 4 (1967): 647–63.
University of Ife. *Small-scale Industries in Mid-Western State, Kwara State, and Lagos State.* Ile-Ife: Industrial Research Unit, 1972.
University of Nigeria. *Small-scale Industries in South-Eastern and Benue-Plateau States.* Nsukka: Industrial Research Unit, 1972.
Usman, Y. B. *For the Liberation of Nigeria.* London: New Beacon, 1979.
———. *Nigeria against the IMF: The Home Market Strategy.* Kaduna: Vanguard, 1986.
Watts, M. *Silent Violence: Food, Famine and Peasantry in Northern Nigeria.* Berkeley: Univ. of California Press, 1983.
———, ed. *State, Oil, and Agriculture in Nigeria.* Berkeley: Institute of International Studies, University of California, 1987.
Webster, James Bertin. *The African Churches among the Yoruba, 1888–1922.* Oxford, U.K.: Oxford Univ. Press, 1964.
Wells, J. C. *Agricultural Policy and Economic Growth in Nigeria.* Ibadan: Oxford Univ. Press, 1974.
Wey, S. O., and E. Osagie. *An Ideology for Social Development.* Lagos: Academy, 1977.
Whitaker, C. S., Jr. *The Politics of Tradition: Continuity and Change in Northern Nigeria, 1946–1966.* Princeton, N.J.: Princeton Univ. Press, 1970.
White, J. *Central Administration in Nigeria, 1914–1948.* London: Frank Cass, 1981.
Wicker, E. R. "Colonial Development and Welfare, 1929–1957: The Evolution of a Policy." *Social and Economic Studies* 7, no.4 (1958): 170–82.
Wickizer, V. D. "Plantation Crops in Tropical Agriculture." *Tropical Agriculture* (July 1958): 167–78.
Wilson, T. *Planning and Growth.* London: Macmillan, 1964.
Williams, Gavin. *State and Society in Nigeria.* Idanre: Afrografika, 1980.
———, ed. *Nigeria: Economy and Society.* London: Rex Collins, 1976.
World Bank. *Background Papers: The Long-Term Perspective Study of Sub-Saharan Africa, II, Economic and Sectoral Policy Issues.* Washington, D.C.: World Bank, 1990.
———. *Report on Economic Conditions in Nigeria.* Washington, DC: World Bank, 1978.
———. *Sub-Saharan Africa: From Crisis to Sustainable Growth.* Washington, D.C.: World Bank, 1990.

———. *World Development Report, 1968*. Washington, D.C.: World Bank, 1968.
Yesufu, T. M. "Nigerian Manpower Problems: A Preliminary Assessment." *Nigerian Journal of Economic and Social Studies* 4, no. 3 (1962): 207–27.
Zachernurk, P. S. "The Lagos Intelligentsia and the Idea of Progress, ca. 1860–1960." In *Yoruba Historiography*, ed. Toyin Falola, 147–65. Madison, Wis.: Program of African Studies, 1991.
Zartman, I. William, ed. *The Political Economy of Nigeria*. New York: Praeger, 1983.

Index

Action Group (AG), 26, 35, 41, 43–44, 48–50, 62, 179; Northern Campaign, 51; split of, 58–60
African Institute for Oil Palm Research, 87, 88
African and Eastern Trade Corporation (AETC), 77
agriculture, 67–74, 78, 81–81, 86–89, 92–93, 160–67, 190–92, 206; commercial, 204–5; decline of, 165–66, 180–81, 184, 203–5; development of, 88, 145–47, 150–53; technology in, 72, 86, 114–15, 128, 149, 165. *See also* marketing boards; plantation farming
Akintola, Chief S. Ladoke, 56, 58–60
Al-Kanemi, 3
anticolonial ideology, 19, 20, 26. *See also* protest; riot; strike
anti-regionalism, 50
Association of West African Merchants, 21
Atlantic Charter, 19–20
Awolowo, Chief Obafemi, 24, 42, 43–44, 48–50, 52, 58–60, 118
Azikiwe, Nnamdi, 24, 25–26, 34, 41–45, 48–50, 52

banking industry, 99, 197
Belewa, Sir Alhaji Abubakar Tafawa, 37, 45, 49, 51, 109
Bello, Sardauna Alhaji Ahmadu, 35, 42, 45–46, 109
Biafra, 169
Britain, 80, 103–4, 126, 167; economy of, 1, 98. *See also* colonial economy; colonial legacy; colonial rule; colonization

Calabar, 128–29
caliphate system, 8
Cameroon, 36–37, 135
capital, 83–84, 92, 117, 172; flight of, 100
capitalism, 157–58
cash crops, 66–67, 69, 72, 74, 86, 87, 124, 153, 161, 163–65, 173, 206. *See also* exports; agriculture
cashew-nut industry, 131–32
cement, 118, 139
Central Bank of Nigeria, 188, 189
Central Marketing Board, 98
civil service, 22–23, 31, 39, 101, 158, 176, 193–94
class, socio-economic, 78, 189–99, 201
Clifford, Hugh, 39–40, 69
cocoa, 69–70, 72–73, 79, 87–88, 97
Colonial Development Corporation, 129
Colonial Development and Welfare Act, 22, 82, 91
colonial economy, 66–68, 184; budget, 75; reform of, 66–67
colonial legacy, 29, 66–67, 174–75
colonial rule: North-South disparity, 12, 15, 16–18, 45–47; objectives, 9–10, 201; resistance to, 6, 7; World War II under, 21–22

colonization, 4–5
conservatism, 47
constitution, federal, 37
constitutional reform, 26, 33, 34–35, 37, 51, 54, 100–101
cooperatives, 116–17
coup d'état, 63–64, 186. *See also* military rule
corruption, 54–55, 60–61, 90, 186, 188, 193, 206
cotton, 72, 87
Council of Ministers, 34
crafts, 75, 89
currency, 80

deficit, 168, 181
democracy, 19
development. *See* economy
domestic consumption, 73–73, 76–66, 92. *See also* imports

East Regional Production Development Board (ERPDB), 122–23, 125–26, 128–30, 132, 137–38
economy, 23, 75, 156–58, 189–200; decentralization of, 107; decline of, 61, 157, 182; development of, 77, 101, 103–5 127–31, 133–34, 144–45, 175, 190; diversification of, 101, 131, 177–78; growth rate and, 169, 170, 178, 180; inflation in, 187; informal sector of, 89; private sector of, 178–79, 180; reform of, 11, 22, 27, 29, 31–32, 64, 82–83, 103, 159–60, 169, 202. *See also* colonial policy; deficit; federalism; Nigeria; World War II
educated elite, 12, 14–15, 23, 43–44
education, 28, 41, 114, 128, 158–59, 204. *See also* Islamic education; Western education
Egbe Omo Oduduwa, 24, 44
elections, 48, 51–52, 58; federalism and, 48–49; fraudulence of, 61–63; parliament and, 51. *See also* regionalism
electricity, 152, 180, 197–98
Electricity Corporation of Nigeria (ECN), 196
elite, 7–9, 18, 27, 92, 154, 199–200. *See also* educated elite; Islamic intelligentsia; Southern intelligentsia; Yoruba elite
employment, 115, 127, 162
Enahoro, Anthony, 35, 51
entrepreneurs: Nigerian, 74, 77–78, 81, 83–84, 92, 99, 185; governmental, 102–103
Enugu Colliery Shooting Incident, 26
environmental degradation, 150, 201, 205
ethnic associations, 14, 198

"ethnic object," 17
ethnicity, 17, 55
Executive Councils of Nigeria, 23
expenditures, 88, 91–92, 103–4, 106, 146, 148, 160, 169, 204
exports, 67–72; crops as, 86, 95, 97, 150, 156–57; minerals as, 72–73; price decrease, 76, 157; price increase, 71–72, 82; restrictions on, 80–81. *See also* cash crops; economy

Farm Settlement Scheme, 163
federalism, 35–36, 37–38, 92, 177; economic reform and, 105–7; revenue sharing under, 37–38
fertilizer scheme, 135–36
First Republic, 54, 58, 157, 174, 181
Fiscal Commission, 38
forced labor, 8, 10, 12
foreign firms, 73, 74, 77, 79, 81, 99, 157, 182, 185, 199
forestry, 86, 130
Fulani, 49, 58, 146–47

Germany, 18–19, 79, 80
gold, 71
Goldie, Sir George, 4–5
government: criticism of, 60–61; decentralization of, 177. *See also* colonial policy; federalism; protest; riot
Grant, William D., 202–3
Gross Domestic Product (GDP), 84, 93, 94, 170, 178, 183, 188, 195
Groundnut Marketing Board, 145

Hausa, 14, 17, 47, 49, 58
House of Chiefs, 33
housing, 137

Igbo, 8, 14, 43, 47, 49, 60
Ijo, 17
Imoudu, Michael, 25
imperialism, 2. *See also* colonial legacy; colonial policy; economy
imports, 86, 92; price increase, 82, 168; restrictions on, 79–80. *See also* domestic consumption; economy
independence, 37, 156
indirect rule, 7–9
Industrial Research Institute, 84
industrialization, 82, 84, 168–72, 181, 184, 195–96

INDEX

industry, 27, 75, 82–82, 83–85, 101, 112, 117–20; development of, 118–20, 153; failure of, 77; technology and, 87, 171. *See also* manufacturing

infrastructure, 27, 29, 90–91, 106, 148; development of, 67–68, 138–39; unequal distribution of, 54. *See also* road construction

International Bank for Reconstruction and Development (IBRD), 105–6, 205

investment, foreign, 172, 180, 198. *See also* foreign firm; Structural Adjustment Program

Islam, 17, 45, 58

Islamic education, 17

Islamic intelligentsia, 17

Kano riots, 35

KKZ Scheme, 146–47

Lafia Canning Factory, 119

labor, 73, 86, 88–89, 106, 135, 179

labor relations, 71

Lagos Youth Movement (LYM), 40–41. *See also* Nigerian Youth Movement (NYM)

land alienation, 72, 130

land settlement scheme, 147–49

land tenure, 162

Legislative Council, 26, 33, 40

licensing, 81, 99

livestock, 134–36, 141, 146–47, 160

Loan Development Board (LDB), 105

loan programs, 92, 105, 139, 140–44, 185; applications for, 141–42, 143–44

Lugard, Lord, 9–10, 11, 16–17

luxury items. *See* domestic consumption; imports

Lyttleton Constitution, 35, 51

McPhee, Allan, 78

Macaulay, Herbert, 40, 43

Macpherson Constitution, 34–35

manufacturing, 85–86, 92–93, 101, 150, 195–97. *See also* industry

marketing boards, 20, 27, 72, 96–101, 102–8, 109–10; regional boards, 150–52, 154. *See also* Nigeria

markets, 67, 68, 82, 89, 136

middle class, 156–57, 187

middlemen, 73–74, 77–78, 99

migration, 13–14

military rule, 182, 186

mining, 66–67, 72–73, 192. *See also* exports

Minorities Commission, 52

minority marginalization, 56–57

missionaries, 3–4, 18

"modernizers," 10

monopolies, government, 195

National Council of Nigeria and the Cameroons (NCNC), 20, 24, 26, 34, 42–43, 44, 47, 48–50, 59, 62; internal difference, 56

National Congress of British West Africa, 39

National Development Plan, First, 174–81

National Development Plan, Second, 185–86

National Development Plan, Third, 185–86, 191

National Economic Council, 179

National Petroleum Corporation (NPC), 194

nationalism, 1, 16, 20–21, 184–85; ethnicity and, 37; radicalism and, 24, 40–42, 101

nationalists, 20–21, 33, 96; politics of, 38–39

neocolonialism, 2. *See also* colonial legacy; economy

"new economy," 66–67, 74–79, 93

Niger Coast Protectorate, 5

Nigeria: Abeokuta province, 118; Eastern Region, 122–40, 151, 152; Kabba province, 150; Katsina province, 148; Middle Belt of, 55, 57–58, 60; Niger province, 88; Northern Region, 144–50, 152; Ogoja province, 130, 137; Owerri provinces, 128, 130–31, 137; Sokoto province, 147; ten-year plan for, 103, 105; Western Region of, 43, 55, 59–60, 111–22, 151; Western Region, economic reform in, 112–24

Nigeria Supply Board, 81

Nigerian Marketing Boards, 139

Nigerian National Alliance (NNA), 61–62

Nigerian National Democratic Party (NNDP), 16, 40, 41

Nigerian Trade Union Congress, 25

Nigerian Union of Students, 43

Nigerian Youth Movement (NYM), 16, 24, 42–43. *See also* Lagos Youth Movement

"Nigerianization," 159

Nkrumah, Kwame, 158

North-South divide, 53–54

Northern Elements Progressive Union (NEPU), 42

Northern intelligentsia, 46

Northern People's Congress (NPC), 26, 35, 45–46, 48–50, 56, 62

Northern Regional Production Development Board, 144–45
Nzeogwu, Chukwuma Kaduna, 63

oil boom, 185–86, 192
oil industry, 169–71, 181, 194, 201–2
oil revenue, 182–83, 184, 192, 199, 203
oil palm, 71, 87, 119, 125
oil palm mills, 125–28, 140, 150
Oil Palm Produce Marketing Board, 122–23
Oil Rivers, 4
Oil Palm Marketing Board, 72
Okigbo, P. N. C., 84
"Operation Wet E," 61

parliamentary system, 56
partition, 4, 5–6
Path to Nigerian Freedom (Obafemi Awolowo), 43
peanuts, 71, 73, 87–88, 98
Phillipson, Sir Sydney, 38
plantation farming, 69–70, 113–14, 115–16, 125, 129, 130–32, 163
political instability, 175, 179
political parties, 16, 24, 26, 38–42, 52, 56–57, 62–63, 176; ethnic base, 46, 59–60. *See also* regionalism
political reform, 23, 54
political violence, 59, 61. *See also* coup d'état
politics, 23, 28, 55, 64, 154–55, 179
popular movements, 20. *See also* protest; riot; strike
poverty, 186, 200–201
Protectorate of Northern Nigeria, 6
protest, 24–25, 60–61, 89, 188
price control, 96–99, 185

railway, 67, 68, 90–91
Raisman Commission, 174
raw materials, 69, 84, 98, 171
reform, 18, 26, 205–6; demands for, 23–24. *See also* constitutional reform; economic reform; political reform.
Regional Production Development Boards (RPDB), 107, 110–11
regional economies, 69–70, 89, 104, 173–74; variation among, 74–75, 109–114, 160–61, 163–67. *See also* economy; marketing boards
regional governments, 37, 99, 106

Regional Loan Board, 107
regionalism, 33, 34, 50–51, 174, 175–76, 198; consolidation of, 46–48; national elections and, 48–49; political parties and, 48–51, 61–62; revenue sharing and, 56. *See also* Nigeria
"rentier state," 202–3
Republic of Biafra, 57
resettlement schemes, 89
retail, 83
revenue, government, 197–98; allocation of, 173–74; public, 67, 71
Richards Constitution, 26, 33–34, 38
Richards, Sir Arthur, 33
riot, 26, 47. *See also* Kano riots; Tiv riots
road construction, 91, 121, 125, 129, 138–39, 149–50, 185
Royal Niger Company (RNC), 4
rubber, 72, 118–19, 133

salaries, 115, 187, 198–99
"savvy boys," 7
secession, 35, 47, 50, 51. *See also* military rule; regionalism
Second Republic, 186
socialist philosophy, 25, 50, 58
Sokoto Caliphate, 45
Southern intelligentsia, 45–46
stereotypes, 10–11, 51
strike, 26, 41, 61
Structural Adjustment Programs (SAP), 186, 188, 194, 197
student movements, 41, 43
surplus, 98, 99, 100–101

taxation, 8, 11–12, 91, 99, 173, 187, 192–93
tsetse fly, 134, 146
theocratic government, 45
tenant farmers, 67, 70
textiles, 170–71, 195
Tiv, 14, 17, 146
Tiv riots, 56–58
trade, foreign, 167–68
trade, local, 68, 89, 138–39, 173. *See also* markets
trade union, 41–42, 61
trade company, 4–6
transatlantic slave trade, 3
transportation, 90–91, 196
Tungar Maidubu, 147–48

underdevelopment, 201–6
unification, 6, 16
United Africa Company, 73
United Middle Belt Congress (UMBC), 52
United Nigeria Democratic Party (UNDP), 56, 62
United People's Party (UPP), 59
United Progressive Grand Alliance (UPGA), 62
University Colleges, 222
urban culture, 13
urban-rural discrepancy, 28
urbanization, 12–13, 14

warrant chiefs, 8, 23
water resources, 149, 152
West African Cocoa Board (WACB), 80
West African Currency Board, 168
West African Frontier Force, 7
West African Pilot, 25, 43
Western education, 12, 14–15, 45
Western ideology, 38–39
Western Regional Production Board, 111, 113–14
Women's War, 12
World War II, 18–20; economy during, 76, 79–82; Nigeria and, 20–23, 201; propaganda, 18–19

Yaba Higher College, 41
Yoruba, 8, 12, 17, 42–43, 47, 49, 58
Yoruba intelligentsia, 44, 60, 62
Yoruba wars, 5, 6

Zikists, 25–26